THOMPSONS

THOMPSONS

*A personal history
of the firm and
its founder*

Steve Allen

MERLIN PRESS

© Steve Allen, 2012

First published in 2012 by
The Merlin Press Ltd.
6 Crane Street Chambers
Crane Street
Pontypool
NP4 6ND
Wales

www.merlinpress.co.uk

ISBN. 978-0-85036-638-9

British Library Cataloguing in Publication Data
is available from the British Library

We have endeavoured to obtain permission from copyright holders of all works reproduced in the book. We apologise if we have failed.

All rights reserved. No part of this publication may be reproduced, stored in a retrieval system, or transmitted, in any form or by any means, electronic, mechanical, photocopying, recording or otherwise, without the prior permission of the publisher.

Printed by Imprint Digital, Exeter

Contents

Foreword by Lord Tom Sawyer	vii
Glossary	xi
Introduction	xv
Chapter 1	
Thompsons today	1
Chapter 2	
The veins of greatness	7
Chapter 3	
Birth and background	17
Chapter 4	
Conscience and convictions	27
Chapter 5	
Joan Beauchamp	43
Chapter 6	
Biscuits and scary reds	55
Chapter 7	
The first major case – Poplar Borough Council	59
Chapter 8	
More scary reds	69
Chapter 9	
Early organisation and some family memories	81
Chapter 10	
Thinking has a colossal future	95
Chapter 11	
Mother Earth and Father Land	102
Chapter 12	
The tree of liberty	112
Chapter 13	
Dying for work	134
Chapter 14	
Harry Thompson – the man: life and death	144
Chapter 15	
The King is dead; long live the king	162

Chapter 16
    People and offices in London   182
Chapter 17
    The opening of regional offices   221
Chapter 18
    Collective action – legal battles   240
Chapter 19
    Everyday life in the offices   249
Chapter 20
    The demise of W.H. Thompson   258
Chapter 21
    The new firms   267
Chapter 22
    Industrial disputes: back to the future   274
Chapter 23
    A national firm   294
Chapter 24
    Personal injury campaigns and test cases   314
Chapter 25
    Employment law starts to bite   334
Chapter 26
    Preparing for life after Robin and Brian   374
Chapter 27
    From 1996-change, challenge and campaigns   388
Chapter 28
    More test cases   395
Chapter 29
    Thompsons Scotland and Northern Ireland   415
Chapter 30
    Robin and Brian Thompson   429
Chapter 31
    My story   446
Bibliography   463
Index of cases   465
Acknowledgements   469

Foreword

It gives me great pleasure to write this short foreword to Steve Allen's immensely readable and well researched history of Thompsons Solicitors.

My interest and knowledge of the firm goes back almost fifty years to the days when I would proudly present cheques for compensation won by Thompsons for members of my union NUPE. In those days as a young official, I had little idea of the hard work and dedication applied by the leaders, the lawyers and the excellent support staff who delivered on behalf of our members.

Over the following years, as my own experience and responsibility in the union began to grow and expand, I learnt much more about this unique team of people who are dedicated, not just to helping my union members but millions of others affiliated to the TUC. During this time, it became a pleasure and indeed an education to get to know both Brian and Robin Thompson, Frank Foy, Geoff Shears, David Thompson, Stephen Cavalier and many more of the men and women who make up this remarkable firm and about whom you will read much about in these pages.

I soon realised that Thompsons was considerably more than a law firm acting on behalf of trade union members. They were, it seemed to me, a band of brothers and sisters dedicated to supporting the labour movement, in the widest possible sense, based on following the sound principles and strong values of fighting for justice wherever injustice may be found.

The lovely thing about this book is that it explains how that vision came about. The opening chapters discuss in some detail the man who had that vision, the founder of the firm, Harry Thompson, or WH as he was better known

He was one of the great founders of the labour

movement, as testified by all who knew or worked with him. Along with his redoubtable wife Joan Beauchamp, Harry Thompson played a pioneering and crucial role in many of the great labour movement campaigns between 1931 and 1939 – some of the most important in labour history: George Lansbury and the Poplar Council, the General Strike of 1926, the formation of the National Council for Civil Liberties; these were just some of the campaigns in which Harry and Joan played a major part.

After the untimely death of Harry Thompson in 1947, the post-war period saw the two Thompson sons, Brian and Robin, lead the firm to continued success and saw a different type of firm emerging. The focus turned to battles of compensation on work related accidents and disabilities and, of course, to representing the unions which were coming increasingly under legal attack in connection with exercising their legitimate activities.

It's no coincidence that when the trade union movement required support when under real threat and attack, such as in the case of Rookes v Barnard or again following the publication of *In Place of Strife*, it was Thompsons to whom they turned for advice and support.

The middle section of Steve Allen's book considers the outstanding success of Thompsons in helping the trade union movement to face the challenges of the 1970s and the 1980s. The emotive moments in time that define our movement in that period such as the miners' strike, Grunwick and Wapping are stories that leap from the pages and we read again of the pivotal role played by Thompsons.

Landmark cases dealing with deafness, asbestos and welders lung are also considered here, along with reflections and opinions of some of the key players who made history in taking these cases and engaging with their colleagues and friends in the trade union movement.

Over the last twenty years, Thompsons has grown and

consolidated its position as the premier trade union law firm. It is widely respected by the legal profession, in politics and, of course, most of all amongst members of the trade union movement. In recent years Thompsons has expanded its work in several countries, South Africa, Columbia and Cuba to name but three.

I had the honour of being a member of Thompsons' supervisory board from 2000 to 2010. During that time I worked closely with Tom Jones on parliamentary matters and had the opportunity to see the contribution made to the firm by Vicky Phillips in employment law and Joanna Stevens in the field of human relations. Throughout my time on the board I was constantly reminded and impressed with how much the firm valued its relationship with the trade union movement, how it continued its efforts to be effective, efficient and give value for money.

Today Thompsons is led by Stephen Cavalier and David Thompson, the grandson of its founder. They manage a team of lawyers in the service of the trade union movement, delivering on the principles and values that were so important to its founders.

Steve Allen is to be congratulated for this excellent book, which will remind young lawyers of the great tradition on which this modern firm is built; I am certain they will be proud of that tremendous heritage.

Tom Sawyer, August 2012

[Lord Sawyer of Darlington. Deputy General Secretary of NUPE from 1981 until the merger to become UNISON in 1994, and General Secretary of the Labour Party 1994 to 1998]

Glossary

Unions

ACAT	Association of Cinematograph Television and Allied Technicians; now part of BECTU.
AEU	The engineering union, now part of Unite. At various times following amalgamations the union was AUEW (which consisted of four sections: Engineering, Construction, Foundry and Technical); the AEEU, and Amicus.
Amicus	See AEU above. Amicus was formed on the amalgamation of the AEEU, and MSF, later joined by GPMU and UNIFI; now part of Unite.
APEX	Association of Professional Executive and Clerical Staff; became part of the GMB.
ASBSBSW	The boilermakers, shipwrights, blacksmiths and structural workers union. Subsequently joined the GMWU to form GMBATU; now part of the GMB.
ASLEF	The train drivers' union.
ASTMS	Association of Scientific and Managerial Staffs. Merged with TASS to become MSF, which subsequently became part of Amicus (now Unite).
ATL	Association of Teachers and Lecturers.
AUEW	See AEU.
AUT	The university teachers' union; now part of UCU.
BALPA	The airline pilots' union.
BECTU	Media and entertainment union.
CAWU	Clerical and Administrative Workers' Union; changed its name to APEX (now part of the GMB).
CEU	The construction union which became part of the AEU.
COHSE	Health service union, now part of UNISON.
CWU	The Communication Workers' Union.
EEPTU	The electrical and plumbers' union; merged with the AEU to become the AEEU.
FBU	The Fire Brigades' Union.
GMB	The general union; currently over 600,000 members.

GMBATU	Now part of the GMB.
GMWU	General workers union which joined ASBSBSW to form GMBATU; now part of the GMB.
GPMU	Paper and print union formed by a merger of SOGAT 82 and NGA; merged with Amicus (now Unite).
MSF	Formed as a result of merger of ASTMS and TASS. Subsequently merged with other unions to become Amicus. Now part of Unite.
NACODS	The mining union for colliery overmen, etc.
NATFHE	The college lecturers' union. Now part of UCU.
NUAAW	The agricultural workers' union which merged with the TGWU (now part of Unite).
NASUWT	The school teachers' union.
NGA	National Graphical Association. Merged with SOGAT 82 to become GPMU.
NIPSA	Northern Ireland Public Service Alliance.
NUCPS	Merged with Inland Revenue Staff Association to form PSTC; now part of PCS.
NUJ	National Union of Journalists.
NUM	National Union of Mineworkers.
NUPB & PW	Union of printers, bookbinders, machine rules and paper workers. Became part of SOGAT.
NUPE	National Union of Public Employees; now part of UNISON.
NUS	National Union of Seamen. Merged with National Union of Railwaymen to form RMT.
NUT	National Union of Teachers.
PCS	Public and Commercial Services Union; now has over 290,000 members. Formed as a result of merger of PSTC (Public Services, Tax and Commerce Union) and CPSA (Civil and Public Services Union).
RCM	The Royal College of Midwives.
RMT	Rail Maritime and Transport Union.
SCPS	Society of Public and Civil Servants; merged with the Inland Revenue Staff Association to form NUCPS; now part of PCS.
SOGAT	Society of Graphical and Allied Trades; print union which, as SOGAT 82, subsequently merged with NGA to form the GPMU, which itself later became part of Amicus (now Unite).

SDTU	Signs and Displays Union; merged with NATSOPA which itself merged with SOGAT in 1982 to become SOGAT 82 (and is now part of Unite).
SGA	Scottish Graphical Association. Merged with SOGAT to become SOGAT 75.
STUC	The Scottish TUC.
TASS	The draughtsmen's union. See ASTMS.
TGWU	Transport and General Workers' Union; now part of Unite.
TUC	Trades Union Congress.
UNISON	Public service workers union with over 1.3m members; formed by merger of NUPE, NALGO and COHSE.
UNITE	General union with 1.5m members formed by merger of Amicus and TGWU.
USDAW	Shop workers' union with over 400,000 members.
USBSSW	Union of Boilermakers Shipwrights and Structural Workers; became part of the ASBSBSW; now part of GMB.

Other

ACAS	Advisory Conciliation and Arbitration Service.
APIL	Association of Personal Injury Lawyers.
ATE	After the event insurance.
CAC	Central Arbitration Committee.
CB&E	Chronic bronchitis and emphysema.
CCFA	Collective Conditional Fee Agreement.
CFA	Conditional Fee Agreement.
CICA	Criminal Injuries Compensation Authority.
CICB	Criminal Injuries Compensation Board.
COSHH	Control of Substances Hazardous to Health Regulations 1988.
CP	Communist Party.
ECHR	European Court of Human Rights.
EMF	European Metalworkers Federation.
ET	Employment Tribunal.
EAT	Employment Appeal Tribunal.
HAVS	Hand arm vibration syndrome.
ILO	International Labour Organisation.
ILP	Independent Labour Party.
IRLR	Industrial Relations Law Reports.

IT	Industrial Tribunal.
NCCL	National Council for Civil Liberties, now Liberty.
NIRC	National Industrial Relations Court.
PI	Personal injury.
PTSD	Post traumatic stress disorder.
RCJ	Royal Courts of Justice.
TULRA	Trade Union and Labour Relations Act 1974.
TUPE	Transfer of Undertakings (Protection of Employment) Regulations 1981.
VWF	Vibration white finger.

Introduction
Fighting for Worker's Rights

A few years ago a colleague said to me that working for Thompsons was like playing for Manchester United – anywhere else would be a step down. Not a very apt comment to me as a committed and (at the time) long-suffering Manchester City fan, but I knew what he meant. I spent 32 years with the firm. It was a privilege.

After I left in 2004, I decided to see if I could write a pamphlet. In fact it turned into two pamphlets – one giving a brief account of the firm's history and one dealing with the firm's major cases. The intention was twofold: to produce something for the staff to fire their imagination about the firm they were working for, and for my own personal interest.

All this engaged the interest of the firm's management, and Laurie Flynn was asked to assist with the project. Laurie is a long time friend of the firm. Indeed, the firm acted for him when he was arrested during the Greek Embassy demonstrations in 1968. His father, Vincent, was General Secretary of the print union SOGAT. As time went on I found more and more material, and Laurie also carried out a great deal of research. The result is this book.

I make no claim to be a writer. On the other hand, Laurie is a first class writer and researcher (having worked on World in Action and produced several books and short films). I have therefore wherever possible simply stolen not only Laurie's research but his words as well. Some of the better sections of what follows in the section up to 1947 are Laurie's work, a typical example being the whole of Chapter 2, which consists of his interview of Gary Slapper.

Some of the story is a severely annotated account of

events; for example, the description of the Poplar Borough Council cases. Anyone who wants to read a full account should turn to Nora Branson's book *Poplarism 1919-1925* or the recently published account by Janine Booth, *Guilty and Proud of it!*

I have tried wherever possible to put the firm's cases into some sort of historical perspective, but to do justice to the subject would take many volumes. In any event, this account is not intended to be an academic treatise. It is a story of a firm and its founder and some of the major events and cases with which it has been involved.

For those readers who wish to read a longer version of some of the political cases of the 1920s and 30s, these are set out in Owen Parsons' account *W.H. Thompson and his Cases*, which again I have quoted from extensively.

In at least one respect this account is seriously deficient. It fails to give much in the way of first-hand accounts of the trade unions. The time and research needed was too great to do this aspect justice.

I am indebted for the help of many people who have given interviews or provided written accounts of their own time in the firm, and apologise to those I have failed to contact or track down. Inevitably a history of this nature is in the end nothing more than a personal perspective.

Much of the text was written in the two or three years up to 2010. Some legal points will already be out of date – inevitable in an account of this nature. Sadly, a number of those interviewed or are otherwise referred to have now passed away – most recently the Scottish firm's joint managing partner Frank Maguire.

Finally, I have taken the liberty of including a chapter on my own story, not because it has any greater intrinsic value than scores of others who have worked for the firm over the years, but because it is the one I know best; and I could not resist the temptation.   Steve Allen, November 2011

Chapter 1
Thompsons today

The Thompsons partnership was formed on 1 May 1996 with Geoff Shears and Frank Foy at the helm as joint managing partners, and the key role of chair of the policy group held by Robin Thompson's son David Thompson.

The firm had been on a long journey since its inception in 1921 by W.H. Thompson, through the early years of fighting for civil liberties and for health and safety at work together with compensation for the injured and bereaved. It had faced up to the death of WH in 1947, brought many test cases, particularly for asbestos injuries and chest diseases, undergone a major expansion becoming the biggest solicitors to the trade union movement with regional offices in the larger industrial conurbations before eventually splitting into two parts in 1974, led respectively by W.H.'s sons Robin and Brian.

During the following two decades the practices grew; and more test cases brought massive influxes of work. But by 1996 both Robin and Brian had retired and the practices merged, not as two component parts stuck back together again – the differences by then were too great – but as a new firm.

The new firm bears little resemblance to the one created in 1921 and which for a number of years had strong links to the Communist Party.

Over the years the firm became much more aligned with mainstream Labour values and, driven by the necessity to survive, more commercially focused.

By 1996 the economic and industrial landscape of the country had changed; and the trade unions, which provided the bulk of the firm's work, were having to adapt to maintain membership. Even professional firms were under pressure. The banks no longer saw them as blue chip clients to whom they could offer money without risk. Clients no longer saw lawyers as professionals who were always unquestionably right. Competition for work had taken on a new complexion, not least with the advent of claims companies; and computerisation was causing big changes in the way the work was done.

1996 was a new beginning.

The new firm adopted a structure which attempted to combine the ability to take action quickly and decisively whenever required with accountability through a policy group responsible for overseeing senior management.

The Senior Managing Partners set about professionalising the support services. IT and Finance Managers were appointed, along with Vineeta Kaura who, as Human Resources Manager, set about the task of updating all the firm's staffing policies, and indeed introducing policies such as appraisals that were long overdue. The staff union sought a grading structure to ensure consistency to all staff, and lengthy and productive negotiations were set in motion, aided by the good sense provided by Sean Keating from the GMB and the senior staff representative Mike Collier.

The administration system was reorganised. It was the era of management consultants and gurus of all descriptions, all recommending change, and Thompsons were by no means immune to this culture. In September 1999 the Policy Group was replaced by a new Partnership Board following a review of the governance structure facilitated by KPMG.

In 2001 the firm adopted a corporate style. The Senior Managing Partners' roles were redesignated as Chief Executive Officer and Chief Operating Officer, positions

THOMPSONS
SOLICITORS

PLEASE QUOTE
THIS REFERENCE

CONGRESS HOUSE
GREAT RUSSELL STREET
LONDON
WC1B 3LW

DX 157722 BLOOMSBURY

TEL 0171 637 9761
FAX 0171 637 0000

1st May 1996

Dear Steve,

Today is a significant day in the history of W.H. Thompson, Robin Thompson & Partners and Brian Thompson & Partners. From today we are officially one firm.

It is only through the commitment and dedication of every member of staff that we are now creating what will be the largest Plaintiff personal injury practice (and one of the largest law practices) in the UK. The firm will have over 800 staff, 14 offices in England and Wales and two associated offices in Scotland. As a combined firm, Thompsons has legal successes that are second to none.

As a memento of the creation of the firm of Thompsons, a commemorative mug has been produced. Every member of staff will be receiving one of these to mark the day.

Geoff Shears and Frank Foy have the responsibility for leading our firm into the future. I have no doubt that working together as a team and with your help, Thompsons will go from strength to strength. I am sure that we will be successful.

Best wishes.

DAVID THOMPSON

The letter sent to every member of staff of the new firm by David Thompson, grandson of the founder WH Thompson

Geoff Shears at the Thompsons' National Conference, March 2007

held by Geoff Shears and Frank Foy respectively, and Regional Managing Directors were appointed.

An Executive Board, responsible for all day-to-day control as well as policy making, was established. Lord Sawyer who had been General Secretary of the Labour Party took the position of Chairman of a newly constituted Supervisory Board (replacing the Partnership Board) in May 2001. It was the start of a process of recruiting onto the Board skilled professionals from outside the narrow legal world, and recognition of the benefits to be gained from a broader perspective.

When Frank Foy retired as a result of illness in 2002, and following a period of cover provided by Andrew Herbert,

Stephen Cavalier – Thompsons' Chief Executive, 2008

he was replaced by Phil Smith, with the writer also joining the Executive Board until May 2004.

By the summer of 2004 the Executive Board comprised Geoff as Chief Executive Officer (CEO), Phil Smith as Chief Operations Officer (COO), Carolyn Hurley as Chief Finance Officer (CFO), and Stephen Cavalier as Client Director.

On 30 August 2006 Geoff Shears announced that from 1 May 2007 he would take on the role of Executive Chair with responsibility for chairing the Supervisory Board and for senior union relationships, and that Stephen Cavalier would become CEO designate from 1 September 2006 and full CEO from 1 May 2007.

The stage was now set for a new generation. Under

Stephen Cavalier's leadership Joanna Stevens and Doug Christie joined the Executive Board, followed by David Stothard (as Phil Smith's replacement in 2009) as Operations Director. In 2008 and 2009 respectively the firm acquired Whittles and Rowley Ashworth, two other trade union law firms, and at the end of October 2009 Geoff left the partnership on a consultancy to set up a new international venture Unions Solidarity International. David Thompson, the grandson of the founder W.H., is now Chairman of the Supervisory Board.

Aside from the Executive and Supervisory Boards, each of the main offices is run by a branch manager, and the firm has a number of professional departments including HR, Training, IT, Accounts, etc.

The complexity of the work these days is such that all the lawyers specialise. The majority deal with personal injury work, but each region has a dedicated team of specialist employment rights unit lawyers (ERU) headed nationally by Victoria Phillips, and a specialist criminal team led by Paula Porter.

Other partners perform critical functions within the firm, for example in relation to case handling where Judith Gledhill is Head of Personal Injury.

Thompsons has never acted for employers or insurance companies and its commitment to the trades unions and their members remains the cornerstone of the reason for the firm's existence and renders the firm unique.

The writing of a history can deal only with the past. To that extent, the account of Thompsons as it is now is nothing but a snapshot of a moment in time.

Let us now go back and start the story of the founder of the firm W.H. (Harry) Thompson.

Chapter 2
The veins of greatness

In 2004 Times On Line asked Gary Slapper, Professor of Law at the Open University, to select a list of the ten greatest lawyers of all time. Nearly six decades after Thompson's death, Professor Slapper unhesitatingly excluded other far more famous names and put W.H. (Harry) Thompson on his list. He explained in interview with Laurie Flynn how he came to this decision.

It was an agonising task for me when *The Times* asked me to draw up a list of the top ten lawyers of all time for *Times On Line*. Some candidates were of course very obvious, well known people such as Nelson Mandela, Cicero, Helena Kennedy and Lord Denning.

Harry Thompson isn't famous or even widely recognised in his own profession. Yet he is such an important and influential figure and I view him as one of the greatest lawyers of all time.

For me what Harry Thompson contributes was a clear and most singular identification of the needs of a very large part of the British population – people whose concerns were either being ignored or systematically under-represented in our society. That group was the working population. If the law is to mean anything in relation to the claims it makes when it speaks with reverence of the rule of law and the promise of equality before the law then it must mean that the same rules apply to everyone across the whole of society.

People just will not voluntarily accept a legal system which preferentially favours a minority and which applies unfavourably to the majority because they are poor, powerless and unrepresented. But we know that the law is formed cumulatively over historical time, laid down in periods of huge inequality, during the reign of priests and kings, under the power of the landed aristocracy and later of the rising business class.

It is a definite historical truth that huge inequalities existed in the British legal system throughout the industrial revolution and that some of these inequalities still persist, albeit to a lesser degree. And the idea that the law has always been applied evenly in congruence with our highest ideals can readily be disproven by reference to the hundreds and hundreds of cases where the ordinary people who produce goods and services and teach and nurse had a much more perilous time than any other social group with the system of regulations known as law.

The people who managed and ran the legal system also added to the difficulties by a heady cocktail of decisions, repeatedly interpreting the law to the disadvantage of the majority of the population who worked in factories, mines and mills. But along then comes a man who is dedicated to making things altogether different and who, when he qualifies as a lawyer, insists on taking up important cases even when there is no economic gain for him.

When it comes to his reading of the law he insists on the most careful examination of the label on the outside of the tin and demands that the contents inside must begin to match those promises on the outside. In his professional life he persistently and repeatedly underlines just how important it is to realise these aspirations, these promises of justice for all in society. He defends lost causes, people attacked as subversives and insists that the law is applied to them in spite of all the pressures in the opposite direction. He does this in dark and difficult times and at great cost to himself.

This is a most singular contribution, the work of someone unusually principled who, in a social setting of extreme privilege which dominated the law, refused to go with the professional flow. In his conscientious objection and imprisonment during the first world war, in his support for the rights of women, the right to dissent and civil liberty which led him to help found the National Council for Civil Liberties, we see that this is a person who is marked by a distinctive political and philosophical stance; and who fully integrates his beliefs with his professional life as a lawyer, asking awkward questions in his legal practice and acting to change the law so that it assists in solving the problems, the real life struggles of the majority of the population.

Harry Thompson never set out to become a rich and important lawyer by tending to the legal needs of industrial and commercial tycoons, aristocrats and powerful political figures. Instead he sides with the disadvantaged – no easy thing to do in the nineteen twenties and thirties and not always easy even now. We now take it for granted in our society that everybody has equal rights to access and use the law, a huge step forward and one to which Thompson greatly contributed. Of course, Harry Thompson did not achieve this on his own – like every other decisive individual he built on the efforts of others who came before him and found colleagues and allies he could work with.

But before he came on the field of play the situation for those injured by accidents at work or crippled by industrial disease was no less than a disgrace. Compensation law had been partly reformed but belatedly, inadequately and at great human cost. What Thompson found was that the big players in the legal system, the judges and the influential advocates who worked for powerful defendant businesses strove to maintain narrow and restricted interpretations of the law so as to exclude whole classes of types of human suffering and injury caused by bad conditions at work.

In his professional life Thompson vindicated what were paper rights at best and took up cases that had never ever been argued or represented in the law courts and which were not therefore really worthy of the term `rights´ because they had never been materialised via the legal process. Anyone who does this was of great social and legal significance and deserves the widest recognition.

The truth about Harry Thompson is that there are few finer examples in British legal history of lawyers acting in this selfless way. He could so easily have used his qualities and talents in more conventional legal directions – to get more money and recognition, more apparent influence and power. But that was not his way. Instead he chose to act in a remarkable selfless way which we can only call heroic. The fact that he combined all he achieved within the law with other significant activities beyond its borders (while also productively deploying his professional knowledge in these areas) makes him an unusual man indeed.

We can say this quietly years after his death – we can see the veins of greatness in his hands.

By his efforts Harry Thompson changed the way British people and British society perceived the law. He seriously broadened the range of possibilities as to what could be done with and through the law. And he did something else too – he permanently expanded the conception of who could be in the law professionally so that it included whole groups who had never been represented before, women, working class boys, people from outside the elite, people from below.

Now that we can look back over the changes in Britain in the twentieth century and try to see how the law can help us in the future, this inspirational component is very important. By his life and work Harry Thompson had a major cascading effect inspiring people to work in the law and then to stretch themselves to take up difficult and innovative cases. By professional example Thompson personally cut a hefty swathe through the prejudice and conservatism of the law and enlarged the mental universe of a whole range of people in politics, in the unions and in the legal profession, including myself.

People he acted for, people he inspired became lawyers or legal executives, went on to write books or become campaigners. The second and third generation of such people may not always have heard much about him but they walk in his footsteps. Thompson was a visionary, but in my view one with an unusual practicality and sharpness of mind. That's why he belongs in the list of the top ten lawyers of all time.

TIMESONLINE

The greatest lawyers in history

Marcus Tullius Cicero
106-43BC
A lawyer widely respected for his philosophical writing, understanding of Greek philosophy and the structure that his analyses gave to Roman law. He viewed justice as the highest human virtue, and his work is a cornucopia of percipient observations about law. He was murdered as an opponent of Octavian.

Domitius Ulpianus
AD160-228
An outstandingly thoughtful jurist and prolific writer whose influence upon the theory and practice of law has been extensive. He forged the systematisation of rules, and the exposition of legal principles, in a way that has since shaped the law of more than 60 countries. When the Emperor Justinian published the unprecedented Digest of Roman Law in AD533, one third of it was extracts from Ulpianus' work.

Sir Thomas More
1477-1535
A barrister of Lincoln's Inn in the 16th century, and later Lord Chancellor. A very successful commercial lawyer, and legal writer. Perhaps best known for writing *Utopia* (Greek for nowhere) a marvellous book depicting a society that rules itself by reason,and in which there are no lawyers!

Louis Dembitz Brandeis
1856-1941
Deeply concerned with issues of social justice, and the originator of what became a ubiquitous form of legal argument, the "Brandeis brief". In a US Supreme Court case in 1907 about a state statute, Brandeis, who later became a Supreme Court judge, innovated a form of legislative interpretation by introducing social study reports to assist the court in construing the law.

Clarence Darrow
1857-1938
Celebrated American defence lawyer and formidable orator, committed to defending freedom of expression and opposing the death penalty. He defended war protesters charged with having violated sedition laws, and in 1925 defended John Scopes, a high school teacher who had broken state law by presenting the Darwinian theory of evolution. In 1926 he won an acquittal for a black family, that of Dr Ossian Sweet, who had resisted a savage racist mob trying to expel it from a white district in Detroit.

Mohandas Karamchand Gandhi
1869-1948
The world-famous advocate of non-violent social reform qualified as a barrister and joined Inner Temple, London. His practice flowered in South Africa and became more socially angled after he was asked to take off his turban in court. He refused. He was later imprisoned in South Africa and India for his activities. A superb exponent of the arts of negotiation and mediation.

William Henry Thompson
1885-1947

A solicitor from Preston, Lancashire, who qualified in 1908, was imprisoned as a conscientious objector, and became the country's leading expert on working people's compensation. A supporter of the suffragettes and co-founder of the National Council for Civil Liberties (now Liberty), he established a law firm in 1921 to act for workers. Today, Thompsons is the largest personal injury and employment rights firm in the UK with 50,000 cases being run at any time.

Lord Denning of Whitchurch
1899-1999

A man of monumental influence on the development of English law, both in its substance and style. His time at Oxford as a mathematical scholar was followed by legal study, and then a highly successful career as a barrister. During his forty years as a judge he reformed many areas of English law including the law of contract, of unmarried partners, and of judicial review. Not, though, an unblemished record of greatness as his views on racial issues were somewhat contentious.

Nelson Mandela
1918-

A Nobel Peace Prize-winner and former President of South Africa who has helped to shape modem history. He was the only black student in his law faculty. He set up his own practice in 1952 and acted for clients who were victims of apartheid. He insisted on using the "whites only" entrance to courts, and campaigned relentlessly for an end to apartheid. He successfully resisted an attempt by the Transvaal Law Society to have him struck off the rolls of attorneys.

Helena Kennedy, QC
1950-

Baroness Kennedy of the Shaws, ennobled in 1997, was called to the Bar at Gray's Inn in 1972 and took silk in 1991. Her juridical prowess has been combined with a breathtaking range of book writing, and legal campaigning on behalf of women, children, crime victims and other groups. The benefits of her technical legal accomplishments ramify into many areas through work as varied as being chairwoman of the British Council, and chairwoman of the Human Genetics Commission.

Professor Gary Slapper is Director of the Centre for Law at The Open University

W.H. Thompson
*the original photograph is inscribed
'Before he went to Prison'*

Chapter 3
Birth and background

William Henry Thompson, known to his friends and family as 'Harry', was born on 15 October 1885 in Preston, the younger son of a family of five daughters and two sons.

His father, also William Henry Thompson (c.1830-1904) was born out of wedlock to a woman with the surname Martin. Family members have speculated that the father could have been the half-brother of another gifted dreamer, the English poet Francis Thompson. William Henry Thompson, Harry's father, ran a wholesale grocery business in Preston, although it is said that he neglected this in favour of the Methodist Sunday School to which he was devoted.

After his first wife died in childbirth, William Henry Thompson senior married Martha Thompson (confusingly, Thompson was her maiden name as well as her married name). They had seven children: Florence (1876-1939), Sally (1877-1892), Constance (1878-1946), Kate (1880-1953), John (1883-1939), William Henry 'Harry', and Madge (1887-1965).

Constance, one of Harry's older sisters, married Percy Taylor, a wealthy second-generation Preston cotton merchant who, together with his father, ran James Taylor and Sons, a company with offices in Manchester and a prosperous business selling finished cotton goods primarily to India. One of their children, and therefore Harry Thompson's nephew, was the historian A.J.P. Taylor.

Harry's father was a 'pro-Boer' during the Boer War – a sign of radical views.

Professor Chris Wrigley in his book *A.J.P. Taylor – Radical Historian of Europe*, published in October, 2006 notes:

... Martha was the daughter of John Thompson, who as a boy had walked with his mother from Brampton, Cumberland, to Preston. He had been a handloom weaver and then an owner of several handlooms, selling out as handloom weaving collapsed in the face of steam-powered factory production. He became a miller, making much money from grain. He married a Sumner from Blackburn and they had three boys (John, William and Joseph) and two girls (Martha and Matilda, `Taidy´). He established his family as among the wealthiest in Preston. When he died, his widow, according to Alan Taylor, was the only one in their area, Ashton on Ribble, ´who kept her own carriage ... in which she drove out every afternoon`. John Thompson was also radical, at least when young ... . In turn his eldest son, John, was also radical, working as a journalist on the Preston Herald, in which he denounced the Anti-Corn Law League. The other sons, William and Joseph, were very successful solicitors.

Chris Wrigley continues:

Martha was the toughest of the Thompsons. Her three brothers ruined their health by excessive drinking, John apparently dying young in the Preston workhouse hospital. Martha and her children were vehemently anti-alcohol and had in them a stern streak of Puritanism. One niece recalled of Harry Thompson and another of his nieces, "Puritanical in the extreme Thompson way, he once washed the make-up off Joy's face. She was eighteen at the time". Alan Taylor recalled Martha as "a hard woman ... a terrible woman". She was the only person who struck fear into Harry.

The Thompsons lived at 27 Beech Grove, Preston. On the death of her husband in 1904, Martha lived with her eldest daughter, Florence, in Blackton Road, Preston, and money was very tight. Martha Thompson's second and third brothers, Harry's uncles, Joseph and William were both successful solicitors. According to Alan Taylor, as recounted by Chris Wrigley:

… to be a solicitor in Preston was to put you up in the society of the Earls of Derby and people like that. If you go back to the eighteenth century you'll find that the two Members [of Parliament for Preston], one was always a Stanley, and the other was always a Fazackerley, who were hereditary solicitors …
[The Fazackerleys] handled all those north Lancashire, Roman Catholic landowners of the eighteenth century … They were … the Derby's solicitors, they handled people like the Welds and the Blundells who owned all the land of North Lancashire.
… The Thompsons, because of the two uncles, belonged to this different society.

Harry (arrowed) with classmates at school in Preston and at home

A.J.P. Taylor in his autobiography *A Personal History* comments that W.H. 'Harry' was 'the cleverest of the lot' and according to his brother John, he gave up cricket because he could not bat all the time. He played billiards, tennis and bridge supremely well and when he was winning, as he nearly always was, kept up a jeering commentary on the mistakes of his opponents.

Harry attended Preston Grammar School along with his brother John. According to Ruth McInroy, daughter of his youngest sister Madge, Harry was supposed, in his youth, to be 'not very strong', and accordingly got away with murder, behaving very badly at school. The punishment for such behaviour was caning. John, aware of his mother's fondness for Harry, used to go to the headmaster. 'I'll take the cane for Thompson H.' This seemed to be acceptable for all parties!

Percy Taylor, Connie's husband was not only a wealthy businessman but one of Lancashire's most committed socialist pioneers. A staunch supporter of the newly founded Independent Labour Party, Taylor was a close personal friend of George Lansbury. Years later, after he moved to London, Harry Thompson would work especially closely with Lansbury and act as the legal adviser and solicitor to Poplar Borough Council (which Lansbury led). It seems highly likely that Lansbury first met Harry Thompson on one of his many visits to Preston to discuss with his friends Percy and Connie Taylor how best to spread the word about 'Socialism – the hope of the world' in Lancashire.

Percy Taylor helped to provide for Martha after 1904, and when Martha died in 1921 provided a generous lump sum for Florence. Martha had also benefited from the early death of her brother Joseph, the Preston solicitor, who had no heir and left her all his money.

Again funded by Connie's husband Percy, on completing his education at Preston Grammar School,

Harry commenced his training as a solicitor in an old Preston firm, William Bramwell & Co in June 1902. Harry later repaid the kindness to his sister Connie and his brother-in-law by taking on their son Alan Taylor to train as a solicitor. But Alan Taylor had another profession in mind and broke his indentures to become a historian teaching at Manchester University and then at Oxford, and presenting radio and television programmes and writing highly regarded and sometimes best-selling books.

Alan Taylor, it is clear, shared a good many of his uncle Harry's radical views, later playing a particularly decisive part in opposing the arms race in the 1960s by helping to found and develop the Campaign for Nuclear Disarmament into a mass movement.

Professor Wrigley's biography also contains some further clues about the strong radical tradition the Taylors and Thompsons forged over generations. One ancestor came from an old Quaker family (with levelling traditions going back to the English civil war) and took the persistent denial of his democratic rights seriously enough to demonstrate at Peterloo. The unfortunate man was killed outright when troops attacked the demonstrators (a massacre commemorated by Percy Shelley in *The Mask of Anarchy*). Another relative was one of the radical voters actually on the electoral roll at Preston who voted for Henry 'Orator' Hunt, a persistent and inspiring nineteenth advocate of peoples' rights.

The Preston where Harry Thompson grew up was in the middle of a social explosion with the emergence in Lancashire of the first industrial society anywhere in the world. How would it have seemed to a young man growing up in the area, particularly one from a family with such dissenting, radical views?

Fortunately, we can picture the times and something of the feelings of the local people through an outstanding recent book – Charles Nevin's *Lancashire – where women die of love*. In it, Nevin paints an affectionate and respectful picture of Lancashire people and the conditions in which they made their lives. But he doesn't pull his punches. Sensitive to issues of injustice and equality, he forcefully describes the shaming conditions and inhumanity on which the fortunes of the rich and the misfortunes of the poor were founded. Particularly haunting is a one paragraph reminder of an 1847 demonstration of factory children marching for the ten hours bill.

During the march they carried with them some examples of the techniques of factory discipline applied to them on a daily basis as part of their normal conditions of work. These included an overseer's whip and a thonged strap with which they were beaten if they dared to falter or fall asleep during their fourteen hour working day.

Above them as they marched they also carried a banner: 'Behold and Weep'.

Robert Owen's son Robert Dale Owen recorded his reaction to local conditions in his autobiography *Threading my Way*:

The facts we collected seemed to me terrible almost beyond belief ... in all the cotton factories they breathed an atmosphere more or less injurious to the lungs because of the dust.

We found that greed had driven the mill owners to still greater excesses of inhumanity utterly disgusting to a civilised nation.

Following a bitter strike in Preston, another man with an open mind and clear eyesight visited Preston and decided to set a novel there. Charles Dickens called Preston 'Coketown' and named his novel *Hard Times*. In drawing his portrait Dickens described the town carefully and

Above: *Women weavers in Preston, who have decorated their shed for Christmas.* Below: *Workers in a Preston cotton mill, winding twist and ring spinning*

created memorable characters to embody the cruelty of those who piled up wealth at the expense of others.

We cannot be certain that Harry Thompson read *Hard*

Times. But it seems very likely that he did. Certainly he devoted the curve of his life to those who suffered (like Stephen Blackpool in the novel), taking on individual cases and later working for the Kent miners and the Miners Federation. And although he left Preston to pursue his profession, first in the Potteries and then in London, he clearly never forgot what he had seen with his own eyes and heard with his own ears as a young man in radical company. And we do know that Thompson maintained a lifelong interest in mining injuries and disease and in the scandal of silicosis. His evidence to a Royal Commission in 1939 strongly features these injustices as does one of his very last speeches before he died, given to an Amalgamated Engineering Union conference in Holborn in 1947.

When, later, building up his own firm, Thompson seems likely to have been setting out quite consciously to build a counterveiling power to the amalgam of greedy manufacturers, engineering bosses, pit owners and insurance companies who by their carelessness and greed inflicted such grievous wounds on other people. Dickens pilloried them in his magazine *Household Words*, calling them the National Union for the Mangling of Operatives. Like Dickens, Harry Thompson found their values repellent and wanted to put a spoke in their wheel and change the way they conducted commerce.

Harry Thompson began his legal career with William Bramwell & Co., Solicitors, of Preston. He was articled for a period of five years from 4 June 1902 (aged just 16) to Mr Bramwell and completed his final examinations in June 1907. The firm Bramwells carried on trading for decades, latterly as Wharton Bramwells.

Life as an articled clerk (a trainee solicitor) was sufficiently leisurely for Harry to play billiards most afternoons. Brian Thompson his younger son, later recalled the story that his father had fallen out at some point with his principals and started playing billiards in the mornings as well and that Harry's mother had to patch up the quarrel!

After qualifying as a solicitor he received his first practising certificate on 16 November 1909 and practised in Longton, Staffordshire. Law Society records indicate that he practised alone, and Kelly's Directory for 1916 lists W.H. Thompson, Solicitor, at Market Street, Longton. The reason for moving to the Potteries is not known, but it was during this period that Harry Thompson gained his introduction to trade union work through John Ward, the one-time Social Democratic Federation and Independent Labour activist who later became Liberal MP for Stoke-on-Trent. Ward was General Secretary of the Navvies, Bricklayers and General Labourers' Union whose early record of militancy subsequently disappeared when he became a colonel in the British Army during the First World War and an aggressive opponent of Bolshevism. The union disintegrated in the 1920s.

It was a time of the growth of the Labour movement, which saw the formation of the Independent Labour Party and the Marxist Social–Democrat Federation along with great political and social upheavals, an explosion in literature as well as a significant increase in industrial unrest. Real wages of the working class had doubled over the last half of the nineteenth century (although 25 per cent of the population still lived at or below the poverty line) but had started to decline in the first decade of the twentieth. Workers sought to regain lost ground and the new unions began to expand. The years from 1911 to 1914 were a period of exceptional industrial militancy. Tom Mann launched a journal in 1910 called the Industrial Syndicalist which called for organisation across economic sectors and promoted direct action. But the biggest upheaval of all was just around the corner: the Great War.

W.H.T. posing for this photograph in a Sergeant's uniform, holding his prison mug and an unidentified document

Chapter 4
Conscience and convictions – the lawyer as prisoner of war

The great mass of peaceful citizens never want a war. It is thrust upon them willy nilly by powers whom they cannot even identify. Somewhere, somehow, someone presses the button and carnage begins: journalist Alexander Thompson writing in the *Clarion*.

What does the responsible citizen do when faced with an unjust and probably illegal war? And what if the citizen is a lawyer with special obligations to protect the public interest by upholding hard won freedoms enshrined in law? What does he or she do in 1916 say, when the rachet is tightened further still with the introduction of forcible conscription for all adult males fit for military service?

That was the precise dilemma that Harry Thompson faced only six years after he qualified as a solicitor when he was called up for military service. He refused to be conscripted and spent the next two years in various prisons as an absolutist (an out-and-out conscientious objector who declined to help with the war effort or cooperate with the authorities in any way).

The pressure ranged against the people who stood out against the 'war to end war' was way beyond extreme. Denounced from pulpits every week and attacked on a daily basis by the Northcliffe press, the atmosphere of jingoistic warmongering is difficult to capture ninety years later. But it ranged from menacing white feathers in the post to repeated physical attacks on those who dared to dissent and call for something other than the brutality of war as a way of solving conflict. In Britain, 16,000 conscientious objectors upheld the right of the citizen not to kill other human beings and to live in accord with their deep seated beliefs – whatever the consequences. Between the people in jail and their supporters on the outside they worked to break the spell of militarism. The young lawyer Harry Thompson was among them.

The historian A.J.P Taylor remembers his uncle arriving by motorbike from Longton in 1916. 'I heard this one phrase', Taylor recalled. 'I'm not going'.

Compulsory military service had just been introduced for single men under the provisions of the Military Service Act, 1916, nicknamed the 'Batchelor's Bill' because to start with conscription only included unmarried men between 18 and 41. (This was extended in May 1916 to include married men, and again in April 1918 to include all men up to 51). According to A.J.P. Taylor, Harry was among the first conscientious objectors. He applied for unconditional exemption, was refused and was drafted into the Royal Northern Staffordshire regiment. There he refused to obey an order and was put in the guardroom at Lichfield. He was sentenced to six months' imprisonment, then back to the guardroom and another six months' sentence. In 1917 he got two years.

One of Thompson's supporters on the outside was his sister Connie, Alan's mother.

With the introduction of conscription in 1916 Connie Taylor became vigorously anti-war and in favour of those who opposed continuing it. A.J.P. Taylor commented:

Here was a new and more exciting opening for my mother's romantic disposition. She became Harry's devoted supporter. Whenever he was in the guardroom, which happened for quite a long period between each court martial, she moved to a hotel in Lichfield and supplied Harry's needs for food and newspapers. Once he was in prison, first at Durham and

Army Form W. 3236.

NOTICE PAPER to be sent to men who belong to the **Army Reserve** under the provisions of the Military Service Act, 1916.

[In accordance with the provisions of Section 24 (2) of the Reserve Forces Act, 1882, " evidence of the delivery at the last registered place of abode of a man belonging to the Army Reserve of a Notice, or of a letter addressed to such man, and containing a notice, shall be evidence that such Notice was brought to the knowledge of such man."]

Surname _Thompson_   No. in Milty. Register (A. B. 414) _100_

Christian Name _Lo. H._

Address _The Hollies, Beurton, Stoke on Trent_   Class Number _12_

You are hereby warned that you will be required to join for service with the colours on the _24 July_ 1916.

You should therefore present yourself at _____ RECRUITING OFFICER, STOKE-ON-TRENT._

on the above date, not later than _8/30_ o'clock, bringing this paper with you.

~~A Railway Warrant is enclosed herewith.~~*

* This will be struck out if the man resides within 5 miles of the place at which he is required to present himself.

G. W. Dutton Signature.
_11 · 7 · 16_ Date.   _Major_ Rank.
Stoke on Trent Place.   Appointment.

N.B.—Particular attention is called to Section 15 of the Reserve Forces Act, 1882, which provides that where a man belonging to the Army Reserve is called out on Permanent service, and such man, without leave lawfully granted or such sickness or other reasonable excuse as may be allowed in the prescribed manner, fails to appear at any time and place at which he is required on such calling out to attend, he shall be guilty, according to the circumstances, of deserting within the meaning of Section 12, or of absenting himself without leave within the meaning of Section 15 of the Army Act, 1881.

(4275 Wt. W1321/M476 (E. 49) 1mm. McA. & W. 5/16 (P765/2) Forms/W. 3236/2

The paper that started it all: Harry Thompson's call-up

then at Newcastle-on-Tyne, she went there also. Harry, being a lawyer, understood his rights and soon established an ascendancy over the prison governor, who was not used to dealing with educated men. Harry also grasped which warders were venal and put them in touch with my mother, who ran a supply of food, cigarettes and newspapers into the prison. It was almost a fulltime occupation. The governor left well alone, and Harry had a pretty comfortable time.

Chris Wrigley gives a rather different view on what W.H.'s time inside would have been like:

… As an absolutist he was treated badly. He was among those sent to Wakefield Prison for the `Wakefield experiment´ of offering `absolutists´ better conditions in return for less intransigent attitudes to cooperation. Harry Thompson was one of an advisory committee…which organised the absolutists … and rejected the Home Office's proposals for them.

There is little doubt that conditions and food would have been atrocious. Inside the jails there were all sorts of ploys to break the spirit of the "conchies" – isolation, the imposition of silence rules, masking of prisoners so they would not recognise one another in the exercise yards to which they were very infrequently taken (sometimes as seldom as once a month).

The best account is probably given in *Conscription and Conscience: a history 1916-1919* by J.W. Graham, published in 1922:

A last trial came to some of the Absolutists in September 1918 when most of them had been in prison for two years or more.

The Government, under growing pressure from the leaders of thought in the country, realised that those who spoke for the national conscience were being rendered increasingly unhappy by the persistence of the imprisonment of the sufferers for conscience' sake, and decided to ease matters for those who had actually served over two years' hard labour.

Men were quietly transferred to the gaol at Wakefield from other gaols all over the country. A well-informed contributor to the Manchester Guardian of September 27 continues the story:

`The early arrivals discovered the hesitation in the mind of the Home Office. While they were congregating, under escort, from the four corners of the land, the Home Office was still wondering what it should do. They descended on a gaol which was not ready to receive them, and which, when it had taken them in did not know, in the absence of instructions, how to treat them. But there was food and shelter, and assured of these necessities, the inmates began to organise the life of the place according to a model of their own. The Governor of the gaol, having no instructions, had to let them do pretty much as they liked.

The staff of warders numbered less than a dozen; the prisoners were counted by scores. The locks which were taken off the cell doors when the other conscientious objectors, those who had accepted the Home Office scheme, were in the gaol as a work centre, have not been replaced; and their successors, within the limits of the high boundary walls, have so far been free to do pretty much as they have wanted. They have appointed an advisory committee, with Councillor Walter Ayles of Bristol for its chairman, and P.T. Davies for its secretary; Scott Duckers of London, W.H.Thompson (a North Staffordshire solicitor), and Mr T.W.H. Sara (a social lecturer) are among its members.

There is a house sub-committee, which details the men required to do each days' cooking and the rest of the kitchen work. The warder in charge is `permitted to help´ (I was told) if he likes. There is also a labour sub-committee, which arranges for the cleaning and tidying of the cells. The prisoners, by the bye, call the lockless cells their private rooms. They have only once been in conflict with the prison authorities. This was last Tuesday when the Governor proposed to give them tasks. They refused to perform them, and when no punishment followed they learned that the Home Office had left him without instructions.

Finally the instructions were communicated to the

prisoners at a mass meeting. It would seem that, as a matter of convenience, or perhaps expediency, the prisoners' organisation has a certain amount of `recognition´. The Governor, at any rate, asked Mr Ayles to make known the Home Office intentions. The Home Office evidently hopes that the Absolutists, now that they are all together and fortified by each others' companionship, will undertake to do work at Wakefield which they have refused to do for two years past when left to their individual resolution.

The Home Office `terms´ are that the Absolutists should work with regularity and diligence, and then, in addition to concessions regarding correspondence and visitors, they will be allowed three-pence a day and the opportunity to spend these three-pences (but no more) at a prison canteen, which will be sanctioned if they run it themselves. The work expected of them was not specified in the communication. The making of mailbags is a customary prison employment, and Wakefield gaol has a small foundry, and it used also to have a ropewalk.

The Wakefield experiment did not quite have the intended effect. Instead it resulted in a historic declaration of absolute non-cooperation with the war, a declaration which Harry Thompson as one of the elected committee members would surely have had at least a part in drafting. As always, the prisoners showed that they were not out for easy terms or for personal relief, however great might be the temptation to worn and partially broken men, but that they were determined to maintain their testimony to the end. Their statement ran as follows:

H.M. Prison, Wakefield
In view of the great misunderstanding and misrepresentation concerning the principles of the Absolutist conscientious objectors, we issue the following brief statement:-

1. Our vital principle as Absolutists is not a refusal to serve our community. It is that we cannot accept either military service or any compulsory work organised to facilitate the prosecution of the war
2. Therefore we cannot accept any scheme of work involving our actual or implied consent to the carrying out of any such purpose
3. We are faced with a situation, submission to which may involve the complete denial of our principles, by implicitly introducing an element of voluntary or semi-voluntary co-operation on our part
4. It appears that the Government still misunderstand our principles, in that they take for granted that any safe or easy conditions can meet the imperative demands of our conscience. No offer of schemes or concessions can do this. We stand for the inviolable rights of conscience in the affairs of life. We ask for liberty to serve, and if necessary to suffer, for the community and its well-being. As long as the Government deny us this right, we can only take with cheerfulness and unmistakable determination whatever penalties are imposed upon us. We want no concessions. We desire only the liberty to serve.

Signed on behalf of the Absolutists in Wakefield Prison, Walter H. Ayles, Chairman; P.T. Davies, General Secretary; W.H. Thompson, Eric P. Southall, Henry Sara, J. Scott Duckers, Geo. Horwill, Members of the Advisory Committee.

September 14, 1918.

J.W. Graham comments that

tens of thousands of copies of this manifesto, written by men with no prospect of release before them, were circulated by the No-Conscription Fellowship. It was thus clearer than ever that no plan of concessions would meet the case. These unconquerable men were then returned to their prisons to continue their sentences.

The No-Conscription Fellowship was founded by ILP socialists and Quakers with a parallel tradition of resisting militarism and defending liberty.

They produced a leaflet which called for the repeal of the Act and condemned Parliament for imposing conscription, arguing that it violated hard-won liberties, involved the subordination of civil liberties to military dictation, imperilled the freedom of individual conscience and established 'militarism which menaces all social graces and divides the people of all nations'.

The men who signed the leaflet were Clifford Allen, Edward Grubb, A. Fenner Brockway, W.J Chamberlain, W.H. Ayles, Morgan Jones, A. Barrett Brown, John Fletcher, C.H. Norman and Rev. Leyton Richards. All were charged under the Defence of the Realm Act. They were all fined. Those that refused to pay the fine were sent to prison.

So poor were the conditions in British prisons and so fierce the attack upon the objectors that seventy of them died in prison. Others were cruelly marked for life with illness and disease. Some were taken secretly to France by rail with the clear intention of murdering them by extra judicial torture and execution. After this early form of what some now call 'extraordinary rendition' they were to be forced on to the field of battle, the idea being to order them to fight. Then when they refused to do so, as everybody knew they surely would, they were to be executed – by firing squad.

This official war crime was, it seems, only narrowly averted when a train carrying a batch of men destined for France passed through a busy London suburb and one of the prisoners succeeded in throwing a written message into the crowd. The No-Conscription Fellowship was alerted immediately and acted directly to bring massive legal and political pressure on the government to avoid this outrage.

What was the philosophical basis to Harry Thompson's refusal to serve in the First World War? Owen Parsons, who worked with him from 1935 to 1946, gives his opinion:

He was not…a pacifist. Some wars were justified, including the war against Hitler or revolutionary wars of national liberation or social revolt …'It was the wrong kind of war', he said of the 1914 war … . He had a conscientious objection to engaging in a war for the defence of British imperialist interests, his objection was essentially political. But actually his objection went a good deal further than that. He did not like being pushed around; he liked, indeed demanded, the right to make his own decisions; scarcely the attitude of a good soldier. I think on that account he would have been a conscientious objector even in the anti-Hitler war and would not have been recruited in the I.R.A. in 1916 or the Soviet rebel forces in 1917. In exactly the same way as he would have refused a Labour Party whip if he had been a Labour Member of Parliament, so he would have refused to accept orders from others – especially on so crucial a matter of killing people – even in a good cause. To some extent the `wrongness´ of the war concerned was merely a supplementary justification to his basic objection to being ordered about and being pushed around. I argued that he got pushed around and ordered about in prison but he contended that this was quite different. 'In the army I would have been a willing obeyor, in prison I and everyone else obeyed because we had to and anyhow the orders were different. It's very different being ordered to kill someone and being ordered to put your slops out.'

W.H. Thompson was released from prison in April 1919.

According to Alan Taylor, in the summer of 1919 the Taylors gave holidays at their rented holiday house in Hawkshead to a stream of conscientious objectors newly released from

The original photo is inscribed 'ex prisoners 1919 Jordans'

The postcard below is of Old Jordans hostel. On the reverse is the list of those attending 25 -29 July 1919

prison and selected by Harry Thompson. It appears that a number of them also gathered for a few days at Old Jordans Hostel, a hostelry with strong Quaker links at Beaconsfield. The list, written by Joan Beauchamp (who later married

*Joan Beauchamp's list of attendees at Old Jordan's Hostel
25 -29 July 1919*

Harry Thompson) of those who attended at the hostel in July 1919 is worth examining.

It includes *Fenner Brockway*, who became editor of Labour Elector in 1913 at the age of 25 and formed, with his pacifist friend Clifford Allen, the No-Conscription Fellowship in 1914. Brockway served several spells in prison, including one period in the Tower of London. After the war he campaigned for Indian independence as organiser of the India League and during the General Strike in 1926 was editor of the *British Worker*, the TUC newspaper. He was elected to Parliament as successful Labour Party candidate at East Leyton in 1929, but lost his seat in the 1931 election having opposed the formation of the National Government. Brockway and the ILP disaffiliated from the Labour Party at this time and did not rejoin until 1950 when he was elected as MP at Eton and Slough, becoming a member of the Tribune Group led by Nye Bevan.

Brockway disagreed with Bevan on the issue of nuclear weapons and in 1958 joined with Bertrand Russell, Victor Gollancz, J.B. Priestley, Canon John Collins and Michael Foot to form the Campaign for Nuclear Disarmament (CND). He lost his seat in 1964 but subsequently became a life peer. He was chairman at one time for the Movement for Colonial Freedom (with which Joan's sister Kay was also closely involved), and of the World Disarmament Campaign from 1979 to 1990. He was a prolific author of books on politics before his death in 1988 a few months before his 100th birthday.

One of his books was *Bermondsey Story: the Life of Alfred Salter*. *Alfred Salter* was another attendee at Jordans Hostel, according to Joan's list, along with his wife *Ada Salter*. Alfred studied medicine at Guy's Hospital and set up in practice in Bermondsey in 1900. He and his wife Ada became involved in local government and politics in an attempt to improve conditions for the poor in the area. Alfred became Bermondsey's MP in 1922 as a member of the Independent Labour Party. Ada became the first woman councillor in 1910 and Mayor of Bermondsey in 1922. They were Quakers and dedicated their lives to the poor. The

Quaker newspaper *The Friend* notes:

Alfred Salter, a brilliant student and researcher, could have achieved wealth and eminence in his profession; instead he chose to serve as a GP and later MP for Bermondsey. Ada, who loved the countryside, remained in the city, becoming the first woman councillor and woman mayor in London and the first Labour mayor in Britain.

Their names and memories live on in the annual Salter lecture sponsored by the Quaker Socialist Society, in the family statue near the Angel Inn, the flower garden in Southwark Park (named after Ada) and the 'Salter Cottages' – various streets built in 1928 as one of the first attempts in London to provide municipal housing in a garden village form.

Similarly Morgan Jones Park in Nantgarw Road, Caerphilly is dedicated to the memory of the man who was Rhymney Valley's most notable conscientious objector. *Morgan Jones* was the first conscientious objector to be returned to parliament after the war, later becoming the Labour Party's expert on education. There are a number of photographic portraits of him held at the National Gallery.

Another remarkable person present at Jordans was *Clifford Allen*. Born in Newport, South Wales in 1889 and the son of a drapery merchant, he attended university at Bristol and won a scholarship to Cambridge where he was elected president of the Fabian Society. On leaving Cambridge he was employed as a manager of the first Labour Party daily newspaper, the *Daily Citizen* and became close friends with Ramsay MacDonald. When war was declared, Allen joined with Fenner Brockway to form the No-Conscription Fellowship.

Allen suffered badly in prison and contracted tuberculosis; he was released, close to death, in December

1917, but lost the use of a lung and was thereafter dogged by ill health, declining a safe seat in the Gorbals as Independent Labour Party candidate as a result. He produced various ILP policy documents and pamphlets, was made a life peer and supported Ramsay MacDonald in 1931, an act seen as a betrayal of socialism by some. He subsequently tried, unsuccessfully, to form his own political organisation, The Next Five Years Group. He died in a Swiss sanatorium in 1939 aged 49.

Yet another there with a fascinating history was *Francis Meynell*, the publisher, poet and typographer. He may not have had a park named after him, but he did receive a knighthood. Meynell began his career in his father's publishing house, in 1916 helped to found the Pelican Press and then in 1923 founded the Nonesuch Press, which designed and published 140 fine editions of poetry and literature. It is noteworthy that in 1926 when Harry Thompson responded to the miners' union call for help in relation to Noah Ablett he did so on Nonesuch Press notepaper. Meynell was also typographer and designer of George Lansbury's Daily Herald when it was launched.

Other attendees included *Hubert Peet*, Editor of The Friend, the Quaker publication, *Scott Duckers*, a solicitor with whom Thompson was to go into partnership on moving to London in 1919, C.H. Norman, author of publications such as *Empire and Murder* (1906) and *Our Factory Workers: the conditions under which they work* (1907), and *W.H. Ayles*. Ayles, like Norman (and Morgan Jones) was one of the committee of the No-Conscription Fellowship. He was chairman of the Absolutist committee in Wakefield prison which drafted the famous resolution quoted above. He subsequently became MP for Southall from 1945 to 1950 and for Hayes and Harlington from 1950 to 1953. His memory is also graced by portraits in the National Gallery.

The list also includes Joan Beauchamp's close friend

Lydia Smith, who helped her to keep the Fellowship's publication *The Tribunal* going when the authorities were making desperate attempts to close it down. Lydia's husband Percy was a well-known artist who exhibited frequently at the Royal Academy.

The Jordans Hostel photograph shows a group of people enjoying a few summer days relaxation. But it was a most remarkable group of people who had not only been united in fighting against the injustice of war and were prepared to go to jail for their convictions, but also included many who were to go on and play an important role in the public life and politics of the next era.

Joan Beauchamp (c.1920)

Chapter 5
Joan Beauchamp

Whilst he was in prison Harry Thompson began corresponding with his future wife, the remarkable Joan Beauchamp, a valued member of the head office staff of the No-Conscription Fellowship.

Joan, born on 8 November 1890, was brought up in Somerset. Her paternal ancestors were farmers, landlords and coal owners, Anglican in religion and Conservative in politics. Joan was one of seven children, but two brothers died in infancy.

Joan entered London University in 1908 to study at the Royal Holloway College, and was almost immediately caught up in the movement for women's suffrage. It is believed that she became a member of Charlotte Despard's Women's Freedom League, and worked with Sylvia Pankhurst in the Women's Suffrage Federation. Many of the suffragettes were politically right wing and Joan soon parted company with them as a result. She was a keen supporter of the socialist press and in particular the *Daily Herald*, then edited by George Lansbury. She strongly opposed the government in the 1914-1918 war, playing a leading part as parliamentary secretary in the No-Conscription Fellowship.

The Fellowship published a monthly journal *The Tribunal* which gave factual accounts of proceedings involving conscientious objectors before tribunals, courts martial, as well as questions and answers in parliament on relevant issues etc. It was not popular with the authorities who attempted to stifle any expression of dissent by making arrests under the so called Defence of the Realm Act for alleged "illegal" and "seditious" material before leaflets had been printed or dispatched. An article by Bertrand Russell in 1918 brought him six months' imprisonment and a heavy fine for Joan Beauchamp as publisher. She refused to pay it and was imprisoned for a month.

More harassment followed, printing machinery was located and smashed up by the police and a cat and mouse game developed with Joan assuming sole responsibility for the printing and publication whilst the new location of the printing remained secret. Joan became an expert at printing in secret, lying low for days in the obscure premises she identified and equipped. Eventually, fresh charges were brought and Joan was convicted and sentenced to three weeks in gaol in 1920. W.H. Thompson, by then of course on the outside, was heavily involved in the campaign to have her released, along with George Lansbury. The campaign was successful and Joan was released after eight days.

After a short period teaching and travelling in Italy, Joan returned to London, joining the Communist Party at its formation in 1920 as one of the Guild Communist Group, a group which included Walter Holmes, Robin Page Arnot, William Mellor, W.N. Ewer, and Ellen Wilkinson. She became secretary of the Trinity Trust in 1921 and first business manager of its publication *Labour Monthly*.

Harry and Joan married on 1 August 1921 at the Quaker Meeting House in Hampstead and had two sons, Robin born on 15 September 1924 and Brian on 13 April 1926. After Harry's death in 1947 and studies to qualify as solicitors, the sons took over the firm.

Joan remained heavily involved in political organisations, mostly those controlled directly by the Communist Party, and through the 1930s gave most of her time to the Labour Research department where she not only produced a number of books – *Agriculture in Soviet Russia* (1931), published by Victor Gollancz, *British Imperialism in India* (1934), published by Martin Lawrence, and *Women*

THE TRIBUNAL

EDITORIAL OFFICES: 5 YORK BUILDINGS, ADELPHI
LONDON, W.C.2

AVE ATQUE VALE

With this issue of the "Tribunal" we complete a year's work on our secret press. When, in April, 1918, after two printers had been dismantled on our account, our publisher began to print the paper herself, we were assured by our friends that if we ran for two months we should do well. We have run for 12 months and the whereabouts of our press is still unknown to Scotland Yard, in spite of their most strenuous efforts!

Of the difficulties that have confronted us during these 12 months our readers can form no idea. If they knew all, they would, we believe, view our deficiences with leniency. In particular, we wish to apologise for the errors which have appeared in our pages; when it is realised that it has been impossible to correct the proofs, perhaps these sins may be forgiven us. For our subscribers' patient endurance of late publishing dates and other irregularities, we render our heartfelt thanks.

Our next issue for April 24 will have a new printer, a new publisher and a new editor. We rejoice that this change coincides by chance, with the release of the two-year men from prison, and we feel that this is a happy omen for the future. There will be no limit to the number that can be printed, and we hope the circulation will go up by leaps and bounds.

We cannot close this chapter of the history of the "Tribunal" without recording the deep obligation we are under to the compositor and machinist who have worked so devotedly for us for the past twelve months. When we think how these two comrades have toiled for us, in spite of drudgery and danger, words of thanks seem totally inadequate. They have produced this paper, week by week on a tiny hand press in a back room, under difficulties hard to realise. At one time, when Scotland Yard was following us about all day long, they were obliged to remain indoors for weeks at a time in our tiny printing house. Sometime we hope to give fuller accounts of the adventures of the past twelve months under such headings as "Paper Smuggling in Wartime," "A Discourse on the Noise made by Various Types of Printing Presses with some Remarks on How to Disguise the Same from Neighbours," "The Ideal Messenger," "How to Make Your Title Fit Your Type," "The Plaint of the Patient Printer," etc., etc.

LYDIA S. SMITH
JOAN BEAUCHAMP

Extract from The Tribunal *10 April 1919*

The piece Rex v Beauchamp *in* The Tribunal *8 January 1920 describes the case against Joan Beauchamp*

who Work (1937), published by Lawrence and Wishart – but wrote articles and helped to edit Labour Research. *Agriculture in Soviet Russia* followed a visit to the Soviet Union in 1927, the first of several visits which concentrated on the countryside.

Her work on the position of women in the workplace would have been regarded as progressive fifty years later. *Women who Work* was introduced with the following words, an early statement of the socialist feminist position as the entry for Joan in the Dictionary of Labour Biography Volume 10, aptly puts it:

Since Mrs Drake's valuable book on Women in Trade Unions, published in 1920, very little has been written on this subject, and the women who work outside industry have been even more shamefully neglected. In this book I have tried, so far as it is possible to deal with such a vast subject in a handy and convenient form, to show under what conditions and in what variety of ways the great mass of the women of this country earn their daily bread. I have included the housewife, for in the great majority of the workers' homes she undoubtedly works longer hours and under worse conditions than most industrial workers, and yet less study and attention has been given to her work, mainly, I think, because it is unpaid and taken for granted.

Women who Work had an international impact. In the conference proceedings of the Australian Society for the Study of Labour History in 2006, Wendy Paterson presented a paper on Eileen Powell, an Australian who campaigned for the improvement of wages for working women. Eileen Powell, during her time with the Australian Railways Union wrote book reviews for the union journal *The Railroad*, and Wendy Paterson comments

the union ... published and distributed pamphlets, reviewed books such as Joan Beauchamp's *Women who Work*, urged its readers to contact the media and politicians, and utilised free air-time on Labor's radio station, 2KY, to inform and influence the general public and government.

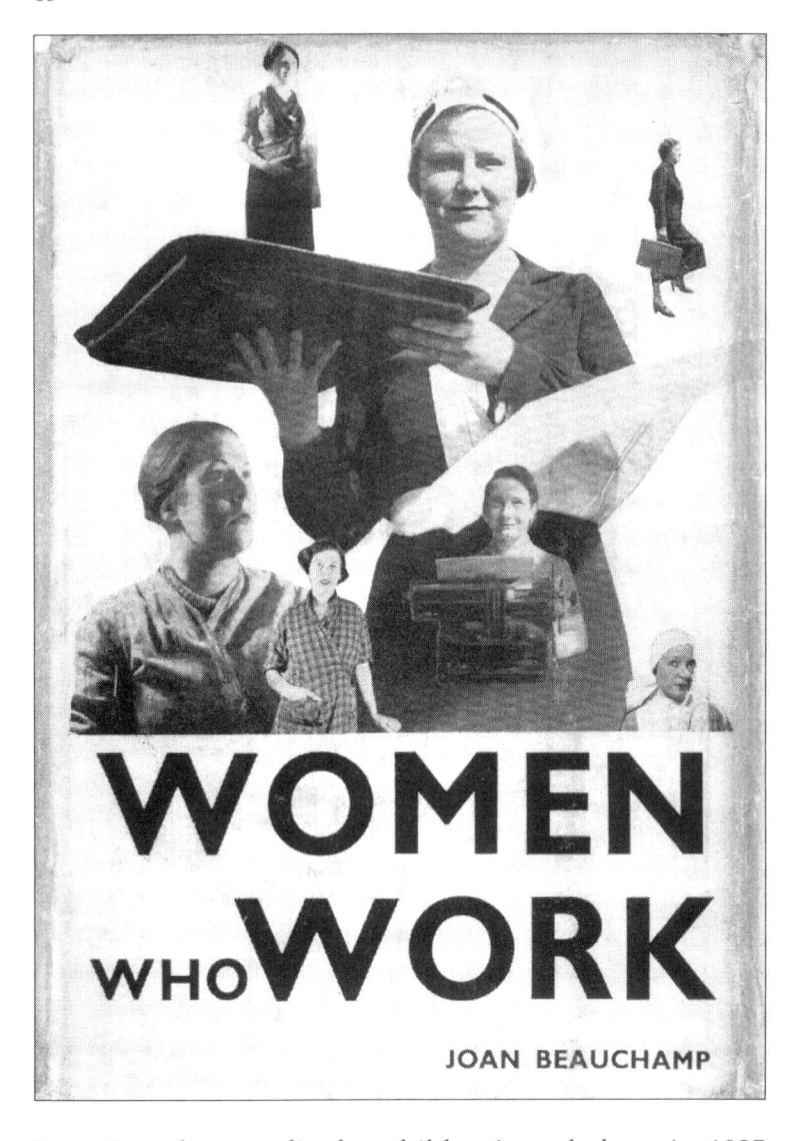

Joan Beauchamp edited a children's anthology in 1935 *Martin's Annual*, one of the stories from which, *ABC for Martin*, was on the reading list as recently as 2004 for a course at Kansas State University entitled *Children's Literature and the Left*.

She published an anthology of poetry, *Poems of Revolt*, in

A B C FOR MARTIN

A stands for Armaments—
war-mongers' pride;

B is for Bolshie,
the thorn in their side.

C stands for Capitalists,
fighting for gold;

D for Destruction
they've practised of old.

Extract from Martin's Annual, 1935

1924, became a Justice of the Peace (one of the few communists to do so), and spent much of her time involved in the children's courts. She was vigorously critical of the attitudes that prevailed in these courts and in general of the ways in which magistrates were appointed. She wrote a play about juvenile delinquency, *John Brown had a Soul*, performed at Gateway Theatre, and her last signed article in Labour Research on the subject appeared in November 1950.

Joan produced numerous pamphlets, such as *Secondary Education Survey – an analysis of LEA Development Plans for Secondary Education*, Fabian Research Series No. 148, published in January 1952 under her married name Joan Thompson. Notes to this publication indicate that she was a member of the L.C.C. (London County Council) and chairman of a secondary school group as well as standing for parliament in 1951 in West Harrow. The pamphlet argues the case for comprehensive schooling and notes in conclusion that: 'The purpose of secondary education for all is that there should not only be equality of opportunity but more equality in our society.' She also wrote a novel *Under the Tulip Tree* which has not been published.

After the Soviet Union joined the Second World War she trained for war work and worked for a short time as an inspector in a factory at High Wycombe making Mosquito war planes.

The war years took their toll. Joan suffered periodically from what was described as neuritis in her limbs and was in hospital in Regent's Park for this condition in June 1944 when she suffered serious injuries as a result of a V1/Doodlebug bomb. Out of a ward of fourteen beds, only Joan and a nurse, Margaret Paterson, (who was blinded) survived. Joan suffered multiple fractures which hospitalised her for the next two years.

She was treated initially at University College London, and then transferred to the Wingfield Morris Hospital at Headington, Oxford.

In an undated letter to Esme Epton, Harry Thompson comments:

This awful business of Joan is very disturbing. There she is with both her legs broken, her ulnar nerve on the right hand severed and her left arm lacerated. Her right foot is … injured and may have to be amputated. She has a lot of pain but bears it like a heroine and when she is not in pain she lies there talking brightly and still interested in everything and still more in other people than in her own troubles. She looks so well and beautiful. She is a standing reproach to us all.

In a letter to her son Brian written on 6 July 1944 from her hospital bed in Oxford, Joan reminisces about her time in the gliding club at Dunstable, and then, after referring to various operations she has either just had or is about to have, begs Brian to get a few days leave to come and stay nearby and 'write letters for me and hold my head up while I drink and otherwise be a ray of sunshine … . There is nobody else who could do it or whom I should find such good company …'

Brian clearly spent a good deal of time visiting his mother in hospital and his relationship with her was of great importance to him throughout his life. According to his father in a letter to Esme Epton, 'Brian has practically lived at the hospital with Joan'. Brian regarded himself as her clear favourite, presumably because of his glittering intellect for which he received constant encouragement and praise. In later life he often spoke of her, what she did and what she said.

Apart from her immediate family, one of those who gave Joan most comfort at this difficult time was Harry Pollitt who, in the midst of his busy life as General Secretary of the Communist Party, wrote her 27 letters between June and December 1944.

Joan's health was permanently affected by her injuries and she endured constant pain for the remaining twenty years of her life.

Years later in 1998 Brian wrote to Eric Heather, a colleague who had just retired:

When I saw your address I was prompted to write to you…about an old friend/acquaintance of mine. I have not seen her for about 7 years or so, but we exchange Xmas cards, and I pay her some money every year, which was started by my mother: I have kept it up and increased the amount, but whether I have kept up with inflation I do not know.

Her name is Margaret Paterson…She was a nurse in the hospital where my mother was bombed in 1944; they were the only two survivors in that wing of the hospital. She was blinded totally and I would say disfigured somewhat…

I feel if you could contact her and keep an eye on her from time to time you could do her a good turn.

Eric duly called on the old lady and reported back that 'as soon as I uttered the magic password Brian Thompson I was invited in'. He found a vigorous, loud and self-sufficient lady without a scintilla of self-pity.

Much the same could have been said about Joan. Until the bomb in 1944 she was a very physically active woman, engaging in ice skating, gliding, horse riding and walking, and bore her considerable physical problems with fortitude. She died on 29 July 1964. The entry in the *Dictionary of Labour Biography* describes her as 'a strong-minded yet modest and selfless woman who was loved and respected by her many friends'.

In 2002, Robin, after regretting that his father had kept no written record of his personal history, noted:

With regard to my mother, she had a fascinating period after leaving Holloway College. There was her work in the suffragettes followed by her anti-war activities that resulted in her going into Holloway Prison. I should not think that there is anyone else who has been to both.

Many years ago I switched on the radio and there was a play on the suffragettes. An actress was taking the part of my mother...If only my mother had also provided her written recollections.

Joan's sister Kay joined the Communist Party of Great Britain shortly after Joan in the early 1920s, and was one of the eight people who produced the first ever edition of the *Daily Worker* which appeared on 1 January 1930. Kay was editor of the women's page. In 1930, the business manager, Frank Priestley, and three partners in the press were imprisoned for an editorial description of a judge as 'a bewigged puppet'. More imprisonments followed in 1931 under the Incitement to Mutiny Act, 1797, when sailors at Invergordon mutinied against a 25 per cent pay cut and the paper published their manifesto. Those gaoled included the owner of the press, and Kay then became Managing Director. She herself spent five months in Holloway prison for contempt of court for refusing to pay a fine of £500 imposed when the paper described the conviction of an unemployed workers' leader Sid Elias as a 'frame-up'. Joan visited her sister regularly. At various times Kay served on Finsbury Borough Council as a Communist councillor from 1945 to 1949, worked in the International Department of the CPGB and for the Labour Research Department and in later years was active in the Movement for Colonial Freedom (later renamed Liberation[1]) and various other anti-racist and anti-imperialist campaigns. She participated in the organisation of major left-wing campaigns over several decades, including solidarity with Republican Spain, opposition to Fascism and to Munich, and many others. Much of her work was done in the capacity of Education

Secretary for the London District of the Communist Party.

Unlike either W.H. Thompson or her sister Joan, Kay managed to get listed in the TUC secret file on subversives!

Note (1) The Liberation archives are held by the Working Class Movement Library in Salford. Kay was born in 1899 and died in 1992, the same year as her second husband Tony Gilbert, another leftwing activist with an amazing history.

A W.H. Thompson's dinner, date unknown but probably early 1950s. Freddie Oaten is speaking; in the foreground is Brian and to his right (next to Freddie) is Kay Beauchamp.

Chapter 6
Biscuits and scary reds

By the time of his release from prison in April 1919, Harry Thompson had numerous friends with connections with the Labour Movement, including Josiah Wedgewood MP, John Ward MP, George Lansbury and James Ramsay MacDonald who was to become Labour's first Prime Minister. With their support he decided to move to London and started to practise in partnership with a fellow conscientious objector. He set up in London in on 1 September 1919, initially with James Scott Duckers, in a basement at 2, New Court, Carey Street close to Lincoln's Inn Fields. The firm was called Scott Duckers & Thompson. Chris Wrigley writes:

He had met Duckers when they had both been in gaol as conscientious objectors. However, he and Duckers differed increasingly on politics. Duckers was a Liberal, who after the war was Asquithian. He went on to be Liberal candidate in one of the most famous inter-war by-elections, the Westminster Abbey by-election of March 1924. In this the local Liberals effectively ran him as a candidate to spoil Winston Churchill's chances of returning to Parliament as an independent Conservative. Churchill lost ... Alan Taylor later recalled, "they were totally incompatible. I can remember Harry complaining of Scott Duckers always having a top hat in the office".

In contrast, Thompson's political trajectory was to the Left, especially so in the three or four years after the end of the First World War. He was a member of the Central London branch of the Independent Labour Party (ILP) one of the branches which seceded to join the Communist Party of

Great Britain (CPGB) on its formation in early 1921. He stayed in the CPGB for up to two years.

Thompson became a trusted confidant of Ramsay MacDonald. In the MacDonald letters held in the National Archives at Kew, there is a substantial correspondence between the two men, one the client, one the solicitor. The correspondence covers a range of matters from house purchases (in which Harry acted for MacDonald and his son Malcolm to purchase homes in London) through to attempts to get political offenders regraded and therefore introduced to a slightly less harsh prison regime.

In the immediate aftermath of the General Strike Harry Thompson also wrote letters before action on MacDonald's behalf, with a view to forcing speedy apologies from mendacious newspapers which smeared all and sundry including the former Prime Minister as mindless cat's-paws for godless Communism and the Russian state. In one such case on behalf of the former P.M. Harry Thompson took on

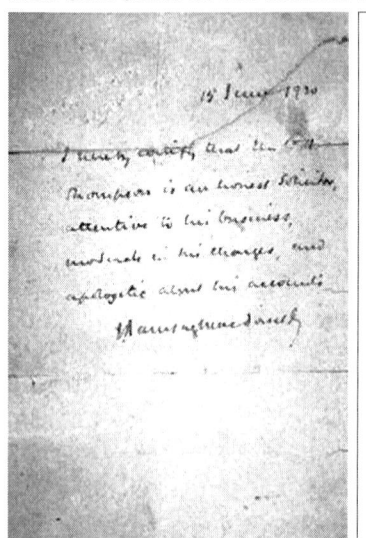

> 9 Howitt Road
> Hampstead N.W.
> 15th June 1920
>
> *I hereby certify that Mr. W. H. Thompson is an honest Solicitor, attentive to his business, moderate in his charges, and apologetic about his accounts.*
>
> *Ramsay Macdonald*

A copy of the reference supplied by Ramsay Macdonald dated 15 June 1920 the *Daily Record and Mail* ('The All Scotland newspaper' as it billed itself) over its London letter of 26 June 1926. His efforts were soon rewarded.

'I regret very much indeed', the editor replied to Thompson's forcefully drafted letter before action 'that through a telegraphic error Mr Ramsay MacDonald was referred to as having been an active Communist and that he had got private letters in the uncensored dispatch bags of the Russian Trade delegation. There is of course no foundation for these statements.'

An unreserved apology was proffered for the so-called 'telegraphic error' and MacDonald, who could have made serious money from pursuing the paper further, decided to let it go at that. MacDonald was by this time a saddened and severely wounded man who privately wondered if a Labour government would ever be able to navigate a way past the propaganda and vicious hostility of those who controlled the British press.

From the very first his 1924 government had been greeted by hysterical class prejudice – Lady Cunard wondered if government ministers knew how to use a knife and fork – and finally buckled under press witch-hunts and the forged Zinoviev Letter which helped to bring about a heavy election defeat. Fabricated by corrupt elements in British intelligence the letter was sneakily delivered into the trusted hands of journalists and editors of the *Daily Mail* and published as if an easily detectable forgery was gospel truth. This letter, published in the *Daily Mail* a few days before the election, purported to be from Zinoviev, President of the Communist International calling on the sympathetic section of the Labour Party to bring pressure to bear on the Government to ratify the Russian treaties, and instructing the British Communist party to form a military think-tank and infiltrate other military institutions, in preparation for the outbreak of revolution. The letter caused press hysteria and the Conservatives under Stanley Baldwin were elected.

Thompson maintained a keen interest in the forgery and its use to bring down the first Labour government and continued actively to advise MacDonald on the matter after his fall from power, urging the former PM to press for a proper no-holds-barred inquiry which could compel witnesses to give evidence, produce documents and tell something of the truth.

To people like Harry Thompson the truth mattered and for those who follow in his footsteps it still does. Today in Britain the Zinoviev letter forgery is a matter of high controversy in the history of the militarised state. So when Labour came to power in 1997 the new Foreign Secretary Robin Cook set out to open up the full spectrum of government and intelligence files on the forgery to some sort of scrutiny. But in the run up to the Iraq war he resigned and later died before the full details of an investigation by an FO historian could be published.

Thompson also gave Ramsay MacDonald sound advice about another matter – his finances. Ramsay MacDonald came by the offer of the loan of a car and £40,000 in securities in 1924 from a childhood friend in Lossiemouth who had risen to prominence in the bread and digestives baking firm McVitie and Price. He wrote to 'his solicitor W.H. Thompson' to set up the appropriate legal framework. Thompson warned him that he should be very careful over offers of donations and financial help. His arrangements should be above reproach. Instead MacDonald muddled through and failed miserably to structure the provision of the car and shares to pay for its maintenance and fuel.

MacDonald paid a high price for ignoring the advice. For many months during the 1925 'Red Scare' election his punishing schedule of election meetings was made more painful by the repeated cry 'Biscuits'.

Chapter 7
The first major case –
Poplar Borough Council

The partnership with Scott Duckers, in which conveyancing work was a prime aspect, lasted only two years, coming to an end on 31 August 1921. Harry Thompson was ready to move on and set up his own practice. According to Brian, his father wrote to Joan when she was in Italy, saying that he couldn't stand partnership with Scott Duckers but was not quite sure he could manage on his own. On Joan's return from Italy they married and set up home in Oxford and within a month Thompson had set up his own firm W.H. Thompson, Solicitor.

The end of the partnership with Duckers was difficult. Thompson brought arbitration proceedings in relation to the financial issues, and these were finally resolved by a deed dated 1 March 1924. The deed is of considerable interest since it lists various outstanding cases and sums outstanding from Duckers. The biggest sums relate to The Poplar Borough Council case, of which more shortly, and The Communist Party 're. various accounts', and also shows that W.H. Thompson already acted for the Amalgamated Union of Building Trade Workers, and the Plumbers' Union. [Documents still in existence amongst Thompson's papers also include an original copy of the Rule Book for the Printers' Labourers Union – a union formed in 1889 which by 1899 had undergone the first of many name changes – suggesting a very early link with the printers].

Harry Thompson did not remain a member of the Communist Party for long – probably no more than two

W.H. Thompson

15 October 1885 – 4 August 1947

years. According to Joan's sister Kay, Thompson and his sister Connie, both strictly teetotal, left the CP because of the acceptance of alcohol. Another of Joan's sisters, Ethel, recalled that when she and her husband stayed with the Thompsons they had to hide the whisky they drank! Joan fairly quickly rejoined the party but Harry never did. It seems likely that as an independent free thinker, Thompson could never belong to an organisation which in any way shackled his own deeply held beliefs and convictions, not to mention his spirit. Nevertheless, throughout the remainder of his life the Party was of fundamental importance not just to Joan, but to Harry Thompson himself, and helped to shape the firm he created. Most of the leading lawyers in the practice, as it developed, were Party members.

In an interview later in her life, in reply to the question, 'How did you get to know Harry Pollitt?' Kay commented:

Through my brother-in-law – Harry Thompson. Harry Thompson was then the Solicitor for the Communist Party and also helped Harry[Pollitt] with any problem, personal and legal… . Although my brother in law had left the CP – my sister rejoined – I told you they disagreed with some of the activities of the Communist Party in the early days but she rejoined the Party but he didn't and I think that partly the reason was he started the first Solicitors firm that dealt with workmen's compensation and tenants' problems and would not have anything to do with employers or landlords and so he was building up his solicitors practice with the trade unions – he had been in prison throughout the First World War – and I think he felt he could not be a member of the Communist Party but he worked very closely with the left wing unions leading up to the strike in 1926.

Harry Thompson set up in practice on his own with a staff of two at 27 Chancery Lane on 1 September 1921. It was to be an exceptional period of social history, as described by Owen Parsons in his account written in 1979:

The inter-war period, 1919-1939, was one where the class struggle reached an intensity as great as any period before or, up to 1979 at any rate, since. The halcyon days of British imperialism were over. The Empire had its back to the wall. One-sixth of the world had gone Socialist. India was in an increasing state of rebellion. The belts – the workers' belts of course – were being tightened at home. Crisis followed crisis in our basic industries. The General Strike brought British capitalism closer to rebellion than at any time since the Chartist movement, the bitterness of labour battles in the coalfields soured a generation of industrial relations, the world economic crisis of 1930 to 1933, fascism and the threat of war loomed over the nation like a thunder cloud.

During the next decades, when Thompson became the leading expert in the country on workmen's compensation and civil liberties, he became also, in Owen Parsons' words, 'the outstanding champion of the left'.

The first major case was in 1921 as solicitor to Poplar Borough Council, a case Thompson was already heavily involved in when he started his new practice.
 The Labour council, led by George Lansbury, had set about a public works programme to cut unemployment, improve services and assist the poor.
 All borough councils were charged precepts to pay for cross-capital authorities such as the London County Council, Metropolitan Police Authority, Metropolitan Asylum Board and the Water Board. The problem was that precepts were not based on the Borough's ability to pay, so that poor boroughs paid towards the costs of rich boroughs for certain common services whilst at the same time did not

receive similar pooling to help with poor relief. So the council refused to pay the levy demanded for broader city-wide services, with the intention of using the money raised for its own local purposes. Legal action followed. Noreen Branson, in her book *Poplarism 1919 -1925: George Lansbury and the Councillors' Revolt* notes:

> The councillors had long since been preparing their legal defence. Their solicitor was W.H. Thompson ... He was not only an exceptionally able lawyer, but held socialist views and was convinced of the political importance of the case. With Lansbury and others he discussed the legal problems. The councillors knew that they had little chance of winning the battle in the law courts, and in preparing their defence they had one main object in view: delay.

W.H. Thompson briefed Henry Slesser, KC for the defence and the case was eventually heard. The court issued an order of mandamus, (a form of injunction requiring positive action) requiring the councillors to levy the 'correct' rate, and thirty Labour councillors were imprisoned for failing to obey a court ruling to impose the rate.

Harry Thompson's role in the case then became critical. A resolution was forced by a mixture of pressure from the TUC, the public and Thompson's ingenious legal approach which persuaded the court to release the councillors, notwithstanding the fact that they had not only still not complied with the court order but were still not offering to do so, to enable them to participate in a conference convened by the Ministry of Health, the upshot being that agreement was reached to give relief to the poorer boroughs including Poplar. In all this he conferred closely with Harry Gosling, leader of the Labour group on London County Council and C.J. Mathew, another member of the Labour group on the LCC who was also a KC.

Councillor George and Mrs Lansbury

The councillors were set free on 12 October. As John Scurr, one of the imprisoned aldermen commented in his booklet *The Rate Protest of Poplar*:

At six o'clock on Wednesday, 12 October 1921, the Brixton prisoners marched out singing the `Red Flag´. At the gate, waiting for them, were their devoted women colleagues released from Holloway, together with their good friends, Harry Gosling and W.H. Thompson.

Soon the cabs started for home, where on their arrival they were greeted with cheers and bands and banners of the people of Poplar.

The struggle was over. It had been short sharp and strenuous and the victory was great.

This well-documented case was an example of the power of collective action in a period which saw the birth of the Communist Party, the growth of the Labour Party and a period of serious unrest and political upheaval. During a

The Council summoned to the High Court

time when the rise of fascism was to end up in a world war, the authorities seemed to be more concerned about the threat they perceived from the rise of the left. An assault on civil liberties was underway. As Thompson noted in his 1938 publication *Civil Liberties*:

> ... in the first instance it will always be the extreme and comparatively small minority who will be attacked when an attack on civil liberties is in progress. People in the working-class movement and Liberals know quite well that it is the rights of such minorities which must be protected if the democratic rights of the people are to be preserved. If the police have a right to enter meetings, it may be only Communist meetings that they enter now, but if and when it is thought necessary in the interests of the capitalist State that trade union meetings should be entered by the police, or that their meetings should be stopped, the precedents referred to in this book will be invoked for this purpose. Readers should remember that when the Tolpuddle martyrs were transported

On release outside Brixton Prison
Front row: J.J. Heales Goodway, W.H. Thompson (solicitor), C.E. Williams, B. Fleming, Mrs Scurr, J.T. O'Callaghan, C.J. Cressall, J.H. Jones. Standing: T.E. Kelly, J.A. Rugless, D. Adams, J.H. Banks, Walter Green, George Lansbury, Harry Gosling, Edgar Lansbury, Sam March, A. Baker, Mrs M. Lansbury, John Scurr, Cr Oakes, C.E. Petherick, R.J. Hopwood, C.E. Sumner, A.V. Farr

it was not because they were Communists, but because they were trade unionists and modern instances have been provided at Meerut, in Trinidad, and elsewhere.

Poplar Town Hall has various records of this great struggle of the 1920s, a struggle prosecuted to defend the right to make proper arrangements to feed the hungry and give useful work at fair wages to unemployed people and also to develop a tax and rating system that spreads the cost fairly across the whole community, rich and poor.

Eight decades later this problem has not gone away and is indeed being posed with increasing ferocity at the international level. Here in Britain it has been attenuated and locally we live in more passive times, perhaps in part because of the great changes and reforms the Labour movement has been able to produce for us. But these pictures still speak to us, reminding us that reforms do not fall from the sky and that they are the fruit of constructive dissent and serious professional commitment to create a better world with fair rules which apply to all.

In one of the photographs of Poplar's marches against the jailing of the local councillors, there is a huge hoarding advertising the *Sunday Pictorial*, and beneath it an unnamed marcher is carrying a banner. Looking at the photograph eighty five years after it was given to Harry Thompson, we can try to imagine how he felt when he first saw the image presented to him by the councillors whose release he had helped to secure.

The banner simply reads:

LET
JUSTICE
PREVAIL
OR THE
HEAVENS
FALL.

The imprisonment of the Poplar councillors was just part of a running battle between Poplar Borough Council and the authorities over a period of years. The Poplar councillors and aldermen figured again in the courts in 1925, but this time they were unsuccessful. Again they were represented by W.H. Thompson. The case reached the House of Lords. The case was *Roberts v Hopwood [1925] All ER 24*.

The Poplar councillors decided to award pay increases so as to bring the minimum rate of pay for Poplar employees to £4 per week regardless of the work done (or the sex of the person doing it). In affidavit evidence they said that wages should not be exclusively related to the cost of living and that a public authority should be a model employer. The district auditor disagreed and applied a surcharge to the councillors.

By the time of the hearing in the Lords the issue related mainly to the issue of women's pay. Lord Atkinson, in the course of his judgment stated:

> ... it does not appear to me that there is any rational proportion between the rate of wages at which the labour of these women is paid and the rates at which they would be reasonably remunerated for their services to the council. I concur with the auditor in thinking that what has been given to the women as wages are really to a great extent gifts and gratuities disguised as wages, and are, therefore, illegal.

Professor Keith Ewing recently described this judgment by the Lords as 'an attack on equal pay as an eccentric principle of socialist philosophy and feminist ambition to secure equal pay'! The case is a leading authority in relation to the power of the courts to interfere in the exercise of a local authority's functions.

Chapter 8
More scary reds

The end of the First World War in November 1918 was followed by a period of political and economic instability. Chronic unemployment was rife particularly in the industrial heartlands. The Russian Revolution of 1917, news of the workers' rising in Hungary and Germany and the growth of the USSR gave rise to anticipation (hope or dread depending on your perspective) of a workers' revolution in Britain. 1919 saw a massive wave of strikes Thirty five million working days were lost in strike action – six times as many as in the previous year, and the highest number by far in the twentieth century.

The focal point of action was the Triple Alliance of the industrial unions of miners, railwaymen and transport workers, with the Clyde Workers' Committee in the forefront. But the action extended further, right into the heart of the state. In 1918, 2,000 soldiers refused to board the waiting boats in Folkestone, instead leading a protest march through the town, leading to more mutinies with troops refusing to fight in Russia. In August 1918 the unthinkable happened – there was a police strike (mainly over the refusal of the government to recognise the union formed in 1913, the National Union of Police and Prison Workers – NUPPO). The settlement of that dispute involving the reinstatement of sacked NUPPO officers brought only a pyrrhic victory. A further strike by the police in July 1919 was unsuccessful and all the strikers were dismissed and never reinstated. After setting up his practice in 1921, Harry Thompson acted for a number of the dismissed men who were being subjected to routine harassment.

By 1920, the fear that the government might declare war on the Soviet Union led to the formation of Councils of Action all over the country which pledged to organise mass strikes should the threat prove real. The Communist Party of Great Britain was formed and although its membership was small, its influence was great.

In 1925, following the fall of the first minority government of Ramsay MacDonald (and the infamous Zinoviev letter), the new Conservative Government under Stanley Baldwin was so disturbed by the alleged communist danger in a period of continuing unrest that police raids were ordered on the party's King Street headquarters and the offices of the London District, the Young Communist league and the National Minority Movement. On the morning of the raid, 14 October, the *Daily Mail* reported:

> It is interesting that the Cabinet at its meeting yesterday discussed the desirability of taking firm action against Communist agitators, and decided to give the fullest support to the Home Secretary in any prosecution he may consider necessary ... Ministers have apparently been brought to realise that these revolutionaries must either be imprisoned, in the case of British subjects, or deported in the case of aliens.

The *Daily Express* on 16 October noted: 'It is understood that the Cabinet considered a list containing the names of 40 Communists and authorised the immediate arrest of 8 of them.'

Large quantities of papers were seized and twelve arrests made.

By this time Harry Thompson had ceased to be a member of the Communist Party. But Thompson could see the obvious civil liberties implications and immediately made himself available to defend the arrested men. They decided that some would defend themselves so their political views could be heard in court while others would be represented by a defence solicitor. Pollitt, Gallagher and Campbell defended themselves and Thompson acted as solicitor to the others.

He instructed a barrister he respected and worked with him painstakingly constructing a legal defence for his clients. As ever he worked quietly behind the scenes, contacting and briefing the Labour leader James Ramsay MacDonald on their behalf and drawing in the influential Labour Party figure Harold Laski, a Professor at the London School of Economics, and a man with a fearsome grasp of the history of freedom, to help with the defence.

With his instinctive understanding of the temper of the times and a shrewd grasp of the government strategy in staging regular 'red scares' and trials, Harry Thompson must have known that his clients would now soon be following in his footsteps and heading for jail.

The charges included conspiracy to publish a seditious libel and incitement to commit breaches of the Incitement to Mutiny Act, 1797. The trial was held before Judge Rigby Swift who commented in summing up that it was 'no crime to be a communist' or 'hold communist opinions', but 'it was a crime to belong to this Communist Party.' Five of the accused, Harry Pollitt, William Gallagher, Wal Hannington, William Rust and Albert Inkpin were jailed for one year. The remaining defendants (who included Robin Page Arnot) received six months. The original official shorthand notes of the judgment are still in existence and held at The John Rylands University Library, Manchester. After the foreman of the jury had given the verdicts, Mr Henderson, counsel for the accused addressed the judge:

May I draw your Lordship's attention to Section 40 of the Prison Act which provides that the court may if it thinks fit, having regard to the nature of the defence and the antecedents of the offender, direct that he be treated as an offender of the first division.

The document contains a handwritten margin note made by W.H. Thompson: 'Under this Section the court has no alternative. The word may should have been shall and the words "if it thinks fit" are not correct. W.H.T.'

In the event the point was of little consequence. The charge was of conspiracy rather than the substantive offence of sedition, and the judge peremptorily refused to accept that the offence was political (which would have resulted in a less harsh prison regime). The judge then passed sentence:

The jury have found you twelve men guilty of the serious offence of a conspiracy to publish seditious libels and to incite people to induce soldiers and sailors to break their oath of allegiance. It is obvious from the evidence that was given before the jury that you are members of an illegal party carrying on illegal work in this country and it must stop.

After sentencing five of the men to a year in prison, the judge continued:

You remaining seven have heard what I have to say about the party to which you belong and you have heard me say that it must stop. I am not anxious, if I can avoid it, to send you to prison …Those of you who promise me that you will have nothing more to do with this association or the doctrines which it preaches I shall bind over to be of good behaviour in the future; those of you who do not promise will go to prison.

One by one the remaining defendants were asked whether

> THE COMMUNIST PARTY ON TRIAL
>
> WM. GALLACHER'S DEFENCE
> And JUDGE RIGBY SWIFTS' SUMMING-UP
>
> The Speech for the defence by Wm. Gallacher, member of the Central Committee of the Communist Party of Great Britain, and one of the twelve defendants against the charge of conspiring to publish seditious libels and incite to mutiny. Begun on Nov. 19, 1925
>
> Price: Twopence
>
> PUBLISHED BY:
> THE COMMUNIST PARTY OF GREAT BRITAIN
> 16, KING STREET, COVENT GARDEN, LONDON, W.C.2

they agreed to be bound over, and one by one they refused and received a sentence of six months.

These sentences kept the men confined during many crucial months of acute social conflict.

The judge was a former Tory M.P. As Owen Parsons later commented:

Not surprisingly the behaviour of an ex-Tory M.P., now elevated to the Bench, indulging in plea bargaining in open court between Judge and Prisoner, the price being the prisoner's readiness to surrender his deeply held beliefs and his membership of a perfectly legal political party, gave rise to considerable concern.

Ramsay MacDonald clearly had a keen interest in all this. The original shorthand note was amongst his papers and is now held in the Ramsay MacDonald archive as Document RMD/1/5/3. Given that the document is an original one on which Thompson had written notes, one can surmise that W.H. Thompson sent it to him.

The same archive at RMD/1/5/4 contains a lengthy hand written critique of the case by Harold Laski in which he doubts both the legality and morality of the trial. One brief extract gives a flavour of the note:

The government had better remember the wise words of the late President Wilson to Congress. "The only way to keep men from agitating against grievances is to remove the grievances. An unwillingness even to discuss them produces only dissatisfaction and gives comfort to the extreme elements in our country which endeavour to stir up grievance in order to provoke governments to embark upon a course of retaliation and repression. The seed of revolution is suppression".

From his cell in Brixton Prison, one of the jailed men, the Scotsman Robin Page Arnot communicated his thoughts and the occasional polite request to the outside world. Some of the prison letters he wrote are preserved today in the Philip Larkin suite at the University of Hull Library. Written in exquisite copper-plate handwriting and neatly miniaturised to obtain maximum use of the pro-forma prison notepaper provided by the authorities for all letters, they are also arranged in neat columns and addressed to Page Arnot's friend and Labour Research colleague Harry Thompson.

The General Strike

1926 was the year of the General Strike, which began when one million miners were locked out by their employers for refusing to take a pay cut.

The General Strike began on 3 May 1926 and was called in defence of miners' wages and hours. Harry Thompson worked tirelessly to help the miners and anyone else he could assist. Some contemporaneous evidence still exists on the TUC's website in the form of correspondence from the Miners' Federation dated 10 May 1926 asking him to represent Noah Ablett at the South Western Police Court the following day, and the response handwritten on The Nonesuch Press notepaper.

Noah Ablett was a miner from the Rhondda Valley who had won a scholarship to Ruskin College, Oxford and on

```
                                              10th May, 1926.

Dear Thompson,
          I am instructed by Arthur Cook to ask you
to defend Noah Ablett tomorrow (Tuesday) morning at
the South Western Police Court at 10 o'clock.
          Will you please be at the Miners' Federation
Offices at Russell Square at 9.15 in the morning, when
you can see Ablett and some of the Miners' leaders.
Arrangements can be made to take you to the Court.
Please do not fail as the Miners' Federation is anxious
that the best possible defence should be put up to
deal with an impossible case.
                    Yours fraternally,



W. H. Thompson, Esq.,
```

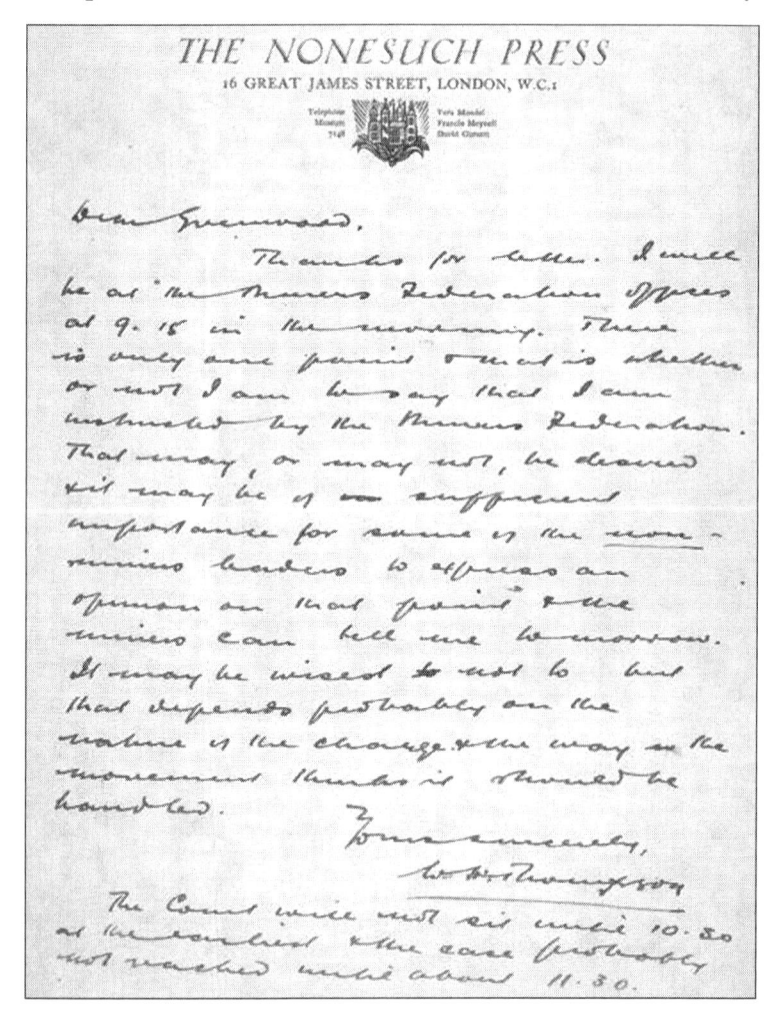

his return helped to set up the Unofficial Reform Committee which was the group which published *The Miners' Next Step* in the wake of the national coal strike of 1911. This revolutionary publication proposed that the miners' unions should reorganise themselves on industrial lines with a strong central direction of policy, the object of which would be to bring the industry to a standstill, with strike after strike, until the system of private ownership collapsed. Then the miners would take over the industry and reorganise it on the basis of workers' control. The ultimate aim was to see their lead followed by the trade unions in other industries. Syndicalism played its part in the growth of industrial unionism including the formal alliance between the NUR (newly formed in 1912 by an amalgamation of three railway unions), the Miners' Federation and the Transport Workers' Federation with a view to joint action for mutual assistance. Ablett was just the sort of person the authorities wished to suppress at this critical moment.

Thompson's reply to the request to represent Ablett is subtly political. It is not easy to decipher but appears to read as follows:

Dear Greenwood
      Thanks for the letter. I will be at the Miners' Federation Offices at 9.15 in the morning. There is only one point & that is whether or not I am to say that I am instructed by the Miners' Federation. That may, or may not, be desired and it may be of sufficient importance for some of the non miners leaders to express an opinion on that point & the miners can tell me tomorrow. It may be wisest not to but that depends probably on the nature of the charge & the way the movement thinks it should be handled.
                        Yours sincerely
                        W H Thompson
The Court will not sit until 10.30 at the earliest and the case probably not reached until about 11.30.

Quite what the charge was, or indeed the result of this particular case is not known.

    The history of ASLEF, the train drivers' union, mentions Thompson speaking at the regular mass meetings near his home, then at Coulsdon, Surrey where the railway workers were strong in numbers. Thompson also continued his work for the Labour Research department solving problems and healing wounds in the difficult, strife-torn times after the General Strike was called off and the miners left isolated for months and months until they were starved back to work.

Joan's sister Kay, a Communist Party activist in St. Pancras took part in the events which preceded the 1926 General Strike. The St. Pancras Communist Party met on the eve of Red Friday 1925 and exulted in the development of the struggle. There were only eight CP members in Hampstead, including Emile Burns and his wife, but 150 in the branch area from the Thames to Hertfordshire. When police raided the branch offices at 44 Maiden Road, Kay burnt the membership records in the back room while comrades delayed them by talking in the front office.

The outbreak of the General Strike in 1926 was hot news in the 1926 May Day march in which Kay participated. She assisted Emile Burns in producing a journal for the St. Pancras Council of Action, and became Chairman of the Women's Committee, of which the Secretary was a leading Co-op Guildwoman. They were preparing to set up soup kitchens, but the end of the strike overtook them. Thereafter for nine months Kay spearheaded the work of raising money for the miners who were on strike, duplicating and sending out endless appeals for donations.

Although the railwaymen had not been prominent in local activities before the General Strike, they were responsible for the bulk of the work of organising during the nine days.

The government's response to the strike? In 1927 the Trade Disputes and Trade Union Act was passed which, amongst other things, outlawed sympathetic strikes and mass picketing. In his 1927 pamphlet *The Trade Union Bill – A*

Critical Analysis, Harry Thompson attempted to explain the intricacies and ambiguities of the new law, a summary of which he gave as follows:

1. All strikes for other than industrial purposes are to be illegal if they are designed or calculated to coerce the Government, or to intimidate the community or any substantial portion of the community
2. All sympathetic strikes if designed or calculated to coerce the Government, or to intimidate the community or a substantial portion of the community, are to be illegal provided they are not within the trade or industry in which the original dispute arose
3. Picketing is to be restricted to the most innocent forms of persuasion by small numbers of pickets and even this may be dangerous.
4. Watching or besetting of a blackleg's house is to be illegal.
5. Civil Servants may not join any Trade Union which is not confined to any employees of the Crown or pursue political objects within their own organisations, nor may their organisations associate with any outside industrial or political body.
6. Local Authorities cannot impose Trade Union membership upon their employees or in any way penalise a non-unionist employee."

He goes on to note that the Bill did not make illegal lock-outs by the employers, coercion by the employer to an employee to leave a union, price fixing by employers, and goes on: "it does not make it illegal for an employer to discharge an employee or for a landlord to evict a tenant for voting labour or for indulging in working class activities; it does not make it illegal for the Tory Party to obtain funds by selling honours; it does not make it illegal for employers to coerce employees into acceptance of slave conditions of employment …

Lansbury's *Labour Weekly* for 23 April 1927 contains a long article by Thompson. It is prefaced by editorial comment:

Will You Surrender what your fathers Won?
For all its most deadly attacks on the workers the governing class turns to the lawyers. The cant of politicians and the guns of soldiers each have their use, but for two hundred years the ruling class has known that in doing damage that is both deep and lasting there is nothing like the legal profession …

The editorial continues in this vein and suggests that the 1927 Bill is designed to drive the Trade Unions and (as a result) the Labour Party out of existence. It concludes:

We have asked Mr W.H. Thompson to analyse for us the new Combination Bill … All can draw their own conclusions. Will you lose what your fathers gained?

Harry Thompson's critique follows and concludes: 'The Labour movement must not concern itself with amendments; it must treat the Bill as a move in the class-war … and must deal with it as such.'

Chapter 9
Early organisation and some family memories

In 1927, A.J.P. (Alan) Taylor joined the practice as an articled clerk. He had intended to become a barrister, relying on the flow of work that W.H. could give him. In his autobiography he says:

After the general strike Harry made a new suggestion. He had a flourishing practice and two sons who would probably be too young to take over from him when he wanted to retire. Why should I not become his partner and fill the gap?

Chris Wrigley notes:

By the time Taylor joined his uncle's practice it was well-established and thriving. Harry Thompson was ably assisted by Mr Cornish, his managing clerk, and two young women, Miss Crisply and Miss Mowbray (later Mrs Cornish). He also employed another qualified solicitor. Shortly before Taylor arrived, this had been Mr Winter, a chess champion, but he had left and been replaced by Peter Stone, who later became music critic of the Jewish Chronicle. Alan Taylor did not fit in … He disliked the work from day one … . He made clear his preference to be judged an Oxford `reading man´ by reading in the office whenever the opportunity arose … .

 Alan Taylor did not get on well with his uncle. They were both used to being the centres of attention, and had been spoilt by their parents. They were also both used to getting their way. Thompson, unlike his nephew, `was a tall, handsome, athletic fellow, excelling in all games´ who had a

Pamphlet produced in 1927

strong sense of humour. This humour he liked to exercise on his nephew, who did not care to be the butt of his jokes. His son [Robin] later commented, "My father was outstanding at putting anyone down and had an extremely strong personality. I would not think anyone got the better of him. I am sure it would not suit Alan to be dominated by such a personality". Taylor did not care for either the work or for playing second fiddle to his uncle.

Alan Taylor records the episode as a ghastly mistake. He broke his articles after six months 'and became a free man'.

Front row, left to right: *Harry Thompson, Joan Beauchamp, A J P Taylor*; row behind, left to right: *John Thompson, Connie Taylor, Sara Thompson*; at back: *a brother in law*.

Taylor seems to have felt that the Thompsons regarded themselves as a cut above his father's family, perhaps a question of old money as compared to new, and reflected in their accents. He says in his autobiography 'These Thompsons thought themselves rather grand', whereas the Taylors, 'though rich, were common'. He felt that his own family spoke with broad Lancashire accents whereas the Thompsons spoke 'beautiful English'. How true this was is open to some doubt. One of the Thompson cousins, Bridget, reflected in 1985 that her memory of her aunts and uncles was of a fairly strong Lancashire accent.

Alan Taylor's point of view may also have been influenced by the generous provision made by his father Percy to Harry Thompson's mother and Harry himself. He notes that Harry's sister Kate married the lodger and comments on this 'nagging symbol of their poverty'. This was of course after the father's death. The lodger, Gustave Juhlin, was actually not a bad catch. He went on to become chief electrical engineer with Metropolitan Vickers (as well as being described as a man with no sense of humour at all).

Taylor describes how he saw the Thompson children as being divided into two camps, one taking after their father 'soft and kind', and the other after their mother Martha 'sharp tongued and arrogant'. His mother Connie, he says, was one of Martha's children, and Harry was another, the cleverest of the lot, 'in the Lancashire phrase a clever-clogs'; and

Later the two brothers thought themselves much cleverer than my father. As a little boy I resented their treatment of him and thought that he knew much more about the things that really mattered, such as Lancashire, the cotton trade and English literature.

Whatever personal antipathy Taylor felt towards him Harry did provide Alan Taylor with many valuable left-wing contacts and introductions, an example of which was securing for him a letter of introduction from the British Prime Minister, James Ramsay MacDonald to Otto Bauer, leader of the Social Democratic Party in Austria when Taylor travelled to Vienna in pursuit of his studies.

In 1933, the practice moved from 27 to 88 Chancery Lane.

Owen Parsons gives a valuable insight into the personalities in the firm at that time in his lengthy manuscript *W.H. Thompson and his Cases*, The manuscript was probably written in 1979 and a copy given to Robin

Thompson in 1984. Parsons had joined the firm in 1935 (probably) and was articled to W.H Thompson from 29 June 1936 for three years, qualifying as a solicitor on 15 November 1939. He remained until 1946.

There were at that time two non-qualified managing clerks, Cornish who was about 35 and Clayton who was about 30. I was 21. I became qualified in 1939.

Later on, during the war, John Williams joined the business and later still one or two others whose names I cannot remember, but as far as I was concerned the outfit consisted of Thompson, Cornish, Clayton and myself.

All surnames be it noted; none of this modern habit of Christian names on five minute acquaintance. In fact I never did get to know any of their Christian names … I heard him (W.H.) called "Harry" – usually by pushers whom he did not like … It was "Mr Thompson" or "Sir" or, very occasionally in the course of a somewhat intimate discussion, "boss". For the rest it was "Cornish", "Clayton" and "Parsons", always without the "Mr" for the rest of us. Young people today will regard this as stuffy; we regarded ourselves as somewhat progressive and indeed we were for those days; anyhow, stuffy or not, we got by.

Clayton was an exuberant extrovert, quick witted, loud and bumptious. Yet behind this flamboyant exterior there was a very shrewd mind and considerable organising ability. To a casual observer he gave the picture of a playboy. In fact he was hardworking, conscientious and a thorough organiser. All this was demonstrated after Thompson's death when he left the firm and, under the umbrella of another solicitor, was, even though not himself qualified, substantially instrumental in building up and establishing and running for many years a large trade union practice.

Parsons continues his account with various anecdotes about Clayton:

The waiting room at Thompson's office in Chancery Lane was at one end of the passage; Clayton's room was at the other. Thompson's room was about half-way down. It used to be Clayton's lazy practice to stand about half-way down the passage and shout for the next customer.

He did this one day: "Mr Hunt". Thompson must have just been coming out of his room because he popped his head out like a jack-in-a-box "Did you say pig or fig?" he asked.

"I don't know" said Clayton, "all I know is that the office boy spells it with a K. Oh, come this way please Mr Hunt."

Parsons also gives some detail about Cornish:

I gathered the impression … that Cornish was the eldest of a poor family who had to leave school early to help in the family finances, and that he slogged his guts out both at work and at night school, learning shorthand and stylised writing, and getting training to qualify as a lawyer's clerk. He joined Thompson quite by chance – the one looking for a clerk, the other looking for a change of job – at the counter of the Law Society's registry, as a young man in his mid-twenties. By the time I met him he was a thoroughly efficient, widely respected, managing clerk with an extensive knowledge of law and practice. He was an indispensable asset to the firm.

After describing Cornish's insecurity, Parsons continues:

I learnt a tremendous amount from Cornish…It was not possible to be in close contact with him for any length of time without a great deal of his skill and judgment rubbing off onto his associates.

In appearance he was much more of the dapper well-turned –out professional than any of the rest of us. Black jacket, striped trousers, wing collar with black tie, rolled up umbrella, bowler hat.

He was a glutton for work. "Work" he would cry, "is the very spice of life." One day he was packing a newly issued Supreme Court Rules and Annual Practice, a reference book of some 1,000 pages into his briefcase. Thompson asked him what he was going to do with it. "Annotate it" said Cornish with enthusiasm, and sure enough, back it came with lots of scribbles all through it and pages of notes in Cornish's spidery writing … .

One of my jobs when working in Cornish's room as his general dogsbody was that of fetcher and carrier of The Board. Thompson acted for the Constructional Engineering Union, the steel erectors, and Cornish did their cases. Very commonly steel erectors worked in rubber-soled tennis shoes when working up aloft because they found that it gave them a better grip … . This practice had the disadvantage of making them vulnerable to foot injuries when on the ground, especially from nails left projecting from shuttering and scaffolding boards lying around the site … . In those days it was necessary to allege negligence against the head contractor and hope for the best. Invariably when the insurance man came in to discuss it, the defence was the same … it was not our board, we had no scaffold boards, we did not do the shuttering, the responsibility must rest on some … subcontractors unknown. Whereupon Cornish would wax eloquent at the skulduggery of building contractors and insurance companies who sank to unspeakable depths to avoid paying damages to poor innocent injured workmen. The insurance man sat back waiting for a suggestion of an ex gratia sympathetic payment, but no, little did he know Cornish's low cunning. It turned out that, in fact, the contractors' denials could be disproved. The plank was available. It was here in the office. `Parsons´ he would order, `fetch the plank in´ (a quick glance at the file to make sure he had the name right) `Jones against Lindsay Parkinson´. And out I would go to the filing room where the office board was kept. A six-feet long piece of timber with a dirty great, rusty, bloodstained nail sticking out of it. I checked that there were no labels left on from previous use, stuck a fresh label on it, wrote Jones v Lindsay Parkinson on it and lugged it into Cornish. Now there are two interesting points about this. First on the slightest consideration it is obvious that there is no conceivable connection between the production of a board even with a label on it and its ownership; the two were utterly unrelated. Secondly, despite all this, there is the fact that it worked without fail every single time; production of this board led to collapse of the defence and a full liability settlement of the claim.

The battle for compensation was fought out in savage fashion. Parsons recalls an occasion when he looked into W.H. Thompson's room:

… there seemed to be some kind of crisis in force. An insurance representative was obviously livid with rage about something. Thompson was leaning back in his chair looking smug and, manifestly, at his most irritating.
 "Mr So-and-so has just paid me what he regards as an insult´ he said, `Perhaps you would care to share your views with Parsons here."
 "Of course I will. I don't mind who hears it. I'll shout it from the housetops"; he was clearly besotted with anger. He stood up and leant over the desk. "I've just said, Thompson, and I'll say it again. You and your office stink in the nostrils of every decent insurance company in Britain. There, I've said it in front of a witness. Now sue me."
 I at once … strode across the room with my arm at full

stretch and began shaking his hand. "Congratulations, boss. At last you've made it. The fulfilment of twenty five years work. Every decent insurance company. They all loathe you. Jolly well done." ... When at last he was able to rescue his hand, Thompson himself grasped his hands and waved them above his head in a boxer's salute. A truly touching scene, from which the insurance chap quietly slipped away.

Parsons describes how on another occasion Cornish came back from court *"with his bowler hat dented by a determined lady who used to represent the Excess Insurance Company…some dispute about the calculation of pre-accident earnings, we gathered"*. This particular incident happened at court in Kent – at the time an important area for Thompson who acted for the Kent Area of the Mineworkers' Union.

Parsons left W.H. Thompson taking a number of unions with him, including the sheet metal workers, dock workers, Kent miners and others too. For years he became unmentionable to the Thompson brothers.

Sir Stephen Sedley, Lord Justice of Appeal, was called to the Bar in 1964, joining the renowned Cloisters Chambers a few years later. He carried out a great deal of work both for Thompsons and O.H. Parsons:

Parsons built up a good practice and took a personal interest in all [the firm's] cases. He instructed me often. On one occasion when we had been on a case in Bristol he spent much of the return train journey reminiscing about his days with W.H.Thompson.

Parsons said that when he joined W.H.Thompson, the insurance companies would not negotiate with Thompson at all. Thompson had to litigate them all. He developed a strategy, with the agreement of the unions, that if the firm lost a hard case the union would refuse to pay the costs. The Iron Trades would put the bailiffs in to the member's home, furniture would be removed and put up for auction. Thompson would then send Parsons down to the sheriff's auction with £30 of union funds to buy the property back (at knock down prices). It was a war of attrition, the purpose of which was to ensure that the insurers lost out even if they were winning cases.

The upshot was that the insurers started to come and negotiate.

Sir Stephen was later involved where Parsons had refused to pay the costs of a lost case. The matter went to the Court of Appeal.

I got a hammering from Fred [Lord Justice] Lawton and the defendants got an order for payment against the union – which put an end to that strategy.

Parsons also recounted the tale of how at a later date the Iron Trades turned up with a stack of files to try and settle. When they got to the last one, they said "sorry about this one Mr Thompson, you're out of time". Thompson replied "oh, that's OK – you're my professional liability insurers."

Early family memories

When Brian died in February 2000, Robin committed some of his memories to paper, and these are laced with his typical sense of humour and irony:

Before I was 6 years old I really cannot remember anything about Brian. That year we went on our usual summer holiday to North Devon. As usual it rained. As it was raining my father said we will go for a drive in the car. My mother sat in the front and Brian and I in the back. As we approached Coombe Martin my father said he would buy each of us a present which we could choose. Brian chose a small book. I a hammer. We returned to the car and drove on. Brian finished the book in a few moments. I went on examining the hammer and said how nice it was. I passed it to my mother so she could admire it and then I stroked it and held it up to the light. I referred to its design and continued in this vein. Suddenly Brian snatched the hammer from me and hit me on the head with it. Dad stopped the car and remonstrated with Brian and I rubbed my head. Henceforth I always regarded Brian as a gentle person but if riled he could become very angry.

Over the 50+ years we were together in Thompsons he only really got angry with me once, fortunately he did not have a hammer with him; but maybe he did get nearly angry on a few other occasions. But we were so different. I was always out and about playing games or cycling with the boys (and girls). He would spend his time reading or doing things with our mother. During the school lunch break I would cycle home from school have a quick steak and within 20 minutes be playing hockey. He would spend time with our mother.

We were at school together and we went to boarding school together but after about 2 days we went our separate ways as our interests were very different. We would meet occasionally. When I started to smoke I had to see him slightly more in order to borrow some money. When the debt got so high I had to tell my father and he increased my pocket money no doubt on my mother's insistence.

My father was fed up with my slow progress at school particularly compared to Brian. So when I was just 16 he decided that as I could tell the difference between a screwdriver and a spanner, which was more than he could, I would make a good engineer. So I was sent off to Loughborough College, which was recommended to him by John Platts-Mills who had been billeted there in the RAF. Henceforth I was not to see much of Brian except a little in the holidays and virtually not at all when I was away in the Army for 4 years.

In 2002, Dominic Carman, son of the late George Carman QC, produced a biography of his father, in the course of which he commented 'The Thompson brothers, Brian and Robin, were champagne socialists, brought up in comfortable affluence on the edge of Hampstead Heath. This did not affect their close links with traditional left-wing and communist trade union leaders.'

In another memoir, mainly about his time in the army, Robin commented on this and gave a few more glimpses into his childhood:

I was amused by his description of Brian and me …

In fact from the age of about 11 we moved to the Hampstead Garden Suburb, which both Brian and I detested. It was a long way to the tube, the shops, and everywhere else. There was no public transport, not many people in those days had cars and consequently it was inconvenient for visitors. There were no pubs and perhaps that is what attracted my father to it.

As young children we lived in Welwyn Garden City. I enjoyed this but I think my mother felt frustrated, politically. Every year on 1 May she would fly a large red flag from the nursery window on the first floor. A Tory councillor lived next door and he was heard to say that: "if it were still hanging on Empire day he would climb up and pull it down."

The family lived outside London, first at Oxted in Surrey, then from 1929 at Welwyn Garden City, next at the Garden Suburb at Hampstead and finally, from shortly before the war at Naphill near High Wycombe.

The house in Welwyn Garden City sporting The Red Flag

The house at Naphill, taken in August 1951

Early family pictures
15 September 1926,
1932 and 1941

Chapter 10
Thinking has a colossal future – Harry Thompson and the Labour Research Department

The life of the law is in essence a life of words, of drafting and writing, thinking and contesting in a specialist language. This language, as James Boyd White, Professor of Law at the University of Michigan, has reminded us in a cascade of elegant recent writing, has the idea of justice at its very core.

Boyd White stresses that this has important consequences. It means, for example, that the true lawyer can never allow himself to be a mere cog in an unquestioned and unquestioning system of social control, nor a profit-maximising service provider in a legal factory providing strokes for powerful and wealthy clients.

Harry Thompson was no such intellectual mercenary and would only take on cases he approved of. In his lifelong exploration of his calling and the way it could interact with the unjust and cruel realities of the society around him, Harry Thompson operated by certain rules. He was deeply interested in evidence, painstaking research and thorough inquiry. He knew that he could only give true service to his clients and have a chance of winning a dissenting case in a time of enormous class and other prejudice if he worked extraordinarily hard. Having built a dissenting case thoroughly and with craftsmanship he had no need to fear any judge striking his clients down for want of evidence or preparation.

He also gave expression to his respect for hard

information in the pamphlets he wrote for the I L P's *Daily Herald* about the radical new Rent Act after the First World War; in his campaigning letters to the *Times* and *Reynolds news*; and in the book length exploration of civil liberty he produced for Victor Gollancz and the Left Book Club.

He wrote this book in dangerous times during the rise of fascism and authoritarianism worldwide. In it he reminds us that our human rights can only be properly protected by the 'ceaseless vigilance of all those who believe that freedom and democracy are the inalienable rights of mankind.'

To Thompson, vigilance did not mean getting angry and sounding off in the pub. As a life-long tee-totaller he was seldom to be found there. Instead he found ammunition in literature and fine books, in the company of writers and artists and politicians and union activists. For him this vigilance also necessarily extended beyond his individual cases to exploring the broader social injustices of which they were usually the symptom.

This led him to work in another field – nurturing an organisation called the Labour Research Department. Labour Research was founded after the First World War from the divisions in the Fabian Society and the Fabian Research Bureau which had itself done some remarkable work of pioneering social investigation. Incorporated under its new name and led by Robin Page Arnot, the idea was to build up a proper informational picture of the structures of inequality and injustice that were hidden factors behind so many social conflicts and to provide unions with information and guidance that would enable them to win rather than lose disputes.

Robin Page Arnot was a truly gifted investigator who devoted endless effort to documenting the heart-breaking struggles of British miners for social justice, for a living wage, better housing and some serious approximation to industrial safety. He embodied his concerns in the outstanding book length Labour Research publication *Facts from the Coal Commission*. Splendidly written, without fat or spurious political rhetoric it can still be read with pleasure and enlightenment eighty years after publication.

As a political activist Page Arnot was also one of the leaders of the newly formed Communist Party of Great Britain who, as we have seen, was provocatively arrested by the Baldwin government in 1925 and imprisoned for his beliefs.

Joan Beauchamp also wrote and worked for Labour Research. The Department had high aspirations to provide proper investigations of the whole range of British industries, inquiring into details of stock ownership and how and in whose interests these industries were actually run. Although there was seldom enough time or money to complete such studies, Joan was able to write and complete her pioneering works on British imperialism in India and women in the workplace.

Despite endless crises due to poverty and lack of resources, Labour Research survived and Harry Thompson found time to put pen to paper again preparing a new edition of his seminal work on industrial safety and compensation during the Second World War. The 1943-44 annual report of the department noted the success of the work as follows:

Of non-periodical publications there is a margin of £900; of this one half is attributable to Mr W.H. Thompson's book Workmen's Compensation; this indicated how dependent the Department is on so profitable a best seller.

Occasionally cases would come the firm's way as a result of the link with the Labour Research Department. Someone who helped out there was Owen Parsons. In his manuscript

'W.H. Thompson and his Cases' he describes an event which says much about the times:

Although articled and busy with my legal studies, I did not desert the Labour Research Department entirely and one evening I was at their offices when a bus conductor turned up. He wanted advice. He had found this on his bus and he wanted guidance before turning it in to his lost property department. 'This' turned out to be Instructions to Counsel to Advise as to the National Union of Fascists, Mosley's Blackshirts, recruiting among H.M. Armed Forces. Included in the bundle was Counsel's Opinion.

    Now clearly this was political dynamite. For years we had been alleging that in Britain as elsewhere, particularly France and Germany, the Fascists had been trying to weasel their way into the police, armed forces and prison service, and here – stated with all the political naivety that only a lawyer can produce – was dramatic proof of our allegations. Clearly we had to publish and the Daily Worker was the appropriate place.

    Equally clearly I had to cover my informant. I had to get the documents copied in a form capable of press reproduction whilst at the same time delivering the documents to the solicitors' office overnight … I worked on the theory that the fool of a clerk concerned would most certainly not know where he had lost the papers, even if he realised that he had lost them at all, and if he was anything like me or any other articled clerk would be only too glad to put them back in the main filing stream with no questions asked. My problem was not with him but in getting the documents copied.

    A reader in 1979 with his copying machines ready to hand will find this problem of 1937 an odd one. In fact it was very real. It took a great deal of phoning around before I ran to earth a politically sympathetic doctor who made a hobby of photography and had the apparatus to photograph the documents sufficiently clearly for newspaper reproduction. A taxi to his surgery in Southwark, lengthy photography and reproduction, drop the originals in at the solicitors to get them mixed up with their morning mail, a phone call to Walter Holmes and delivery of the copies to him, and home to bed, tired but happy …

The following day, Thompson … had hardly got his coat off when Pollitt was on the phone burbling of writs and applications for injunctions. He came round in ten minutes and he and Thompson went into a session and I was allowed to sit in as a spectator. Thompson read exhibit one, that morning's *Daily Worker*. His eyes nearly popped out of his head. His first question was professional. "Who the devil passed this for publication?" Pollitt's eyes were dancing. "Ask your boy there," he said. "Oh", said Thompson, "you, I might have guessed it". He read the endorsement on the writ and the details of the claim for an injunction. "They're basing their claim on breach of copyright. No allegation of libel. Some vague talk of theft. Who wrote the story?"

Pollitt shrugged his shoulders. "Who do you think? Ask your boy."

The injunction application was at 12 o'clock. Counsel Elwyn Jones (later to become Attorney General and then Lord Chancellor in successive Labour Governments) was briefed. Parsons was instructed to attend with counsel. The injunction was granted, but of course by then was too late, and there was no order as to costs. In Parson's account, he continues:

Again Thompson and I sat down at Twinings for a pot of tea and cream cakes.

"I'm sorry about all this, boss".

"What are you feeling sorry about? As far as I can see you did alright."

Thompson's political role is highlighted by D.N. Pritt in his autobiography Part 1, *From Right to Left* when he talks about meetings that took place in the early 1930s:

EASTON LODGE MEETINGS

About this time I was invited to take part in the "Easton Lodge meetings".

 The meetings which I attended were held once or twice a month and the attendance constituted a vague Shadow Cabinet. We discussed all sorts of Socialist problems; some of us read papers for discussion, but talk roamed pretty freely, being largely directed to the practical problems that would have to be faced when the Labour Party would take office with a clear majority. I remember Colin Clark, the statistician, W.H. Thompson, a very fine left-wing solicitor; Ernest Bevin occasionally; Richard Mitchison; Raymond Postgate; Hugh Dalton; and many others.

Apart from *Civil Liberties*, published in 1938, W.H produced a number of pamphlets. Copies of some which have survived are:
The Trade Union Bill, 1927,
Workmen's Compensation – The New Act Explained, 1940,
Workmen's Compensation Up-to-Date, 1944,
EWO Questions and Answers (by W.H. and O.H. Parsons), October 1944, and
Your New Home and the New Rent Act.

The New People's Library
VOL X
Simple, Short, Authoritative

CIVIL LIBERTIES

by
W. H. THOMPSON

1/6

W.H. Thompson's book Civil Liberties published in 1938 was reprinted in 1988. As Robin and Brian said in the foreword "what he wrote then is just as relevant in 1988".

Chapter 11
Mother Earth and Father Land; the international dimension

Looking back over a remarkable life it is clear that Harry Thompson represents a political tradition where justice and human rights are not only a consideration but *the key consideration* in the struggle to overcome injustice and exploitation.

Reflecting on what he stood for and how he worked is not of some slight, marginal importance at a time of speeding globalisation, massive industrialisation on a scale that dwarfs anything that happened in Britain, all taking place when industrialisation is polluting and destroying the very planet we live on.

Harry Thompson's friend Francis Meynell tried to find a way to communicate some of the issues at stake with one of his headlines: 'We are internationalists. We believe in Mother Earth as well as Father Land'.

Thompson himself also tried to put his shoulder to the wheel in the fight for global justice in the Meerut conspiracy case when the King Emperor or rather the law officers of the British Empire took it upon themselves to crush strikes of textile workers in India by brutalising and jailing strikers in Meerut. Coming from Preston in the heartland of Britain's textile industry Harry Thompson had an instinctive understanding of what was at stake and worked to help the defence of the 32 accused.

India was very important in the twenties and thirties in the context of both British Imperialism and the British Labour Movement and Communist Party. In India throughout 1928 and 1929 there was a wave of strikes on the railways, in ironworks, and in the textile industry where a general strike lasted for nearly six months. 31 million working days were lost through industrial disputes in 1928 alone.

The Bombay Textile and Labour Union, which was the established and registered trade union for textile workers in Bombay, had tried to persuade the workers not to strike, but was defeated by the Girni Kamgar (Red Flag) Union which succeeded in bringing the men out.

The workers were persuaded to go back to work on the old conditions pending a government enquiry under a committee headed by Sir Charles Fawcett. Three days before the report of the enquiry was issued, the majority of the accused in the Meerut case were arrested – among them the whole of the Girni Kamgar executive. Those arrested were nearly all well-known officials of trade unions, including the Assistant Secretary of the All-India TUC. Attempts were made to justify the case by denouncing the men as Communists. Undoubtedly some were, but many had no connection with the movement. Lester Hutchinson, who was arrested as an afterthought when he took up the task of carrying out some of the trade union work after the arrest of the others, was a journalist on the *Indian Daily Mail* and unconnected with the labour movement.

This case is commonly referred to as the Meerut Communist conspiracy case, but its full title was: *King-Emperor v Spratt & ors [1932]*

The arrests took place on about 20 March 1929, amidst wholesale raids and house searches, and took place to a backdrop of a show of force throughout the country. Although these events occurred in India, there was much disquiet about various aspects of the case in Britain, not least the fact that the men were denied bail, held in jail unnecessarily for many months, were being refused a proper jury trial and that the trial was to take place hundreds of miles from where the accused lived and worked.

Thompson was retained by the three British defendants Ben Bradley, Phil Spratt and Lester Hutchinson. On paper the case against all the accused looked weak, as Thompson commented in a letter he wrote to Bradley after considering the depositions. And behind the scenes Thompson was

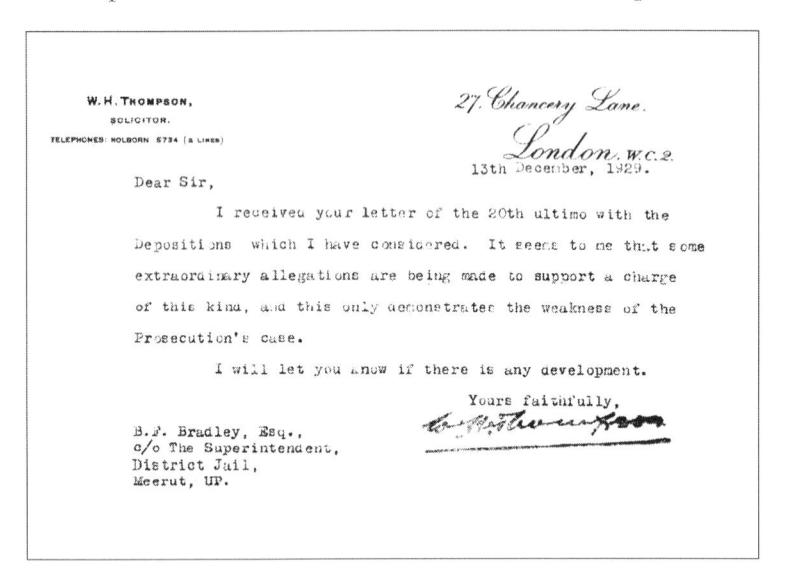

> W. H. THOMPSON,
> SOLICITOR.
> TELEPHONES: HOLBORN 5734 (2 LINES)
>
> 27 Chancery Lane.
> London, W.C.2.
> 13th December, 1929.
>
> Dear Sir,
>
> I received your letter of the 20th ultimo with the Depositions which I have considered. It seems to me that some extraordinary allegations are being made to support a charge of this kind, and this only demonstrates the weakness of the Prosecution's case.
>
> I will let you know if there is any development.
>
> Yours faithfully,
>
> B.F. Bradley, Esq.,
> c/o The Superintendent,
> District Jail,
> Meerut, UP.

busy, prompting a letter from H.G. Wells, Harold Laski, R.H. Tawney and Walter Walsh to the *Manchester Guardian* in defence of their human rights.

Joan Beauchamp, in her book *British Imperialism in India*, comments:

The alleged reason for the choice of this out of the way place for the trial (Meerut) was that a Conference of the Workers' and Peasants' Party was held here in 1928, but the real reason was that, had they been tried in Bombay or Calcutta (from which places the majority of the prisoners came), they would have been entitled to a trial before a High Court Judge and Jury, whereas at Meerut the trial took place

MEERUT CONSPIRACY PROSECUTION.

The Elementary Rights of British Citizens.

To the Editor of the Manchester Guardian.

Sir,—The present ' situation with regard to India makes it desirable to call attention to certain disquieting features of the prosecution of thirty-three persons at Meerut. The charge against the prisoners is that

> they have conspired with each other and with other persons known or unknown to deprive the King Emperor of the sovereignty of British India, and for such purpose to use methods and carry out the programme and plan of campaign outlined and ordained by the Communist International, and in fact they used such, methods and carried out such plan of campaign with the assistance of, and financial support from, the Communist International.

We understand that a large number of the persons charged were officials of a trade union which took part in i a bitter strike in Bombay in 1928, and it has been suggested that this is merely a strike-breaking prosecution.

It is not, however, with this debatable point or with the wisdom of embarking upon this prosecution that we are concerned; there appear to be certain facts which are not "open to challenge. They are (1) that the accused were arrested in March, 1920, and the preliminary inquiry by the magistrate has not yet been completed, but bail has been refused, with the result that the prisoners have been in gaol already for eight months: (2) that ' trial by jury has beer* refused; and (3) that for some obscure reason this trial is taking place at Meerut—800 j miles from Calcutta and Bombay. It is difficult to understand why these men, at present presumed to be innocent, have been refused bail. It is still more difficult to understand why they are to be denied trial by jury.

If the Government cannot see their way to grant an amnesty to these prisoners, as desired in the recent message from the leaders of Indian political opinion, they can surely see to it that the prisoners are at once admitted to bail, and that they are tried by a jury in such a locality as will give them easy access to their friends and advisers.

We are expressing no opinion as to the guilt or innocence of the accused; but the ordinary principles of fair play and traditional justice demand that these people shall be allowed the elementary rights of British citizens on trial.—Yours, &c.,

H. G. WELLS.
H. J. LASKI.
R.H TAWNEY.
WALTER WALSH.

London, December 8.

Manchester Guardian 10 December 1929

before a District Judge (an ordinary Civil Servant) and five assessors. All applications for a transference to a High Court were refused, the final application, made on January 24th 1930 being rejected by the Chief Justice who said "a jury might not take a judicial view".

The prosecution against the 32 men had been sanctioned by the Conservative government, and once it was underway the incoming Labour government declined to intervene. The men were charged under Section 121A of the Indian Penal Code with 'conspiring together and with others to deprive the King-Emperor of his sovereignty'. The case proceeded, involved a detailed examination of a mountain of paper comprising more than 2,600 documents many of which related to the Communist Party, and tens of thousands of printed pages. Evidence was given by numerous witnesses both Indian and British.

Joan Beauchamp:

Throughout the trial not one of the accused was charged with committing any "overt act" violent or otherwise. One of the judges in the High Court, examining an application from the prisoners, pointed out that the counsel for the prosecution had himself conceded that the accused persons had not been charged with having done any illegal act in pursuance of the conspiracy. On another occasion the prosecution claimed that the mere fact that some of the prisoners were members of the Communist Party and the Workers' and Peasants' Party proved them to be guilty…

In August 1932 the Assessors gave their verdict, finding seventeen of the prisoners guilty, but even these findings were rejected by the Judge who passed guilty verdicts against no less than twenty seven. The judgment was given in 1933, four years after the arrests, in a document 676 pages long. Savage sentences were passed; some prisoners were sentenced to transportation, in one case for life, in others for up to 12 years and others to 'rigorous' imprisonment.

One of the Indian defendants was Shaukat Usmani who, from his prison cell in India, stood unsuccessfully as a candidate for the British Communist Party in the General Election of 1929 for the seat of Spen Valley in Yorkshire. Spen Valley was significant as it was the focus of an attempt by the leader of right leaning Liberals, Sir John Simon, to get back into Parliament. Simon had also led the commission whose report was named after him in 1930 on the situation in India. Although Usmani's campaign was unsuccessful in getting him elected, it succeeded in bringing the issue of Meerut to public attention, and was repeated in 1931 when Usmani again stood, this time in St. Pancras South East against a Tory South African mining millionaire associated with the Cliveden set, Sir Alfred Lane Beit. Usmani was sentenced to ten years transportation.

MEERUT CONSPIRACY CASE

27 INDIAN AND BRITISH WORKERS JAILED IN INDIA

1 sentenced to transportation for life.

26 sentenced to 170 years imprisonment.

In March, 1929, thirty-two leaders of the Indian Trade Union and Political Movement were arrested in India and sent handcuffed under armed guard to Meerut and charged with "Conspiracy against the King."

In June, 1929, legal proceedings were begun. They continued until January 16th, 1933, and during this 3½ years the majority of the prisoners were confined to jail, and were subjected to all the misery and humiliation of Indian jail life.

Meerut Jail has the reputation of being one of the worst in India.

The Trial was before a Sessions Judge and five Court Assessors—Trial by Jury being refused. The Court Assessors found 14 Not Guilty. The judge, however, is not bound to accept their findings. He declared 27 guilty, including 11 whom the Assessors found not guilty, and then proceeded to pass the following vicious sentences:—

1—Transportation for life.

5—Transportation for 12 years.	4—Transportation for 5 years.
3—Transportation for 10 years.	6—4 years' rigorous imprisonment.
3—Transportation for 7 years.	5—3 years' rigorous imprisonment.

SENTENCED for WHAT?

No act of violence or criminal offence has been committed by these standard-bearers of the working-class movement. The charge of "Conspiracy against the King" includes among other things:

"**The incitement of antagonism between Capital and Labour,**" "**The encouragement of strikes, hartals, and agitation,**" "**Propaganda by speeches, literature, newspapers, the celebration of anniversaries connected with the Russian Revolution,**" etc., etc.

This was the basis for the whole case of the Government of India, which has spent over £120,000 on the prosecution.

The anti-working-class attitude of the Judge is brought out by the following observation:—

"Perhaps of deeper gravity was the hold acquired over the Bombay Textile Workers, illustrated by the 1928 strike and the revolutionary policy of the Girni Kamgar Union."

The whole of the Executive Committee of this Union was arrested.

The only "crime" committed by those sentenced was the building of the workers' and peasants' independent trade union and political organisations. Prior to 1920 strikes were practically unknown: trade unions were managed by Government agents. In the ten years that followed 1,739 strikes took place, and of these 924 were caused by attacks on the miserable wages and the appalling working conditions that existed in India. In practically all these strikes Trade Union recognition was one of the chief points in the workers' demands. Trade Union activity is regarded as Conspiracy. The prosecutor stated:—
"*That Mitra's—one of the accused—career in the conspiracy began when he participated in the Calcutta scavengers' strike.*"

Those accused in the Meerut Conspiracy Case have been sentenced to these vicious sentences because they have assisted the workers and peasants of India in their struggles to build their own trade union and political organisation, and because they led the workers in some of the most heroic strikes in the history of the international working-class movement.

These savage sentences have been imposed by the British Government, and the responsibility for the release of these militant leaders lies at the door of every Trade Unionist and politically-conscious worker.

Get your organisations to adopt resolutions to the Government demanding their release. Organise Demonstrations of Protest and for the solidarity of the Indian and British working-class movements.

Send donations for the Prisoners' Appeal Fund to the Treasurer, Meerut Prisoners Release Committee, Alex Gossip, Bedford House, 58, Theobald's Road, London, W.C.1.

One of the information leaflets produced by The Prisoners Release Committee. The statement by Professor Laski appears on the reverse side of the leaflet.

MEERUT CONSPIRACY CASE

Memorial

FOR THE RELEASE OF THE PRISONERS

WE have seen with a profound sense of disturbance the verdict and sentences in the Meerut trial. We desire emphatically to record our belief that the proceedings in this case violate all the accepted canons of British justice. We do so on the following grounds:

1. The prisoners were deliberately tried in Meerut to escape the possible inconveniences of trial by jury.
2. The prisoners have been in jail, under conditions so bad that hunger strikes have had to be taken in protest against them, for a period of almost four years. The terrible sentences imposed take no account of this.
3. No overt acts amounting to conspiracy have been proved against the accused. Acknowledged or presumed sympathy (in several cases denied) with Communism has been taken as sufficient ground for conviction. It is as though Englishmen were sent to jail for being, or being presumed to be, members of the Communist Party.
4. Proper facilities for the organisation of their defence were withheld from the accused from the outset.
5. The main evidence alleged for the conviction which relates to the Indian activities of the accused describes only the normal activities of trade union officials in this country.
6. The acquittal of fourteen of the accused (including Hutchinson) was actually recommended by the Assessors to the trial Judge, who overruled their finding in his judgment. We suggest that this is evidence of a will to conviction highly undesirable in political cases of this kind.

We do not need to point out that for some years now this case has been closely watched, both in India and in this country, as the acid test of British justice in India. We believe that the findings of the Court confirm all the doubts and misgivings which accompanied its origination. We do not believe that the maintenance of the result is possible if any reputation for British integrity in India is to be preserved.

PROFESSOR HAROLD J. LASKI.

London, March, 1933.

Published by Meerut Prisoners Release Committee, c/o Alex Gossip, Treasurer, Bedford House, 58, Theobald's Road, London, W.C.1, and Printed by The Utopia Press, Ltd. (T.U.), 44, Worship Street, London, E.C.2.

The three British citizens represented by Thompson were:

Ben Bradley, formerly a London District Committee member of the AEU. He was sentenced to 10 years transportation;

Phil Spratt who as 'a Cambridge man' and 'traitor to his class' got 12 years transportation; and

Lester Hutchinson, who received four years imprisonment. Mr Hutchinson later became a Labour MP, being elected to Manchester Rusholme in 1945. He wrote a book about the case.

The League against Imperialism held a meeting about Meerut at Caxton Hall in 1932, and the Manchester street theatre group the Red Megaphones performed a sketch.

On appeal, in July 1933, nine of the defendants were acquitted, including Lester Hutchinson, and the sentences of the remainder greatly reduced, the most severe being reduced to three years 'rigorous imprisonment'. The remaining British defendants, Bradley and Spratt had their sentences reduced to one and two years respectively and, not surprisingly as they had already spent over four years in prison, were swiftly deported back to Britain.

Even so, the import of the appeal court judgment was, in Joan Beauchamp's words,

> to make it perfectly clear that the British authorities regard membership of the Communist Party of India as illegal and a sufficient pretext for a lengthy term of imprisonment.
>
> The chief crime of the Communists in the eyes of the Indian Government is that they help to organize militant trade unions. The object of the Government in arresting the Meerut prisoners was to get all the militant trade union leaders safely out of the way at a time when not only were the workers and peasants in revolt against the imperial

power, but many thousands of workers were in revolt against the local bourgeoisie.

Within a decade, and coincidentally also within months of Harry Thompson's own premature death, the clock moved on beyond midnight towards a new morning. India won her freedom from her colonial masters. The King Emperor would jail no more textile workers.

After Meerut and all the publicity it generated the Communist Party of India and its offshoots went on to become a major electoral force.

Note: Various files of papers relating to this case including original correspondence from W.H. Thompson are held by the Peoples History Museum in Manchester and a detailed account is given in *British Imperialism in India*.

Chapter 12
The tree of liberty

The 1930s was a time of major upheaval, deep economic depression, hunger marches, and demonstrations against fascist authoritarianism whether it be in Spain or at Olympia or Cable Street in London.

Three cases Harry Thompson became involved in were regarded as of sufficient legal importance to be reported in the Law Reports. They also feature in some length in Thompson's own book *Civil Liberties*. The first was *Elias v Pasmore [1934] 2 KB 164*

The case and its background are explained in this extract from *Civil Liberties* at page 57 et seq:

In 1932 the National Unemployed Workers' Movement was organising a hunger march which was expected to reach London from various parts of the country. The march created considerable controversy, and newspapers of a certain colour were calling for the arrest of the leaders. A warrant was issued for the arrest of Wal Hannington on a charge of attempting to cause disaffection among members of the Metropolitan Police Force contrary to the provisions of the Police Act 1919 ... On the 1 November 1932, Hannington attended the offices of the N.U.M.W to attend to his work and was confronted by several police officers, who prevented any of the people in the building from leaving, packed up many parcels of papers...loaded them in conveyances and, with Hannington, departed to Scotland Yard ... . The effect was to disrupt the work of the N.U.W.M. for the time being.

Scores of documents had been removed without any

investigation as to their relevance, and in any event the charge against Hannington related only to a speech he had made. Most of the documents were returned, but some were retained and used as the basis of a charge against Elias.

W.H. Thompson's account continues:

There appeared to be no legal justification for this conduct, and an action was started … . When the case came on for trial there was no dispute about the facts. The defence was that the papers were seized "for the purpose of examination and investigation in connection with the arrest". In respect of the documents which formed the subject of the charge against Elias, the police claimed the right to retain these … . The case was tried by Mr. Justice Horridge, and he came to the conclusion that the police had seized and removed the documents which were returned without any legal justification, and he awarded damages against them. It is, therefore quite clear that the wholesale removal of documents was quite illegal, and that the police were acting illegally, and it is important to observe that this illegality was defended by the Home Office.

As the account above indicates, Thompson successfully obtained damages for trespass on behalf of the National Unemployed Workers Movement in respect of the unlawful seizure of documents by the police. However, the decision of the court was not entirely favourable as Thompson explains:

There was however part of the decision in this case which appears to have established a principle for which no legal precedent can be found. The court decided that, although the police seizure of documents without examination might be illegal, yet if some of those documents were evidence of crime committed either by the defendant or by any other person, the illegality of the police in seizing those documents was made legal because by chance the documents were found to be evidence of crime. The effect of this part of the decision is stated in a standard text-book as follows: "The interest of State excuses the seizure, otherwise unlawful, of documents or articles in the possession or control of the person arrested if subsequently it should appear in fact that they are evidence of a crime committed by anyone."

In these matters it is becoming more and more apparent how elastic legal principles appear to be when "the interests of State" are affected.

The second case was Thomas v Sawkins [1935] 2 KB 249

Let us consider the right of the police to enter a meeting … . After the scenes at the Mosley meeting at Olympia, when complaints were made that the police made no attempt to enter the hall and stop the brutality which was going on there, the Home Secretary in the House of Commons said on the 14 June 1934: "The law provides that unless the promoters of a meeting ask the police to be present in the actual meeting they cannot go in unless they have reason to believe that an actual breach of the peace is being committed."

The account goes on to explain the similar expression in a reference to the Departmental Committee of the Home Office, and continues:

These statements of the law seemed at the time to be open to no question and the Home Secretary had all legal authority on his side; it may be a matter of surprise that even on this statement of the law the police did not enter to put a stop to brutality and breaches of the peace which were taking place to the knowledge of everyone except apparently the police.

In view of the events at the Albert Hall and other places, it is perhaps not difficult to find an explanation of this. The cynic may think it depends on who is being "beaten up".

Prior to the events just mentioned, the police in certain parts of England had always claimed the right to enter meetings, and in South Wales it was decided to put the Home Secretary's views to the test. On 17 August 1934, a meeting was held for the purpose of protesting against the Incitement to Disaffection Bill, and to demand the dismissal of the Chief Constable of the County. The steward at the entrance to the hall informed the police that he had instructions not to admit the police, but they insisted on entering. When the chief speaker and chairman arrived – it ought to be said that they were both Communists – they repeated the request to the police to leave, quoted the Home Secretary, made a complaint in writing, and the speaker laid his hand on a police sergeant, who resisted removal. This was a technical assault. The meeting proceeded, but there was no breach of the peace or disorder. The police sergeant was summoned for assault – of which he was plainly guilty if he had no right to remain at the meeting. The magistrates dismissed the summons on the ground that the police were entitled to enter the hall and remain there throughout the meeting because they had ground for their belief that if they were not present seditious speeches might be made or that breaches of the peace might occur.

The speaker appealed to the High Court but lost. Thompson goes on to note, sarcastically, that:

The right of the police to enter and remain at a meeting depends on whether their apprehension that there will be seditious speeches made or other offences committed is reasonable, and the reasonableness of that apprehension is to be determined by a bench of magistrates.

The third was *Duncan v Jones [1936] 1KB 218*. The case arose out of a Home Office Circular to the Metropolitan Police instructing them, arbitrarily, to prevent the holding of a public meeting within 100 yards of the Employment Exchange where unemployed workers went to sign on. The NCCL, which included Thompson as a founder member, challenged the Circular and organised a public political meeting within the relevant area, deploying observers to watch and be available to give evidence if necessary. The observers included Harry Thompson (and as a potential witness he did not act in the subsequent case).

On 30 July 1934 the meeting was held in Deptford, and the speaker was Kath Duncan, a Communist. She spoke on the Incitement to Disaffection Bill, then before parliament. Mrs Duncan was advised by a policeman that she was not allowed to speak and invited to move to a new meeting place 175 yards away, beyond the relevant limit. Mrs Duncan declined, indicating that she had committed no offence and that in speaking she would be committing no offence. She was then arrested. There was no suggestion of breach of the peace or obstruction of the highway. It was based entirely on the policeman's subjective opinion that he apprehended a breach of the peace if a political meeting were held in the vicinity of the relevant venue.

Mrs Duncan was convicted and fined and her appeal was dismissed. Ronald Kidd, founder of the National Council for Civil Liberties commented in his book *British Liberty in Danger*:

The police are set up by this judgment as the arbiters of what political parties or religious sects shall or shall not be accorded the rights of freedom of assembly – two civil rights which even the judges of earlier times were jealous to protect.

During the 1930s the effects of the depression were still

being felt. Unemployment was massive and the cuts in unemployment benefit introduced at the turn of the decade as an emergency measure were still in force. Many were forced onto public assistance (supplementary benefit) and the rates for that were cut at the end of 1933. The government sponsored a scheme by which the unemployed were made to work in order to qualify for their benefit (with some extra 'pocket money'). This undercut the wages of those who were working. There was a national hunger march in 1932, followed by a series of local hunger marches organised by the Unemployed Workers Movement in 1933. The Movement then organised a national march from every part of the kingdom into London in 1933. This was due to arrive at Hyde Park on 25 February 1934. Wal Hannington was in charge of the organisation.

Harry Pollitt, General Secretary of the Communist Party, and Tom Mann, former General Secretary of the Amalgamated Engineering Union and treasurer of the National Unemployed Workers Union were scheduled to address the Delegate Congress of Action on 24 February and the Hyde Park demonstration the following day. Both were outstanding speakers. Both had addressed meetings the previous Sunday in South Wales at Ferndale and Trelaw. In an effort to remove Pollitt and Mann and prevent them addressing the Hyde Park marchers, the Government arranged for them to be arrested on the evening of 23 February and taken to Pontypridd Magistrates Court where they were charged with sedition – alleged to have been committed in their speeches on the previous Sunday. Owen Parsons describes what happened next:

Thompson was down there on the Saturday morning applying for bail. The magistrate ... very reluctantly and in face of Thompson's threat to get an order from a High Court judge who will "have a more realistic sense of justice than local jacks-in-office" overruled the police objections to bail but set it at a high sum. Thompson at once produced a surety of such wealth and probity "that" as he told the magistrate "not even the most biased of policemen or magistrates could refuse him". The gloves were well and truly off from the start.

By the time the Saturday morning hearing and formalities were over it was already too late to get from Pontypridd to London in time to address the Council of Action that evening and their speeches were read by someone else. The real question was whether Pollitt and Mann should address the Hyde Park demonstration …

Bail had been granted for one week only, and the magistrate had made it clear that any further grant would depend on the conduct of the accused in the meantime. Parsons notes that Thompson gave Pollitt and Mann purely legal advice. They were experienced enough to make up their own minds as to whether to continue with the Hyde Park address. In the event they decided not to.

The case against them was listed for a committal hearing (effectively a rehearsal of the police evidence so that the magistrate can decide whether the evidence is strong enough to commit the case to trial before the higher court). The only evidence of relevance was that of two shorthand writers who actually heard and recorded the allegedly seditious comments. They were both police constables. Parsons account continues:

It seemed incredible that any competent shorthand writer capable of taking down a speech by Pollitt, who was a very fast orator, or Mann, who tended to meander, would only be of the rank of constable in a South Wales mining village. Even in advance of their evidence, Thompson had good grounds for doubting their bona fides.

Finally, and he would always insist that this was the

determining factor, the names of the two witnesses were Police Constable Onions and Police Constable Fudge. `Chaps with names like that,´ he said, `are made for suffering. I felt it was my job in life to make them suffer.´

Thompson turned what should by rights have been a nice gentlemanly committal proceeding into a brawl involving the Government, the Glamorgan police, the Magistrate and, of course, the unfortunate Onions and Fudge.

It soon turned out that neither P.C. Onions nor P.C. Fudge in fact knew shorthand at all. They were unable to take down a statement dictated by Thompson at almost longhand speed.

It turned out that the shorthand notes of both sets of speeches only filled four or five pages of each notebook.

"How come?", asked Thompson, having first ascertained that each speech occupied about half-an-hour. It turned out that the policemen did not set out to take down the whole speech. "I waited until I heard him say something seditious and then began to take it down."

"So you started behind him?"

"Yes."

"And then caught him up?"

"Yes."

"And passed him?"

"Yes…I mean no, sir."

A great row developed when Thompson insisted on the Magistrates Clerk, whose job it was to make a note of the evidence for use later at the Assizes, entering the full contradictory reply.

"But he clearly meant 'no', Mr Thompson."

"I have not the faintest idea what he `clearly meant´" said Thompson, "nor, I suspect, have you. All that I am concerned with, and all that you should be concerned with if you are doing your duty, and most certainly all that the learned Judge will be concerned with at the Assizes, is what the witness said, not what he meant."

"But his reply was contradictory. It did not make sense."

"I'm sure it didn't," said Thompson, "but if you're going to leave out all the nonsensical evidence this witness has given you'll be sending the Clerk of the Assizes a lot of blank sheets of paper." Finally, "Of course the witness has been committing perjury all through his evidence but it is not your job to cover for him. I have a competent official shorthand writer here. If you don't perform your statutory duty and enter the evidence correctly, I'll apply for an order of mandamus to force you to do so."

Despite the weakness of the evidence, the magistrate duly committed the case to trial and Thompson briefed D.N. Pritt. There was great public interest and the International Labour Defence got 75,000 signatures to a petition of protest at the charges – based largely on Thompson's exposure of the hollowness of the case.

Before the trial Thompson saw the Associate of the Assize and told him that a dozen or so special friends of the accused were anxious to be allowed into court, and the Associate was courteous enough to give special passes to enable the people concerned to be let in. There was then an incident where the Chief Constable refused admission, notwithstanding the passes on the basis that they 'looked like communists'. Thompson complained, the judge intervened and the friends were allowed in.

Thompson went back to the public gallery and personally supervised the removal of a dozen policemen in uniform – the usual trick of packing the court having been adopted – and their replacement …

As he got back to his bench in front of Counsel, Thompson leant across a couple of solicitors clerks towards the Chief Constable. In a stage whisper designed to reach the ears of the jury Thompson asked him: "How do you like your onions fried?".

As he used to say when recounting this yarn, rather fourth form but he enjoyed saying it. One can well understand how he might.

Thanks to the shorthand notes of the evidence given at the Magistrates committal proceedings, and particularly the answers of police constables Onions and Fudge in cross-examination which tied them well and truly to their fake notebooks and lying evidence, Pritt had a field day … . To be savaged by Thompson and then after three months of anticipation to be torn apart by Pritt was no joke.

During the first day thousands of people had gathered to demonstrate outside court. The judge in the case was Mr Justice Talbot, described by Pritt in his book *From Right to Left* as 'of quite icy impartiality, capable of trying a question of alleged conspiracy by a Communist with as little emotion as a question of the quality of a tin plate'. The judge needed to get back to his lodgings, as Parsons describes 'in style in accordance with time honoured custom and practice…to the accompaniment of trumpeters, outriders and a good deal of bowing and general paraphernalia.'

The Chief Constable offered his solution; he was quite sure he would be able to clear a way – he had 'a hundred mounted officers and 250 foot in reserve'.

'Oh, my god, another Blaina riot Thompson thought …'

Thompson offered the alternative suggestion – 'The prisoner Pollittt is extremely popular with the people concerned…I suggest that his help is invoked so that he can influence the attitude of the crowd.'

Pollitt was called, and to the Chief Constable's chagrin, the Judge agreed with his suggestion that two of his friends should address the crowd and explain the position to them, and that the troops should be withdrawn.

And so it was arranged. Thompson went to collect the two local lads who were duly briefed by Pollitt. The Chief went to withdraw the troops.

Within five minutes, the trumpets rang out, the police guard sprang to attention, His Lordship, his Clerk, the Associate, the Bailiff and, last but not least, the Chief Constable made their dignified procession to their waiting cars. As they did so, the cheers of the assembled multitude rang out, Sosban Fach, Land of My Fathers and other music swelled out over Swansea Bay. Never had an Assize Judge had so magnificent a send-off.

The next day the prosecution decided not to proceed further with Mann's Ferndale speech. The Judge indicated that Mann's Trelaw speech only had one passage which "even if the shorthand evidence is to be believed" was capable of being construed as seditious. Pursuant to this very strong hint, the Jury found Mann not guilty on all counts. Following this the prosecution announced that they were calling no evidence against Pollitt so he, of course, was found "not guilty". A complete victory.

The reference to Blaina was to the Blaina Riot of 1935. Martyn Thomas gives an account both graphic and erudite of what happened in Blaina in South Wales in his lengthy article *The Blaina Riots 1935*. The Unemployment Insurance Fund, from which benefit to insured workers was intended to be paid, was supposed to be self-supporting through the contribution system. However, the fund had fallen deeply into debt because of the level of unemployment. The May Committee was set up to report on public expenditure and recommended swingeing cuts in unemployment benefit. (The argument that this gave rise to led to Ramsay MacDonald leaving the Labour Party to become Prime Minister of the national government). Subsequently unemployment benefit was cut and the Means Test system

Women hunger marchers in Wales, March 1934
Photograph taken from *Women Who Work*

set up. Changes to the benefit system were designed to improve the level of benefit paid, but at the same time removed local discretion, and many mass rallies were held as a result. A march was planned in Blaina, South Wales which the police attempted to ban, a factor which turned the planned march into a demonstration of the right to free speech and free assembly.

The march went ahead on 21 March 1935. Unemployed people in their thousands marched on the local Public

Assistance Committee offices. They were prevented from reaching the offices by a cordon of police and a pitched battle broke out. Numerous men were charged with assault, some with riot. W.H. Thompson was retained by the defence. He represented a number of men charged following a similar event at Abertillery on 15 March 1935 and secured their acquittal. The Blaina trial proceeded amid great publicity; Nye Bevan and Jennie Lee were among the defendants' well-wishers. Notwithstanding the overtly political nature of the evidence the prosecution led and the transparent unreliability of at least some of the police evidence (as a result of which some of those accused of assault were acquitted), a number of those charged with riot were found guilty and imprisoned.

The National Council for Civil Liberties

W.H. Thompson was a founder member of the National Council for Civil Liberties in 1934, a member of the Executive Committee and Chairman from 1939. The NCCL devoted much time in the 1930s to defending members of the anti-fascist movement who were prosecuted by the police for their action against Mosley and the blackshirts.

The formation of the Council for Civil Liberties was announced in the Manchester Guardian and the Times on 24 February 1934. The organisation was renamed the National Council for Civil Liberties in November of the same year. The founder Ronald Kidd was convinced of the need for such an organisation after he observed the use of Agent Provocateurs who were inciting violence during the hunger marches in 1932. His idea was to bring together eminent journalists, writers, lawyers and MPs to observe the behaviour of police at mass public gatherings. Kidd became the first General Secretary and E.M. Forster was the first President. Harry Thompson was the chairman of the General Purposes Sub-Committee the purpose of which was to plan the immediate programme and which met each week for this purpose. The executive originally met where Kidd and Sylvia Crowther-Smith (later Scaffardi) lived, in a tiny flat, 3 Dansey Yard, off Shaftsbury Avenue, but soon moved to an office in Charing Cross Road.

In the early years the NCCL was run by Kidd and Sylvia Scaffardi, supported by an Executive Committee which included Vera Brittain, Claud Cockburn, Rev. Dick Shepherd, Harold Laski and Kingsley Martin, along with D.N. Pritt and Harry Thompson on the General Purposes Committee.

Sylvia Scaffardi describes Harry Thompson's work for the NCCL in her book *Fire under the Carpet: Working for Civil Liberties in the 1930s*:

Thompson was generous in the time he devoted to the Council. He turned up every week. His buoyant, decisive presence reassuring, stimulating – but demanding. He wanted results, was impatient, intolerant of delays, uninterested in the reason why – he had no use for waffling, time-wasting frills.

He was Chairman also of the monthly Executive Committee … . In the few minutes of chat before we sat down to the agenda, Thompson was juxtaposed with Forster. Thompson, a man of the world with an air of success, a practical approach, a way of life cut down to his essentials, as rationalised and streamlined as his own well-integrated office … . He had the greatest respect for Forster, for his literary standing, his integrity on matters of principle, and indeed for his courage in accepting ultimate responsibility as President in such acute times, especially with his vulnerability as an undeclared homosexual. Forster deceptively hesitant, with a tentative approach that almost gave the impression of timidity. He always declined a place at the head of the table. Thompson unbending genially, making a big effort to meet him on his own plane. Almost a *Howard's End* encounter!

The NCCL was involved in many campaigns in the 1930s, many against the activities of the Union of Fascists and the apparent official bias on the part of the authorities in favour of the Blackshirts and against the anti-fascist demonstrators. During this period the Council campaigned against the Sedition (Incitement to Disaffection) Act which replaced the Incitement to Mutiny Act, 1797.

The NCCL was one of Harry Thompson's proudest achievements. The essence of their method was to foster and build loose alliances which would be all the stronger for defending the space for people to think their own thoughts and unite around what they had in common.

We can see the NCCL/Thompson coalition building method at work in two cases – one involving the freedom to publish a children's book, the other the liberty to show a radical foreign film which suggested that in certain circumstances people could perhaps even change the world for the better. The book was edited by Thompson's wife Joan Beauchamp. The film was by a Russian, Sergei Eisenstein.

First the book and a story within it called *Men Who March By*. In this story one character in South Wales suggests to another youngster that it's not in her experience always a good idea to cheer men in uniform and blindly sway to the drumbeat of war. The book *Martin's Annual* was planned to appear for the Christmas market in 1934, just as the government of the day was trying to push a new Sedition Bill through parliament.

The publishers of the annual, the firm Martin Lawrence, received a letter from its printers suggesting all sorts of cuts to the story in view of the Sedition Bill then before the House of Commons and warning their customers that the Head Printer had been told to cut everything he felt might be seditious before printing went ahead. The NCCL was already campaigning vociferously against this bill at the time and behind the scenes mobilising a powerful alliance to oppose it.

Within a week of the threat an important letter appeared in the *Manchester Guardian* arguing just how sinister such censorship of books was. Signed by a formidable list of names of Britain's leading publishers, there is little doubt who had initiated the round-robin – *Martin's Annual* editor Joan Beauchamp and her husband Harry Thompson.

The second case involved miners exhibiting two films at the Miners Hall in Bolden Colliery near Newcastle before an audience of 400 people. The two films were Eisenstein's *Battleship Potemkin* and a British made documentary called *Hunger March*.

By the 1930s these inexpensive 16mm films were being used increasingly for education, for documentaries and propaganda purposes. Miniature versions of many classic films were available. Films such as Potemkin (as Ms Scaffardi says, 'dangerous revolutionary stuff!') were being shown in halls. In addition, privately made films on topics concerned directly or indirectly with civil liberty, such as police brutality, colonial repression, and the Spanish war, were being shown at meetings all over the country, and the government was very anxious to prevent this. Commercial inflammable films could only be shown under licence from the local authority under the terms of the Cinematograph Act, 1909, and the Home Office drew up plans to bring miniature films under the same regulatory system. But were miniature films flammable and therefore capable of being subject to the same rules? To get a ruling, the police served summonses on eleven miners at the Bolden Colliery Miners' Lodge for showing a miniature film in the Miners' Hall, on the grounds of public safety. The NCCL, with financial support from the British Institute of Adult Education, undertook the defence.

Sylvia Scaffardi recounts what happened:

In the Jarrow Police Court, a lawyer from London caused something of a stir. W.H. Thompson had come up himself, and brought technical experts with him. He took by surprise the men from the Home Office who had hoped to have it all their own way. Thompson gave a demonstration in court with samples of film and matches. The celluloid of the commercial strip flared up explosively, the cellulose acetate of the miniature film crumpled, charred and refused to burn. The magistrate dismissed the case, with costs against the police.

The Home Office reacted furiously threatening an appeal and continued to press ahead with another similar prosecution at Stockton-on-Tees. Four months later the *Daily Herald* reported the final outcome. There would be no Home Office appeal in the Bolden case. And as for Stockton: '…Mr Thompson, solicitor to the NCCL, has been informed by the solicitor for the police that the proceedings are abandoned'.

The specialist newspaper the *Kinematograph Weekly* on 7 February 1935 reported a protest meeting in Cambridge which unanimously passed a resolution deprecating the introduction of new special regulations regarding the use of such film. The meeting was sponsored by the Cambridge University Film Society, Education Society and Film Club, along with the Association of Scientific Workers and the NCCL. The principal speaker was W.H. Thompson. In commenting on the censorship issue raised, he said:

People who have studied kinema art know that some of the Russian films are magnificent productions. Whether it is a case of Conservatives banning a Communist film or Communists banning a Conservative film does not seem to matter. If it is you and I who want to see the film, we should be allowed to see it unless they can say that it is obscene, seditious or blasphemous.

After this, some local authorities continued to attempt to ban miniature film exhibitions in their area, but in due course an Advisory Committee set up by the Home Office advised that both the content and safety precautions should be left to the good sense of the exhibitors and that the small minority of licensing authorities that still attempted to control them should come into line, and accept that these films were outside their jurisdiction.

In commenting on the legal services available to the NCCL, Sylvia Scaffardi notes:

With W.H. Thompson, another solicitor and three young barristers on our General Purposes Committee, legal defence for police court cases could be arranged at short notice. Thompson, the barristers, and indeed all the lawyers who acted for us, generously gave their services free.

These cases can give little more than a flavour of the type of work W.H. was engaged in during the 1930s. Owen Parsons' account gives details of a number of other political cases: the Percy Glading espionage trial; the defence on behalf of the two Welshmen who blew up the bombing school in North Wales in 1936 in which an overtly political defence was run with the result that whilst guilty, very lenient sentences were passed; various cases involving the *Daily Worker*; and the Cove Camp.

Thompson drew this appreciation from Harry Pollitt: 'a valiant champion, strong and independent character, a great friend and a great socialist.'

Margaret Cole in her book *Growing up into Revolution* gives a pithy view of the type of work Thompson was sometimes involved in:

*Women demonstrate against war and fascism,
International Women's Day 1935*
Photograph taken from *Women Who Work*

The Communist Party in its early days was conspiratorial to the point of being a joke. I remember one comrade being instructed to meet a higher-up comrade in the middle of Blackfriars Bridge; he did so, and received a sign to walk to the south side of the bridge and then return. After a repetition of this manoeuvre, the two, having, I suppose, successfully thrown the police off the scent, sat down together and transacted their business in a convenient Lyons. On another occasion, members of a Party cell were told to rendezvous in an unfashionable part of Bloomsbury at 11 p.m. <u>in separate taxicabs</u>, a proceeding which naturally concentrated the attention of the entire neighbourhood on their activities – it may have been then or at another time that the assembled comrades succeeded in setting afire the flat in which they were having their secret meeting, and had to be rescued in a literal blaze of publicity by the London Fire Brigade. Harry Thompson, who was more-or-less honorary solicitor to a good many bunches of crack-pots, used to have a fund of anecdotes of this kind.

Some may have been 'crack-pots'; most were ordinary citizens simply trying to exercise their rights – to freedom of speech freedom of association, and freedom from oppression. If they happened to be crack-pots, no matter; if they were communists, no matter; and, as he made clear at the Cambridge University debate, if they were conservatives, no matter. All were entitled to inalienable rights under the law and were deserving of representation. No one was beneath the radar. A street seller of the *Daily Star* who was arrested and charged with obstruction brought the full force of Thompson's growing army of lawyers in his expanding practice to her rescue. But a comrade on the left who departed from Thompson's view of justice equally brought his wrath and condemnation.

The build up to, and outbreak of, war in 1939 stretched

loyalties to the limit. Even though Thompson was not a member of the Communist Party, he was involved in the thick of the debate. In Stan Newens' unpublished biography of Kay Beauchamp he describes some of the fall out.

When the Second World War broke out on 3rd September 1939 the Communist Party leadership had little faith in Chamberlain's will to conduct a genuine struggle against Nazi Germany, but Harry Pollitt produced a pamphlet, *How to Win the War*, which argued it was a just war which the British working class should support to defeat Hitler and fascism. A Manifesto of 2nd September took the same view, and was initially endorsed by the Party.

Kay said there was widespread disagreement with this line within the CPGB, even before D. J. Springhall, a CC member, who had been working in Moscow, returned to Britain on 24th September and reported that the Comintern had denounced the war as an 'out and out imperialist war to which the working class in no country could give any support.' (ECC1 Manifesto of 6.11.39.)

Kay therefore took the view of the majority of members in the London District, led by Ted Bramley, that Harry Pollitt was wrong, and she had no difficulty in supporting the decision of the Central Committee to withdraw the Manifesto of 2nd September which led to Pollitt's removal from the post of General Secretary. She wrote to Harry Pollitt to express her view that it was an imperialist war which the Party should oppose, and was told by Harry Thompson, when the latter put his disagreement with support for the war to Pollitt, that Pollitt could accept this from him, but resented being told what to do by Kay, who was, after all, an employee of the Party.

Notwithstanding this, when the *Daily Worker*, having started off by attacking German fascism, increasingly aimed its ire at the Allies for 'spreading the war', Thompson waded into the fray and wrote to Ranji Palme Dutt on 29 April 1940 from the firm's offices at 88 Chancery Lane, making clear his unhappiness about the Worker's editorial stance.

The Communist Party only changed course and supported the war after Hitler attacked the Soviet Union, and Harry Pollitt duly resumed his position in the Party. None of this debate affected Harry Pollitt's close personal friendship with Harry, Joan or for that matter Kay. Debate was healthy and occasional disagreements inevitable. When Joan was seriously injured in 1944 Pollitt sent her numerous letters, an exercise he repeated on other occasions over the years when Joan was in hospital; he was an exceptionally kind and considerate man.

Chapter 13
Dying for work

In parallel with his work among dissenting, largely Communist-led lobby groups and protest movements, Thompson spent much of his time helping the Trades Union Congress, individual union leaders and their members. A typical example is given in John Saville's appendix to *Forged in Fire – the History of the Fire Brigades Union* (1992):

When for instance, the National Fire Service was established in the summer of 1941, Herbert Morrison, the Home Secretary, told John Horner (FBU General Secretary) and John Burns (FBU President) that FBU members were now no longer employees of local authorities and that the government was giving serious thought to the application of the 1927 Trade Disputes Act to the FBU. Strictly applied this could mean insisting on the FBU disassociating itself from the TUC and the Labour Party, as the civil service unions were obliged to do. When Horner consulted W.H. Thompson the latter said it was 'bluff' and explained to John Horner what the arguments were. With these Horner then went to see Walter Citrine, general secretary of the TUC, and Citrine said he would take action. He did, and soon Morrison was explaining to the House of Commons that the Trade Disputes Act would not apply to the newly established National Fire Service.

According to John Saville, John Horner and his future wife Pat were evening students at a Quaker educational settlement where Thompson and his wife Joan were well known among the circle of pacifists and progressives who managed and taught there. John and Pat's favourite tutor was Fred Parsons, a close friend of W.H. and the father of Owen.

In the 1930s, many people were desperate for work – to avoid poverty and starvation. Those lucky enough to have work, unfortunately literally ran the risk of dying for it – being killed or maimed or suffering disabling illness as a result of the conditions they encountered. Thompson's busy professional schedule and his family life as the father of two growing sons was stretched still further to accommodate regular TUC and summer schools where he spread his unique knowledge about the epidemic of avoidable industrial injury and disease and about the grossly inadequate arrangements employers and insurance companies wanted to keep in place so victims were not properly compensated.

Throughout the 1930s there is reference after reference to him in the reports of the TUC Conference recorded in the TUC's outstanding website, all with the movement's thanks for the generous efforts Thompson put in, free of charge as always.

A Summer School was held each year at Ruskin College, Oxford, and W.H. Thompson was listed as the speaker on Workmen's Compensation in 1930, 1931, 1933 and 1935. In 1931 it is recorded that, along with Sir Thomas Legge, medical adviser to the General Council, he addressed six district conferences around the country on industrial diseases. This was so successful that the conferences were repeated the following year, and the TUC Conference Proceedings note for 1932 makes interesting reading. At each session the main topic was industrial diseases locally prevalent. In Birmingham they dealt with injurious dust and fumes including silica dust, chromium plating fumes, nitrous fumes, solvents and thinners, and lead poisoning.

In Swansea they dealt with pitch and tar cancer, silicosis including anthracosis prevalent among South Wales miners, and dermatitis (in engineers from oil, and bakery workers from dough).

So pronounced was the interest in silicosis in Sheffield that a second conference was held on this subject alone. The note reads:

With the assistance of sections of a silicotic lung which he had been able to borrow from the Pathological Museum and lantern slides of x ray photographs, Sir Thomas Legge was able to indicate very clearly the causation and progress of silicosis.

At Plymouth they dealt with the effects of rapidly vibrating machinery, dermatitis, silicosis and asbestosis, carbon monoxide and lead poisoning. Following questions as to whether anything could be done to alleviate noise for boilermakers and men using pneumatic tools, arrangements were made for a visit by Doctor C.P. Crowden, Lecturer in Industrial Physiology at the London School of Hygiene. Dr Crowden, who had been closely studying the question of vibration and noise from pneumatic tools for a report to the Industrial Health Research Board, then spent a week testing workmen's hearing and visiting the dockyard. The report notes:

What is more to the point, he distributed a number of simple ear stops for the prevention of deafness and ear shock from noise produced by pneumatic tools, riveting hammers, gunfire, etc. Dr. Crowden expressed his pleasure at the reception the men had given him, and stated that the supply of ear stops he had taken down was exhausted in a quarter of an hour, such was the demand for them.

At Carlisle, the subjects dealt with included dermatitis, silicosis and the various forms of industrial poisoning, and, at Bristol, rapidly vibrating machinery, dust diseases and woods.

W.H. Thompson dealt with the legal issues at these conferences including an outline of the 'provisions of the various silicosis schemes'.

The battle for compensation for industrial diseases had begun and was to be fought out in the courts over many decades. It took over fifty years to gain a precedent ruling on industrial deafness in the case of *Thompson v Smith's Shiprepairers* reported in the Law Reports at *[1984] 1 All ER 881*, and even then the courts found that employers were only responsible for damage caused to workers' hearing for excessive noise exposure without adequate hearing protection from 1963!

The effects of Vibration White Finger continue to blight the lives today of many exposed to excessive vibration, a large number of whom would not even have commenced their working lives (or even been born), at the date of the conferences referred to above; and the biggest tragedy of all, the asbestos debacle, was barely getting underway. That was also to unfold over many decades and the legal battles continue to this day.

Owen Parsons summed up W.H. Thompson's work:

Fundamentally, Thompson believed in using his great skill and knowledge and courage as a lawyer in the interests of the oppressed against the rich and powerful, on behalf of injured workmen against insurance companies, on behalf of tenants against landlords, on behalf of trade unions and trade unionists against employers, on behalf of political demonstrators against the police, on behalf of the citizen against the bureaucrat, in short on behalf of the poor against the wealthy, on behalf of the mass of people against those who sought to govern and control them.

Owen Parsons   Ralph Thompson   Lord Hailsham
Photograph taken at the Centenary Function, October 1985

The struggle to obtain damages for injured workers remained a difficult one. The Workmen's Compensation Acts provided some compensation, but forced the injured person into an election – to accept the Acts' often very small award or to pursue a civil case for damages, but not both; and the Acts were extraordinarily complex and difficult to fathom.

The first Workmen's Compensation Act had been passed in 1897, but as Harry Thompson said in his introduction to the booklet published in 1940 *Workmen's Compensation Up-to-Date*:

The history of the Workmen's Compensation Acts should start in 1897, but it is a long and complicated story … . The Workmen's Compensation Act of 1925, with the many schemes made under it and the numerous amendments made to it, together with the thousands of decisions in the courts of appeal and the House of Lords, forms the basis of the present system. The whole subject is full of technicalities and the

Wilfred Clayton and W.H. Thompson, taken at Budleigh Salterton in 1947 in the pose of 'Master and Servant'.

decisions of the courts are numerous and in many cases contradictory.

Thompson gave evidence to the Royal Commission on Workmen's Compensation in 1940, in the course of which he said:

The present law as to election of remedies is preposterous, although it ought to be said that it is in such a chaotic condition that one of His Majesty's Judges recently declared that he did not know what it was and the Appeal in that case has demonstrated the extraordinary distinctions which the Courts are being driven to make on this subject. When a man meets with an accident which may well give rise to a common law claim against his employer, it is quite common for the man to be sent for at once and paid 30s.[£1.50p] and, without any advice, he signs a form of receipt expressing his election to claim under the Workmen's Compensation Act – and his rights may well be taken away without his knowing anything about it …

Any payment under the Workmen's Compensation Acts was made by the insurer or employer. As the booklet produced 'by the staff of the late W.H. Thompson', *A New Era for the Injured Worker,* later explained:

At one time some insurance companies used to run a very prompt messenger service to take a payment of compensation to an injured workman whilst he was still in hospital and obtain his signature to a receipt, and were then able to say that the workman had elected to take compensation. The Courts have tried to mitigate the harshness of this rule, but even up to 1948 many claims for damages had to be abandoned, not because the employer was innocent of negligence, but because the workman could not afford to wait until his case was decided, and had to accept Workman's Compensation payments to prevent himself and his family from starving.

A classic example of this is given in a case involving Harry Thompson, recounted by Owen Parsons:

The facts were brutally simple. The client was a young man of just over 21 years of age. He was set to work on an unguarded machine in breach of the Factories Act and had his right arm torn off as a result. The employers were prosecuted for this breach of the criminal code, pleaded guilty and fined.

Obviously a clear cut case. The only snag was that three days after the accident he was visited in hospital by a representative of the employers' insurance company and was given 35s [£1.75p], one week's compensation under the Workmen's Compensation Act, had explained to him that this was in payment of his rights under the Act and signed a document which had been read to him confirming this. The representative concerned gave evidence along these lines and produced the document concerned and his evidence was accepted by the High Court Judge who tried the case. On that evidence the judge decided, rightly, that he had no alternative, and the injured worker's claim accordingly failed.

Thompson understandably was furious. In a fit of bad temper, indeed in a tearing rage, in breach of all the good advice he had meted out to others, he appealed and briefed Cripps.

Sir Stafford Cripps was a highly experienced advocate. He knew when to let the facts speak for themselves. When the case was heard by the Court of Appeal he outlined the facts and Lord Justice Greer intervened:

"This case seems to raise points of public importance," he said. He glanced across at the empty press bench. "I notice that there is no representative of the Press present. I propose to adjourn the hearing in the hope that they can be notified."

Parsons, on Thompson's instructions duly went off in

search of some press, a mission successfully accomplished when he found two reporters and a photographer waiting for judgment to be given in a society divorce case. The appeal was then re-opened.

"Now, please remind me, Sir Stafford. Just which insurance company was that?"

"The Midland Employers Mutual Assurance Company of such-and-such an address, Birmingham, My Lord."

"Ah," said Greer with a glance at the press box, and at dictation speed, "the Midland Employers Mutual Assurance Company Limited of such-and-such an address, Birmingham."

The pattern of the court's attack was becoming clear. It soon developed further. Cripps and Greer conducted a duet in which the dominant and oft-recurring theme was the Midland Employers Mutual Assurance Company Limited.

After eliciting that the defence was being financed by the insurance company, Lord Justice Greer suggested to the defendants that they might like an adjournment. Parsons account continues:

At long last came the white flag. Paull [the defendants' counsel] asked for a short adjournment. Thompson went out. Cripps stayed in his seat. Greer looked a little surprised and Cripps indicated that he felt that the plaintiff's interests would be better served in any discussion by "Mr Thompson, my instructing solicitor than I could hope to do", a singularly gracious remark.

In the corridor, Paull came up to Thompson. "Well Thompson, you've got us over a barrel. What's your figure?"

Thompson gave a figure for damages and another for costs, each being at least double the going rate. Paull's solicitor whistled. "It's bloody blackmail," he said.

Thompson turned to Paull. "Mr Paull...if this person opens his mouth once more, it will be the end of our discussion and we will all go back into court if the Midland Employers really want that sort of publicity. Of course it's blackmail and I'm enjoying every minute of it, but blackmail or no blackmail, those are my terms, take them or leave them."

The parties duly settled on Thompson's terms, and the press, having been advised by Lord Justice Greer that in the circumstances the case was not particularly newsworthy, rushed back to their society divorce, disappearing like 'snow in the summer sunshine'.

There were other big obstacles in the way of successful civil claims, not least the common law doctrines of common employment – which prevented a claim if the accident was the fault of a fellow employee employed by the same employer – and the rule which defeated any claim where the worker was partly to blame. These two doctrines were ones Thompson campaigned against tirelessly and subjected to withering criticism in his booklets.

All this, and much else besides, was the subject of Thompson's evidence to the Royal Commission on Workmen's Compensation, given in oral evidence and supported by a written memorandum which is included in his 1940 pamphlet *Workmen's Compensation - The New Act Explained* published by the Labour Research Department.

Chapter 14
Harry Thompson – the man: life and death

Sylvia Scaffardi describes Thompson in her book *Fire under the Carpet: Working for Civil Liberties in the 1930s*:

Thompson was a tough Lancastrian, a big personable man with a large presence, a genial manner, the successful single boss of a lucrative solicitor's firm that specialised in the industrial field and had a thriving trade union practice. His good friends among the trade union and Labour men, and his regular attendance at the annual Trades Union Congress offered very useful contacts for the Council. An uncompromising radical, a fighter against injustice and privilege, he also had friends among leading Communists. He was too rugged an individualist to toe strictly any party line. A powerful advocate, once convinced, he admitted he saw no other point of view than his own. As an opponent he would have been ruthless and implacable. His worldly common sense judgement of what was practicable brought decisions very much down to earth. A man's man, in a man's world, he was probably something of a philistine, with little time or place in his busy life for the aesthetic, the gentler side.

This last comment may not be entirely accurate bearing in mind the Thompson's literary and academic friends, but it gives some insight to the qualities W.H. brought to the Committee.
    She continues:

He had been interested in Mosley's New Party in its very

early days. On a political weekend at Denham – Mosley's Tudor mansion outside London – he was a guest with John Strachey and the writer Lawrence Meynell. After dinner Mosley offered, with the coffee, a box of chocolates. Thompson never ate chocolates, but Meynell took one, bit into it and swallowed castor-oil instead of cream. The genial host apparently used the practical joke on guests that irked him.

"I think he was a bit twisted," Thompson commented.

I should think that in this case it was Thompson who was Mosley's intended target. Thompson who was no respecter of persons, unimpressed by rank or privilege, who had nothing of the sexual ambivalence of so many of the men who gravitated towards Mosley, and, most antagonising, who had been a conscientious objector in the 1914 war, and treasured, and took away with him at weekends, the prison mug he had purloined as a memento.

A W.H. Thompson employee from that era, **Esme Epton** (nee Heller), gave her recollections. She recalled joining the firm in 1939:

Most of the staff had moved from 88 Chancery Lane, with just Miss Hore left behind. The men at High Wycombe were W.H. Thompson (Tom, behind his back to me), Owen Parsons (for whom I started to work), John Williams who had one eye (he had, I think, lost the other in the RAF) and the chief clerk Mr Cornish – I don't think I ever knew his first name. Arthur Petch, then a solicitor but afterwards a barrister in Manchester, joined later.

Tom was a wonderful man, though at first I was rather afraid of him. I remember that I called him Sir at first, and he replied: "For Christ's sake don't Sir me". Things were easier after that.

He used to pull my leg about an incident in my first job

when I went with a clerk to Brixton Prison to take down the statement of an alleged murderer. He joked to Harry Pollitt to whom he introduced me: "A client of hers was hanged because she couldn't transcribe her notes".

Tom used to see details of all the new cases. Over the years he encouraged me to work on my own on some he called "Money for old rope". At the end I was dealing with more than a hundred.

He was an expert on workmen's compensation, and in 1940 published a book *Workmen's Compensation – The New Act Explained*. I still own a copy inside which he wrote "To those who need an explanation, but not to Esme."

Tom offered me articles, for which he would pay, but I decided to get married, instead. He gave me a wedding present of £50 – an absolute fortune then.

Esme moved to Manchester where on W.H's recommendation she got a job in the legal department of USDAW – NUDAW as it then was.

Peggy Peake also worked at the same time as Esme (and became her sister-in-law). Peggy later made a successful career out of writing romantic fiction – more than 60 books for Mills and Boon. She recalled:

As an employer he was considerate and generous. For instance, he became the guardian of a young woman employee and her sister when their mother died. Then again, he employed a girl he knew to be an epileptic, and, after she was taken ill one day, he paid for her medical treatment.

In 1943, I, too, became ill, and he sent me to top specialists, paying for it all. Eventually, an operation became necessary, and he paid my salary for three months of convalescence that followed. Who could ever forget such an employer?

Just before I left, W.H.T. invited me to tea. Brian was there, and W.H.T's wife Joan was on crutches. I shall never forget the moment when he stood on the other side of the lawn, held out his arms to Joan and said: "Walk across to me". With great difficulty she did.

Another employee from that era was **Marg Craner**. Marg and Miriam Edelman are two of the very few people left alive with direct, personal memories of working for Harry Thompson. Marg, a delightful woman looking much younger than her years, left school at 14 and joined the Co-op. Not long afterwards a customer got talking to her and said that her daughter worked for a firm which was desperate for staff.

She went for an interview with W.H. Thompson and Owen Parsons and was appointed as an office junior/telephonist at age 15 in October 1942. She gave her notice in at the end of the first week but was persuaded to stay by W.H. and his secretary Kay Garrod.

The office by then was based mainly in High Wycombe. Thompson had opened an office at 13 London Road, High Wycombe in 1939 and subsequently moved to 2 Rectory Avenue, a large house with a garden off the Amersham Hill. At the time, they also retained the 88 Chancery Lane office, but only Miss Hore worked there (she did the court work), the rest having vacated because of the bombing. In 1946/7, the practice also took accommodation at 52 Bedford Row, WC1, in the same building as the Fire Brigades Union.

Marg recalled Harold Cornish the managing clerk who had been with the practice for many years. She said he wore a ring, and when he wanted assistance, e g from his secretary he would bang his ring on the wall – he made a large dent in the wall. John Williams was the other significant lawyer, and David Phillips joined quite soon after.

She recalled Thompson as 'a lovely man, kind to all the staff, no matter how junior'.

Within a few years of the end of the war all the staff moved out of High Wycombe and back to London. By then, Marg had joined the conveyancing department, and she remained in this department. She moved offices from 88 Chancery Lane to Moorgate, then back to Chancery Lane before they all went into Serjeants' Inn. She finally left the firm in 1987 after 45 years.

The conveyancing work of the practice was for union members generally. Marg recalled that they acted for Poplar Borough Council, and she recalled Ellen Wilkinson as another client.

Barbara Hands (nee Oxley) joined the firm in April 1945 as a 16 year old, having been offered the job by Henry Schramek in a friend's kitchen! She was based in Chancery Lane 'which was like something out of a Dickens book' but remembers Harry Thompson visiting from High Wycombe.

Miriam Edelman is now a spry and elegant woman well into her nineties, a lover of Beethoven, Mozart and Delius who now lives in a spacious and beautifully maintained flat just outside Glasgow.

Her parents came from Latvia and Lithuania respectively, refugees escaping racial discrimination and seeking a better life. They met and married in London where her father entered the cigar trade – one of relatively few trades open to Jewish people. They later moved to Glasgow where they educated and brought up their children. Miriam was one of nine children, but such was the extreme poverty and lack of healthcare provision in the days before the National Health Service, five of them died before reaching adulthood.

As a young woman, Miriam became involved in the

Labour Movement first in Scotland, then in London where she joined the Labour Party Highgate Branch. Later, through the Clerical Workers' Union, Miriam went to work in the London district office of the Amalgamated Engineering Union dealing, among other matters, with the union's industrial accident cases.

Working at the AEU, the forerunner of Unite, the Union brought her into contact with the union's lawyer Harry Thompson who encouraged her to come and work for him. He hoped that Miriam would qualify as a solicitor one day but in the end Miriam didn't follow that route and instead worked for the firm as a legal executive for thirty-five years, retiring in 1975.

Thompson was a most remarkable man and the truth is he more or less single-handedly invented civil actions for damages for industrial disease and injury. Before he began running cases for the unions the best the injured worker got was the travesty known as scheme payments which left the sick and injured to struggle on a fraction of their wages, something like two pounds fifty a week

Harry Thompson was so organised, so determined to change what was a horrible, terrible situation which caused so much unnecessary suffering.

I knew nothing about the law when I was introduced to the office in Chancery Lane round the corner from the High Court in 1940 and was stuck right in at the deep end and sent off to court to supervise cases for which I felt ill prepared.

There was such a deep sense of concern for the injured people who were our clients and this made me very, very nervous to begin with. It seems five hundred years ago now when I first went to court, relying completely on my barrister until I got the hang of things. But before long you started to enjoy what you were doing. You felt such a sense of dignity, even importance because you were helping ordinary people to begin to get their rights.

After a while it became great fun particularly when you won a case you didn't think you would win. Then you came back to the office with whatever you had for a tail wagging wildly. Occasionally if there was a really significant victory we would go and have a drink to celebrate but you had to be strict with yourself because you had to drive home. As for Harry Thompson, looking back he was a very brilliant and charming man, kind and generous, friendly with his staff and supportive. If we went out from the office for lunch he invariably paid or so it seemed.

It was very sad that he died in 1947 just as his life's work was bearing fruit. I then worked with Brian and Robin Thompson his sons after they qualified and later with Tony Woolf and I just did not want to retire at all because work was so important to me. As I said I didn't get much formal training and in the end I decided not to try to qualify as a solicitor. But just to be in the office of such a brilliant lawyer was an enormous privilege. For Thompson was extraordinary in many ways, truly extraordinary without the backward attitude of so many male lawyers, someone who wanted women and ordinary people to get ahead in the profession, who cared deeply about the world and who translated those cares into his professional life in an admirable, memorable way.

Thompson was demanding too. He set high standards and somehow encouraged you to live up to them which is just as well since in the job we did against the insurance companies and powerful employers you needed to be very sharp and very quick.

Asked to sum up Thompson in the context of the legal profession of his time Miriam paused to reflect and then made it clear that Thompson was a 'rare orchid' among dank weeds. And if they were to get the justice they deserved, the ordinary people of Britain still needed more lawyers like Harry Thompson. More orchids and fewer weeds.

Miriam's partner at one time was Joe Scott, a leading member of the Communist Party for many years and executive committee member for the AEU.

David Phillips was another lawyer recruited by Harry Thompson. David was born with a considerable disablement of one arm and one leg and was therefore rejected for the forces. As soon as he qualified as a solicitor he was ordered into government service – first the Estate Duty office and then the Public Trustee office until the end of the war. He was introduced to Harry Thompson as a prospective employee by John Williams, who was already working there. (John and David knew each other at Cardiff High School). His widow Freda recalls David's interview:

David was instructed to get a bus to Golders Green on a cold winter evening – I think it must have been 1947 – and find a man (W.H.T.) sitting in a car under the railway bridge. Harry Thompson was much more concerned to talk about David's politics than qualifications for the job. I think the fact that we were both members of the Communist Party at the time clinched the job.

The firm was working in a big old house on the steep hill down into High Wycombe. We lived in North Kensington so David had to travel by train through a very cold winter with fuel shortages and long delays out to Wycombe. W.H.T. frequently took the whole (small) staff out for a pub lunch (no beer or other alcohol).

In 1952 he attended a conference in East Germany. As Freda says 'I think Thompsons must have funded him for that as we never had any money in those days'.

Ted Lewis was also recruited by the firm at around the same time as David Phillips. His widow **Margery Lewis**, now over 90 years old, spent a few weeks herself at the High Wycombe office, and it was during this short period that she met Ted:

> I was active in the Communist Party and sold the *Daily Worker* in Oxford at one time, sleeping on a camp bed in the Party offices. During the war I was an ambulance driver. I knew Joan Beauchamp, a brilliant woman, through the Women's Cooperative Guild. I also knew John Williams. He rang me one day: "Get off that couch, Margery – come and work with us." I had tons of letters to type and only lasted a month.
>
> Harry Thompson was there. I remember one day he took us all out for lunch. He was really nice. I remember he was fun in the office and used to tease me.

When Ted and Margery set up home together they lived in Anson Road NW2 and attended the local Communist Party meetings in Willesden. A young man they met at these meetings was John Lebor, and Ted encouraged John, after John completed his National Service in 1954, to join Thompsons: 'not many solicitors know the Labour Movement – you should come and work for us'. John joined and remained with the firm until 1995. Coincidentally he also bought a house in Anson Road where he continues to live after more than 35 years.

John Bowden became a lawyer who worked for Thompsons with distinction for more than 25 years after joining in 1953. But in the mid 1940s he was an apprentice toolmaker, already active in the Engineers' Union, the AEU. He met and saw Harry Thompson speak, first at a shop stewards' quarterly meeting in Kingston and then at a weekend course:

I recall attending a shop stewards' quarterly meeting in Kingston when Harry Thompson came ... .

As a result of that shop stewards' quarterly meeting, Harry Thompson came again, this time to a big house in Surrey called Wisley where he did a course – it was probably a shop stewards' course. I recall seeing Harry Thompson speak. I remember him as a quiet man but as one who could raise his voice if necessary and who did not hesitate to correct people if he needed to, but in a kindly sort of way. He gave tuition on workmen's compensation. He was clearly political and quite riveting as a speaker.
I also recall that when he sat at the table for meals he would sit at different ones to give everyone a chance to talk to him.

John Horner was a working seaman who rose through the ranks to become an officer in the merchant navy, travelling all over the world. His experiences during the general strike in Argentina in 1930 had a particular effect on him because he witnessed at first hand and later wrote about a remarkable display of solidarity from his crew. This was in sympathy with striking Argentinian workers on the River Plate.

Horner's ship was delivering iron rails and cement hundreds of miles up the River Parana for the Central Argentinian Rail Company and the crew declined to unload their vessel until the strike was settled.

Back in Britain on the outbreak of the Second World War John Horner joined the Fire Service, which was in a state of some turmoil at the time because of poor organisation and the many challenges and emergencies total war involved. He agreed to stand as a protest candidate against the sitting general secretary of the union. But serious obstacles were placed in his way. After at first being flatly denied the right to stand for the post, he won the election. This is how he recalled Harry Thompson:

In those days I was the most privileged of union secretaries for I had in the room just above my head the sharpest of intellects, the most liberal of minds and the possessor of the widest experience of the law.

At that time the firm had offices in Bedford Row in the building occupied by the Fire Brigades Union.

Margaret Cole was another close friend. She gave up her job as a classics teacher at St Paul's school to work for the newly founded Labour Research Department where the Thompsons were heavily involved. An important scholar in her own right, she married the radical socialist and ground-breaking historian of the early labour movement, G.D.H. Cole.

Margaret moved in the same literary artistic and political circles as Harry Thompson. She was also a productive writer of detective stories, often with a dissenting tinge and titles such as *Death at the Quarry* and *Big Business Murder*. In *Growing up into Revolution* she wrote as follows of her friend:

I remember particularly W.H. Thompson, solicitor and absolutist [in opposition to conscription] who spent long terms imprisoned in various jails, which he always said had been of great value to him in his practice, since he had inside knowledge of the kind of treatment which was likely to fall to the lot of his clients.

Harry Thompson was a tall, handsome athletic fellow, excelling in all games; he married Joan Beauchamp a militant left-wing suffragette, and worked up a large and socially very valuable practice in the defence of Trade Unionists, strikers, persons accused of treason or mutiny – and above all in cases of workmen's compensation.

He was one of the few men I know who managed to

devote his life to "causes" without ever losing his sense of humour or his power of enjoying himself.

Harry and Joan's circle of friends also included well known literary figures as well as politicians and communist and labour movement activists. In later life, Brian Thompson would recall H.G Wells as a regular visitor and, as a child, being bounced on his knee. David, Robin's son, acquired on Robin's death a number of H.G. Wells' first editions some inscribed 'to Joan'.

Brian also recalled that as lawyers and politicians the family would argue rather than discuss. The children were encouraged to assert themselves. No one ever let a point go. They learned how to achieve and then maintain supremacy through debate. If all else failed voices were raised. Brian said that 'H.G. Wells was the only man I heard talk my father down'. Arguments were about winning and losing. Brian and Robin learned these skills to good advantage in later life. They played family games at home which all concerned were determined to win, although Brian at least learned later that the game was the thing rather than the victory save in real life. He may have been unusual among the Thompsons in this respect.

Another close friend from the literary world was the poet and writer W.H Davies, author of the acclaimed memoir *Autobiography of a Supertramp.*

A friend from the world of academia was Professor Cyril M. Joad, Head of the Department of Philosophy at Birkbeck College, London, best remembered now for his work on the radio programme *The Brains Trust.*

Other visitors to the home as recalled by Brian included Cheddi Jagan and Paul Robeson. Cheddi Jagan, a labour activist, subsequently became Chief Minister (1957-1964) and President (1992-1997) of Guyana. Paul Robeson of course was amongst other things a concert singer, writer and civil rights activist.

Brian's recollections indicate that the family was close and home life stimulating. He remembered that his father idolised his mother but there may have been less affection the other way. He also recalled fondly long sunny holidays on the north Devon coast during the 1930s where the family would take a house for weeks on end.

W.H. Thompson was a lifelong non-drinker. A.J.P. Taylor recalls 'when he took you out to dinner, at the end of the meal when he was paying the bill, he would say to the waiter, "Give Mr. Taylor a separate bill for the drink"'. Muriel Thompson (one of the daughters of W.H.'s brother John) remembers Joan Beauchamp having wine when they travelled together to the Soviet Union and saying *'Well I can't drink at home, and I do rather like it'*. Harry Thompson was cautious with money. He did not entertain clients, but would happily attend football matches with them.

In 1947 Thompson began to suffer worsening health, as a result of what was thought to be leukaemia. Brian, in a letter dated 31 July, commented:

This week we decided to call another opinion and finally got hold of a Dr Piney who was recommended by several people and turned out to be quite well known to Dad at the office. He doesn't think the disease is lymphatic leukaemia at all and has confirmed himself in this opinion by blood tests and a sternum puncture to sample the bone marrow which he carried out on Tuesday. He is now convinced that the disease is primarily due to the spleen and might be entirely cured by its removal… In any event in Dad's present condition the operation is extremely dangerous and the chances of survival have been variously assessed as between 10 and 50%. After discussions with the doctors and Robin and myself Mum did finally decide to have the operation, which will accordingly take place on Saturday morning. You will appreciate that the decision was an extremely difficult one but I myself have no doubt that whatever my own views may be Dad himself would have chosen likewise were he in a position to judge for himself, and that he is going in to this operation with his eyes wide open: he has said himself that he would rather die on the table feeling that something is being done for him than lie here in misery for another month … .

The operation was carried out but was not successful, and Harry Thompson died in the Hendon Cottage Hospital on Monday 4 August 1947. The death certificate records the cause of death as follows: 1a. Cerebral thrombosis; b. Operation for spleenectomy Bantis disease.

He was cremated at Golders Green Crematorium where the ashes were scattered.

The Times newspaper published an obituary by the Communist barrister and former Labour M.P., D.N. Pritt KC on Saturday 9 August 1947.

I knew Harry Thompson as a friend, as a worker's compensation solicitor and as a solicitor for the left wing of the Labour Movement in political cases. As a friend he was staunch and loyal, intolerant of humbug, lively and witty. As a worker's compensation solicitor he was effective and vigorous; he was disliked by (insurance company) claims departments and saved many families from being broken up by poverty.

He had one clear and definite principle: "As much money as possible to my clients, the workers", and he applied his vast and ever-growing knowledge of a very complex field of law whole-heartedly to the realisation of this principle. One insurance company even had to keep a special section of its office to deal with him, and he must also have made a difference to the dividends of some of them.

Of recent years, his pre-eminence in this field, and the

natural determination of several of the larger Unions to have the best legal advice, practically forced him to build up one of the biggest solicitors' practices in the country, with a well trained team of experts to help him.

But as a political solicitor he was unique in the true sense of the word.

A man can be a good politician and a good lawyer and still not be able to conduct political cases. This calls for specialised heroism – and certainly for a rare combination of qualities.

For plain integrity and courage; for the patience to endure, and the skill to neutralise as far as possible the unconscious but deeply seated prejudices of judges, juries and magistrates; for the self-sacrifice, not easy for a lawyer, involved in going down to defeat in cases which could be won by a small sacrifice of one's client's principles, which of course he would not permit. And for a readiness to endure the unceasing hostility of three quarters of one's own profession and a fairly large section of the Labour Movement itself.

All these qualities are needed: Thompson had all of them. It will not be easy to train a successor. His many friends will not feel their personal loss any the less for the sense of the almost irretrievable loss of this great fighter.

Denis Nowell Pritt, the author of this obituary, was an original member and founder of Cloisters Chambers; for a period he was a Labour MP, but was expelled in 1940 for defending the Red Army invasion of Finland. He subsequently served as an independent and then, with others including John Platts-Mills formed the Labour Independent Group. His work as a Civil Liberties lawyer was legendary.

The National Council for Civil Liberties (NCCL) in its annual report for 1947-8 reported:

DEATH OF W.H.THOMPSON

Before reporting in detail on the Council's work mention must be made of an irreparable loss the Council has suffered in the death of our Chairman for so many years, that brilliant and courageous lawyer, to whom every lover of liberty and every democratic organisation owes a very great deal of debt of gratitude – W. H. Thompson. We all know how much the N.C.C.L. owed to the single- minded devotion of the late Ronald Kidd, to the wide humanity of Henry Nevinson. But it is perhaps difficult to estimate as yet just how great is the incalculable debt we owe to the wise guidance of Harry Thompson with his penetrating mind, generous spirit and unshakable integrity.

The Daily Worker reported the funeral on Monday 11 August under the headline 'Thompson to be buried today'.

Leading members of all sections of the Labour Movement will pay their tribute to W.H. Thompson, outstanding fighter for socialism, whose funeral takes place at 2 o'clock this afternoon at the Golders Green Crematorium.

The sudden death last Monday of this brilliant lawyer, expert on worker's compensation, came as a shock to many thousands of trade unionists for whom he acted so successfully in the courts.

In another edition the newspaper added:

Among all the virile and dynamic figures of the Labour Movement of our generation, Thompson was outstanding in energy and achievement.

Of the best Lancashire type, alert, combative and irrepressible, Thompson was a godsend to the trade union movement when he gave his energies to the business of mastering workmen's compensation ... . Not only did he undertake innumerable cases, winning large sums in compensation but his accumulated experience was embodied in the best current text book on the subject.

Thompson acted as a solicitor to the Amalgamated Engineering Union, the National Union of Distributive and Allied Workers and a number of others. He was a leading member of the National Council for Civil Liberties.

During the years of struggle against fascism he was constantly occupied by the legal defence of democrats whose activities brought them within the grip of the law … . Besides all these activities W.H. Thompson was a genial and entertaining friend and a formidable opponent at tennis, his favourite game.

Owen Parsons, in the preface to his account, *W.H. Thompson and his Cases*, said that he hoped his notes 'would serve as a small measure of tribute to a man who served the labour and trade union movement with conspicuous courage, wit and skill throughout a tempestuous generation'.

By the time of his death in 1947, the firm had grown in size to 70 staff and W.H. Thompson was the leading firm of solicitors to the British trade union movement. The end of the war had seen the return of large numbers of soldiers and a consequent increase in the working population, moreover a working population that was increasingly based in heavy manufacturing industry and heavily unionised. This was the firm that he left.

W. H. THOMPSON

W. H. THOMPSON, who died on 4th August at the age of 62, was one of the most valued supporters and contributors of the Labour Monthly. He was a unique figure in the British Labour Movement.

As a steadfast opponent of the Imperialist war of 1914-18 Harry Thompson knew the inside of a prison for over two years. This experience gave him something not shared by any other reputable solicitor in Britain. He came to London after 1918 and from the beginning he set all his professional skill at the service of the working class and its organisations.

It was not long before his special talent as legal adviser was widely recognised by the trade unions, while in the Labour Party his powers as speaker and organizer attracted an attention that would have made it easy for him to attain high office.

But Thompson was cast in a different mould from the political climbers. He would not depart from what he believed to be socialist principles: and preferred to help in necessary activities that the leaders of his party ignored or contemned. Thus he became the Executive Chairman and guide of the National Council for Civil Liberties. He was earlier an Executive member of the Labour Research Department to which he contributed some of its most widely read publications. At the historic Labour Monthly Conference of February, 1940, in the midst of anti-Soviet frenzy over Finland, it was W. H. Thompson who presided.

He was distinctive within the Labour Party by his outspoken refusal to recite the shibboleths of anti-communism. Often though he differed from the Communists, he never failed to lend his aid at times of difficulty. Thus both in 1921 and in 1926, when endeavours were made to suppress the Communist Party, Thompson took up the legal defence—as he did in hundreds of cases where persecution of strikers by a prejudiced and unscrupulous officialdom required a defender of high courage and high principle. In the long history of the British Labour Movement, there are only two outstanding solicitors, W. P. Roberts, who defended the Chartists and the early Trade Union fighters, and W. H. Thompson, who did as much, perhaps even more, for their successors in the present century.

Thompson specialized in Workmen's Compensation. He did more than anyone else to make this a burning question for over twenty years, both by his skilful handling of difficult cases and by his persistent agitation for an alteration of the law. On principle he never handled a case for an employer or an employer's organisation against a workman or against a Trade Union. In this branch of law he had an unexcelled experience and knowledge, while in his personal conduct of cases he was a peerless fighter. There are many widows and disabled men in Britain who owe what compensation they have to the fighting qualities of Harry Thompson. His hatred of the shabby treatment of injured workmen was part of his deep hatred for Capitalism, and of his loathing for the corruption which Capitalism bred even inside the Labour Movement.

R. P. A.

Obituary in Labour Research written by his friend and co-founder of Labour Research, Robin Page Arnot

Chapter 15
The King is dead; long live the king

When Harry Thompson died in 1947 there was no other partner, and by that time neither of his sons Robin or Brian had become lawyers. O.H. (Owen) Parsons had left in 1946, and it is said that John L. Williams wished to assume control. Joan consulted Harry Pollitt (a close friend and General Secretary of the Communist Party from 1929 to 1956, apart from a brief period during the Second World War) whose views were decisive, and Henry Schramek agreed to become sole partner for the duration on the instructions of the Communist Party.

Schramek, a communist, was a gentle, unassuming and undemanding man, hugely respected throughout the firm. He had joined the firm on demobilisation having by then already acquired a reputation for voluntary legal work. He served in the National Fire Service (along with Peter Pain, later a famous judge) and had been a leading member of the FBU regional council for the London Civil Defence Region and had formed and trained a team of 'accused friends' from among union members to assist those accused under the National Fire Service disciplinary code.

Ivor Walker comments:

After W.H. Thompson had died the firm was run by sole partner Henry Schramek. He was asked by the Communist Party to hold the reins until Robin and Brian qualified. He was a Hungarian who had qualified as an English solicitor and was trusted to hold the firm together.

At the time, Robin was just concluding his National Service in the Army (REME), having joined in 1943 following a course in engineering at Loughborough College. By then Robin had decided he wished for a career in law, and he joined the practice as an articled clerk. As he recorded in a memoir on his war time experiences:

I was…on a course in Croydon, which received many V1 bombs. I arranged to go to the theatre with Clayton, my father's right hand managing clerk. After the theatre we travelled back by train that was frequently stopped because of the bombs. I asked Clayton what would his reaction be to my entering my father's firm and he was most enthusiastic. I think he thought I would be off playing tennis most of the time and he would run the firm. Anyway, he discussed the matter with my father and he was keen. I had already acted on a number of Court Martials both prosecuting and defending and I continued to do more …

I left the army in July 1947. Shortly afterwards I was called for an interview at the Law Society. I turned up in my captain's uniform … . They decided that I should do only two years articles and that I should be exempt from all examinations, except the final and accounts.

My mother was still badly disabled and sadly my father died in August that year. I entered into my Articles in September.

Brian had studied chemistry at Imperial College, London and had started work at South Eastern Agricultural College (part of the University of London) at Ashford in Kent in October 1945 as a Junior Assistant Chemist 'to assist in the investigation on Hop Verticillium Wilt'. Their mother approached Brian to see if he would transfer to law and join Robin in W.H. Thompson's. He agreed to do so.

Brian started his articles in the High Wycombe office on the same day as Robin, 15 September 1947. He had three years articles as against Robin's two.

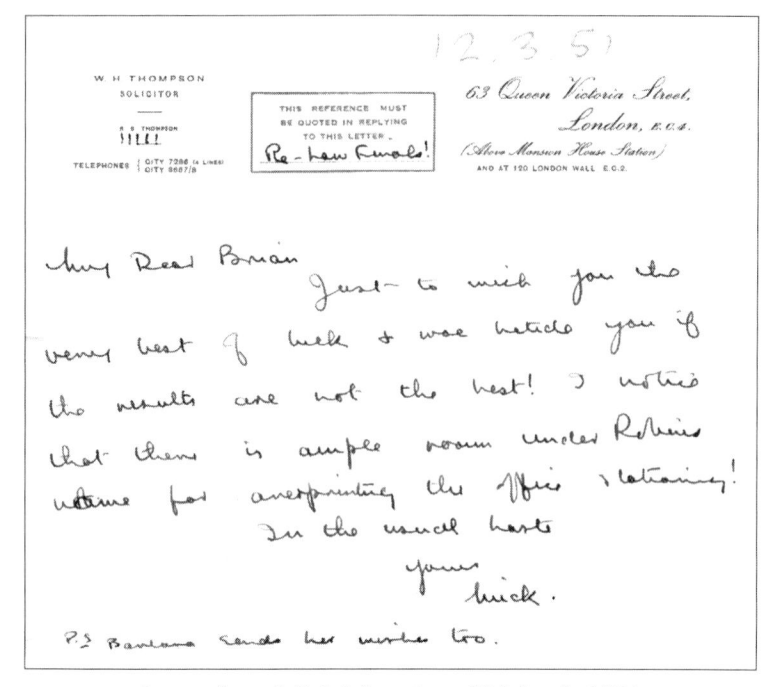

Letter from Mick Manning, 12 March 1951

Brian was articled to Robin. This required an exemption from the usual strict rules on experience necessary for the principal. As Robin noted,

… to my amazement with the help of William Charles Crocker, ex-President of the Law Society, we got him articled to me. He was required to attend Law School where everyone took verbatim notes of all lectures. Brian sat with folded arms and never took a note. He read the books later and in the end stopped going to the Law School. He sailed through the exams.

Robin qualified in May 1950 and became sole principal of the firm at the age of 26, with 70 staff, two offices in London and one (the largest at that time) in High Wycombe. The ever amenable Henry Schramek stood down as partner but continued to perform an invaluable role in the firm until his retirement in 1969. Unfortunately he died shortly afterwards. As Freda, widow of the late David Phillips remarked, 'The few years under the titular headship of the unflappable Henry Schramek ... seemed (to us) to run comparatively smoothly'.

When Brian qualified as a solicitor, the two brothers became joint partners, with no written agreement.

In the post-war years, and despite Harry Thompson's death, the firm grew very fast. The prospects of recovering compensation for injured workmen had improved with the Factories Act 1937, and the common law doctrine of negligence was growing. Thompson did not quite live long enough to see the abolition of two old common law doctrines which had frustrated many claims; the first was the rule that an injured person could not recover compensation if he was even only partly to blame for the accident. That rule was replaced by the Law Reform (Contributory Negligence) Act, 1948 which established by statute that a person's own blameworthiness in causing an accident should only be reflected by a suitable deduction from the compensation, not the complete abrogation of any right to compensation at all. The second, another old common law rule, was the doctrine of common employment by which an injured person was unable to sue his employer for compensation if his injury was caused by the fault of a fellow employee employed by the same employer, was also abolished at around the same time under the Law Reform (Personal Injuries) Act, 1948.

The biggest change, however, was the repeal of the Workmen's Compensation Acts and introduction of the Industrial Injuries Act which came into force on 5 July 1948. Under the new legislation, workmen injured in accidents or as a result of listed prescribed diseases would be entitled to injury benefit and, where the injury was serious enough, disablement benefit, from the state without proof of fault and without in any way affecting their right to claim compensation through the courts.

As a result of all this, the late 1940s saw an explosion of personal injury litigation. As the unions became stronger they developed their legal services and turned to W.H. Thompson which had stood by them during the hard times in the twenties and thirties. W.H. Thompson's was in the courts constantly, bringing one challenge after another. Lunchtimes were spent in impromptu case conferences deciding which cases were to be pursued through the appeal courts, and the Factories Act legislation and numerous regulations passed under it began to take shape as a result as a coherent code designed to protect workmen.

Many important precedents were set over the next few years. One such case was *Paris v Stepney Borough Council [1951] AC 367*

The crucial issue which arose was whether the standard of care was one which should change in the light of the particular circumstances of an employee, or whether it was a general overall standard in which individual requirements were irrelevant.

Mr Paris, the claimant (or plaintiff as the claimant was known in those days) worked as a fitter in the council's garage. His employers knew that he only had one eye. He was using a hammer to remove a bolt when a chip of metal flew off into his good eye as a result of which he became totally blind.

It was not normal practice at the time to provide goggles or other protective eyewear for such work.

The House of Lords, overturning the decision of the Court of Appeal, found that in the circumstances the employers owed a special duty of care to Mr Paris and should have provided goggles. An employer had to take

Fred Oaten, Robin and Brian

into account all factors including the known condition of Mr Paris' eyes, the likelihood of an accident happening, and the gravity of the consequences should an accident occur.

The case was recognised at the time and stated by the

Lords to be one of general importance. It had a profound impact on the development of the common law. The Law Lords decision that responsibility for safety by the employers was not just a general duty but also a personal duty owed to each individual in the light of their own circumstances was a crucial development in the law of negligence and remains one of the leading cases in the field to this day.

Mr Paris not only suffered a terrible injury but also an agonising time as his case was taken through the courts. He won before the judge, lost in the Court of Appeal and won in the House of Lords. His lawyer Fred Oaten was rightly proud of the final success.

Another case from this period was *John Summers & Sons Ltd v Frost [1955] 1 All ER 870*

In the post-war years the interpretation of the Factories Act was a significant feature of the development of health and safety. The Act had been passed to provide a code of protection for factory workers backed up by criminal sanctions, but the approach of the courts enabled civil claims to be brought for breach of some of the Act's provisions. For years one of the biggest causes of accidents in factories was dangerous machinery. The Factories Act 1937 included a provision designed to remove the dangers from unguarded machines, and Section 14 provided that 'every dangerous part of any machinery shall be securely fenced…'.

Mr Frost was using a power driven grinding machine when his thumb came into contact with the grindstone. The relevant question for the courts was to decide the nature and extent of the duty to fence (guard) the dangerous moving part of the machine.

The House of Lords decided that the duty was absolute, that the employers were liable and that it did not matter that the consequences of securely fencing the machine in

Dinner dance at the Cafe Royal in the 1950s.

Top table along wall includes (from left to right):
Bert Ross & wife, Ted & Margery Lewis, Fred and Edna Oaten, Henry Schramek and wife, Robin and Queenie, Brian, Cyril Wener & wife, Mick Manning and Ron Smith.

accordance with statutory obligation would be to render it commercially unusable.

This classic victory established the absolute duty of the employer to protect his workers from dangerous moving parts of machinery, a case which alone brought compensation to thousands of workers over many years (despite the House of Lords subsequent rather bizarre ruling that the purpose of the legislation was to keep the worker out rather than the machinery in, the result of which being that if a worker was injured as a result of some part of the machinery flying out of the machine the absolute duty did not apply!)

The decision stood as the benchmark of interpretation of Section 14 of the Factories Act 1937 and its replacement in 1961 until the relevant legislation was changed with the Provision and Use of Work Equipment Regulations, 1998. It brought compensation to many thousands of workers who were injured by machinery and, perhaps of more long term value, helped to bring about a change in the culture of machinery safety where safety features were incorporated in the design to avoid any possibility of injury.

Of course, the abolition of the Workmen's Compensation Acts still left many cases where statutory compensation under those provisions continued – all the cases where the accident had occurred prior to 1948 or where the allowances under the Acts needed to be challenged. Brian Thompson took up the mantle, using his extraordinary intellect to understand and pursue the cases. He became the country's leading expert. The concept of statutory entitlement to benefits for industrial injuries of course continued with the Industrial Injuries Acts (with the important differences that the workman did not have to choose between benefits and a common law case – he could claim both, and the benefits under the Industrial Injuries Act were paid by the state as part of the new system of social welfare). During the 1950s and '60s, Brian took appeals to the Court of Appeal and the House of Lords. He challenged the conservative application of benefits legislation to the victims of industrial accidents, often succeeding only to face new regulations designed to defeat his success.

Years later, in his written evidence in 1973 to the Royal Commission on Civil Liability and Compensation for Personal Injury (the Pearson Commission) Brian commented:

I have had a fair amount of experience of dealing with claims under the Industrial Injuries Acts. It has been a sad, frustrating, bitter experience. I could write a book about the anomalies and injustices and maladministration under those Acts.

The Construction Regulations passed by Parliament during this era were typical of the increasing emphasis being given to the protection of workmen. Brian virtually wrote key passages of these regulations.

By the 1950s, W.H. Thompson was litigating significant numbers of disease cases, many of which were on behalf of Scottish workmen. One of them was *Bonnington Castings v Wardlaw [1956] 1 All ER 615*, a landmark case which still forms an essential part of the law fifty years after the House of Lords gave its judgment.

Mr Wardlaw worked in a foundry for eight years and was exposed to silica dust and contracted pneumoconiosis. The main source of dust was from pneumatic hammers and at the time there was no known way of protecting against this. Another source was from swing grinders, and the company was in breach of statutory duty in respect of the dust extraction for these.

The situation therefore was that one source of the dust which caused the damage was 'innocent' in law but the other was negligent. The company said that as there was no evidence to show the proportions of dust from each of the relevant sources they could not be held liable.

The House of Lords decided that as the negligent source (from the swing grinders) had made a material contribution to the contraction of pneumoconiosis, the defendants were liable to pay compensation.

The principle of material contribution remains highly relevant today. Wardlaw, dealt with by Fred Oaten, was part of the trail blazed in respect of pneumoconiosis and then asbestos-related disease in a whole series of cases establishing the employers' responsibility and liability under the Factories Act and regulations. The Law Reports are littered with vast numbers of reported cases fought by the firm, many of them pursued to the House of Lords, challenging and extending the law – in the majority of cases successfully. More unions retained the firm, more union members claimed compensation, and at the same time the

Robin, Queenie and Brian, 12 October 1955

unions were growing in power.

Test cases continued through the 1960s and '70s with a particular spotlight on disease cases. A major problem for any victim of a disease was in bringing his case within the period prescribed by law – the 'limitation period'. This presented an almost insurmountable difficulty for those victims whose condition was contracted as a result of exposure to a substance many years previously. This was always the case with diseases related to asbestos exposure with a minimum latency period of at least ten years (and usually many more) from the date of exposure to the onset of symptoms. An example was the infamous case of *Cartledge v E Jopling & Sons Ltd [1963]* where a workman had contracted pneumoconiosis by inhaling noxious dust before 1950. In 1955 he discovered that his lungs had been damaged. The courts were 'forced' by the operation of the limitation rules to reject the claim because it was not brought within three years of the date the damage was caused, even though there was no way of knowing at the time that any damage had occurred.

As a result the Limitation Act, 1963 was passed. It was obscure in its language, but amongst other things provided that time did not begin to run until the material facts of a decisive nature were known. The Act was stunningly complex and obscure.

Tony Woolf, one of the firm's solicitors, and a remarkable lawyer of immense talent, started to apply the new law to forge the precedents for pursuing disease cases, particularly those related to asbestos exposure. There were two major cases: *Pickles v National Coal Board [1968] 2 All ER 598*, and *Central Asbestos Co Ltd v Dodd [1972] 2 All ER 1135*

Woolf was probably the country's leading expert on limitation in disease cases. Geoff Shears who had recently joined the firm and was at the time an articled clerk (trainee solicitor in today's language), assisted Tony as part of the team in Mr Dodd's case.

In the Pickles case, Mr Pickles worked as a miner from 1947 to 1960 before leaving the industry to become a lathe operator. In February 1966 he became ill with chest trouble and in September 1966 he was told by his doctor that he suffered silicosis from his work underground. Because of some delay in processing the form, the relevant application to the court under the 1963 Act for leave to bring court proceedings was not made until more than 12 months after the date of diagnosis.

The Court of Appeal found in Mr Pickles favour. He had taken all such action as was reasonable to take, and the application to the court was made within 12 months of the date he was advised that he might have a legal claim against the Board. Lord Denning commented that this was 'one more case on this very complicated and obscure Act'.

In the Dodd case, Mr Dodd was exposed to asbestos from 1952 to 1965 in circumstances where the company was clearly at fault. He was diagnosed with an asbestos disease in January 1964, awarded disablement benefit in 1965 and left the company's employment in September 1965 to avoid further exposure. However, he did not know that he could bring a claim for damages having been told by the works manager that if he got asbestosis there was a panel which would pay compensation 'but you can't sue your employers'.

In 1967 he consulted W.H. Thompson on learning that a fellow workman was bringing a claim. The company contested the claim on the basis that it was out of time.

By a majority of 3 to 2, the House of Lords found in his favour saying that he did not have knowledge of a material fact – that he had a legal remedy against the employer – until April 1967.

The result of these landmark decisions was that large numbers of workers who would otherwise have had their cases dismissed on grounds of being brought out of time were able to bring legal proceedings for their diseases and recover compensation.

The bare facts of these cases cannot do justice to the impact they had at the time. For example in Pickles, the union which funded the case was the Engineers' Union, the AEU. This was the union Mr Pickles had joined on becoming a lathe operator. Despite the fact that the case arose from exposure that occurred entirely before Mr Pickles joined them, the AEU agreed to cover all the legal costs in a case which was very expensive to pursue and carried considerable risks.

Mr Dodd's case was an example of the lengths to which the insurers would go to avoid payment, even where they accepted that the employers were to blame and had been in flagrant breach of the safety regulations designed to protect workers. A similar example was seen in more recent times in the Fairchild litigation in which Thompsons also played a part.

The Dodd case remained the leading authority on the interpretation of the 1963 Act until it was replaced by a new Act in 1980, and was one of the very first judgments in an asbestos disease case.

Both cases served to accelerate the drive for compensation for the victims of dust disease, a battle which W.H. Thompson was fighting almost single handed, ably supported by the trade unions.

Geoff Shears:

At the time I joined Tony was the leading authority on limitation issues in personal injury cases and had indeed written the only book of substance on the issue. He had fought the Central Asbestos cases, the first successful asbestos trial, and was very busy pursuing litigation against the National Coal Board in respect of coal miners' pneumoconiosis. This followed on from the successful action in the Pickles case. Having won on limitation the case had settled at the door of the court for a sum in excess of what a judge might have awarded, the Coal Board being anxious to avoid a precedent.

Pickles was sponsored by the AEU, the union Mr Pickles had joined after leaving the coal industry, but now some mining unions started to instruct Thompsons in respect of members'/former members' pneumoconiosis. Cases came in from the Durham area, from NACODS in Kent, and there were some from South Wales and the North West. Apart from Tony, other lawyers in the firm handling them were Freddie Oaten, Miriam Edelman and John Pickering.

Ted Constable who joined the practice in 1964 also recalls being part of the team working on this large and important batch of cases:

Tony fought a series of cases against Central Asbestos in the time I was privileged to work as his assistant.

When working on the Pickles case I went with Tony to the Durham coalfield to interview miners and learn about the working conditions. I remember the concern we had that the pits seemed to be quite wet – they extended out under the sea – and we were seeking to establish the extent of exposure to dust. I still remember my feeling of pride when we settled at court just as the case was starting. Tony, who was a fearless litigator, had gone where no one had dared to go before. I learned a lot from him.

I was good friends with Tony. He was eccentric, very clever, loved music and chess. He took me to his chess club in the Strand, but I was easy meat and he didn't invite me again! He took on all sorts of cases. I went on Rent Tribunal cases with him. I remember an escape of animals road traffic accident case which broke new ground at the time. He was the firm's expert on limitation, and knew the Construction and Building Regulations inside out. I had the highest regard for him as a lawyer. I heard sometime later when I was working in Cardiff that Tony had "become a law unto himself", and had left disenchanted. I was very sorry that his unique talent was lost to the firm.

Geoff Shears:

Tony Woolf was a former CP member – I believe he had left the party in 1956 after Hungary – but was still very radical. He had a considerable intellect as well as being very cultured. His wife Alexa was becoming well known as a sculptress.

Tony had, I recall, been involved in direct action in the past, leading an occupation at Claridges, and after he left Thompsons he joined a commercial firm dealing with construction work, initially in a junior capacity but subsequently as a senior partner specialising in environmental issues – he must have been one of the first lawyers to do so. But all that was in the future.

Another critical issue which arises in many disease cases was resolved around the same time. The issue was: when should a reasonable employer have become aware of the health risk to which he was exposing the worker and thus taken steps to avoid or minimise the risk? The relevant test was established in the case of *Wallhead v Ruston and Hornsby Ltd [1973)]14 KIR 285*

Mr Wallhead was employed in a foundry as a moulder from 1942 to 1949. In 1949 the employer set up a new foundry, and he then worked as a sand miller until 1964. In 1968 Mr Wallhead brought a legal action on account of his chronic bronchitis and emphysema.

The judge held that from 1950 a reasonable prudent employer should have known of the risk it was exposing Mr Wallhead to from noxious dust; and further, that although the exposure after 1950 was not the cause of the illness it nevertheless aggravated it and compensation would be payable.

This case, dealt with by Colin Dove, is still regarded as the leading case on constructive knowledge. As with many such cases, the principle now seems self evident, but it had to be fought for and established against insurers representing employers who fought against it tooth and nail.

The investment of resources by the unions into cases such as this was immense. Geoff Shears recalls that when it came to the judgment being given, Colin Dove was not available, and Tony Woolf asked him to attend court to take a note with the comment that 'if the case is lost the Foundry Workers will go bust'!

As it happened, the judge found against the claimant on almost all the issues in the case save for the final crucial point, and the union could breathe again. Judges would always give their judgment in such a way as to leave it open until the last moment what the decision was going to be. Sitting in court on such occasions, attempting to make an accurate note of what the judge was saying, and wondering how you were going to break the news – if it was bad – back at the office was trying to say the least.

The battle for compensation for industrial diseases continued relentlessly. Numerous successes were achieved in relation to various chest diseases, skin conditions such as dermatitis.

Lawyers within the firm, as they gained expertise, prepared notes and guidance to help their colleagues. Frank Foy joined the firm in 1970:

I recall being given a note prepared by Don Wilson, another Thompson's lawyer, explaining how to deal with dermatitis cases. This note became very well known throughout the firm as being a good example of how to prepare a note of guidance which was useful without being so long as to be off-putting.

There were many battles still to be fought. Most of these were played out in the 1980s and '90s, but progress continued to be made on many different fronts. Until 1969 there was very limited scope for judges to award interest on awards of damages. Peter Gornall recalls briefing counsel in a case to argue the point. 'I had dug out a very ancient case; the judge said it was an unusual submission but he could see no reason why interest should not be awarded.' He raised the matter with Labour MP Ben Whitaker who introduced the Justice for Victims (Interest) Bill under the 10 minute procedure. As luck would have it, there was already an Administration of Justice Bill proceeding through Parliament and the government took it up. The result was the enactment in Section 22 of the 1969 Act (since re-enacted in Section 35A of the Supreme Court

Act, 1981) of a compulsory requirement to award interest on awards in personal injury cases 'unless there are special reasons to the contrary'.

In the early 1970s there were two important enquiries, governing health and safety in the workplace and then civil liability and compensation for personal injury. Brian gave evidence to both. The first was the Robens Committee report on Health and Safety at Work (and gave rise in 1974 to the Act of the same name). Robens argued for a more consensual approach to the issue of safety at work along with the creation of a central national authority for health and safety at work. He recommended that there should be a set of general duties on all employers with more emphasis on health and safety management, with less reliance on prescriptive regulatory requirements.

Some of this was undoubtedly good – the existing system allowed some employers to slip the statutory net completely. Some of it was bad, and Brian argued the case much as his late father would have done: that employers and others had failed to protect workers despite the existence of a criminal as well as a civil statutory framework, and were even less likely to do so if the law was watered down; on the contrary it needed to be strengthened and properly enforced.

The new Act, when it was passed by the incoming Labour Government in 1974, relied significantly on the detailed advice that Brian and the firm was able to provide. The general purpose of the Act fulfilled Robens' vision with the introduction of a set of general duties on all employers and the creation of the Health and Safety Inspectorate covering all workplaces, but left in place most of the detailed regulations covering specific workplaces.

In the course of his report Lord Robens also made a number of critical comments about the system of compensation, and the Royal Commission on Civil Liability and Compensation for Personal Injury under the chairmanship of Lord Pearson was set up partly as a result.

Robens had concluded that claims for damages for accidents at work had a deleterious effect upon accident prevention, and noted what he perceived to be a capricious and unsatisfactory system of compensating the victims of injury or disease, the results depending in each case very largely on sheer luck.

Geoff Shears later recalled: *'I can remember as an articled clerk, or a recently admitted solicitor, sitting between Robin and Brian when our evidence was presented to the Pearson Commission. Brian did the talking and Robin lent gravitas.'*

In the summary to his lengthy written submissions Brian concluded:

The first question to consider is the fundamental question: do injured persons at the present time get enough compensation or do they not? In my view they do not, and that I suggest is the main reason this Royal Commission has been established. The object of the exercise as I understand it is to improve the position of injured persons generally and not to take away from them the rights which they have at the present time with a view to substituting different rights which in many cases would produce not more money but less.

The principle of liability without fault established under the Workmen's Compensation Acts and the Industrial Injuries Acts is basically sound. The Industrial Injuries Acts however are inadequate and unsatisfactory in many ways, and should be radically reformed and extended. Provision of a similar kind might well be made for road traffic accidents and for other injuries and diseases. It does not follow that the right of injured persons to claim damages in addition should be taken away.

There is a strong case for extending the liability of the employers to pay damages so as to include all industrial injuries irrespective of fault. This liability should be enforceable by legal action against the employers (or their insurers) and not by means of a claim under an insurance scheme.

If the liability to pay damages is not extended as in (the paragraph) above then the onus of proof should be imposed on the employers (or the driver of a motor vehicle) so that they would have to prove that the injury was not caused by any fault on their part.

The arguments against the common law action for damages mentioned in the Robens Report do not justify or support any proposal to abolish the common law action.

In the event Pearson made a number of worthwhile recommendations including the setting up of a system for provisional damages, but on the central issue of whether the present fault based system should be replaced, recommended a no fault system for road traffic cases only (and not accidents and injuries at work). This was rejected by the Government and it took many years in some cases for various of Pearson's detailed recommendations for improving the system to be implemented.

Chapter 16
People and offices in London

After qualifying as solicitors, Robin and Brian closed the High Wycombe office, but had offices at London Wall, Warnford Court next to the London Stock Exchange, Queen Victoria Street and two small overflows. Robin Thompson was based at London Wall and Cyril Wener also worked there. Brian was at Warnford Court and Mick Manning, who was very close to Brian, also worked there until he opened Mansion House.

In the 1950s the firm recruited many youngsters from working-class backgrounds. In the midst of this, David Skidmore was one of six boys taken on together in 1954 (another was Tony Walker). David's story is extraordinary. He joined W.H. Thompson in 1954 aged 16 as a postroom/filing clerk with no qualifications.

He was based initially at London Wall. At that time the firm also had an annex across the road where Rex Church worked and Warnford Court. Another satellite office was then opened at Mansion House.

David had only been with the firm for a few months, working in the postroom, when John L. Williams, one of the senior lawyers in the firm at the time, who subsequently left to set up his own practice, allowed him six cases to run. In 1956 he had made enough progress to be upgraded from the postroom to become a court clerk. Whilst undertaking national service in Cyprus in October 1958 he lost both his arms in an accident when sitting as rear guard on a lorry. An oncoming lorry crashed into the lorry on which he was travelling, hitting his rifle and right arm. It knocked him from the lorry and his left arm was run over when he fell. After spending a number of months in the Soldiers'

Hospital in Roehampton where he had metal arms fitted in December 1958, Robin and Brian together with Henry Schramek decided to try and accommodate him by taking him back. He was offered a position as a legal executive on one month's trial undertaking the North West work, working under the supervision of Henry Schramek. The difficulties David had to overcome were immense. When he returned to work he could not even use a knife and fork, and one can hardly begin to imagine the problems he would have faced. Nonetheless he made a success of it. He was given articles at age 26, passed the exams and qualified as a solicitor. He went on to become one of the most important figures in Thompsons' history.

A lawyer who was taken on in 1953 was John Bowden. In fact, like many taken on at the time he was not a lawyer at all:

I left school just before my fourteenth birthday and was apprenticed with Kingston Instruments, a well-respected subcontracting firm who made machine tools for major companies such as Hawkers, Vickers etc. As the years progressed I became a shop steward for the AEU and was active in the Communist Party.

In due course I qualified as a tradesman and I loved my job as a journeyman toolmaker. I had by then become an avid Daily Worker reader, and I moved round the trade. It was normal to do so in those days to gain experience. I returned to Napier's working in their tool room and I recall that while I was there the union organised a big social event at Vickers at Brooklands, Weybridge. At this social event Joe Scott asked me if I had met the union's solicitors. I said no but I had heard talks by them. He told me that Robin and Brian Thompson were present and I was introduced to them. One of them said to me could I come and have a talk with them sometime. I forgot about it afterwards or did not follow it up until someone in the district office asked me whether I had phoned Robin or Brian. As a result I rang up and spoke to Robin and after some negotiations over the time I could go for an interview they finally agreed that I could go down and see them at 5 p.m. one day (since to go any earlier would have meant me losing a day's pay). I went to London Wall in my working clothes. They asked me loads of questions and asked what ideas did I have. I really could not understand it. I asked them what it was all about and they replied that it was about me coming to work for them. I was astonished. Brian said they were interested in employing young men like me. I said to them, `Look let's get this clear – I am not applying for your job. You're applying for me´. Brian thought it was funny but Robin was rather stiff and starchy about it.

After this "interview" I went to see Harry Pollitt at King Street to discuss it with him. Everyone would discuss their problems with Harry Pollitt. He explained that the Party wanted to strengthen its links with Thompsons and he advised me to go up again and see what I could negotiate. He told me to go and become a working class lawyer. So I did, and I joined W.H. Thompson in April 1953.

John remained highly active politically:

I would say I was notorious because I was still associated with the Youth Section of the AEU and in particular recall attending three years running the Annual Youth Conference. Together with Jimmy Reid and Aubrey Lytton the three of us led the Apprentices' Strike in 1960. The strike was successful. All the apprentices got a wage increase.

I started to work for the firm at the Mansion House office. Not long afterwards, a number of us moved to Warnford Court and we also had a big influx of school leavers. I recall that when I joined Rex Church was already employed. Ivor and Tony Walker joined later.

The work was very different for me of course. I worked for Ted Lewis. He was a wonderful man. Partly through him I became a member of the Haldane Society who, after a while, asked me if I would organise events for them. One of these events I recall was an Industrial Law Conference at Sidney Sussex College Cambridge, Cromwell's old college. I recall Ted showing me a painting of Cromwell in the college.

I was also a friendly with Harry Nyman, a lawyer who left to become a senior partner in due course in Leo Abse & Cohen in Cardiff.

Ted and I would go on regional visits to various parts of the country to see clients – members who had suffered accidents or contracted diseases. By then I had a Morris Minor motorcar, and we would put a tent in the boot of the car and go into the hills and stay in the tent, even when it was cold and snowing. This was particularly in Wales. However, I had cases from all over the country, the North West, Wales, Greater London, etc.

I was also a member of the Lawyers' Group of the Communist Party. When I joined the firm Ted Lewis said he would take me to a meeting and it was a meeting of a group of communists who are lawyers, some qualified some not. We met at Seifert Sedley's offices and would deal with all sorts of issues as an advisory group of the Communist Party. I participated with enthusiasm and eventually became the Secretary.

One of the key lawyers in those days was Mick Manning. Mick joined the practice shortly after the war when he had served as a flight engineer in the RAF. He was very good at the public relations part of the job, liked to socialise and enjoyed a drink. Each time David Skidmore took law examinations in this period he recalls that Mick bought him champagne to celebrate on the days prior to the results being declared! Mick was a member of the Wheelers Club opposite the courts, being very keen on motor racing. As Ivor Walker commented 'Mick knew everyone – from racing drivers to royalty'. At Christmas in 1973, Mick was killed in a motor vehicle accident, when a mini he was driving belonging to a girlfriend, Kate, was struck by another vehicle skidding on black ice. (Mick himself ran an MGB GT). Brian was devastated.

Many years later at David Skidmore's retirement function at The Waldorf Hotel, Brian mentioned the key people in Thompsons' history. Mick Manning was one of those he named along with W.H. Thompson, Henry Schramek, David Skidmore and John Harris.

In his autobiography in 1990, Clive Jenkins, former General Secretary of the white collar union ASTMS, had this to say about Mick:

One of our members was "Curly" Manning (called Curly because he was very bald indeed), who must surely be the only Communist engineering shop stewards convenor ever to become a managing clerk for a major firm of solicitors, then W.H. Thompson, the leading firm of union lawyers, now so big it is divided into two. He was an immensely attractive personality and deeply concerned about the cases that he had to allocate. He kept a collection of photographs of young women who had been scalped by machines in order to keep up his red flame of resentment against careless employers. But Curly always enjoyed himself and was fun to be with.

Bruce Tyrer who joined the firm in 1954 commented:

Mick Manning was the PR man of the firm. He knew everyone who it was necessary to know. Robin had a difficult personality with people and Mick ran all the public relations. As a result of Mick's PR work he was often out of the office. It tended to get left to me to keep an eye on the cases in his department and he would frequently ask me to go to court hearings for him. His secretary Barbara Oxley was sufficiently skilled to deal with day to day work. Mick would go off to conferences handholding Robin. He had many journalist friends and would knock around in Fleet Street with the leading industrial writers. He loved motor racing and knew many of the drivers and commentators. He lived in a lovely mews flat off Westbourne Road.

Barbara Hands (nee Oxley), Mick's secretary, subsequently became a highly skilled case handler. She worked for the firm for 38 years from April 1945, initially as a junior shorthand typist working for Henry Schramek. Henry shared a room with Mick Manning and one day he suggested they swap typists. Barbara:

"He (Mick) was good to work for and over the years let me do more work on the cases than a secretary normally would. This led to me taking over a lot of his cases when he died."

John Bowden:

Mick had been in the RAF during the war and was returning from a bombing raid over German when the plane developed a fault. He got out onto part of the wing of the plane [while it was in mid air] and carried out a repair job. As a result he was `mentioned in dispatches´. He never talked about it himself. I discovered it from a friend of his. I was present when someone subsequently asked him about it and he simply said he did not want to know about it. Brian subsequently spoke to Mick's son who confirmed that it was true.

John Bowden was a particular friend of Rex Church, another recruit in this era:

Derek Whiting and wife (far left);
Harry Nyman (3rd from left) *and wife Libby* (3rd from right)
John Bowden and wife (centre)
Mick Manning and a secretary (far right)
August 1954

When Rex was interviewed for a job at W.H. Thompson he was working as a labourer at Fry's in their chocolate factory. He managed to get a lift to London on a Fry's lorry that was travelling down to London (contrary to Fry's rules). Rex was in the back of the lorry sitting amongst millions of cocoa beans. He dozed off, and when he awoke his shoes had come off and he was unable to find them in the lorry in all the cocoa beans. He had to get off the lorry to go to the interview wearing no shoes. Fortunately, Mick Manning came to the rescue and gave him a pair!

The rapid expansion of the firm had caused it to take on various new offices. There was an urgent need to rehouse under one roof. In 1955, Brian found newly built 1 Serjeants' Inn and they took a lease for 21 years (at 15 shillings

[£0.75p] a square foot with no rent review). The firm moved in on 21 January 1956.

Robin later recalled one of the issues of the time:

Before we made the move we had one of our major problems. Dad's right hand man had been a Managing Clerk, Wilfred Clayton. Gradually everyone fell out with him and then we did. We wrote him a letter inviting him to resign. He went to his union, the CAWU. We went to Harry Pollitt, an old family friend.

He knocked our heads together and said we must immediately withdraw the letter and the man will be gone within 6 months. He was 100% correct and we never needed his help again. Clayton went to Victor Mishcon who set up a new firm named Blatchfords … 30 years later we invited him to the Centenary party we held on 15 October 1985 to mark the 100 years from our father's birth and he came.

Other significant figures who left in the same period, and went on to have successful careers elsewhere were Bill Stapleton who became a partner in Lawfords, Frank Clifford who left the firm in 1964 after 14 years to set up a practice under his own name, and John Williams, who did likewise.

Ivor Walker recalled John Williams:

John Williams was still with the firm when I joined, but … . I think he thought he should have been the boss. He was a powerful personality although not someone I liked. He had a reputation as a good personal injury lawyer. He had one particular union that he looked after, the plumbers, and a legal executive in the firm, John Jones, who dealt with the plumbers work. John Williams left some years later taking the union and John Jones with him.

Robin, Wilfred Clayton and W. Griffiths, Minister of National Insurance. Labour Party Conference, Scarborough 1947. Wilfred Clayton was a Barnardo boy, and left his estate to Barnardo's on his death.

Over the coming decades Robin and Brian ran the firm as joint and only equity partners. Their roles overlapped to an extent, but broadly Robin dealt with the organisation and efficiency of the firm, and Brian with major legal cases. Both had enormous ability and powerful but very different personalities. Brian was a great intellectual and a lawyer of the first rank.

Starting on 1 July 1960 they began to appoint salaried partners. The concept of salaried partnership is an odd one. The "partner" is paid a fixed salary just like any other employee, but is held out to the world as a partner in the firm (and must be a qualified solicitor). It is often seen as a stepping stone to full equity partnership, but in the period to 1974 none who received a salaried partnership went on to full equity partnership.

The first to be appointed as salaried partners in July 1960 were Henry Schramek, David Phillips and Ted Lewis.

Schramek was a key figure in the firm, highly competent as a lawyer and a Communist who lived by his principles. For the last few years until his retirement on 30 April 1969, Rosina Newton was his secretary:

I joined W.H. Thompson in 1964 at Serjeants' Inn in the typing pool, aged 16. The lady in charge was Mrs Kennedy and I received a first class training.

As part of the normal training I progressed to a department as an assistant secretary and was 18 years of age when I went to work for Henry Schramek and became his secretary.

Henry's room was at the end of a long corridor. He had a small room. He was modest. He did not want a large room and when carpets were introduced he said he did not want them either.

In those days the lawyers did not get their own departments quickly at all. They would carry references of the departmental heads so that David Skidmore at that time for example was HS3. Others in Henry's department at that time were Harry Sedler, Stuart Nicholl and Chris Gilmore.

Henry was a very nice man. He loved his charts which I kept setting out all sorts of dates including of dates of Summons for Directions, trials etc. He was never grumpy or bad tempered and although he was the most senior person in the building he was probably the least affected.

John Lebor:

Henry Schramek was one of the leading people in the firm when I joined. He was a real Central European man, always relaxed and never angry. There was a standing joke about his rich aunt and her longevity. When she eventually died she left him a lot of money and after he retired he went to live in the south of France. Unfortunately, he did not survive long.

Like Schramek and many other senior figures in the firm, Brian was a member of the Communist Party having joined in March 1944. Notwithstanding his criticisms of it, Brian made various gifts to the Party and remained a member until eventually joining the Labour Party during Tom Sawyer's tenure as General Secretary many decades later. Robin was a member of the Labour Party, sat on the Greater London Council for a period and contemplated standing as an MP. As Geoff Shears has since commented:

If the brothers had done it on purpose, they could not have done better for by this means they straddled the politics of the labour movement. However the Cold War inspired volatile consequences, and early in their leadership of the firm the brothers woke up one day to find that half of the AEU's work (then the major client) had been allocated elsewhere for political reasons and the rest was at risk of following. They did the right thing, they said very little, they coped and they kept going. It was like that for years afterwards and in some ways still is. There was always some crisis or other … .

Ivor Walker knew nothing of the firm's politics when he joined in 1953, aged 21 and unqualified, following his National Service and a brief period working as a tax clerk:

I had not long been with the firm when I realised how political it was. I recall a meeting being called because we had lost half of the Engineers' Union (AEU) work to Evill & Colman. Bill Carron was President of the AEU and was a Catholic. There was something of a conflict in unions between Roman Catholics on the one hand and Communist Party members on the other – this was true of many unions.

John Bowden asked why I did not join the Communist Party and I decided to do so. Having done so, I recall being called into Brian's room and being shouted at for joining, despite the fact that Brian himself was a member. The reason he was unhappy was that there were splits in the unions and the firm tried to present two faces – one the Communist Party and the other the face of moderation. Robin was never a member of the Communist Party but I wonder whether he was a sleeping member. Many years later I recall asking Dick, later Lord Marsh, why Robin had never received an honour. He told me that Special Branch had vetoed it.

An important member of the AEU at the time and on the Executive Committee was Joe Scott, a communist who for a time was Miriam Edelman's partner. She was the only female executive.

In my early days, after I joined, Ted Lewis introduced me to meetings of Thompsons' Communist Party members at which Joe Scott would be present.

When John Lebor joined the firm, also in 1954, he was already a communist activist.

As a 16 year old I had joined the Young Communists and I got to know Ted Lewis and his wife Margery because they were in the local Communist Party at Willesden. On completing my National Service, Ted said to me that there were not many solicitors who knew the Labour Movement and that I should come and work for Thompsons. I had been offered another job at £10 per week. Anyway, as a result of Ted's suggestion I applied to Thompsons, was interviewed by Robin Thompson and joined the office just off Moorgate in 1954.

I had only been with W.H. Thompson for a week or two

when I was summoned to a meeting of the caucus of the Communist Party within the firm. The meeting was held at Mick Manning's flat. Present, apart from Mick Manning, were Brian, Rex Church, Tom Smith and others. It also included Joe Scott even though he was a union man and not employed by the firm. One item on the agenda was me. The issue was that I was well known as a very able public speaker on behalf of the Communist Party and was it appropriate in the circumstances that I should carry on with that work bearing in mind the fraught political relations between the firm and the AEU? It was agreed that I would not speak on a platform again for the Communist Party. They had other plans for making use of my speaking ability. I accepted this because it made political sense.

John Williams was another leading character. He was my hero as a boy, typical old school Communist Party. He had quite a temper. He subsequently left taking a managing clerk with him and set up his own firm.

Other characters including Mick Manning who was like a kind of father confessor to Brian, Tom Smith who was also unqualified, Freddie Oaten who was a very nice man, a real gentleman, David Philips, one of the qualified staff and there were others. Lou Holt was the accountant. He had been in the International Brigade.

During my time in the Communist Party I even went to tea at Harry Pollitt's. I had been invited by his daughter Jean. He was very friendly. He showed me his tomatoes (which he grew and of which he was very proud).

In the mid 1960s, the principal players in the firm included Robin, Brian, Henry Schramek, Mick Manning, Ted Lewis and David Phillips. Others of significance included Bert Ross, Fred Oaten, Cyril Wener, Ron Smith, Miriam Edelman and Lou Holt the accounts manager, together with Edna Scharts the Office Manager, George Dawson, Malcolm Lee,

B. Roberts Gen. Secretary NUPE and his wife
W. Hutchison EC of AEU plus wife
B. Gardner Gen. Secretary AEU and wife and 2 daughters
August 1954

Jack Alsop, Arthur Charles, Frank Clifford, Tony Walker, Ivor Walker, David Skidmore, Vic Nicolls, Bruce Tyrer, Tony Woolf, John Lebor, Rex Church and John Bowden amongst others.

Others who joined in this era and who went on to play a major part in the firm over several decades included Nick Carter, Simon Walton, Geoff Thomas, John Pickering and Roger Bent.

David Phillips remained with the firm until his retirement in 1982, and died in October 2003, a few days before his 85th birthday.

He specialised in accident litigation, mostly undertaking work in the North East and Yorkshire and dealing with a lot of construction site accident cases. In later years he did a great deal of work including lecturing for ASTMS (Clive Jenkins), the white collar union, and for ASLEF (Ray

Buckton), the train drivers' union.

His best friend in the office for many years was Tony Woolf, and many W.H. Thompson lawyers were articled to him, including Don Wilson, Geoff Thomas, Andrew Dismore, Stuart Carroll and Tony Woolf himself, among others.

Peter Gornall was one of those who benefited from David's tuition. Peter had joined in 1960 but felt that he was struggling until he sought David's advice and encouragement. *"He was fantastic. He opened my eyes and made me believe I could do the job."* Peter went on to become a renowned case handler, supervisor and member of the firm's Law Committee, remaining with the firm until the end of December 1987.

In his autobiography, Clive Jenkins describes David Phillips as 'the unsung brilliant solicitor'. David Skidmore noted he was 'a perfect gentleman, bald with a white beard'. He travelled into work for a number of years with John Harris who also regarded him as a particular friend. Many others felt the same.

Ron Smith had started work as a 16 year old in 1939 with the Transport and General Workers Union – the TGWU – as a post boy in Transport House. When people were called up for service he gained promotion to the Legal Department as a junior clerk. After four years in the Navy mainly as a Radar Operator he returned to the TGWU in their Area 1 regional office. All T & G members could call at the office without an appointment and it was Ron's job to interview and advise them.

Ron recalled:

It was still the age of Common Employment, Employers' Liability Act 1880, Workman's Compensation Public Authority Protection Act and it was not always easy to tell a docker who had had a load dropped on his head that the person who did it was in Common Employment, or that a person could not claim damages because he had accepted W.C. (workman's compensation).

Ron won promotion to the Head Office legal department where he started to deal with claims. He had a cousin at W.H. Thompson, Tom Smith, who suggested he should apply for a job, which he did. He was interviewed by five senior members of staff, John Williams, Wilf Clayton, Mick Manning, Henry Schramek and Mr Cornish. Following this Brian invited Ron and his wife to his home for tea. He was then offered a position at London Wall and started on 1 May 1950, sharing an office with Cyril Wener, who was very helpful, as was Miriam Edelman.

Ron had been working for the firm for about two years when he contracted T.B. He was off work for 18 months but received his full salary plus sickness benefit in addition. He describes this as something he was 'always grateful for at Thompsons'.

Ron moved to Serjeants' Inn in 1956 and then Ilford in 1968 and eventually retired on 30 April 1987 after 37 years' service. He specialised in disease work and particularly dermatitis cases. At times he had forty or fifty of these proceeding. He never lost a contested case at trial throughout his career. He recalled one case:

Dear old Mrs Ada Reeves who called the Judge "Ducks" and "Ducky" and when he told her he could not be addressed like that she then continued to call him "Dear". After that needless to say she won.

Ron was a case supervisor responsible for supervising and training many lawyers throughout his time at Ilford, and dealt with cases for members from a number of different unions. He was responsible for attracting work from the

TGWU (Albert Blyghton) at Ford Dagenham works.

Ron's cousin Tom Smith was a very large man who was a managing clerk at London Wall until he left to become a used car salesman of vintage motor vehicles (and became very rich in the process). A contemporary was Harry Sedler, most noteworthy for allegedly breaking a bottle over Robin's head and for marrying Thompsons' telephonist at the time.

Arthur Charles joined W.H. Thompson in 1949. He dealt with a great deal of work for the Fire Brigades Union. John Saville in Appendix V to *Forged in Fire – the History of the Fire Brigades Union* records Arthur's speech to the FBU Conference in 1975 after he received a presentation:

When I joined W.H. Thompson back in the dim and distant past they said to me: "Look, there is a little union here, the Fire Brigades Union. Will you take it over? You will never do any work for them, they never have any trouble. It is another union you act for and that is it". We all know how different that is today and I am very, very proud to have played a part in building up the history of the legal work of this union and, more important, putting your union on the map in the league of the world trade unions.

I am sure you won't mind me saying that you are a small organisation. We act for large organisations from the AEUW upwards and downwards. This union historically has played a very, very great part in making industrial history. I heard Dick Foggie tell you about the success of damages and so forth over the years. That is all very fine but I would like to retire thinking that W.H. Thompson never did another case for the Fire Brigades Union because every case I have been involved in, from the £5 claim to the £50,000 claim, as Dick said, means pain and suffering. Only last night I was told of another tragedy. We have done an awful lot to prevent accidents. We made brigades realise that if they do not work properly, if they do not devise a safe system of working, people are going to be injured and it is going to cost money; and I think that many types of accident that I was brought up with in the 1950s have now disappeared. Why? Because the work you have done as a union and the work behind the scenes I have been proud to do for you, make the courts say: "This shall not be. If it is, you will pay money." And even insurance companies are hurt most when they have to pay money. My object of working for you and working amongst friends has been to cut out accidents. I do not thrive on accidents. It is no satisfaction to me to earn a salary because somebody has been killed and left a wife and kiddies. I would rather think the fireman is not injured and none of my work is ever necessary.

Arthur then went on to pay tribute to the help he always got from the union and the rank and file members. He carried on working until March 1981 when he was 71 years old, and died in December 1987.

Bruce Tyrer was yet another of the young men who joined the firm with no qualifications and were given the opportunity to progress:

I was born in 1935 and joined W.H. Thompson in 1954. I had left school at aged 15 with no qualifications working as an office boy at a firm of solicitors.
 The managing clerk at that firm took me under his wing. He knew Richard Brice, the outdoor managing clerk at W.H. Thompson and I got an introduction to the firm through him. I applied when the firm was looking for an outdoor clerk. I was interviewed by Brian and offered the job at £4 7s 6d [£4.37p] per week plus luncheon vouchers.
 I started work in Mansion House office but would go to London Wall every day to see Florence Hore who was

directly in charge of me. She organised all the issuing of proceedings that needed doing, gave me the money to go and issue writs, summonses and other process at the Royal Courts of Justice (RCJ). I would go to the RCJ every day for issuing and I would also have to check the daily cause list to see which of the firm's cases were listed for the next day.

In the Mansion House office, apart from Brian, there were Mick Manning, Ted Lewis, Arthur Charles and Harry Nyman amongst others.

Sometime after I joined Mansion House closed and we all moved into Warnford Court. It was at Warnford Court that I started working in a department doing work on cases in John Jones' department.

There were lots of juniors including a few young men including David Skidmore who joined and stepped into my shoes. However, it was mainly girls who joined and they started as juniors, and then worked their way up into the typing pool, before becoming assistant secretary and then departmental secretary.

It was an extraordinary place to work at that time – a community apart from what was going on in the outside world. The politics were very different. I came in green from a political point of view, although my first job had been in a firm where I was working for a Labour MP. After being at Thompsons for a time I joined the Communist Party. There were many Communist Party members at that time.

Bruce clearly made excellent progress because he was offered articles:

I married in 1961 and in about 1963/64 approximately I started on the road of qualifying as a solicitor.
A little earlier Tony Walker had become articled, I think mainly because Brian liked him. Frank Loeffler was articled to Robin and was his assistant but left soon afterwards and

subsequently became a partner in Gaster Vowles Turner & Loeffler in London.

Before me and many others, Geoff Clark asked for articles. He took on a case called Auton v Rayner. It was a huge commercial case with vast amounts of paperwork. He told Robin and Brian that if he did not get articles he would leave and they would be stuck with this case. They gave in and offered him articles. There could be no justification for singling him out and it opened the door to lots of other people. Ivor Walker was one of those who benefited along with Bill Stapleton, Frank Clifford, Malcolm Lee and John Bowden, as well as me. I made an approach to Robin and Brian. Because I had been a clerk for more than 10 years it was possible under Law Society rules to gain entry into articles by passing the Law Society preliminary examination. Once I passed that, Robin and Brian agreed to my having articles.

Bruce went on to qualify as a solicitor and was given a salaried partnership in March 1970.

Ivor Walker was likewise encouraged to take his professional examinations and subsequently became a partner in Robin's firm in 1974. His brother Tony Walker joined in 1954 became a salaried partner in 1966 but left in 1971 to further his ambitions and become very successful in the commercial field. Ivor started at London Wall:

The firm had two buildings at London Wall on opposite sides of the road. The one I was in was more modern with a lift. The annex on the other side of the road had a sloping floor with a post in the middle to hold onto because of the slope! The area has since been demolished and turned into The Barbican.

I worked as Bert Ross' assistant and stayed with him for

about two years. I did nothing but calculations for him on steel erector cases. Bert was innovative in that he was the first person to calculate future losses taking into account increasing rates of pay. He was a very good shrewd hard litigator and meticulous. He was a hard task master. He would send me to see clients on a Sunday in South Wales, to save money.

The work was very exciting. We were fighting for the working class. Thompsons were not liked. Local solicitors did not get a look in because Thompsons dealt with the work all over the country and there was some resentment from local solicitors and the bar.

Ivor confirms the rather curious background involving Geoff Clark and the Auton case:

… the firm took on someone called Geoff Clark. He brought a non personal injury case Auton a large commercial case. The amount of paperwork was absolutely vast. This case went to trial and was lost. The day after it was lost the defendants' brief arrived in the offices of John Platts-Mills, the defendants' offices having been burgled. The documents showed that Auton should have won. John Platts-Mills applied to the Court of Appeal but the Court threw out the application on the basis that they could not look at documents that were the subject of a burglary. Anyway, half way through this case Geoff Clark said to Robin and Brian that unless that gave him his articles he would leave and leave this case behind. So they decided to give him articles. In a sense of fair play, they also gave my brother articles to save him from National Service which he would otherwise have had to undertake. Articles were also given to Rex Church at the same time, and generally the floodgates were opened. Articles were given to everyone including me.

Not everyone had been in favour of this policy. John Bowden:

I recall Mick Manning was against it as was Frank Clifford. At first I was also against it, but when others got articles I changed my view. I had never swotted or crammed and had no previous experience of taking examinations but with help from Ted Lewis and John Platts-Mills I eventually slogged my way through. After a long struggle with revenue law, I passed them all and qualified.

[John qualified as a solicitor after leaving Thompsons].

Bert Ross was a legendary figure from the era. A passionate ballet aficionado, Bert was known for his particular ability in calculating all aspects of past and future losses in personal injury claims, not least pension losses, an area of work which most lawyers struggled with! Ted Constable who joined the firm in 1964 describes Bert:

Bert was a real gentleman but a man of steel. He was dedicated to the work, and after retiring he couldn't stand not being involved so returned to work at the Ilford office. Bert looked like a City gent, was softly spoken and charming. In Chancery Lane days he handled a large number of steel erector cases. His method of dealing with insurance representatives was the stuff of folk lore. I enjoyed observing him in action. He would first keep the rep waiting, then clear his desk before politely inviting him into his office. He would then sit, arms folded, looking straight at him and say 'Yes?' After the discomfited rep had fumbled his way to an offer, Bert would display irritation that his valuable time had been wasted on such a "piffling" proposal and begin to show the hapless man out. He was an ace operator.

John Lebor joined the firm in 1954, aged 25 and already a qualified solicitor, and stayed for over forty years. John, the son of a high-class tailor, joined the Communist Party as a teenager. As he said in his autobiography:

When I went to my first meetings, held above a shop in Cricklewood Broadway, the young people had a great spirit. We made great efforts to improve ourselves by education and reading. For me it was a chance to use my gift for communication, for public speaking and debate and to be a part of a great movement that, it seemed, was going to change the world.

John started the route to qualification by obtaining articles in 1946 with Tarlo Lyons & Co – the contact came through his father who made suits for Jonas Lyons. John's father had to pay a premium of £300, as John says 'a great deal of money in those days'. He recalls:

I qualified as a solicitor in 1951 and did my National Service.

I believe I got on well during my early years in Thompsons. Mick Manning was particularly known for his ability to entertain union clients and socialise with them and I took this up in a big way particularly with regional visits, developing weekend schools and such like. I got to know many leading figures in the trade union and Labour movement as a result. I was particularly known in the north of England, Yorkshire in particular. I became a very close personal friend of George Caborn, now deceased, father to Richard Caborn the Labour government minister.

With everyone else, of course, I moved to Serjeants' Inn when that office opened in 1956. I got on well with Robin … In the office I was quite friendly with Brian. Brian was openly homosexual at a time when this was still illegal. He said he "liked sailing close to the wind".

I left the Communist Party in 1962. Over the years I had become less and less committed to the party. I was considered a liberal revisionist. The catalyst to me leaving occurred after the case of Stratford –v- Lindley, a case in which I was involved on behalf of the firm. After the case was concluded we wanted to show how dangerous it was for the Labour Movement. Bill Lindley and I saw George Woodcock and Vic Feather. Word got back to me after the meeting that Woodcock had said to Vic Feather: - "Who's that bright young man with Bill Lindley?" Feather had replied "CP". Once George Woodcock knew that he was no longer interested.

I then joined the Labour Party.

In the 1960s Robin asked me to open Manchester office. I had not long then got married and was not keen … I remained working in London, but was transferred to Stanmore office in the 1970s where Cyril Wener was the man in charge.

I had many friends in Thompsons … . I shared a flat [for a time] with Tony Woolf. He was in the Young Communist League and his brother was Peter Woolf the consultant psychiatrist … . John Bowden was my best friend when I first joined. The firm had a commendable policy at that time of bringing in people from the factory floor. John was another one who was in the Communist Party. Unfortunately, our friendship came to an end when I became a partner since he felt that I had joined "the other side".

I was also very friendly with Rex Church and many others.

John was to stay with the firm until 1995, 41 years. He married his wife Rose, a Holocaust survivor, in 1962 and they have lived in Brent ever since.

In 1963 Robin and Brian (but largely Brian) co-authored

Accidents at Work which was distributed free to union stewards. The book went into six reprints in three years and into nearly every major workplace, helping spread knowledge of health safety and accident law, and a message that accidents often happened because employers paid too little attention to the health and safety of the workforce. It contained a swingeing indictment of the law, the legal system and the impact of the profit motive on health and safety standards.

The illustration on the cover of a barrister slipping on a banana skin was a cartoon drawn by Eric Heather, a legal executive for many years. As well as being an excellent lawyer, Eric was a skilled cartoonist. Eric joined the firm in August 1960, answering an advertisement in the *New Statesman*:

I couldn't say that I had ever heard of W.H. Thompson … . But I knew of a mate of mine in the Labour League of Youth, who used to work on the factory floor at Hawker Aircraft at Kingston, and was now working for a firm of solicitors in London. He had met this solicitor (I later found it was Brian Thompson) at a meeting for young trade unionists.

I had started work at 15 and had no educational qualifications. If you failed your 11-plus as I had you simply didn't do school certificate and that sort of thing. By 1960 I was 25. I worked as an artist and sign writer with a firm of screen-printers and display-makers. I didn't feel I was doing all that I was capable of doing. The only thing to recommend me was my politics. I had been a Labour candidate four times in the local elections. And I had stood for Parliament in 1959 – the second youngest candidate that year, in the third strongest Tory seat (Epsom) in the country.

I was interviewed … by four people: Robin Thompson, Brian Thompson, Henry Schramek and the other one I can't remember (I think it may have been David Phillips).

ACCIDENTS AT WORK

A guide to your Legal Rights

THIRD EDITION

by **ROBIN THOMPSON**
and
BRIAN THOMPSON

Eric describes the interviews:

One was with Robin Thompson, then aged 35. His interviewing technique in those days was notorious – long silences – when you didn't know whether you should wait for the next question, or say something to fill the gap, or creep out quietly on the assumption that the interview was over. Henry Schramek was kind, witty and amusing and he put me at my ease. I think the third interviewer was David Phillips – I'm not sure – but I always found him easy to get on with. And the fourth interview was with Brian – the younger brother, aged 34 – but I didn't know what to make of that rising note of interrogation in his way of speaking. He seemed sceptical about my credentials, and I thought him intimidating. I had no idea what any of them thought of me.

Eric was offered a job and accepted, even though it involved a considerable pay cut. (Two other assistant litigation clerks started on the same day, Ronald Frew and Desmond Ball, together with Brenda Long who started as a junior).

I needed a suit, but I had the one I'd been married in the year before. You could only afford one suit at a time, and when it wore out…you bought a new one on the never-never.
    I bought a second-hand copy of Munkman's Employers Liability and read it from cover to cover. When I started I found that it was the same firm that my friend worked for…John Bowden. The Thompson brothers had been recruiting people from the factory-floor – shop stewards – for some years. Those were the days when Britain still had factories. Like me they had missed out educationally, but they learned the job simply by doing it. I think I was probably the last of that era. In the years since then the firm has always looked for good legal qualifications. At the time there were very few qualified solicitors in the firm. Robin and Brian were

the only partners.

There was only one office in those days, occupying three floors at 1, Serjeants' Inn in Fleet Street. Everybody lived in or around London. And every executive had to have an overnight bag in his desk. I say `his´ desk because, except for Miriam Edelman, there were no female litigation executives then. We were dealing with cases at assize courts and county courts all over England and Wales. You might not know till about half-past-three whether, that same evening, you might have to be in Durham, Chester, Liverpool, Manchester or Cardiff. It might be someone else's case – because he might have two of his cases coming on at the same time. Life became very much easier when the other offices opened.

The only law lectures I ever attended … were on a five day course in practical conveyancing. We were about to lose the services of our long-term conveyancing clerk, Roy Degenhart, and the firm had not found any replacement. Although we had Marg Craner with over 30 years' experience in conveyancing and probate…the conveyancing department had to have a man in charge! Somehow I survived six months without any disasters until Barry Samuels was recruited. I have never forgotten how helpful and how completely lacking in resentment Marg Craner was. She never once blamed me for being passed over, and she helped me if I had any problems.

Eric gradually began to specialise in employment cases:

I was rather surprised to find myself in demand as a law lecturer. It was partly because I was one of the few lawyers in the country to know anything about employment law at that time. It's become a major industry since. Ken Brett, Assistant General Secretary of the Engineers' Union, reckoned that my lectures to his shop stewards reminded him of nothing so much as Derek Nimmo in full flight! He seemed to assume that I was a bit odd as a trade union lawyer. He thought I was a bit of a toff and educated at Oxbridge. It amused him to take the micky out of the posh voice I'd carefully cultivated as a teenager. I never had the heart to tell him that my working class credentials were beyond reproach.

Eric dealt with personal injury cases for about the first ten years of his time with the firm, initially in Freddie Oaten's department along with George Dawson and Don Heslop, and eventually under the supervision of Cyril Wener who was 'meticulous and careful'. Within about ten years Eric stopped dealing with personal injury cases completely in order to concentrate on employment work. He specialised in the early legislation such as The Contracts of Employment Act, 1963, The Redundancy Payments Act, 1965 and then unfair dismissal when this was introduced, together with work on collective issues such as industrial disputes. He did a great deal of work for the Construction Section of the AUEW. This had previously been dealt with by Ivor Walker. When Ivor fell out of favour with Robin, John Baldwin the General Secretary threatened to take the work away from the firm. Eric was asked to take it over and made a great success of it, dealing amongst other things with rule book and pension scheme issues (including their own officers' rule book). He became an expert on these matters and over the years drafted a number of union rule books. Whenever something unusual came up such as advising on tax issues, share scheme options and suchlike, Eric was the man for the job.

Eric retired from the firm on 30 April 1998 after 38 years' service.

I look back on my time...with great affection. I have made many friends, some no longer alive. But I can't always put a name to the face … . I remember Robin Thompson … telling the staff how he extracted himself from the social gaffe of not remembering the name of someone he had previously met. He said he used to pull out a piece of paper from his pocket, and say, "Now, tell me, how do you spell your name?" He had to give this up when someone replied, "S.M.I.T.H".

In his last three years before retirement, Eric began training for the priesthood (Church of England), and now carries the prefix Reverend. He has since retired again, although, as he says, this is purely nominal. (In April 2008 Eric officiated at the funeral of Robin's first wife Queenie at Woking crematorium.)

Another important figure that joined in the 1960s and would play a critical role in the work of the firm for thirty years was John Harris. John had worked for a couple of other firms before Robin took him on in April 1966 and doubled his salary. He recalls his time with the firm:

I worked initially with John Bass, a lovely man. He had about 1,400 cases and I took most of these on. I recall having 42 cases set down for trial at one time. Included in the team were Vince O' Callaghan and Pat Cartwright.

I had been used to working very hard. At Thompsons in those days it was much more leisurely, but also very organised with good support staff, a highly efficient Dictaphone room and a court department which again was highly efficient and run by Miss Hore.

I loved the work right from the beginning.

On joining the firm I was allocated 3 particular cases that no one else wanted. One was against the union and involved Bill Keys of the Printers, Bookbinders and Paper Makers Union, SOGAT. Another was a case called Salisbury which went to the House of Lords and was reported in the Law Reports. The case against the union was one which I thought we should win, but our QC Edward Sutcliffe thought otherwise and advised us to settle. Bill Keys decided to back my judgment. The case went to trial, lasted 6 days and we won. I recall that immediately Robin told me to get a firm's car!

After that case I was given the union, SOGAT, to look after. They had previously been dealt with by Robin and John Bass. At that time Tom Smith was the General Secretary, and I hit it off with him and the union generally.

When I joined I did not have a particularly political background, save as a Labour voter, but I discovered that I loved the trade union work. My whole working life then became dominated by the print unions and to a lesser extent by my work for the DPF.

I dealt with personal injury work, a great deal of industrial tribunal work as the years went on, and industrial issues on a daily basis … .

From a professional point of view it was a most enjoyable time.

I had many friends in the firm – I got on well with everyone, but some who spring immediately to mind are Robin, Brian, David Phillips, Mick Manning, John Bass and Cyril Wener. I travelled to and from work for a number of years with David Phillips, and David was a particular friend.

I retired just before the merger (which I was very happy to see take place) in 1996 at 65 years of age.

Ted Constable joined in 1964:

I left university with a law degree but no particular interest in following a career in the law. After 9 months in a central London firm acting for landlords, and villains on criminal legal aid, I knew this was not for me and left.

I saw an advert for W.H. Thompson, walked in to the office unannounced, was interviewed by Bert Ross and Ted

Lewis before seeing Henry Schramek and Brian. I had never been quizzed on my politics before. I knew nothing about the firm so I just plunged in. I must have struck the right note as I was taken on at £11 7s 6d [£11.37p] plus luncheon vouchers, good rates at the time. This was in 1964. I was placed in the Chancery Lane office, sharing a room with Tony Woolf. I was trained up by him, Bert Ross, and later in Serjeants' Inn by Cyril Wener – a pretty high powered line up.

They were a very agreeable crowd in Chancery Lane. Others in the office included Eric Heather, John Bowden, Bill Stapleton, Mike Osborne, Ted Lewis, Rex Church, John Pickering, and the outrageously funny Malcolm Lee. Roger Bent joined about 6 months after me.

I felt at home; as a rebel without a cause. Thompsons was somewhere I felt comfortable. Every other person was a communist – I thought it was great. I took to the work straightaway. It had a real social purpose. Finding Thompsons was the only reason I stayed in the law.

In those days, trainees like Ted frequently went to court on other people's cases. This was a great boon to young lawyers because of the generous travelling expenses paid. Eric Heather, John Harris and Ted Constable were all legal executives: lawyers who were not qualified solicitors. Some unqualified lawyers were given the opportunity to qualify as solicitors, but this period also saw the growth in the recruitment of articled clerks (trainee solicitors) and qualified solicitors. The first graduate trainee ever taken on by the firm was G.W. (Nick) Carter. Nick joined in 1961 and played a crucial part in the firm for almost forty years. Nick explained how his career started:

I graduated from University College, London in 1961 and started looking for articles. I had been brought up in

Norwich but wished to remain in London and needed to earn enough to survive in London. I attended a number of interviews. A couple of the firms I was interviewed by wanted a premium to offer me articles.

In any event I saw Thompsons name, had an interview and was offered £12 per week, starting work in September 1961 at Serjeants' Inn with articles of three years. I knew the firm was a left wing firm and I was a leftish Labour Party member. It was perfect. David Phillips interviewed me and commented that I was "a smart young student with a beard". I had not long started when I was asked to shave off my beard, at the request of Robin Thompson! I had no great problem with this, though ironically within a few years many men, including some in Thompsons, sported beards.

I was trained by Jack Allsopp who hailed from the north. Ann Martin was his secretary and I learnt a great deal from her about practice and procedure. Jack was a nice modest man. I came across Henry Schramek, one of the senior people in the office. He was a pleasant man who I liked. I recall Lou Holt the cashier who smoked fifty cigarettes a day. He told me that by the time I was thirty I would be earning £3,000 a year. Although I was only articled, at the end of my first year I received a bonus of £300 which was a lot of money in those days.

I became friendly with many people in the office but particularly the salaried partners such as Rex Church, Tony and Ivor Walker. The atmosphere in the office was friendly and relaxed. We would play table tennis at lunchtime.

There were many executives who were members of the Communist Party and they held CP meetings. It was said that Thompsons' accounts would be spread across the desk in King Street at the HQ of the Communist Party!

Another graduate who was taken on as an articled clerk in this period, joining in 1964, and who likewise was to play a major part not just in the firm's cases but also in its management over several decades, was Simon Walton:

I read Law at University College, London. I started looking for articles, and saw an advertisement for W.H. Thompson on the university notice board offering £11 per week. This was very attractive in those days, and I applied.

I had a preliminary interview with Ted Lewis and was then called back for a further interview, this time with Brian Thompson and Bert Ross (and one other I cannot now recall). What I remember about this was the discussion with Brian. I explained to him that my father knew the firm because he was a shop steward and AEU member from Coventry and had had a claim for an injury to his foot which W.H. Thompson had dealt with successfully. Brian asked a lot about my father, we talked about politics and about cinema, particularly movies featuring Humphrey Bogart (all subjects we had a common interest in).

I was successful, and was taken on in 1964, in Serjeants' Inn, articled to Robin Thompson. The pay was £11 7s 6d [£11.37p]plus a three shilling [15p] daily luncheon voucher. I was the highest paid articled clerk I knew! I joined Mick Manning's team – his reference was "M", as "M4". My supervisor was Tony Walker and the team also included Bruce Tyrer.

I was admitted as a solicitor in 1967 and in the period prior to 1971 spent a fairly brief period at the Chancery Lane office where I was supervised by Malcolm Lee, before returning to Serjeants' Inn.

One of the "giants" of the firm when I joined was Henry Schramek, a man highly respected by all. He was very friendly with Brian and Mick Manning. Mick Manning was lovely and kind … I still have the wedding gift he gave me when I married my first wife Marianne. He was a creature of Brian's; I recall that Brian showered Tony Walker with gifts which he then decided, for reasons which are not difficult to guess, he wanted back. Mick Manning was the one who asked for their return. Mick ran a volume of cases, took me to trade union schools and I learned that side of the job from him.

The 1960s was a golden period of recruitment. John Pickering joined in 1962:

After leaving school I attended Leeds University and obtained my Law Degree. I then started looking for a job. I did not find most of what was available to be at all appealing – conveyancing type jobs in Blackburn and suchlike. However, I then saw an advertisement after scouring the papers for a number of weeks, and it was an ad from W.H. Thompson, a trade union firm. I thought this sounded good and I was very keen. I went down for an interview with Robin, Brian, Ted Lewis and David Phillips all on one afternoon, and then a further interview with Henry Schramek the next day. I really wanted the job, and I think this is what swung it for me.

I accordingly started work for WH Thompson in March 1962 at Serjeants' Inn at £10 7s 6d [£10.37p] a week. This was a living wage at the time, and in addition I got luncheon vouchers and obtained the benefit of the very favourable expenses regime.

I was technically articled to Brian, but in fact for the first year or so I worked for Bert Ross. Bert was feared and respected, and I would say "on top of his game" at the time. He had previously worked for the Iron Trades, but he was a communist and very committed to the firm's ethos. He insisted on the highest standards and I respected him greatly. I recall that after about three months he said that he did not think I was clever enough for the job. This spurred me on to try even harder.

There was a tremendous atmosphere of political

commitment in the office. Although I did not know him well, Henry Schramek was a very likeable man who treated everyone the same whatever their status. I knew Ted Lewis a lot better and liked him very much.

I worked under Bert until the Chancery Lane office opened a year or so later, and there were just a few of us based at Chancery Lane including Bert Ross, Mike Osborne, Tony Woolf and myself. I would help all three of them.

I knew Tony quite well because I would baby-sit for him. Tony was the pioneer of industrial disease litigation. I remember Mike Osborne as being the most patient, helpful and easy person to work for.

In this period up to 1966 I went on lots of trials. It was great training … . As an articled clerk particularly and then as a young solicitor I got sent on lots of trials all over the country and I learnt a great deal.

Geoff Shears joined on 18 October 1971 in Serjeants' Inn. Geoff was to go on and play a major role in Thompsons and indeed become the leading figure in the firm after the retirement of Robin and Brian. Geoff, who was born in December 1947, was brought up in Plymouth before attending LSE to undertake his Law Degree:

It was a time of student radicalism and the Vietnam War and in my first term at LSE there was a student occupation … . At around the same time I recall attending a debate at the University of London Union where Bill Wedderburn seconded a motion that the United States should get out of Vietnam. He was brilliant in his discourse with an indictment of imperialism and capitalism. It had an impact on me. My political views began to come together.

Geoff's role in the occupation resulted in his suspension, but he returned to finish his degree course. His time at LSE was also punctuated by the Grosvenor Square demonstrations during one of which he enjoyed the physical attentions of the police.

Geoff explains how he ended up at Thompsons:

On Bill Wedderburn's recommendation, after Law School I did an MA in Industrial Relations at Warwick. Warwick was another university where students had been active – I attended the year after the student occupation there inspired by E. P. Thompson. While I was there the Conservative Government was steering the Industrial Relations Bill through Parliament, and as the only lawyer on the course I was expected to become an expert on it!

Subsequently, Wedderburn advised me to apply to W.H. Thompson, there being very few law firms I could imagine being happy to work for. I did not know much about the firm save that they had acted for the trade unions in a number of cases I was familiar with.

I wrote to Brian Thompson and was invited down for interview. Brian, when he saw me had a copy of the book his mother had edited - Poems of Revolt – visibly located on his carefully organised desk. I knew and loved a couple of the poems. He also had a reference from Wedderburn. He asked me to see Robin also, who told me that his brother thought well of me, and I was taken on, joining the firm at Serjeants' Inn on 18 October 1971.

On starting with the firm I was met by Bruce Tyrer who explained that I would be articled to and working with Tony Woolf.

Inevitably he was thrown into a whole range of different issues. As well as the work Tony was undertaking on coal miners' pneumoconiosis there was much else:

The first client I saw in the office was a mesothelioma victim from whom I took a statement dealing with liability. I recall that 6 months later I had to visit him and his family at their home – he was too ill to move and was about to die; we needed a further statement this time dealing with quantum; and the whole family needed reassurance that we would win the case, albeit after our client had died.

My knowledge of the Industrial Relations Act proved to be useful, or so I thought. I was asked to read the Rule Book for the Signs and Displays Trade Union (SDTU) to see what rules needed changing in the light of the Act. In addition we got stuck into a series of cases for TASS. TASS like most of the unions did not recognise the NIRC (the National Industrial Relations Court – set up by the Act) so I would go along incognito to sit at the back of the court to see what happened and report back. In the course of this I got to know Ken Gill who of course duly became General Secretary of the union.

A few weeks after I joined the firm I was asked to go to court on one of Bert Ross' cases. When I arrived the barrister Patrick Mayhew advised me that special damages [actual losses in a personal injury case] was still disputed and would have to be proved. This could only be done by my giving evidence. I barely knew how to calculate special damages! Fortunately we were able to agree the figures by rapid negotiation during counsel's summing up!

In this early period I recall attending the House of Lords with Brian. He had three cases in quick succession in the Lords, all of which resulted in favourable judgments on issues arising out of the Industrial Injuries Acts and in particular the entitlement to benefit for industrial disease. Following each successful judgment the government passed legislation effectively returning the position to what it had been. After that Brian felt that such appeals were a waste of time.

The Serjeants' Inn office was extraordinarily busy. While the High Court was sitting we seemed to have case after case ready for trial. If union leaders needed advice, we seemed to be on their doorstep. If there was a demonstration by print workers in Fleet Street in support of the imprisoned Pentonville Five, it was inevitable that some of us would join in. It was a wonderful introduction to trade union law.

By the early 1970s the firm was undergoing major changes, partly brought about by the opening of regional offices, and to some extent accelerated by the new regional presence. The firm had gained more trade union clients, and at least partly as a result of its own efforts more and more working people who suffered injury or disease were able to claim compensation.

Chapter 17
The opening of regional offices

The continuing growth in the firm along with the desire to provide a service readily available to the unions and their members saw the opening of the first regional offices, starting with Cardiff in 1965, Manchester 1966, Ilford in 1968 and Stanmore in 1971.

Robin described how this came about:

The firm got so large that when an Engineering Union executive member raised with me the question of our opening an office in their office in Cardiff I agreed and made the necessary arrangements. This was not easy as we needed a person in charge. Ted Lewis was the obvious choice but he was living happily in Epping Forest. I went and saw him one evening and after a very friendly chat he decided to move to Cardiff; that was a great help. It was sad that he was to die not many years afterwards. Because we were still pressed for space and the lease at Sergeant's Inn would shortly expire to be replaced with a new lease with a very high rent, we opened other offices in different locations. The one at Manchester was particularly successful, opened by two younger solicitors on our staff. They were Nick Carter and John Pickering.

When the Cardiff office opened on 22 March 1965, Ted Lewis was joined by Fred Oaten, Ron Frew, Don Barkshire and Norman Edwards, and they were soon joined from London by Geoff Thomas, who went on to manage the office after Ted Lewis' death (before moving to London in 1985 to join Robin Thompson's 'A' partners), and Ted Constable in 1970. Roger Bent joined the office, then

Andrew Herbert in April 1971 and the author in 1972.

Several went on to manage various Thompsons' offices. Stuart Henderson also started in Cardiff office before moving to Birmingham where he worked for a rival firm before rejoining Robin Thompsons there. He subsequently left again, this time to join Irwin Mitchell where he is a Regional Managing Partner and has been highly successful.

Don Barkshire dealt with Scottish cases. This was before the firm had opened its first Scottish office. He dealt with those cases where a settlement could be negotiated and sent others which needed to be litigated or were obviously serious up to Scottish agents. When he retired in the 1970s these cases were passed to Eric Heather in London. Don was a Quaker pacifist who was imprisoned in Wormwood Scrubs initially in the Second World War and later served as a nursing orderly dealing with wounded servicemen and blitz casualties.

Norman Edwards was another notable lawyer with significant links with SOGAT. One partner who nearly came to Cardiff but decided to stay in London was Bruce Tyrer. Bruce and his wife were very friendly with Ted and Margery Lewis and were all members of the Communist Party. Another close friend of Ted's and Party member was John Bowden. Like Bruce he considered it but decided against for personal reasons.

Ted Lewis was a warm, kind and generous man. He was steeped in the law and had an encyclopaedic knowledge of health and safety regulations. The author recalls the academic nature of the discussions Ted had, particularly in construction case accidents, with a highly skilled consulting engineer and good friend of the firm Ray Brueton.

Ted met his wife Margery when she joined the practice in High Wycombe for a few weeks shortly after the Second World War. Margery:

I divorced my first husband and Ted and I married in 1948. Before I met him Ted had graduated from Cambridge with a first despite the fact that he had to take a year out for a throat operation. He was also a member of the Communist Party.

We moved to Cardiff in the mid-1960s when Ted opened the Cardiff office.

Margery has a fascinating story of her own, particularly her involvement as one of the original Greenham Common marchers, a story set out in detail in Ann Pettit's book *Walking to Greenham.*

En route and frustrated by the lack of publicity, Ann Pettit describes how the women considered whether to take more direct action on their arrival. The original intention had been simply to march. Now they considered whether to take a leaf from the suffragettes and chain themselves to railings. A meeting was held when they arrived in Devizes. Different views were expressed, and each spoke in turn:

"I only know," said Margery Lewis, "that this is not what I came to do. Coming on this march was a big step, but I felt sure it was right and now I know it was. The other thing, I'm not sure about. I wish my husband was alive, because we always used to discuss everything together, and he was a wise and thoughtful man. Now I don't know what would be the right thing to do." Margery's husband had died not long before … and they had been married for many years. She spoke for many there.

In the event they decided collectively that they would chain themselves to the railings on arrival and purchased suitable equipment including lengths of chain in an old-fashioned ironmonger in Marlborough on the way! The protest and peace camp at Greenham eventually brought worldwide publicity.

Margery's comments about her husband Ted will resonate with all who knew and worked with him; wise, thoughtful and calm, he was admired by the young lawyers he recruited in the Cardiff office.

The monthly law meetings in the Cardiff office were never anything but instructive. Each month one of the lawyers would give a report on recent cases of note. One month the unfortunate person giving the report referred to the McGhee case which had just been heard by the House of Lords, but dismissed its importance. Fred Oaten, who by then was very ill, suddenly roused himself and launched into a vigorous explanation of the critical importance of the case which followed and expanded the concept of material contribution. You could not fail to learn and be enthused. Fred was quite unlike Ted. He liked to go for a drink at lunchtimes with his friends from the insurance industry. At one of the firm's cocktail parties, shortly after the breathalyser law was introduced, his wife Edna said to Barbara Castle that she 'did not know who introduced this breathalyser nonsense'. Barbara Castle was the minister responsible! Unfortunately both Ted and Fred Oaten died prematurely; Fred in 1974 and Ted in March 1981 aged 67. Ted Constable recalls Fred:

Fred Oaten was friendly and jovial; he had his own way of doing things and came from the old insurance school. In London he wore a bowler hat.

Ted Constable moved to Cardiff from Serjeants' Inn in 1970. He dealt with a vast number of NUPE (the public employees union) cases, forging very strong links with that union and various others in South Wales and the West Country. In later years he went to Bristol, opening the office with Andrew Herbert, with Ted as the front man with the clients.

As a result of illness, Ted transferred back to Cardiff in 1998 before leaving the firm in 2001 after 37 years. He continues to work for the firm on a consultancy basis, interviewing clients and witnesses and collecting evidence on cases as requested – particularly for the Cardiff office.

One of the mainstays of Cardiff office for many years was Roger Bent. Roger, after studying at King's College London, saw an advertisement for the firm and was encouraged to apply by Peter Benenson and Neville Vincent, two of the founders of Amnesty International. He joined in February 1965 in Chancery Lane where he was supervised by Bert Ross and undertook his articles. He transferred to Manchester office from late 1966 and worked there for two years before leaving to work for the National Coal Board. He then came back to Thompsons, this time in the Cardiff office, in February 1971 where he was made a salaried partner in March 1973.

Roger took over as managing partner of the office in 1985 a position he held until his retirement from the partnership on 30 April 1998. Always a brilliant case handler, Roger carried on working for the firm until 2001 on a consultancy basis.

The Manchester office was led for over thirty years by Nick Carter. Nick joined the practice in September 1961, qualified as a solicitor in December 1964 and transferred from Serjeants' Inn with John Pickering to open the office on 17 October 1966. Nick:

They needed someone to head up the Manchester office. None of the salaried partners would go – they were too London based. So, as a qualified person, it came down to me. It was a glorious opportunity. I had been covering the North West personal injury work and had made many, many visits to the North West to see clients, had visited numerous union offices. I would travel up with a colleague on the sleeper, arriving in Manchester at 4 or 5 a.m. We would have to kick our heels on the station before travelling on to whichever union office we were going to visit to carry out our interviews.

It was left to me to find premises which I did in Quay House, in a new unpartitioned floor. Robin and Brian came up to look and approved. I arranged the floor plan, ordered the furniture and so on. I was assisted by Ann Martin who by then was Ann Caldwell. She was one of the original contingent who came up from London to start the office off. Others who joined me were John Pickering, Jack Allsopp, Mick Piggott (he was Victor Nicoll's nephew) and Mike Osborne (who had been called to the Bar but did not practice as a barrister and had re-qualified as a solicitor). Subsequently we recruited Ron Waterton and Pat Cartwright.

I was in control, managing the office, including managing Jack which was slightly ironic as while we were in London he had supervised me. The four or five of us who started the office off used to lunch every day together at The Grotto.

John Pickering was also one of the initial group:

I heard on the grapevine that Nick Carter was going to head the new office. I was just married and was thinking that I probably could not afford a house in London and I also thought it would be a good opportunity for me if I could go to Manchester because I would have more immediate involvement. It was agreed that I should go, and I was accordingly one of the original contingent, effectively second in charge to Nick at Quay House. Others who came up to Manchester at that time or shortly afterwards included Mike Osborne, Pat Cartwright, Jack Allsopp and Mike Slaughter.

I became a salaried partner with WH Thompson on 1 March 1968, the same day as Ivor Walker and Anton Bates.

We started doing a considerable amount of disease work

such as pneumoconiosis cases from the Foundry Workers. In addition I started to cut my teeth on asbestos work. There was a doctor in Halifax, Bertie Mann, who was impressed by the preparation Thompsons put into cases. For example, when instructing him we would send him a copy of the client's detailed statement which would save him a fair amount of work. As a result he started passing cases to us, particularly cases from Acre Mill in Hebden Bridge. We started dealing with a lot of them and at the time they were new and complex.

All this was happening at the time that Tony Woolf in particular was fighting the pioneering cases such as Pickles and Smith –v- Central Asbestos (which went to the High Court in 1970 and the Court of Appeal in 1972).

From that time on I dealt with a large amount of complex disease litigation.

As was so often the case, early in the life of the new office it had a major dispute to deal with. Nick explains:

We had not long opened in Manchester in 1966 when we had to deal with a major industrial dispute at Roberts Arundel. This was a textile machine manufacturer in Stockport which had been taken over by an American businessman Robert E. Pomeranz in July 1965. In November 1966 the company began hiring women as cheap labour and refusing to discuss their pay and conditions with the union. The union was the AEU, one of Thompson's main clients, if not the main one.

The dispute really started in earnest when Pomeranz decided to sack all 145 employees and advertise for non-union workers to take their places. As a result the strike became one of the most bitter strikes in the history of the British Trade Union Movement, and is described in detail in Jim Arnison's book *The Million Pound Strike*. Boycotts of

Roberts Arundel goods were organised by the AEU and mass demonstrations began in February 1967 in the course of which the Chief Constable rang the District Secretary of the AEU threatening literally to read the riot act to the strikers. The District Secretary of the AEU was John Tocher who I got to know very well and who became a lifelong friend. The Regional Organiser was Hugh Scanlon and, of course, I got to know him also. Hugh Scanlon went on to become the General Secretary of the union.

I was present in Stockport on occasions when bricks and bottles were thrown. The strike eventually came to an end when the factory was put up for sale in May 1968.

Many pickets were arrested and we arranged rotas in the office to cover the Magistrates' Court hearings, instructing barristers Ben Hytner and George Carman to represent the union members.

There was also a very big case that we brought against the police. Three of the strikers who had been arrested alleged that they were beaten up in the cells and we

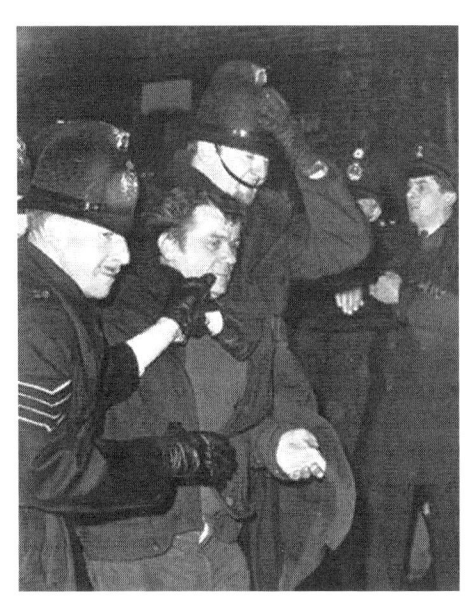

A protester is manhandled away. Police threatened AEU officials with The Riot Act – an extreme measure which entitles officers to make summary arrests and even open fire if a crowd does not disperse.

commenced a claim against the police. I decided that rather than instructing a QC with known political views I would go for an establishment man and we briefed, as a result, Derek Hodgson QC who did an excellent job. I recall that the solicitor acting on behalf of the police was Mike Sachs who later became the first solicitor to be appointed as a High Court Judge.

The case was settled very close to trial and subsequently Thames Television did a half hour documentary on the dispute and the case. I briefed them and appeared in the programme which caused quite a stir particularly as none of the police officers involved had been disciplined. George Carman accompanied me to Thames TV to watch the rushes as it had been a condition of me appearing that we would be able to watch the rushes and correct any errors before the programme went out.

During the course of the dispute there were hundreds of arrests and it placed a lot of strain on the office. I recall being in Stockport dealing with some matter arising out of the dispute when my wife Judi was in labour with my daughter Emma.

For a number of years the barristers most frequently instructed by Manchester were Ben Hytner and George Carman. In the biography of George Carman, his son Dominic comments:

The largest single area of George's practice by this time was personal injury (PI), with factory accident cases being the principal breadwinner. As a junior, he acted for plaintiffs, instructed mostly by the trade union solicitors Thompsons. Between 1966 and 1971, they provided over half of all his work ... . Nic (sic) Carter, who set up the firm's Manchester office, was impressed ... Carter often socialised with his number-one barrister.

All this was true, but Nick was focused on making the office successful, and friendships with barristers did not mean that they were used exclusively. Nick comments:

The office expanded very quickly. The work in those days was vastly different from what it is today. Much of the work came to us from accidents in foundries, on construction sites, in paper mills. Liability wise it was probably not as difficult as cases arising in the service industries but there were many horrendous injuries that we dealt with.

When I came up to Manchester the Chambers we used were the Peter Street Chambers where the Clerk was Ronnie Lynch. The two barristers we used constantly were Ben Hytner and George Carman, both to go on, in later years, to make considerable names for themselves and with both of whom I became friendly. In fact, however, I was not keen in having all our eggs in one basket and, despite some resistance from Robin and Brian, started using Chambers elsewhere in addition.

We had a great deal of work, the case handlers, including myself, handling 400 or 500 cases each. We took on more staff, acquired more disease cases, particularly asbestos, although we had had pneumoconiosis cases from the start.

By and large the legal atmosphere in Manchester was extremely good. It was possible to have a good relationship with opponents. They were professional but pleasant. We built up good relationships with a number of the lawyers from James Chapman & Co. and A. W. Mawers, the firms which represented insurance companies. I recall that I established a decent relationship with Arthur McKenna, the senior partner at that time at James Chapman & Co. when I offered to go and discuss some cases with him at James Chapman's offices. It was the normal protocol that defendant's solicitors would come to the claimant's lawyers' office. However, he was a good deal older than me, so I offered to go to his offices. We got off on a good footing as a result.

We probably looked very unusual to the rest of the profession in Manchester – long hair, flared trousers and the like. Mick Piggott was seen by someone from James Chapman wearing his pink plastic mac – causing considerable consternation!

I felt that it would be in the interests of the firm for us, as a major legal firm, to have a presence on The Manchester Law Society, and I became involved in The Manchester Law Society for many years.

Rodger Pannone was recruited by Nick in 1969.

Rodger, whose half-brother was Rex Church, joined

Casson's in Manchester, a firm set up by Tony Casson, another former employee of Thompsons. During this period he got to know Nick Carter well. After successfully completing his articles with Casson's, he was offered an immediate partnership but turned this down and joined W.H. Thompson at Carter's invitation.

He gave Derry Irvine (later to become Lord Chancellor) his first brief in the National Industrial Relations Court (the NIRC) in a case which dealt with the issue as to whether strike action broke continuity of employment, a case that was successful.

He made very rapid progress, becoming a salaried partner in W.H. Thompson on 1 March 1971. He and his wife socialised with Nick and Judi Carter. Later in his working life Rodger was described as the person who invented class actions, but he himself thought that Tony Woolf was the forerunner of this – with the miners' pneumoconiosis cases, for example.

Rodger left the firm on 28 February 1973. 'I left because of concern about Thompsons' ability to embrace the next stage … I didn't see any chance of that happening, given the structure as it then was.' It was a wrench. He was particularly happy in the Manchester office environment.

After he left Rodger had a stellar career, joining a firm which became Pannones which soon became very well-known and highly respected, and in the course of which he became President of the Law Society in 1993. He also dealt with many high profile cases including the Manchester Air Crash, Piper Alpha, Lockerbie and the John Stalker case.

Another solicitor with the practice in Manchester from 1970 to 1972 was Mike Napier who became Senior Partner with Irwin Mitchell. Like Rodger, Mike also became President of the Law Society – in his case in 2000, and together with Rodger, Simon Walton and John Melville Williams, QC was a founder member of APIL, the

Association of Personal Injury Lawyers.

Manchester recruited during this period many highly talented lawyers, including Frank Foy and Chris Chapman in 1970, John Whelan in 1971, Pauline Chandler in 1973, and Robert Lizar (who subsequently left to set up his own practice). Frank and Chris went on to run various offices, and in Frank's case to become coordinator of Robin's firm and then joint managing partner of Thompsons in 1996.

Pauline Chandler's recruitment is particularly noteworthy in illustrating how far backwards the firm had gone by then in terms of equal opportunities. With typical candour John Pickering explains:

I remember that Pauline was extremely keen to join us. She attended an interview and I admit to my shame now that the decision was taken, after consulting Robin, that we would not take her on because she was a woman. About a year later we discovered that Pauline had still not got herself fixed up and we changed our minds and got in touch with her. She refused to come into the office but agreed to meet us in a nearby pub! We then recruited her.

Pauline later became the first female Thompsons' equity partner in 1983.

Frank Foy describes how he came to join Thompsons and his early days in Manchester office:

After leaving school I obtained work with James Chapman & Co, a decent firm which primarily acted for defendant insurance companies in personal injury litigation.
I was attending night school undertaking my Legal Executive course when Keith Berry, an executive who worked for W.H. Thompson in Manchester, who was in the same class, told me about a vacancy at Thompson's. I was keen to

act for working people – on my father's side my ancestors were miners; an uncle was active in the Miners' Union and reputedly Joe Gormley's right-hand man until he had to cease working, my father worked down the pit for a while, and I had a grandfather killed in a mining explosion.

As a result I applied and had an interview with John Pickering. Although I felt I had not done very well in the interview I was invited back for a second interview with Nick Carter and at the end of that interview Nick offered me a job. I was delighted. I was particularly impressed when he explained about Thompson's pension scheme and social club. Benefits like these were almost unheard of. I also heard that the firm had a reputation of looking after their staff.

I joined the firm in 1970 and worked initially in John Pickering's department. John Pickering's training was amazing, and I worked hard. At first I dealt with small cases but I was gradually given bigger cases to deal with.

After a while I started dealing with some disease cases including heavy metal poisoning cases – i.e. poisoning from lead, cadmium, etc. I remember one day when John was delayed at court and had a client waiting in the office, a foundry worker with pneumoconiosis. As a result I saw the client. I took a very long and detailed statement and John then let me deal with the case which eventually settled. As a result more came my way.

Frank, encouraged by Nick Carter, subsequently took the solicitors course to qualify as a solicitor, although not first without some debate within the firm. The old policy of encouraging unqualified staff to qualify as solicitors had been reversed:

At the time, the policy was not to give articles in-house following some difficulties which had arisen in relation to individuals previously. In any event there was a debate apparently and a vote, and by a narrow majority I was allowed to carry on and do my Law Society exams with a view to qualification as a solicitor. So, I did my articles and then went to Law School to do the final Law Society examinations in January 1978 during which time I was paid my salary as a loan which I then repaid over a period of time.

By that time deafness work had started to come in and I expressed an interest in this and I dealt with many of the early deafness cases, McGuiness v Kirkstall Forge being one particularly noteworthy example.

The opening of the Ilford office on 13 December 1968 was designed to facilitate the handling of work from Ford's Dagenham plant. The office was led for many years by Victor Nicolls and David Skidmore.

Vic Nicolls had qualified as a solicitor a few months before David. They opened and ran the office (actually in Gants Hill) together, with Vic as managing partner.

Vic was made a (salaried) partner in 1967, and David, having qualified as a solicitor in 1969, in 1970. Both were to become 'A' partners in Robin's firm in 1974, and David eventually became Coordinator of Robin Thompsons.

Colin Simpson worked in Ilford from 1971 to 1997, for many years as managing partner of the office. Colin came from a working-class family. He became interested in employment law during his degree course at Queen Mary College in London. His tutor Tony, now Lord, Grabiner encouraged him to apply to Thompsons. After being offered a job by Robin in Serjeants' Inn, Colin had found himself a bedsit near Baker Street and moved in when Robin rang him and said there had been a change of plan and would he mind working at Ilford, offering to pay his tube fare for two years. Colin started at Ilford on 8 March 1971, sharing a room initially with Roger Bronckhurst.

Colin recalls his time in Ilford:

Ilford office included Victor Nicolls, David Skidmore, Bert Ross, Ron Smith, Colin Dove, Michael Giles and others. It ran very well.

The managing partner of Ilford office was Vic Nicolls who I was very fond of and who was very kind to me, but David Skidmore was the driving force and David and I hit it off from a business point of view.

I recall arranging, at some point, to have carpets fitted in the Ilford office, largely to cut down on the noise in the office. Typically, Vic said that this would be the downfall of Thompsons and that the office was "just a workshop". Vic was a genuine socialist and would not budge from his views and principles.

At some point Vic went up to Scotland. He retired to Scotland.

Well before this I became the managing partner of Ilford office. David had become the finance partner in Robin's firm.

Ilford was a successful office, the engine room of Robin Thompsons It was very competitive and I encouraged this. Everyone loved it. We had many characters; we all stuck together and there were very few problems running the office. I recall that we had 27 fee earners and 75 staff in total. Terry Butterfield was brilliant and she ran the technical staff. She was a truly great office manager.

Stanmore office opened on 1 February 1971 with a 35 year lease with no break clause! Its relative proximity to Elstree Studios probably explains why part of it had previously been used as a studio by Diana Dors. One of the upstairs rooms had two way mirrors fitted by a sub tenant which claimed to be a market research company. Quite what market research they undertook is a matter of speculation. Cyril Wener, another important managing clerk from this era, opened the office and was joined by Simon Walton and Anton Bates. Many Thompsons' partners and other senior personnel spent at least some time in Stanmore, including Simon, Alec Frew, Greg Powell, Tony Lawton, and Geoff Shears who went there from Serjeants' Inn and then moved up to Newcastle to open the office there (with Frank Foy). Tony Lawton had joined Thompsons on 17 March 1969, articled to Ivor Walker in Serjeants' Inn and transferred to Stanmore when it opened, working for Simon Walton.

Simon takes up the story:

In 1970, the decision was taken to open an office in Stanmore, mainly because this was a convenient location for Cyril Wener. The office opened on 1 February 1971 with Cyril in charge plus myself and Anton Bates. I remained in Stanmore until 1976 and was joined there over a period of time by various others such as Greg Powell, Chris McGrath, Tony Lawton, Geoff Shears, and so on.

While I was at Stanmore I was given the coalminers' pneumoconiosis cases to deal with. Tony Woolf, a brilliant lawyer and acknowledged expert on limitation, had been handling these. For political reasons these cases did not come from the NUM – they preferred to deal with them themselves. However, W.H. Thompson was instructed by NACODS and also received some cases for former mineworkers who had left the industry and taken up work in engineering where they were members of the AEU who then sponsored their cases. Robin asked me to attend a meeting with him – at his home I think – and asked me to take over these cases. He said that Tony was getting the firm and its clients into potential bankruptcy. As a result the cases were reallocated to me.

There was so much work that I had to give up all my other cases. The List of Documents ran to over 1 million pages, and the legal team included John Hampden Inskip QC, and John Melville Williams. Geoff Shears assisted me on the cases for a while. We had some test cases selected and nearly ready for trial when the NCB entered into negotiations direct with the NUM and agreed a scheme – The Coal Workers Pneumoconiosis Scheme, 1974. When I advised Joe Gormley that the scheme was not good I was firmly put in my place; and once the scheme was agreed the test cases settled under its terms. There was no question of bucking it.

When Simon took on these cases Geoff Shears moved to Stanmore to provide continuity. Geoff:

… the pneumoconiosis litigation was proceeding apace, and Tony Woolf was determined to fight. He wanted me to work full time on the cases and it was a privilege to do so. There were meetings with Thompsons' colleagues and conferences with counsel. We went down Blackhall Colliery in Durham and met many miners.

At this point, as the cases were progressing, Tony Woolf left Thompsons following an irretrievable dispute with Brian. The dispute related to the funding (or lack of it) of the cases from NACODS which the brothers felt was placing the firm at risk.

I had been working with Tony since joining the firm – he was regarded as difficult to work with and would not tolerate error. I was still only halfway through my articles but had the opportunity to help with these precedent cases, deal with other high profile disease cases, attend the House of Lords and deal with union general secretaries.

When Tony left, Robin asked Simon Walton to take on the pneumoconiosis cases. Simon was at Stanmore. To retain some continuity Robin asked, indeed required, me to go to Stanmore to work with Simon. I was happy to carry on working on these cases, but not so happy to be transferring to Stanmore – particularly after all the high profile work I had already been involved with.

As Simon would, he got on with the litigation. The trial

was set for Newcastle with four cases from Durham as the lead cases. At this point the government intervened and persuaded the Coal Board to deal directly with Joe Gormley's NUM. The result was the Coal Workers' Pneumoconiosis Scheme, 1974. This in our view grossly under settled the value of the cases. However, all the cases, including the lead ones, were concluded under the scheme and that was the end of this litigation. Robin's response was one of relief since the scheme at a stroke removed the financial risk faced by the firm. Whether the same would have happened had Tony Woolf still been involved I do not know, and my own feeling at the time was that the opportunity to do our best for our clients had been snatched from us.

Simon (along with Tony Lawton) subsequently moved back to Serjeants' Inn in 1974.

In addition, the accounts department was based at Stanmore. Bernard Ferguson was accounts manager.

The introduction of regional offices in Thompsons' had a number of consequences. The most telling one was that the local presence of lawyers committed to, and themselves part of the trade union movement, led to a significant increase in work. Union officers and elected officials welcomed the newfound ease of access to lawyers who shared their own aspirations and concerns; and members with injuries and diseases preferred to see lawyers based in their own locality rather than ones who, however sympathetic, travelled up from London.

In those days, much of the advice on industrial matters to union officers was given on an ad hoc basis. Industrial issues were determined mostly at a local level through the normal process of negotiation. Collective bargaining ruled the day. But there were some major legal cases in which an attack was made at the heart of the unions' right to take collective action.

Chapter 18
Collective action and trade union immunity – the legal battles of the 1950s, '60s, and '70s

The post-war years following the death of W.H. Thompson saw a different type of firm emerging. The civil liberties battles were no longer so pressing; fascism had been defeated, at least for the time being, a Labour government was in power and had introduced the National Health Service along with the nationalisation of several major industries.

The unions became stronger, aided by a large influx of workers returning from the war, and the focus of the firm turned firmly towards the fight for health and safety at work and proper compensation.

But there was one major area apart from the battle for compensation for work related accidents and diseases where W.H. Thompson was called upon to play a key role. This involved the protection of workers' rights.

In a series of cases the firm represented various unions which came under legal attack in connection with the exercise of their trade union activities.

In a personal memoir in which he recalled some of the big issues from his early days at W.H. Thompson, Robin noted:

We had one very major case, and that concerned D.C. Thomson and involved our clients, the Printing Union. It lasted about a year and arose from the refusal of the defendants to recognise the union. When in court we briefed

Sir Frank Soskice, the TGWU had Hartley Shawcross and another union had Gerald Gardiner.

The case was: *D C Thomson & Co Ltd v Deakin and Others* [1952] 2 All ER 361

D. C. Thomson & Co. Ltd were printers and publishers of the *Beano* and *Dandy* comics and the hugely profitable newspaper *The Sunday Post*. They required all their employees to sign an undertaking not to become members of a trade union. (This had been company policy since the General Strike in 1926) Some workers disregarded this and the employer dismissed one of them. The union called a strike and enlisted the assistance of other unions whose employers supplied materials to the company. One such supplier decided not to call on their employees to load or deliver paper for the company, but then brought proceedings against the various unions concerned, seeking an injunction to 'restrain breaches of contract'.

The first union asserted in affidavits that they had merely asked for help from other unions and nothing more, and the other unions concerned denied that they had given instructions not to handle or move paper intended for delivery to the company.

The judge decided in favour of the unions. He said that while an action would have been justified if, with actual knowledge of the contract and with the intention of damaging the suppliers, they had persuaded the loaders and drivers by unlawful means to render it impossible for the suppliers to perform the contract, this was not the case here. The injunction was refused.

Although the case was successful, and brought a few years of relative peace and protection for unions from legal actions in the courts, the subject was about to return with a vengeance.

In the early 1960s there was an all-out legal assault

against the unions in the celebrated case of *Rookes v Barnard and others [1964] 1 All ER 367*, which Brian handled personally on behalf of the union.

The House of Lords in a decision which was overtly political (as Rodney Bickerstaffe later noted in his obituary of Brian), tried to reverse sixty years of trade union rights by inventing the civil wrong of 'intimidation' during industrial disputes. The decision infuriated the trade unions, caused a political furore and was overturned by the Labour Government which passed the Trade Disputes Act of 1965.

This case is probably the best known industrial case of its generation. The Law Lords used the case to drive a coach and horses through the Trade Disputes Act 1906 which provided that 'an act done ... by two or more persons shall, if done in contemplation or furtherance of a trade dispute, not be actionable unless the act, if done without any such agreement or combination, would be actionable'; and further that 'an act done in contemplation or furtherance of a trade dispute shall not be actionable on the ground only that it induces some other person to break a contract of employment ...'. This law was in effect a statutory immunity for unions so that they could go about their business of representing their members without facing actions based on old common law concepts such as conspiracy. The law had worked tolerably well in keeping most industrial disputes out of the courts, but all that changed with Rookes.

Mr Rookes was employed by BOAC, the forerunner of British Airways, as a draughtsman. He was a member of the Draughtsman's union. There was a closed shop agreement between the union and BOAC and 100 per cent membership. There was also an agreement between the union and BOAC that there would be no strikes and that, in the event of a dispute, direct negotiations would take place and that if these failed, the matter would be referred to the Ministry of Labour.

Rookes resigned from the union which then passed a resolution for strike action unless he was removed from the design office where he worked. As a result the company suspended him and then gave him notice.

The judge found, despite the Trade Disputes Act, that the actions of the relevant union members constituted the unlawful act of intimidation, therefore the protection afforded by the Act did not apply, and damages would be awarded. The decision was overturned in the Court of Appeal but restored in the House of Lords.

At almost the same time as the Rookes case was being heard, Thompsons was back in the courts in the other major case of the mid-1960s: *J T Stratford & Son Ltd v Lindley [1964] 3 All ER 102*, again dealt with by Brian.

This case was heard by the House of Lords just a few months after Rookes. It was a complicated dispute which arose as a result of a disagreement between two unions. The result was that the union lost its immunity under the Trade Disputes Act 1906, as they could not establish that the action they took was in contemplation or furtherance of a trade dispute. It was another blow to the 1906 Act.

The short period of relative legal peace which followed the Trade Disputes Act 1965 was not enjoyed at a political level. The return of a Labour government in 1964 came at a time of a serious economic crisis. In December 1964 the government, representatives of the trade unions and employers' organisations signed a 'Declaration of Intent'. This was partly designed to increase output and was effectively the first phase of a prices and incomes policy. Pressure on the pound, the balance of payments deficit and inflation led to a period of industrial strife with government interventions to try and resolve matters over 'beer and sandwiches'.

This was the context when the Wilson Government announced, on 2 February 1965 that a Royal Commission on Trade Unions would be established – the first of its type since 1903. It was asked:

To consider relations between management and employees and the role of trade unions and employers' associations in promoting the interests of their members and in accelerating the social and economic advance of the nation with particular reference to the law affecting the activities of those bodies.

The Commission took a huge amount of evidence; again Brian Thompson contributed. When it reported, the Commission, which had been heavily influenced by the Oxford school of industrial relations based at Nuffield College (a group including Alan Fox, Hugh Clegg and Allan Flanders among others), resisted calls for legal regulation and opted for voluntary reform.

Barbara Castle's White Paper *In Place of Strife* followed. It went much further and proposed, amongst other things, statutory cooling off periods before strike action, compulsory pre-strike ballots, legal enforceability of some trade union agreements in the courts and an Industrial Board with the power to fine trade unions.

Battle was joined within the Labour Party and indeed within the government, with some notable cabinet members such as Jim Callaghan refusing to support and ultimately blocking the proposals.

When the Conservatives won the 1970 election they had the unions in their sights and passed The Industrial Relations Act, 1971. The Act, which abolished all the old law, was a disaster. Various unions refused to recognise the court – the National Industrial Relations Court, set up to administer the new laws, there were fines and sequestration orders, and the code which was ostensibly designed to regularise industrial conduct (although in truth the purpose was to reduce the power of the unions) simply drew the battle lines and encouraged both sides over the top.

This Act went much further than anything in *In Place of Strife*. Not only were restrictions placed on strike activities and collective agreements made legally binding, but the closed shop was outlawed and a new system of 'unfair industrial practices' introduced, policed by a court, the National Industrial Relations Court. The unions were required to register under the Act. W.H. Thompson's biggest trade union client was the AUEW, the engineering union. They, along with the TGWU, refused to register or to recognise the new court created by the 1971 Act whose first judge was John Donaldson. Sequestration orders followed and industrial relations fell to a new low. The Act was badly thought out. Its aims were contradictory. Unions were undermined by the Act, but the Act required their assistance to operate.

By this time Michael Foot had accepted a place in the shadow cabinet as Shadow Employment Secretary and had immediately set to work to try and repair relations between the Labour party and the trade unions which had been damaged by *In Place of Strife*. At the suggestion of Jack Jones, leader of the TGWU, a Labour Liaison Committee was set up, with six members each from the Shadow Cabinet, the National Executive and the TUC. W.H. Thompson was able to play a significant role in assisting the unions (and therefore the next Labour government) in preparing a legislative programme to be implemented as soon as Labour was re-elected. As Mr Foot confirmed in interview with both the author and with Thompsons' partner Tom Jones on 7 February 2006:

'Relations with your firm were very important to me' and 'the

Labour Government was elected on a platform that was agreed with the TUC Committee and your firm was very much in on that'.

One industrial case handled by W.H. Thompson on behalf of the relevant trade union from the period is worth recounting: *Cory Lighterage Ltd v Transport and General Workers Union and others [1973] 2 All ER 341*

The company were tug and barge owners in the Port of London. Their crews were registered dock workers. For many years 100 per cent trade union membership had been practised in the docks. One employee let his membership lapse and his fellow workers refused to work with him. The company suspended the employee on full pay and applied to the National Dock Labour Board for permission to discharge him. The Board refused, and the company applied to the court for an order restraining the union from directing or recommending that any union member should withhold his labour because of the continued employment of the employee, and claiming intimidation and conspiracy.

The court decided that the dispute was an industrial dispute within the meaning of the Act, and that the complaint was one that should have been made as an 'unfair industrial practice' under the Act and brought to the National Industrial Relations Court rather than the High Court

This was a rare success in the period from 1971 to 1974. It stopped employers relying on the Rookes v Barnard approach rather than the mechanisms set out in the 1971 Act.

A number of years later there was one final attempt by employers to try and get round the statutory immunity and resurrect the tort of intimidation. It came in a case handled this time by Eddie Solomons of Thompsons on behalf of the union, ACTT:

Lord Elwyn Jones and Brian Thompson

Hadmor Productions Ltd and others v Hamilton and others [1982] 1 All ER 1042

Hadmor was a facility company which made TV programmes for sale to network TV stations. In 1979 they made a series of programmes using freelance performers and technicians who were members of the technicians union. The first 2 programmes were transmitted, but the local branch at the TV station decided to black the remainder in accordance with the branch's policy that facility companies should not be used by the station to make programmes when they could be made in the station's own studios using permanent staff who were members of the union and who might be threatened with redundancy if ready-made programmes were bought in from outside. Faced with the possibility of disruption, the TV station withdrew the programmes from transmission. The company then issued writs against three officials from the union seeking an injunction.

In the House of Lords it was held that the union's actions were in contemplation or furtherance of a trade dispute and that the statutory immunity applied not just to the immediate parties to the dispute but also to actions which affected third parties such as Hadmor in this case.

The union had been successful in the High Court, but then lost in the Court of Appeal before winning again in the House of Lords where the Lords decided that in the circumstances Hadmor were not entitled to an injunction.

Chapter 19
Everyday life in the offices

The spirit of Thompsons owed much to its staff, and the staff owed much to the office managers. All the office systems were controlled and directed by them, and the lead role for many years was taken by Edna Scharts who held the position at Warnford Court and then subsequently at Serjeants' Inn from 1956 until her retirement in 1980. Other office managers of particular note include Terry Butterfield at Ilford, Beryl Westwell at Cardiff, Irene Parker at Manchester and Val Fountain at Stanmore. Terry's position was significant because of the way that much of the administration was controlled by David Skidmore, but Edna's role was key.

Edna Scharts answered an advertisement in 1947 for a job with the firm. The advertisement was in the *Daily Worker* for whom she was working at the time. Edna was already politically active and knew about the firm from her membership of the Civil Service Union during the war, when she worked for the Ministry of Supply and from a colleague, Violet Lansbury, an expert on workmen's compensation. Edna's husband had been John Platts-Mills' agent when he was MP for Finsbury. Already a Communist, she was interviewed by David Phillips and worked at 52, Bedford Row. She was 'not in the least surprised to find that the office in which I was interviewed was shared with the Fire Brigades Union and the London Trades Council'.

At that time the firm had offices at Mansion House, 52, Bedford Row and 88, Chancery Lane, along with High Wycombe. Before too long, most staff moved to 120, London Wall, and Bedford Row and High Wycombe were closed. Lack of space soon caused the opening of an overflow at 34, London Wall, and then at Warnford Court and Queen Victoria Street. All these offices closed when the practice moved under one roof in 1956 at Serjeants' Inn. (London Wall, for example, closed on 23 February 1957).

By around that time, the nature of office work began to change with the advent of photocopiers, Dictaphones and electric typewriters. Before this machinery existed, as Edna explains,' the main bugbear for the secretaries and typists was the endless copying. No faxes or photocopies in those days. The courts would accept only original documents, so everything that was used had to come out of a typewriter. Very labour intensive.' All the dictation had to be taken down in longhand. 'After a stint of dictation often as long as two hours, secretaries would stagger with a pile of files over which they could barely see.'

Terry takes up the story 'When copies of documents were required, everything had to be typed – birth, death and marriage certificates, special damages, medical and engineers' reports etc. What a performance!' The new electric typewriters were 'heavy and sluggish, and took up to one plus nineteen carbons typed on very flimsy paper. If you made a mistake, the rubbing out had to be done twenty times.'

The early copying machines bore little resemblance to those used today. In Terry's words:

And then came copying machines. Wet copiers. A small room was set up with lots of shelves and boards. There was a small wringer type machine which contained developing fluid. The document to be copied was placed between two sheets of sensitized paper. It was then necessary to judge the copy, lighter, darker or just right. Expose the copy to the light for the decided number of seconds, then remove the original and place the two sheets in the little tank and pass it through the wringer. Wait for a few seconds then separate the sheets.

Hey presto, a copy appeared. The copies were placed on the boards on the shelves to dry.

Dorrie Collins was a member of the firm's accounts department from 1959 until she retired in 1995. When she joined Lou Holt was in charge. Before him the accounts manager was Miss Cropley. NCR accounting machines were used, state of the art at the time, but again highly labour intensive by today's standards. Dorrie started in Serjeants' Inn, moved with the department to Stanmore in 1970 and then to Harrow.

As office manager, Edna Scharts organised the opening of the Cardiff, Manchester and Ilford offices. All the while she continued with her own political work, spending many years as a member of the British Peace Committee which was affiliated to the World Peace Council, and working for the Communist Party in London where she got to know Kay Beauchamp. She also met Joan Beauchamp from time to time, for example when attending No.10 Downing Street as part of a peace delegation with Dame Sybil Thorndike. Her role at the World Peace Council's Conferences was to organise the technical team. Edna recalls:

A WPC conference was arranged in Buxton in the 1950s. I believe it was a Labour government that banned so many delegates including Picasso, church leaders, etc. from all around the world that the conference was moved to Poland. I used to take some of my holidays in order to attend these conferences ... which were held at various times at Stockholm, Prague, Berlin, Soviet Union, Hungary and the then Ceylon.

In the 1970s Edna was invited to do a similar job for the Union of Democratic Lawyers which was held in Bulgaria. She also worked with the British Committee for Medical and Scientific Aid to Vietnam.

Edna and Terry recall the W.H. Thompson Sports and Social Club which began to flourish in the early 1950s with various sports teams, theatre visits, keep-fit classes and amateur dramatics. Several plays were produced, including *When we are Married* J.B. Priestley's 1938 comedy with Arthur Charles as producer. Many members of staff were involved including John Bass and Robin's wife Queenie. Staff performed the plays at the Cripplegate Theatre (for the staff), at Wormwood Scrubs Prison, Stoke Mandeville Hospital, Springhill Open Prison and Ford Open Prison.

Another person much involved in the social club was Pam Holman. Pam joined in August 1953 at London Wall as Cyril Wener's post room junior. Subsequently she worked in Mansion House and Warnford Court and then Serjeants' Inn and Bainbridge House. For more than 20 years at the end of her career before retiring in November 1996, Pam was secretary to John Harris, who handled the print union work and dealt with a number of major issues including the Wapping Dispute and various print union mergers. In 1987 John produced a paper on the Wapping dispute which he ended with this tribute:

This paper is dedicated to my secretary Pam Holman who has worked with me for a number of years and who readily understood my problems in dealing with this case, moaned very little and got on with the job. Her loyalty to me and to the General Secretary of the union in handling this massive case which involved over 12,000 documents is appreciated. The General Secretary has shown her appreciation on one or two occasions by a bouquet of flowers, (to Pam not to me) but one day I really *will* buy a box of chocolates for Pam Holman.

Pam was one of many backroom staff who not only gave

The Thompson's football team.
Back row L-R: *Les Mitchell (Ilford), Cliff Poole (Ilford at time, also London and later Birmingham), Keith Bailey (London), Dave (a ringer), Stephen Dudley (Ilford), and Neil Hunt (London)*
Front row L-R: *Greg Powell (Stanmore), Terry Morgan (London), Don Wilson (London), Peter Bamford (London and later Birmingham and Sheffield), Tony Lawton.*
Other regular players at the time included Geoff Shears, Alec Frew, Vic Shelley, and David Wallen. WH Thompson were Division 2 champions in the London Legal League 1971-2.

their all for the cause but made the atmosphere of the firm special.

W.H. Thompson's strongly encouraged all staff to belong to the union, and the recognised union for collective bargaining purposes was the Association of Professional, Executive, Clerical and Computer Staff (APEX).

All terms and conditions, including the annual pay round for the technical staff, were negotiated with the union. The policy in respect of technical staff was to recruit youngsters at age 15; they would spend two years in the post room and were normally allowed day release to attend

RULES

(AS REVISED AT ANNUAL CONFERENCE 1974)

ASSOCIATION OF PROFESSIONAL EXECUTIVE, CLERICAL & COMPUTER STAFF (APEX)

ESTABLISHED UNDER THE TITLE OF
"THE CLERKS' UNION"—JUNE 1890

Head Office
22 WORPLE ROAD
LONDON, SW19 4DF
Telephone 01-947 3131/6

APEX

college to learn to touch type. Normally they would progress to copy typing, then the typing pool, and finally to secretarial work. It meant that any secretary had, by then, a comprehensive working knowledge of the firm's systems

W. H. THOMPSON SOLICITOR
1, FITZALAN PLACE, NEWPORT ROAD, CARDIFF CF2 1US   Telephone 0222 41436
and at LONDON MANCHESTER ILFORD and STANMORE

when replying to this letter
please quote this reference

ROBIN THOMPSON BRIAN THOMPSON D. C. PHILLIPS E. A. LEWIS JOHN LEBOR L. V. NICOLLS G. W. CARTER
IVOR WALKER JOHN PICKERING M. OSBORNE BRUCE TYRER D. A. SKIDMORE S. K. WALTON G. J. THOMAS G. R. BENT

A sheet of W.H. Thompson notepaper in 1974

and procedures and was able to undertake much work as a matter of course on her (they were all women) own initiative – work which probably had to be carried out by fee-earners at other firms. A W.H. Thompson training was a passport to another job elsewhere, but few secretaries ever left. The terms and conditions provided for pay rates which, outside London, were very high.

Pay rates for the lawyers, including the partners, were never high. For the non-partner lawyers, earnings were fairly modest for the legal profession; for the partners, their earnings were (and still are) well below what they might have earned elsewhere. Of course all this is relative, given the general level of lawyers' earnings compared to the average earnings in society in general.

Robin Thompson and Brian Thompson

Chapter 20
The demise of WH Thompson

In 1973, the brothers decided to split the practice.

They wrote to all their major union clients on 25 June 1973, and sent a copy of the letter to partners and supervisors in the firm.

Why did the split happen? The growth of the firm, the increase in qualified solicitors, the reluctance of the brothers to cede their complete control, and their very different personalities all contributed.

John Bowden:

There were tensions between the brothers, and I recall endless meetings at the Great Eastern Hotel. We would book ourselves in as the Essex Fishing Club. All of us who were in the Communist Party said that the firm should be preserved in its current form and we must not let personal differences between the brothers split up the firm. It was a difficult period. Younger lawyers had come into the practice and qualified as solicitors, with the blessing and support of Robin and Brian.

I think the brothers suspected that some who were qualifying wanted to become solicitors so as to make inroads into the equity of the firm – at that time the only equity partners were Robin and Brian themselves.

Ivor Walker:

Of course, once some of us started becoming qualified and becoming salaried partners we were anxious to have a bigger say in the firm – more power. The brothers refused to accede to this and in the end Rex went to Pattinson & Brewer and my brother left to join Nicholson Patterson & James, a commercial firm.

John Lebor:

In 1963 I was made a partner in the firm. Apart from Robin and Brian, all the partners were salaried partners only. Three of us, Rex Church, Tony Walker and I approached Robin and Brian to ask for equity partnerships. The firm was becoming very large simply to be run by two people. Our request was bitterly resisted. I think Robin might have been more inclined to consider it but Brian was implacably opposed.

Tony Woolf kept a detailed handwritten diary of the discussions that went on in late 1970. Many issues were raised, including, as he and a number of others saw it,

the Thompsons' power of dismissal, the failure to expand, the rejection of clients and potential clients, the lack of forward planning, and the lack of, especially, financial information on which we could form any view or questions for decision as well, of course, the lack of authority to decide.

Tony canvassed support and put forward proposals for change. The brothers' supporters, such as Mick Manning, did not doubt Tony's integrity – they did not think Tony's proposals for change were motivated by self promotion – but they did doubt the motives of some others.

    Tony records a private conversation with Robin on 16 November 1970:

Robin said that a democratic voting procedure would not necessarily change anything and one would still have, as in any political party, factional organisation and the real decisions taken before the actual vote. You would then get decisions being taken on the basis of a determined group seeking their own benefit, rather than the basis he and Brian try to apply of considering the advantage of the office as a whole. I suggested he was underestimating the power of his and Brian's intellects and personalities in thinking they would be unable to win the votes that matter. He responded that that would be much too hard work, at which we both laughed.

This particular dispute came to a head in January 1971. The demands of a number of the salaried partners for elections to the firm's management committees, decisions as of right by majority vote on those committees, greater power of decisions by partners on questions of employment of individuals, and sharing in control of the firm's assets, were all rejected out of hand.

It is noteworthy that the last of these sought a measure of control of the assets but did not include sharing the assets themselves. It seems the "rebels" were not at that time seeking full equity partnership status. But that was to follow.

Tony's notes go on to describe detailed private discussions initiated by Rex Church and Tony Walker to leave the practice and set up in practice on their own – prompted by the unsatisfactory result to the dispute.

On 7 July 1971 Tony records: 'Time to re-open this diary after several months of depression, lethargy and inner turmoil about the work situation.'

He notes that Tony Walker had been asked to leave in May, when a cash settlement had been proposed, and that discussions were continuing with an ultimatum likely.

The dispute in the firm could not just be broken down to a split between the salaried partners en bloc on the one hand wanting more power and Robin and Brian on the other resisting change. It was certainly true that the senior unqualified staff such as Mick Manning supported the brothers' stance, but some of the qualified staff including partners such as David Skidmore and Vic Nicolls did likewise. Bruce Tyrer confirms that the issue did not simply relate to equity partnerships:

[I] became a salaried partner in March 1970. Around that time I was invited to go on the firm's Policy Committee. The meetings were often lengthy going on for two days. It was very contentious with a lot of personal conflicts and I seemed to start spend a lot more of my time dealing with managerial issues. Having said that, at these meeting Robin and Brian would normally present a united front and as nobody else had any real power their views normally prevailed.

There was a movement within the firm that the firm should broaden its work base. Others thought the opposite. As a result there was quite a lot of conflict. In the end a number of lawyers left, including Tony Walker and Rex Church.

Some discontent began to grow amongst the solicitors who wanted more than salaried partnership. I recall there was a meeting I think convened mainly by Nick Carter. Tony Walker was involved and probably Ivor and Simon Walton (who worked with me when he was articled and with whom I was good friends). This meeting was some time before the brothers announced the split. The meeting was regarded by Robin and Brian as a conspiracy by the qualified solicitors to gain control and that indeed was probably the agenda of some who attended. I attended this meeting. I felt there was a case for Robin and Brian to involve people more. After the meeting when Robin and Brian got to hear about it, they called a meeting of all the staff in London and announced the decision to split. They then set about picking who they would each have.

The proposed split was an important factor that prompted me to decide to leave. I had nothing against Brian nor did I have any ill will towards the firm. Brian had regarded me as part of his management team. However, I felt the firm was being fundamentally damaged and did not, in any event, wish to be manager. I wanted to be a lawyer.

I left therefore on the final date of W.H. Thompson in 1974. It was a very sad day and I had terrible feelings that I was being disloyal to those who had given me … opportunities … . This was particularly so since it happened at a time that Mick Manning had the previous Christmas been killed [and] Brian had in consequence lost the person who was to be his right hand man.

Bruce and Tessa Roxburgh (who had been the first female articled clerk in the firm) set up Tyrer Roxburgh, a successful legal aid practice. Bruce remains grateful for the opportunity given to him by the firm and the way he was treated:

I can only reflect on the period … with pleasure and pride for the work being done for the trade unions and their membership. By and large they were a great firm to work for who cared for their staff. For example in 1956 not long after joining W.H.Thompson I had pulmonary TB and was off work for five months during which time I was paid in full. No other firm at that time would have put up with this or felt obliged to pay for such a long absence. Who would have taken unqualified 17 or 18 year olds with no hope of a professional qualification, and trained them up as lawyers, sponsored them through their training and allowed them to get qualified and give them a career? It was an extraordinary firm.

Geoff Shears was a young articled clerk at the time:

As I came to realise, it was a period of upheaval in the firm. There were no equity partners save Robin and Brian, but there were a number of salaried partners. Some wanted a greater say in the running of the firm. Tony Walker for example had left two weeks before I joined. There was a Policy Committee which considered major issues, and there was also a Communist Party group which effectively considered these issues in advance as a caucus.

It was said that the brothers had decided to divide the firm for 'administrative reasons'. In fact, as Geoff Shears recently commented:

Robin and Brian had a strong mutual respect and commitment and community of interest, but frequently disagreed on issues of policy and could not decide what to do when they disagreed. As a result there was inaction. The split was designed to overcome that problem, but so far as I could tell they agreed more often when apart than they had done when together. Certainly they continued to look after each other and their firms as though for most purposes they were one firm thoroughly committed to the interests of the labour movement.

In a memoir prepared in 2002, Robin commented on the reason for the split:

Ultimately ... the office had become so large that it really could not be carried on by two partners only. Certain difficulties had arisen between Brian and me and in the end we decided to split the firm. Brian and I were the sole partners for nearly twenty-five years.

The explanation of the cause of the split as size seems to have been accepted; as Clive Jenkins said in his 1990 autobiography: 'W.H. Thompson ... now so big it is divided into two'.

The two firms opened separate offices in London although Brian's office there was considerably smaller and Robin took the lead with most though by no means all head office work; Robin took Ilford, and Brian took Manchester, Cardiff and Stanmore.

W.H. Thompson had himself been dead for over 25 years. But Robin and Brian's firms went on to play a significant role over the next decades as the country's leading lawyers to the trade union and labour movement. They expanded, changed and adapted to the issues of the day and eventually remerged in 1996 as Thompsons.

The story of W.H. Thompson had been one of building from scratch, against all the odds, a law practice for the workers and the disadvantaged with civil liberties at its core. The next few decades saw the growth of a practice right at the heart of the labour movement.

Herewith copy letter dated 25.6.73. which has gone to our client Unions.

R.B.T.

Dear

We have been in control of this firm for over twenty years. During this time there has been a considerable expansion both in respect of Partners and Staff and in office premises.

We have throughout maintained the principal motivation of the firm as founded and laid down by our father, that is to provide an efficient and effective service to the Labour movement.

We have now reached the conclusion that in order to maintain this service, we must re-arrange the structure into two units - one led by Robin and one by Brian, in order to give a greater involvement to our Partners and Staff and provide more flexibility with a view to adapting to any changes in the law.

We are engaged in discussions with our Partners and Staff regarding the details of our intention and there are a number of practical aspects to resolve. Meanwhile we are continuing to deal with current matters as in the past.

We will be writing to you again as soon as possible with our detailed proposals for your consideration. There is complete accord and agreement between us and we anticipate that you will find our proposals acceptable and that they will ultimately lead to an improvement in the service we are able to provide with very little change in the relationship between your organisation on the one hand and our Partners and Staff on the other.

If meanwhile there is any point you wish to raise, please do not hesitate to let us know. We will both be away together on a family holiday in July, but our senior colleagues will be available in our absence.

Yours sincerely,

ROBIN THOMPSON   BRIAN THOMPSON

To: Mr. Hugh Scanlon, ENG Sec.   )
    Mr. E. Marsden, CONSTR. Sec.) AUEW
    Mr. W. Simpson, FDY Sec.   )
    Mr. G.H. Doughty, TECH Sec.)

Mr. Alan Fisher, NUPE   Mr. S.W. Parfitt, NUS
Mr. W.H. Keys, SOGAT   Mr. Clive Jenkins, ASTMS
Mr. R.N. Bottini, NUAAW   Mr. R. Grantham, APEX
Mr. D. McGarvey, USBSSW   Mr. A.C. Blyghton, TGWU
Mr. T. Parry, FBU   Mr. G. Eastwood, APAC
Mr. A. Sapper, ACAT

W.H. Thompson Partners from 1951: dates of partnership

(with details of any retirements prior to March 1974)
All save Robin and Brian were salaried partners

Robin Thompson
Brian Thompson
1 July 1960
Henry Schramek   retired 30 April 1969
David Phillips
Ted Lewis
21 April 1963
Rex Church   left 1 March 1972
George Dawson   left 15 November 1965
John Lebor
1 March 1966
Tony Walker   left 31 December 1971
Tony Woolf   left 1973/4 – date uncertain
1 March 1967
Victor Nicolls
Nick Carter
John Davies   left 31 August 1972
1 March 1968
Ivor Walker
John Pickering
Anton Bates   left 1973/4 – date uncertain
1 May 1969
Mike Osborne
1 March 1970
Bruce Tyrer   left 28 February 1974
David Skidmore
Simon Walton
Geoff Thomas
1 March 1971
Rodger Pannone   left 28 February 1973
1 March 1973
Roger Bent

Chapter 21
The new firms

Robin's firm was named Robin Thompson and Partners, and Brian's firm Brian Thompson. The new firms started up on 1 March 1974.

To the outside world the demise of W.H. Thompson involved little more than a straight geographical split of the intake of work between the two new firms. The firms opened separate offices in London although Brian's office there was considerably smaller and Robin took the lead with most though by no means all head office work; Robin took Ilford office, and Brian took Manchester, Cardiff and Stanmore.

The sons and grandson of WHT

Brian's firm

Brian's partners in his firm initially included Ted Lewis, John Lebor, Nick Carter, Geoff Thomas, Roger Bent, John Pickering and Mike Osborne, but control of the practice continued to operate through the Executive Committee, aided by a couple of important folio groups. The Executive Committee included elected representatives, appointed representatives and some partners. Geoff Shears later commented:

> The management of Brian's firm was formally in the hands of an Executive Committee which included elected members of staff. Brian was many years ahead of his time in establishing a "works council" long before they were introduced across Europe. In practice staff members assumed a loyalty to Brian which he and our friends were able to use to secure power within the firm. However it was not necessarily the best way of developing business strategy. In those days it mattered less.

Robin's firm mostly took the lead in administration (at least some of which was still conducted jointly through the Accounts department), and assisted Brian's firm financially from time to time.

Following the split, both firms searched for suitable premises. Brian opened an office in Pimlico on 11 August 1975. His colleagues there included Geoff Shears and John Lebor together with legal executives John Harwood (joined in 1962), Keith Bailey (1965), Vic Shelley and Terry Morgan (1970). Others of note when Pimlico opened were Alf Cooper, Barbara Hands (nee Oxley), Joyce Kane and the office manager Pauline Davin, and they were joined by Eddie Solomons in February 1977 and Roger Maddocks in 1978.

Geoff Shears' return to Central London was facilitated by the conclusion to the miners' litigation. He moved back to Serjeants' Inn briefly as part of Brian's firm and then spent about two years in Pimlico after it opened before returning to Stanmore. His next move was north to open the Newcastle office with Frank Foy in 1980.

John Harwood was a key figure at this time. He had joined in November 1962 and became very close to Brian, a role which became more significant following Mick Manning's unfortunate death in 1973. He made rapid progress in the firm, becoming a case supervisor in 1970, a member of the firm's management committee before the split, and a member of the Executive Committee in Brian's firm after it:

Over the years, I went to 19 TUC conferences, a similar number of Labour Party conferences as well as numerous union conferences. I became good friends with Hugh Scanlon and various members of the AUEW executive including Len Edmundson, Gerry Russell, John Weakley and Roger Butler. The other union I had most contact with was the Agricultural Workers (NUAAW). When the retired General Secretary of that union Jack Boddy remarried, I was best man. He also had much contact with Gerry Eastwood of the Patternmakers. (The Patternmakers later became part of MSF with Eastwood as Trade Group Secretary).

John left the firm aged 60 and subsequently had a spell at Rowley Ashworth. Whilst he was there, another legal executive formerly at Pimlico, Terry Morgan, collapsed and died in the office. This was in 1995 and Terry was aged just 47.

Robin's firm

Robin's firm started with six partners – Robin, Vic Nicolls, David Skidmore, Simon Walton, David Phillips and Ivor Walker.

Robin adopted a more traditional partnership structure. Ivor Walker:

… in the early 1970s Robin and Brian decided to split the firm. I recall one evening Robin invited me and my wife to dinner. In fact at the time I had been looking to move out of the firm myself. Out of the blue Robin said he was thinking of splitting the firm and would I join him in his new practice. He wanted to have full equity partners with him in an equal partnership. I was delighted. Robin took the people he wanted and the people he did not want went off with Brian.

Simon Walton was then a young salaried partner:

Around this time, in 1973, the brothers decided to split the practice, a split which took effect in 1974. The salaried partners like me were not involved in any way in the lead up to this. Brian took the lion's share of the firm including Manchester, Cardiff and Stanmore. Robin took Ilford. I was asked to return to Serjeants' Inn along with Tony Lawton and became part of Robin's firm.

Robin chose his partners very carefully, and decided to have equal equity partners from the outset … I was overwhelmed at becoming an equity partner at 33 years of age in an equal partnership. We were given the deeds and accounts to look at. It was clear that the brothers had been very modest in their earnings considering they had been the sole owners of the practice. I also recall that Robin was clear that he did not want any special arrangements for his son David.

In a way I was not that certain about joining Robin's firm rather than Brian's. All my friends were the old lefties who were becoming part of Brian Thompson's firm. What was noteworthy is that Brian's firm did not have the phrase "and Partners".

Robin was particularly proud of the partnership clause he drafted, which was also adopted by Brian and which is a fundamental clause of today's Thompsons' partnership:

The principal object of the practice shall be to assist Trade Unions and their members. It shall not be an object of the Partnership to earn for their Partners the maximum income which in general practice they are capable of earning.

Robin was a good administrator himself but preferred to delegate the administration work, mostly to David Skidmore who then controlled finance, created the accounts system and indeed all financial and many administrative systems for all the firms. Finance was run on behalf of both firms through W.H. Thompson at Harrow. The office managers were key players in these developments together with the accounts function. Nick Carter became the finance partner in Brian's firm and he and David Skidmore liaised together over many years, with David taking the lead.

Robin's firm moved into Bainbridge House. It was the TUC building, the office entrance to which was at the back of the building on Bainbridge Street, on 25 July 1977.

Robin described how he found these offices:

One day I sat next to Norman Willis at a dinner and he mentioned an office they were letting which was part of Congress House but with a different name and we had not heard of this vacancy. I visited it the next day and we decided it would be most suitable for us and moved in accordingly. Since then it has turned out most successfully with the extended premises within Congress House.

John Harris recalls it slightly differently:

I was instrumental in helping the firm find the offices in Congress House. I was at a SOGAT lunch in the Kenilworth Hotel on Great Russell Street and was talking to Norman Willis, with whom I had become friendly. He told me that the TUC was struggling to let a number of floors in the block. At the time I knew we were looking for premises. Norman showed me the available space. It was in quite a state but clearly had potential. I told Robin and he came with Ivor Walker and the decision was made to move from Serjeants' Inn.

Ivor Walker left the firm in 1982, and Vic Nicolls retired in 1988. In Ivor's case he was required to leave when Robin became disenchanted with him or rather his perceived lack of effort on the firm's business.

Ivor subsequently set up his own practice before joining Pritchard Englefield and Tobin for a period, then Capsticks, before working on his own account again. For a number of years he sat on various tribunals including a period as a part-time Chairman of the Employment Tribunal.

Liaison

The risk in 1973/4 was that the split into two separate firms would result in firms that would not only diverge in ethos but might start to compete with each other, to the detriment of the trade unions and their members. An inter-firm liaison committee was set up and masterminded by David Skidmore. It was to play a crucial part in ensuring that the firms stayed close and would act as one in all major issues, examples over the years being various major industrial disputes such as Grunwick and the miners' strike, as well as major test cases such as the deafness cases and the massive new case intakes which resulted.

An example of the continued level of cooperation was the firms' annual cocktail party which was attended by senior trade union officials, Labour politicians, and some judges as well as barristers and doctors who did relevant work. Robin explained how these started:

When we moved in there [Serjeants' Inn] we held an opening party which was very successful. We held one or two more annually but then they got too big and we proceeded to hold one cocktail party at a hotel each year.

In due course Simon Walton became a prime mover in the organisation of these functions which were held as a joint function for many years at the Waldorf Hotel before eventually transferring to The Law Society's Hall. Politicians who attended included Michael Foot, Barbara Castle, Elwyn Jones and Tony Benn, amongst many others.

In *The Castle Diaries 1974-1976*, Barbara Castle describes a discussion with Jack Jones at the Thompsons' cocktail party on 24 April 1974, and adds 'The Thompsons are solicitors who do a great deal of work for various trade unions. Their party is one of the highlights of the political year'. In the entry for 23 March 1976 she notes 'Later that evening I went to the Thompsons annual party. Though Ted was in Brussels, I didn't want to miss it. One meets more union chaps there than anywhere else.'

Chapter 22
Industrial Disputes – Back to the Future

The period from 1974 to 1976 was a momentous one in terms of development of the law. Michael Foot, now Secretary of State for Employment, framed and piloted through the Commons three major pieces of legislation. The first was the Health and Safety at Work Act 1974. This followed on from the Robens Report, but went a good deal further, establishing the Health and Safety Commission and setting up Safety Committees and Safety Representatives. As Michael Foot noted in interview, the legislation 'was worked out in detail with your firm. It wouldn't have been the same if it hadn't been.' The second was the Trade Unions and Labour Relations Act 1974 (TULRA) which swept away the Industrial Relations Act, restored the old 'immunities' and guaranteed the right to recruit and organise, the right of recognition, the right to collective bargaining and the right to strike. (Two battles were lost – one within the Cabinet, and one at the hands of Labour's opponents – in relation to picketing and the closed shop; the price for failing to carry the day on the picketing point was to be paid at Grunwick and in the miners' strike…). The third leg followed in 1975 with the Employment Protection Act, one of whose lasting legacies was the creation of the conciliation service ACAS. In addition, following on from Barbara Castle's Equal Pay Act of 1970, this period saw the Sex Discrimination Act 1975 and the Race Relations Act 1976.

In the meantime, and prior to the enactment of TULRA, Hugh Scanlon of the engineers was smarting under a £75,000 fine imposed by John Donaldson of the industrial court (the NIRC). A solution needed to be found, and Brian was consulted. Brian provided the idea of payment of outstanding fines by third parties, a solution which was eagerly accepted. Michael Foot's personal letter of appreciation to Brian is reproduced below.

Dear Brian Thompson,
I cannot let this afternoon pass without writing to thank you for the expert help you gave us this morning. What would have happened if we had not had that meeting, heaven knows. It seems that things have turned out as they should, & Hugh Scanlon who has just left here is almost as relieved as I am.

   I have not quite had time to calculate how many tens of millions you have helped to save the country but the total figure must considerably exceed anything even Sir John Donaldson* might have sequestered, legally or illegally.
Thank you again,
Michael Foot

*My reports suggest that he was a bit sick when he had to improvise the final words of his judgement in court today.

But any hope that the balance of power in industrial relations was about to be restored was swiftly dashed. Political disputes came back to the fore with the attack on trade unions and their members. The hard won rights recovered under TULRA were viciously attacked by employers who adopted new strategies to counter them, and in the all-out assault on trades unions which took place following the election of the Thatcher government in 1979. The post-entry closed shop was outlawed in 1988 and the pre-entry shop in 1990. In the meantime legislation impaired union security in another way, by interfering in check-off arrangements. The strike threat was weakened by a succession of laws which permitted a union to be sued,

Personal

8 ST JAMES'S SQUARE, LONDON SW1
Telephone 01-930 6200

13/4/8

Dear Brian Thompson,

I cannot let this afternoon pass without writing to thank you for the expert help you gave us this morning. What would have happened if we had not had that meeting, heaven knows. It seems that things have turned out as they should, & Hugh Scanlon who has just left here is almost as relieved as I am.

I have not quite had time to calculate how many tens of millions you have helped

> *to save the country but the total figure must considerably exceed anything* *x* *even Sir John Donaldsons might have sequestered, legally or illegally,*
>
> *Thank you again*
>
> *Michael Foot*
>
> *x my reports suggest that Lawsn [?] looks sick when he had to improve the final words of his judgment in court to-day.*

introduced ballots prior to a strike, and outlawed both secondary and unofficial action.

All this was combined with an economic policy which resulted in the closure or decimation of large parts of manufacturing industry in particular and the deliberate targeting of particular industries or unions (the mining industry being the classic example). Thompsons represented thousands of mineworkers in the mid 1980s when criminal and other proceedings were brought arising out of the mineworkers' dispute. The firms also played a leading part on behalf of the unions in the Grunwick and

Wapping disputes and in many others when some employers seized the opportunity to attack the collective power of working people. These were bitter disputes. In all of them Thompsons acted on behalf of the trades unions concerned, not only in relation to the legal proceedings brought against the unions including sequestration orders, injunctions and so on, but also the criminal cases brought against individual members who were attempting to assert their long held rights such as the right to strike as well as the right to support colleagues by picketing and demonstration. The first such major dispute of the period, and one which achieved national notoriety, was at Grunwick.

The Grunswick Dispute

The dispute began in August 1976 when 137 workers, who were predominantly East African South Asian, walked out of the Grunwick film processing plant in Willesden, north London. The dispute, which centred on the lack of union recognition at Grunwick, involved the Association of Professional, Executive, Clerical and Computer Staffs (APEX) for whom Thompsons acted. Thompsons represented the union throughout.

It was claimed that conditions in the plant, particularly in the mail order department, were poor, and pay rates low. Mrs Jayaben Desai refused to work overtime and, together with her son, resigned. She then picketed the plant, asking the other workers to sign a petition demanding trade union recognition. Others followed her example and the strike had begun.

A Strike Committee was set up, and the strike became a cause celebre for the union movement attracting a wide range of activist support to picket lines, where much violence occurred.

Geoff Shears from Stanmore took on and coordinated all the cases and matters arising from the dispute.

Our first involvement was modest. APEX instructed us in relation to six teachers who were arrested and charged after refusing to comply with a request from a police constable to move. I felt this was a perfect case to try and establish the legal right to picket. [Although such a right technically existed, it was always subject to being overridden by a demand from a police officer to move]. I briefed Jeffrey Burke for the Magistrates Court. We lost and appealed to a judge. I briefed John Hampden Inskip QC along with Jeffrey Burke. Inskip's cross examination of the policeman was brilliant and at the end of it the judge found that our clients were exercising their right to peacefully picket – so we won. In a sense we did too well. I would have preferred to have won in the Court of Appeal and set a precedent!

In due course the call went out for there to be a mass picket, and APEX decided to offer legal support to anyone arrested in the course of peaceful picketing. The local Law Centre was also involved – along with just about all those involved on behalf of the civil liberties movement. We had a team of lawyers and ten barristers acting non-stop.

During the course of the strike, the union applied for recognition under the Employment Protection Act 1975. ACAS, acting pursuant to its duties under the Act, sent confidential questionnaires to those dismissed workers who were union members, and wished to be re-employed, but not to the rest of the workers, whose names and addresses it was unable to obtain from Grunwick. As a result of the answers to the questionnaires the ACAS report recommended recognition of the union. Grunwick applied for a declaration that the report was void. Geoff Shears explains what happened next:

We were instructed in the litigation between ACAS and Grunwick on the consultation issue in which APEX was joined as a third party. Once again we had John Hampden Inskip QC and Jeffrey Burke. Inskip was once again brilliant. The case came before the Lord Chief Justice, Lord Widgery, known as being right wing. Despite this, we won. The decision was made on the first or second day of the Scarman enquiry where we briefed Stuart Shields QC.

The action proceeded to the Court of Appeal chaired by Lord Denning. He found against the union despite once again a brilliant speech from John Hampden Inskip (which caused a spontaneous outburst of applause from some American observers sitting in court). By the time the case went to the House of Lords we had ceased to be involved. The case in the Lords was lost.

Grunwick Processing Laboratories Ltd v ACAS & anor [1978] ICR 232
The House of Lords agreed with the Court of Appeal that the duty of ACAS under the Act to 'ascertain the opinion of the workers to whom the issue relates' was mandatory without any such qualification as 'so far as reasonably practicable'. As a result of their inability to obtain the

opinions of that part of the workforce whose addresses they could not obtain, the report was void.

The strike finally ran out of steam in July 1978 after 670 days, and although the strikers failed to win their immediate goal of trade union recognition, the case represents an important landmark in the history of British industrial action, and indeed black workers' rights. The national impact of the dispute was such that the then Labour government set up a cabinet committee to deal with the issues it raised. A Court of Inquiry (where again Thompsons represented the union) chaired by Lord Scarman reported, recommending, amongst other things, reinstatement of the workers to the extent that this could be achieved with ex gratia payments to the extent that it could not. Scarman also stated that 'we have no doubt that union representation, if properly encouraged and responsibly exercised, could in the future help the company as well as its employees'. (See Cmnd.6922 Sessional Papers 1977).

As Geoff Shears recently commented, 'notwithstanding Scarman's findings, Mr Ward and Grunwick ignored all the recommendations. At the time, this was unprecedented'.

The Miners' Strike 1984/85

The 1984 strike followed on from the disputes in 1972 and 1974. In 1972 the miners came out on strike for higher pay, with a successful result. But by 1974 they had slipped back again. The government of Edward Heath refused to compromise on a 7 per cent rise and a strike began whereupon the government declared a state of emergency, imposed a three-day week and called an election which they duly lost.

The incoming Secretary of State for Employment, Michael Foot, implemented a Pay Board report which showed how miners' pay had dropped since 1972. As well as increases in pay, there were two other important results

CONCLUSIONS AND RECOMMENDATIONS

Conclusions

65 The underlying cause of the walk-out on 23 August 1976 was a genuine, even if not clearly formulated, sense of discontent and grievance amongst a substantial number of staff—particularly in the mail order department. The demand for a union, which was the cry of those who went on strike, summed up accurately their sense of grievance: they wanted some body independent of management with the knowledge to advise them and the strength to make some impact upon the company.

66 Their discontent and grievances arose from the company's lack of a properly developed industrial relations policy including effective machinery for the examination and redress of grievances.

67 The company by dismissing all the strikers, refusing to consider the reinstatement of any of them, refusing to seek a negotiated settlement to the strike and rejecting ACAS offers of conciliation, has acted within the letter but outside the spirit of the law. Further, such action on the part of the company was unreasonable when judged by the norms of good industrial relations practice. The company has thus added to the bitterness of the dispute, and contributed to its development into a threat of civil disorder.

68 Once the recognition issue was referred to ACAS by the union, the company recognised that by law it must co-operate with ACAS in its inquiries. It is not for us to pass judgment on the legal differences which arose between the company and ACAS: nor are we in a position to determine whether the company "dragged its heels" or ACAS was justified in deciding on 20 December to proceed without the assistance of the company. We merely note that the company has exercised its undoubted right of access to the courts to test the validity of the ACAS report, and that the consequent legal proceedings have added to the delays which have so greatly embittered the dispute.

69 The union acted reasonably in responding to the strikers' call for help, in enrolling them as members and in seeking to negotiate with the company. When the strikers were dismissed, the union had no choice but to add a claim for their reinstatement to its existing claim to be recognised by the company for the purpose of collective bargaining.

70 In all the circumstances the union was fully justified in raising the dispute at the Trades Union Congress and invoking the support of the trade union movement as a whole. It was also fully justified in referring on 15 October 1976 a recognition issue to ACAS.

71 The union, however, when frustrated by the seemingly indefinite prolongation of the dispute in 1977, in calling for further industrial action by members of the UPW took a step which led to breaches of the criminal law. Although it was never the intention of the union the mass picket on occasion has led to forms of civil disorder. It could have been foreseen that this was likely.

72 In our judgment, good industrial relations depend upon a willingness to co-operate and compromise. The law favours collective bargaining and encourages the use by workers of independent trade unions for the purpose. The

Extracts from the Scarman Report

policy of the law is to exclude "trade disputes" from judicial review by the courts and to rely not on the compulsory processes of the law but on the voluntary approach backed by advice, conciliation, and arbitration to promote good industrial relations. The efficacy of such a law depends upon goodwill. If men act unreasonably, by which we mean in obedience to the letter but not the spirit of the law, it will not work. It does not, however, follow that judicial review would be an effective substitute: for, whatever the sanctions imposed by law, its efficacy depends upon the consent of the people.

RECOMMENDATIONS

73 **(1) Reinstatement**

In the conduct of industrial relations in this country, and no matter what the legalities are, it is the exception rather than the rule for employees who are dismissed during the course of a strike not to be re-engaged after the dispute is ended. Ideally in our view Grunwick should therefore offer re-employment to all those strikers who before the dispute were full time employees of the company and who wish to be taken back. It is our recommendation that this should be done if it be at all practicable. We recognise however that the nature of the company's business is such that the necessary number of vacancies may not now exist, although it seems to us that a seasonal business dependent on overtime must have at least some vacancies.

In the absence of any established relationship between Grunwick and APEX the question of determining the number of vacancies which do exist could well, and we recommend should, be considered by a mediator either agreed by the company and the union, or appointed by yourself in the absence of such agreement.

It would in our opinion be reasonable for the company to make to those for whom there are no vacancies, an ex gratia payment commensurate with their length of service. The amounts of such payments are a matter on which the mediator might well be able to offer helpful advice.

(2) Individual rights of representation

We were pleased to hear it said on behalf of the company during the course of our inquiry that if an individual employee who was a member of the union had a grievance which he or she could not settle directly with the management, and wished to be represented by the union in pursuance of that grievance, the company would accept that right. We recommend that the company give effect to this declaration.

(3) Recognition for the purposes of collective bargaining

Whatever the result of the company's case against ACAS (which is now for the House of Lords to decide), ACAS is the body established by law to determine the recognition issue in the absence of agreement. We do not propose to pre-judge the issue. Nevertheless, we have no doubt that union representation, if properly encouraged and responsibly exercised, could in the future help the company as well as its employees.

Stuart Shields QC, Jeffrey Burke and Peter Clark instructed by Thompsons represented APEX at the Court of Inquiry of the strike; the implementation of a scheme for compensation of pneumoconiosis sufferers (which arose as a result of the pioneering litigation run by Tony Woolf and then Simon Walton), and a new superannuation scheme which commenced in 1975.

In 1984 the Conservatives were back in power, and this time they were prepared, ready and waiting. They had many months' supply of coal stockpiled in readiness for a prolonged dispute. In March 1984 NCB Chairman Ian MacGregor announced that twenty pits would have to close, putting 20,000 miners out of work. Miners at Cortonwood colliery in Yorkshire, the first earmarked for closure, walked out at midnight on 5 March in protest.

Arthur Scargill, the NUM's president, on 12 March called on members across the country to join the action in a national strike against pit closures.

By then, Thompsons were acting for the Yorkshire Area of the NUM, dealing with 50 per cent of the region's personal injury cases, and handling some head office matters. One such matter related to complex litigation over the Mineworkers' Pension Scheme. Chris Chapman, who had been responsible for acquiring the NUM as a client, as described elsewhere, was handling this case with assistance from Virginia Kerridge a solicitor in Brian's London office. The court hearing from 26 March to 5 April (with judgment on 13 April) coincided with the start of the national strike: *Cowan & Ors v Scargill & Ors [1984] ICR 647*

Under the mineworkers' pension scheme, a committee of management was formed to administer the scheme. The committee had ten trustees, five appointed by the NCB and five by the union. A formal plan was set up in 1980 and amended in 1982 for the investment of the pension funds in various categories, including, amongst other things, overseas investments, oil and gas. The union trustees objected to the plan on the grounds that such investments were contrary to union policy. The board trustees brought legal proceedings against the union trustees.

At trial the judge found that the union trustees' moral reservations were irrelevant, and found against them.

The strike turned into one of the bitterest disputes Britain has ever seen. The year-long strike brought hardship and involved violence as pit communities fought to retain their local collieries – for many the only source of employment.

Debate still continues over the tactics used by all parties; the use of the Metropolitan Police in local mining villages, biased press coverage, flying pickets, and so on.

There were major confrontations between pickets and police, a key one occurring at Orgreave in June 1984 where pickets were met by police in riot gear, police horses and dogs.

An important source of support for the miners came from other trade unionists such as the dockers and railway workers, and from within their own communities, particularly the women. Locally they set up action groups, organised the Women against Pit Closures conference, joined the picket lines and travelled the country speaking at political meetings and fundraising.

Throughout all this Thompsons was involved. There were sequestration proceedings against the union, and many criminal charges against individual trade unionists, often brought in the Crown Courts involving charges of conspiracy. Thompsons not only attempted to look after the interests of the union as a whole but also represented with considerable success many individual workers who faced these serious criminal charges.

Some of the issues involved in the strike ended up in the law reports. One example was Thomas v NUM, a case which highlighted a number of issues, and where Thompsons once again represented the union:

Thomas & ors v National Union of Mineworkers (South Wales Area) & Ors [1985] ICR 887

On 9 March 1984 the South Wales area of the NUM passed a resolution to support the national union in strike action and to stop work on 12 March. In November 1984, some members including a number of the plaintiffs, returned to work. They were met by large scale picketing. Six pickets were selected by lodge officials to stand at the colliery gates and a large number of others were kept back from the approach road by police. There was evidence of picketing near the homes of working miners and in one case outside a college one of the miners was attending, together with evidence of action outside other industrial premises. The plaintiffs sought injunctions restraining the NUM (South Wales Area) from organising unlawful picketing or demonstrations and from funding and organising secondary picketing outside South Wales.

The judge decided that the working miners were entitled to use the highway without unreasonable harassment and the picketing at the colliery gates, at miners' homes and at the college was unreasonable. The pickets should be limited to peaceful picketing by numbers not exceeding six. However, the judge refused to grant any injunction to restrain picketing at other collieries or secondary picketing since it was by no means inevitable that the same would involve criminal acts. He also rejected the claim brought against the national union and co-ordinating committee.

Two other cases, both handled by Chris Chapman, are worth noting, one the 'road blocks' case, and the other the picketing conditions case; both had significant civil liberties implications:

Moss v McLachlan [1985] IRLR 76.

The 4 appellants, all striking miners, were travelling in a convoy of vehicles on the M1 when they were stopped by a police cordon. The police inspector told them he feared a breach of the peace and asked them to turn back. After blocking the road with their vehicles, a group of men including the appellants attempted to push their way through the police cordon and were arrested. The Mansfield Magistrates convicted them of wilfully obstructing a police officer in the execution of his duty. The men appealed. The appeal failed, the Divisional Court finding that it was not necessary to show from the words and deeds of the men concerned that a breach of the peace was intended. On the facts a breach of the peace was 'a real possibility, imminent, immediate and not remote'.

R v Mansfield Justices, ex parte Sharkey [1985] 1 AER 193.

The applicants were striking miners who regularly picketed East Midlands' collieries. Each faced charges of threatening behaviour under the Public Order Act 1936, or obstructing a police officer under the Police Act 1964. All were of good character. The magistrates, when granting bail, imposed a condition that they were not to visit any premises for the purposes of picketing or demonstration save for peaceful picketing at the person's own usual place of employment. The applicants applied for judicial review on the grounds that such a condition could only be applied under the Bail Act 1976 if the court was satisfied that there were substantial grounds for believing that the bailed person would commit an offence while on bail. The application for judicial review was refused, the court holding that the magistrates had a wide discretion and were entitled to use their knowledge of local events and conditions.

By January 1985 the strike was beginning to disintegrate as miners facing increasing financial hardship began to return to work. The strike came to an end on 3 March 1985. By 2002 there were just 13 deep coal mines in the country where once there were 170, and the membership of the NUM had fallen to 5,000 compared to 187,000 in 1984. The work may now be gone, but its legacy continues to live on in the shape of tens of thousands of claims for compensation for diseases such as occupational deafness, chronic bronchitis and emphysema and vibration white finger.

The Wapping Dispute

The result of the miners' strike was watched closely by other employers, who were prepared to adopt an aggressive approach which involved no compromise and which was intent on breaking the unions.

On 24 January 1986, 6,000 trade unionists went on strike after a successful ballot for strike action and months of protracted negotiations with their employers News International and Times Group Newspapers. The company claimed to be seeking a legally binding agreement at their new plant at Wapping which incorporated flexible working, a no-strike clause, new technology and the abandonment of the closed shop. The new plant was set up allegedly to produce a new London evening paper.

The company immediately secured an injunction to restrain the union SOGAT from interfering with contracts between the company and their wholesale distributors, an injunction which the union did not obey. Sequestration proceedings quickly followed and the union was fined £25,000 and had its assets seized.

As soon as the strike was announced, dismissal notices were served on all those taking part in the industrial action. The company replaced the print workers with workers from another union, and transferred its four major titles to Wapping. Some claim that it was the company's intention all along, and the company never had any intention of negotiating with the unions.

In support of their colleagues, the print unions organised regular marches and demonstrations at the company's premises. John Harris describes what happened:

With the authority of SOGAT's NEC, their London District Council organised the picketing of Grays Inn Road, Bouverie Street and Wapping … . In addition on Wednesday and Saturday nights rallies, marches or demonstrations took place. Marches usually assembled at Tower Hill or Temple for a procession to Wapping. The majority of arrests took place on Wednesday or Saturday nights … . Most of you will have seen the television reports…there were two very violent nights, namely the 3 May 1986 and the 23 January 1987. I was present on both occasions and never thought that I would see English police behave in the … way they did. The charges by the mounted police were particularly frightening and obviously the reason it was done was to terrorise people. I hadn't done anything wrong and it was the first time in my life that I ran away from the police as I was frightened I would get trampled on by the horses or beaten about the head with a policeman's baton. The majority of union members were in exactly the same position as I was, completely innocent and exercising a free and democratic right. It has to be said that there were some football type hooligans about, but it is my view those persons could have been isolated by the police and the unions allowed to carry out its peaceful rallies and demonstrations ... . On another occasion I went on the march from Temple to Wapping. The band was playing, marchers were singing; wives kids and dogs were all there marching. The mood was good and the march had carnival flavour. Within ten minutes of the march reaching Wapping, the police had turned this great march into a violent frightening shambles.

The General Secretary complained to the Home Office about the police behaviour but things did not improve and the innocent continued to suffer. When you see a woman charging up the road pushing her baby on a wheelchair with the police in hot pursuit, something has got to be wrong ... .

Once again there was much work done in connection with the dispute both in acting for the union and for many individual members who were charged with criminal offences. As with the other disputes, Thompsons' staff attended regularly on the picket lines to assist members of unions who were arrested, and represented them in any criminal proceedings which followed.

John continues the story:

By the time the dispute was in full swing we had a team of people dealing with the magistrates' court issues, and someone would be on duty every night. In the early days I dealt with all this myself and had much success in persuading the police not to press charges and let men off with warnings. However, once the violence started this was no longer possible. In the end there were about 1,400 magistrates' court cases.

One significant case which proceeded to trial was brought by the employers against the union, again represented by Thompsons, and once more involved the issue of picketing:

News Group Newspapers Ltd & Ors v SOGAT '82 & Ors
[1987] ICR 182

The judge found that picketing, marches and demonstrations ceased to be lawful if there was an unreasonable obstruction of the highway; that the court could grant injunctions to prevent this along with threats to employees if the threats were serious; and that although the Trade Union and Labour Relations Act 1974 provided immunity to the union in relation to the tort of interference with contracts, this immunity could not apply to the case since none of the pickets had been employed at Wapping! However the injunctions granted would be limited so as to permit peaceful picketing and marches.

During the course of the dispute about 4,000 SOGAT members were dismissed. A vast exercise was undertaken and the majority made applications for unfair dismissal. These were all still pending in the Industrial Tribunal when the dispute came to an end.

News International was certainly on the back foot in the publicity war. Brenda Dean, the union's General Secretary, presented the case skilfully – her members had lawfully balloted for industrial action but the law had allowed their peremptory dismissal, and the company had opened up new printing works in Wapping and was demanding they transfer there on different terms and conditions of employment.

Nevertheless, the legal battle continued. The earlier sequestration had been satisfied, but by early 1987 new sequestration proceedings were threatened. The union decided to negotiate the best deal available. John Harris was able to avert any further sequestration and secure offers of compensation for the dismissed workers. The NGA and AEU, the other unions involved, soon followed suit.

These disputes, and the Tory legislation designed to curb trade union power, changed the face of industrial relations for the time being. Individual battles were lost, but others were fought off, and the unions adapted and survived.

John Harris describes one success and his involvement in some of the major industrial issues of the time:

One campaign which was highly successful involved the change in the law introduced by Margaret Thatcher requiring union members to contract in to the political levy (as compared to the previous position where they had had the right only to contract out). It was critical for the unions that their memberships should contract in. The unions gave the job of marshalling the campaign to Bill Keys of SOGAT and Graham Allen MP. I helped organise this and the result was that we won 43 out of 46 union ballots. At a celebratory event Neil Kinnock gave Bill Keys a cup.

There were many industrial disputes which I had to deal with. Robert Maxwell who owned the *Daily Mirror* at the time was a regular opponent. I met him on many occasions and got on well with him. I recall one dispute where the union had been fined £75,000. Bill Keys rang me one evening and asked me to go to Maxwell's office the next morning to settle the dispute. At the same time the £75,000 had to be paid into court by 12 o'clock. The intention was that Maxwell would refund the money if the matter was settled. The next morning I explained the position to Robin who arranged for a cheque for £75,000 to be given to me. I duly attended the negotiations, having insisted that I be accompanied by a member of the union's executive. The negotiations were protracted, and 12 o'clock was fast approaching. Maxwell realised the risk if the money was not received by the court in time and sent me round to the Royal Courts in his Rolls Royce!

Subsequently we were able to settle the dispute and Maxwell honoured his word and refunded the money.

I was involved at various levels in some major disputes including the miners' strike and Grunwick. The flat in the offices [Robin Thompson's London office] was used for meetings. I recall that on one occasion in the miners' dispute at a meeting involving Arthur Scargill and Peter Heathfield it was so full of smoke that Norman Willis, then General Secretary of the TUC and a talented artist, drew a picture (which Thompsons still have) – the picture is of a room so full of smoke that any other distinguishing feature is impossible to ascertain. On one occasion I recall me and Peter Heathfield going out and bringing back thirty lots of fish and chips for those assembled for the discussions! It was much appreciated.

One consequence of the attack on the collective power of unions was that their efforts and representation moved into different areas such as the struggle for improved employment rights, a struggle which was all the more possible because of European regulations incorporated into British labour law. This has a certain irony bearing in mind that the Tory government took the country into Europe and much of this regulation occurred during the Thatcher era.

Geoff Thomas, John Hughes (Ruskin College), John Lebor Geoff Shears and Simon Walton

Chapter 23
A national firm

In the period following the split both firms expanded, opening more offices and gradually providing between them truly national coverage.

Birmingham/Newcastle

On 12th January 1976 Robin's firm opened an office in Birmingham. Simon Walton went there as the managing partner and was joined by Tony Lawton (by then already a salaried partner), Cliff Poole, Paul Malone, Peter Bamford and Vic Shelley.

Simon had huge energy and organisational skills as well as very strong contacts with a number of the trade unions:

Birmingham was ideal for me; it was near my home town of Coventry. I stayed in Birmingham until 1980, and it was a period I thoroughly enjoyed, building up the office, making the important contact with our union clients and so on. When I returned to London Graham Dickinson and Colin Ettinger took over.

Colin Ettinger had started as an articled clerk at Ilford in 1976 and was just 27 years old when he went to Birmingham, by then already quite a sizeable office with more than fifty staff.

Another important office, this time in Newcastle was opened by Brian's firm on 21 April 1980.

The volume of work received from the unions in the North East was considerable, but there was another underlying feature. Frank Clifford, after leaving W.H. Thompson, had set up his own successful practice and had close links with the construction union, the CEU (by then AUEW (Constructional Section)). Clifford had an office in Stockton and there was pressure from some parts of the union for Clifford to be allocated all the union's north-eastern work.

Geoff Shears transferred from Stanmore and Frank Foy was recruited from Manchester. Together with Philip Ballard they opened an office in Erik House and were joined by Mark Berry from Manchester and Tony Briscoe from Ilford. Newcastle quickly became very successful, building important and long-lasting links with a number of trade unions and becoming, inevitably, the focal point and centre of operations for the huge number of deafness cases the firm was acquiring.

After a couple of years in Birmingham, and at Robin's request, Colin Ettinger returned to London and within another year Graham Dickinson had also departed from Birmingham.

As a result, Frank Foy transferred, at the request of Robin's firm, from Newcastle to become the managing partner in Birmingham, leaving Geoff in sole charge of Newcastle. Geoff remained in Newcastle until he moved to Pimlico in the summer of 1991, and Philip Ballard then took charge of Newcastle.

Frank's team in Birmingham included Sarah Goodman and Terry Loughrey, and he also recruited many lawyers, including Peter Mulhern now the branch manager. Tony Lawton who had left to join Rowley Ashworth in July 1977, also re-joined as a full partner on 1 May 1986.

Frank's move to Birmingham came just before the judgment in the deafness test cases being pursued by the firm:

Between the end of the hearing and the announcement of the judgment, I transferred from Brian Thompson's in Newcastle to Robin Thompson's in Birmingham in October 1983. Birmingham was becoming a strategic office. It was a big thing at the time for a Brian Thompson partner to go and take over a Robin Thompson office. From my point of view it was all Thompsons. I drew no great distinction between Brian's firm and Robin's firm.

I enjoyed the job and was fortunate in pulling in quite a bit of new work. The Boilermakers had merged into the General & Municipal Workers to become the GMB. Early on in my time in Birmingham I was introduced to the GMB Legal Officer and I dealt with some complicated disablement benefit cases arising out of deafness. I also recall meeting the Divisional Organiser of NUPE (National Union of Public Employees, now part of UNISON) Barry Shuttleworth. As it happened he was from Manchester and when I met him I recognised him and vice versa. We got on well. He was introduced to me by Simon Walton. He told me that the regional secretaries of all the major unions in the West Midlands met from time to time and he invited me to go and meet them all and to give a talk. As a result I met the T&G and GMB regional secretaries and it went very well.

At the time in Birmingham we had a lot of deafness scheme cases [following the successful conclusion of the deafness test cases] but not much of this was local work and I was a bit concerned that when that work ran out the office would be short of work. However, because of acquiring work from the GMB and T&GWU, we were able to expand significantly. When I went to Birmingham we had two-thirds of one floor in the McLaren Building which in due course became two full floors. I recall Nigel Tomkins being in charge of all the new T&G work and I also recall Geoff Wheatley was the GMB regional secretary from whom we first acquired the West Midlands work.

Manchester, Moss Side and Sheffield

By the mid 1970s Manchester office was already well established. Philip Ballard and Jane Litherland joined in 1976, Mark Berry in 1978 and Julie Wood, Francine O'Gorman and Alicia Rendell in 1979. Of these, all became full partners and Philip, Mark, Julie and Francine went on to become managing partners of offices.

Pauline Chandler established herself as a fearless litigator, and trained and encouraged everyone else in the office to follow suit. She developed numerous internal archive systems, the asbestos archive being an example, to ensure that documents, statements and reports in cases were kept and categorised for use in future cases; manuals such as the Damages Manual and the Costs Manual, loose leaf manuals of materials to assist all lawyers in the firm; files of court transcripts of Thompsons' cases; and much else. She worked tirelessly.

In 1976, Manchester opened a satellite office in Moss Side. John Pickering:

In the early 1970s the whole future of personal injury litigation was under a cloud with the Pearson Commission. There was a real fear that personal injury litigation might be abolished and that the government might adopt a no fault system rather like that which had been adopted in New Zealand. Accordingly, the firm started to give serious consideration to diversification, and this was the background in which we decided to open an office in Moss Side, a deprived area of South Manchester. The intention was to take on other forms of law work and in particular deal with what was called in those days 'neighbourhood law'. I was quite interested in doing other forms of law, and was keen on the project generally, and therefore I went and opened Moss Side in 1976. I was the anchor man in the office. Others in the office included Rhys Vaughan and Robert Lizar, both of whom loved advocacy. I still did personal injury work.

John left Thompsons in 1979 to set up his own practice:

Although I was a full partner, I soon discovered that I did not particularly like committee work. I began to feel restless and started to wonder whether I could manage on my own. I felt I was in a comfort zone. I got on well with Brian. I liked the office but I decided to see whether I could set up my own firm.

At Moss Side I had just dealt with the first byssinosis case which I settled. The cotton workers' unions were interested, and it gave me a start when I decided to leave Brian Thompson's in 1979. It was agreed that the cotton workers' unions would instruct me, and it gave me a real start. I found a little room in Ancoats in North Manchester and started off my firm there. Over the years I dealt with a considerable number of byssinosis cases and then increasingly over the years almost exclusively asbestos work.

Nick Carter:

John ... was a brilliant case handler and I admire him for what he did in going off and opening his own practice (in 1979) and making such a success of it. We always got on well.

After John departed, Chris Chapman took over in Moss Side. Chris had joined W. H. Thompson in Manchester on 2 March 1970, the same day as Mike Napier, Chris as an articled clerk and Mike as a solicitor:

In the early days I was trained by Pat Cartwright and was mentored by a whole variety of people and had much contact with Rodger Pannone, got used to attending weekend schools and such like.

Around that time the Pearson Commission Report was published and I recall John Pickering saying that there was "no future in PI". I had been doing some work for the NCCL for the Anti-Nazi League, and I was spotted by Tony Casson in the Magistrates' Court. He courted me and I left W. H. Thompson in 1973 and did not return to the firm until 1979. During that period I worked for Casson's and was busy as it was at the time when Casson's were acting for the Shrewsbury pickets. During my time away from Thompsons I never really lost touch with the firm. I used to see Ron Waterton and Pat Cartwright and started to meet Nick Carter in the Film Exchange. When Rhys Vaughan, Robert Lizar and John Pickering left Moss Side Nick offered me a job back with the firm. I accordingly re-joined what was by then Brian Thompson at the Moss Side office.

The Moss Side office grew in size, but its location proved troublesome. Chris Chapman:

There were riots in Moss Side in 1981 and there were one or two incidents involving members of staff. At the time some technical staff used to come over daily from the Manchester office by taxi to assist with typing and secretarial work. The union expressed concerns about the safety of the staff. The result of this was that … we felt it was best to simply relocate. Space became available in Quay House where the rest of Manchester office was based, and we returned therefore to the main office in Quay House.

By that time we were already having discussions in the firm about setting up a Yorkshire office. Sheffield was the best location for a Yorkshire office, rather than Leeds, because of the increasing contact we were having with the NUM. I had not long been in Moss Side when I received a telephone call from Mick Clapham (now an MP) who at the time worked for the NUM. He referred to a Current Law Report of a pneumoconiosis case where John Pickering had recovered compensation for a former mineworker in excess of what the Pneumoconiosis Scheme would have given. Mick Clapham had alerted Arthur Scargill, and I got an invitation to speak to the Yorkshire area of the NUM. I made it clear that John Pickering had dealt with the claim (and that John had left to set up his own practice), but they likewise made it clear that they wanted to use a firm with wider coverage. I saw Arthur Scargill and Mick Clapham and explained the basis on which Thompsons were prepared to take their work.

We were allocated 50 per cent of the region's personal injury work with the other 50 per cent remaining with Raleys, the existing solicitors, on a strict geographical allocation of collieries.

It was partly as a result of this contact with the Yorkshire NUM that Thompsons' Newcastle office began to acquire work from the North Eastern coalfields.

Arthur Scargill became National President in 1981 and we started dealing with some aspects of the National Union's work. Accordingly, shortly after the closure of Moss Side on 11 February 1983, we opened up an office in Sheffield on 5 September 1983.

The Current Law case Mick Clapham called Chris about was:

Spencer v British Steel Corporation [1979] CL 703. It involved a foundry worker whose disability was attributable to pneumoconiosis. The case is better known on the issue of the non-deductibility from damages of redundancy payments.

Chris also played a part in bringing work to the firm from COHSE (one of the health unions). As he said:

The success in bringing that work in was based on hard work attending weekend schools and delivering services and solving problems often at very short notice and inconvenient times.

In addition, and as was often the case, the strong personal relationship forged by Geoff Shears in particular with senior union officers was crucial.

A number of the lawyers who were based in Moss Side transferred to Sheffield office including Jane Litherland, Pam Kenworthy and Pat Cartwright.

The early days of the Sheffield office coincided with the miners' strike. Again Chris takes up the story:

At that time we were dealing with a major case on behalf of the union in respect of the mineworkers' pension scheme, an issue that went to full litigation and which fully occupied me although I also had help from Virginia Kerridge, a solicitor in Brian Thompson's office in London.

The beginning of the two week trial over the pension scheme coincided with the calling of the National Strike in 1984. It was a very busy period for the office. The Yorkshire area pulled us in to deal with high profile cases such as Moss –v– McLachlan and R. –v– Mansfield Justices, ex p. Sharkey and I handled these.

The Newcastle office helped out considerably with the bulk of the picketing cases. We also dealt with other political high profile cases arising out of the dispute. We managed to get through this period without dislocating the office, and we got through it without ever having to face a successful order either against the National Union or the Yorkshire Area for an injunction or damages.

After the strike we were inundated with work, including much deafness and vibration white finger (VWF) work on behalf of miners/former miners. The office expanded very

David Blunkett and Chris Chapman at the Thompson's Reception to celebrate Rodney Bickerstaffe becoming Chairman of the TUC and Tom Sawyer becoming Chairman of the Labour Party, 29 September 1991

quickly and the mining work was the mainstay of our income. As the years went on, mining work decreased in volume, and the work of the office became very much centred on service industry work.

Chris remained managing partner of Sheffield office until 1994. He left the practice in 1995. In his words: 'For a number of years it was largely Brian, Geoff Shears, Nick Carter and I who ran Brian's firm ... and took all the key decisions'.

Cardiff

Cardiff office was part of Brian Thompsons when the firm split in 1974. In 1978 the office was effectively given financial independence (and Brian's firm gained the addition to the firm's name of 'and partners'). Andrew Herbert:

There was … a major event in 1978, when Cardiff broke away from Brian Thompson's. The discussions were led by Geoff [Thomas] and I was happy to go along with it. I felt we would do better under our own steam than under Brian. Ted Lewis was still around at that time but was nearing the end of his career and Geoff was the leading force in the Cardiff breakaway.

The new firm was formed on 1 September 1978, and I became an equity partner. Chris Short was also an equity partner on a reduced share. The two of us joined the existing equity partners of Ted Lewis, Geoff Thomas and Roger Bent.

Nick Carter would have taken the same approach in Manchester if he had had enough support: 'In the late 1970s Cardiff office split away from Brian Thompson's and I was enthusiastic to follow suit. However, it did not happen.'

In 1985, the office which by then was led by Geoff Thomas, Ted Lewis having died, wished to return to the fold but as part of Robin Thompson's rather than Brian Thompson's. Andrew Herbert:

The arrangement with Brian under which we in Cardiff operated independently was a seven year arrangement. As the seven years began to draw to a close it seemed inevitable that we would not carry on as we were, and I was probably in favour of the move that then took place to re-amalgamate, but with Robin Thompson & Partners. The only material difference that took place was that the firm felt more of a commercial organisation. Of course, there were significant internal changes in that Geoff Thomas went to London, Steve Allen to Manchester, and subsequently Paul Llewellyn to Nottingham. By then Chris Short had left under something of a cloud, and it left me and Roger running the office – Roger as managing partner.

Scotland

The firms' geographical coverage was gradually becoming more extensive. Cases arising in Scotland were handled from the English and Welsh offices, and very often agents in Scotland were instructed if court proceedings were required and had to be commenced in Scotland. However, even then it was often possible for the proceedings to be pursued by Thompsons in the English and Welsh courts if the defendants had a place of business in England and Wales – more often than not this is what happened in the era of major construction work arising out of North Sea oil.

All this came to an end with the MacShannon case:
MacShannon v Rockware Glass Ltd [1978] 1 All ER 625
The claimant, a Scotsman living in Scotland, was employed by the defendants, a company registered in England, at their Scottish factory. As a member of the union, he instructed Robin Thompsons in England and, following the usual practice at the time, an action was commenced on his behalf in England. The defendants applied for the action to be stayed leaving the claimant at liberty to bring his proceedings in Scotland. The judge refused to stay the action, a decision which was upheld by the Court of Appeal. However, the House of Lords disagreed. A stay would be granted, and the proceedings must be brought in Scotland

Thompsons' action was immediate. Within five months David Skidmore had successfully argued in favour of and then organised and implemented the opening of the first Scottish office in Edinburgh which opened on 1 November 1979. David Stevenson, whose background was personal injuries, and Manus McGuire, an expert in Labour Law, were taken on, trained in Thompsons' systems in Ilford and were sent 900 cases on the train to get them started in an office in Edinburgh. An office in Glasgow followed on 9 November 1987, managed by Frank Maguire which has

Ron Todd, David Skidmore and Robin Thompson

built a formidable reputation for asbestos and other chest disease litigation in particular.

Robin's London office

In 1980 Simon Walton returned from Birmingham to become managing partner in Robin's London office:

By this time there were just the four of us remaining from the original Robin Thompson partners – Robin, David Skidmore, me and Victor Nicolls … . Between us we ran a very tight ship. The firm grew, both in terms of size and financial stability. A great deal was done which effectively carried both firms. David Skidmore ran the accounts function and much else in terms of administration. I too enjoyed administration and for example for a number of years dealt with staffing and salaries. In addition I built up a number of strong union relationships.

David Phillips was the key player with Clive Jenkins and ASTMS, but I became close to Clive particularly after David left, a contact which had begun some years earlier when I dealt with the Birmingham smallpox cases in the early 1970s (the last fatal outbreak of smallpox in the Western world).

David Phillips was also responsible for us getting the ASLEF (the train drivers' union) work, Ray Buckton being a friend of Clive Jenkins. When David left I took over responsibility for this union and very much enjoyed the work and the relationship, advising on industrial disputes and doing the work as well as the entertaining.

I looked after the FBU (Fire Brigades' Union) folio for a time after Arthur Charles retired and before Andrew Dismore took that over, and was instrumental in the firm acquiring the AUT (University Teachers) work. I was close to Roger Lyons, having been at university with him, had strong links with NASUWT (one of the teaching unions), and so on. I was in my element in Congress House looking after clients.

In 1983, Colin Ettinger received the call to return to London from Birmingham; David Phillips had retired, Stuart Carroll had left and Denise Kingsmill was to leave not long after. Colin:

We had just started a libel action for Clive Jenkins of ASTMS against *Private Eye*, and I took this up, and I recall going to ASTMS to discuss the *Private Eye* defence to the claim (which involved an allegation that Clive had crossed a picket line). In any event we got an offer from *Private Eye* and the case was settled. Clive Jenkins was delighted, and I handled the ASTMS folio until I left Thompsons.

I was appointed an equity partner on 1 May 1982 and as well as dealing with personal injury and employment cases I dealt with a considerable amount of folio work in London. I had dealt with employment work in Birmingham including union issues, and I carried on with all of this in London as well. I handled work for the SCPS as well as ASTMS.

In 1983 Colin transferred to Stanmore which, until then, had been one of Brian's offices, but now became part of Robin's firm. He stayed there until 1993 when he again moved back to Bainbridge House, and dealt with head office work. Colin's colleagues included Lesley Wicks (until she moved to France), Paul McMahon, Bronwen Jenkins, Doug Christie, John Pickering's daughter Anna, John Skinner, who subsequently became managing partner there, and Alison Eddy.

All the while the Ilford office, rather like Brian's Manchester office, drove the firm's success in terms of case handling, with a stable core of highly experienced lawyers.

The expansion of the firms gathered pace from 1986, assisted by the income generated by deafness work, and almost every new office brought with it an increase in work from the trade unions.

Nottingham, Liverpool, Hull, Leeds, Bristol and Stoke

1986 saw the opening of a new Robin Thompson office in Nottingham on 2 June of that year. David Thompson, Robin's son who had joined the firm in January 1979, transferred from Ilford and became managing partner, and was joined by Karen Mitchell and Nigel Saunders amongst others, and by Phil King who joined the firm from Rowley Ashworth. David remained as managing partner until 1995 when he transferred to Congress House. David was succeeded by Phil King and, more recently, by Nigel Saunders, under both of whose wise leadership, ably supported by Susan Harris and others, it has prospered.

Brian's firm opened an office in Liverpool on 24 March 1986, with Mike Humphreys at the helm. Mike took with him his wife Caroline, Len Edwards and Ron Pringle together with Rose Malcolm to run the court department. All of them came from Manchester office. Ron Pringle soon left, the caseload expanded fast and, with a few notable exceptions, it proved difficult at the time to recruit top quality committed lawyers. When at the end of 1990 Mike Humphreys left, Tony Briscoe, assisted by Dave Armitage from Manchester, answered the call to take over.

Tony's story was another remarkable one. Having left school in 1964 at age 16 he did his A levels by evening class, took a Diploma in Law and then started five years articles with a city law firm. His trade union activities brought him into contact with Thompsons, and he transferred his articles to Brian Thompson's in 1973. He left the firm and travelled to East Berlin where he worked as a translator for 18 months, before spending a politically active period in Paris for six months. After returning to the UK he spent three years working for another trade union firm John L Williams before re-joining Thompsons in 1980 at Ilford. He transferred to Newcastle where his work during the miners' strike and in relation to deafness cases was legendary, and then moved to Liverpool. In 1995, Tony once more answered the call and moved back to London, first to Congress House and then Ilford in 1996. He finally left the practice in 2001 to work for the *Morning Star*.

One of a number of partners who learnt her craft in Ilford is Karen Mitchell. Like Tony Briscoe, Karen was always ready to answer the call at a time of expansion and rapid change. She moved to Nottingham, and then opened Hull office in July 1989. Hull proved unsuccessful and closed down. Karen took over the running of Sheffield from Chris Chapman in 1994 before returning to Ilford to become managing partner there in 1997.

1990 saw the opening of Leeds office by Brian's firm and a Bristol office by Robin's. Mark Berry became managing partner in Leeds, and Andrew Herbert in Bristol. Andrew explains how Bristol came about:

In 1990 I was involved in discussions about opening an office in Bristol. The South Western work was a large part of our intake into Cardiff and was important. We had no other office between Cardiff and London. I made out a written case to present at a partners' meeting and it was agreed that we should proceed. I found the premises in Bristol and accordingly then worked in the Bristol office which opened in 1990. Six of us started up the office including myself, Ted Constable and Gavin Roberts, together with three others. I very much enjoyed the place, the office and was happy there. I ran the office, and Ted's role was getting out with the clients particularly the FBU, UNISON, etc.

Both offices went on to become important within the Thompsons' framework, under the stewardship of Judith Gledhill in Leeds and Gavin Roberts in Bristol.

The expansion continued when Robin opened an office in Stoke on 1 November 1991 with Tony Lawton as managing partner. The original proposal from David Skidmore had been that the office would be a joint one, but eventually only Robin's firm proceeded. Tony moved back to the Birmingham office in October 1992 as managing partner when Frank Foy succeeded David Skidmore as Coordinator of Robin's firm.

Tony was followed as managing partner by David Wallen, a veteran of a number of offices, and then in January 1996 by Francine O' Gorman. Francine transferred from Manchester where she had started in July 1979. Her work there had included not just the usual personal injury but large numbers of deafness cases and, increasingly as the years went on, employment law.

Harrow

David Skidmore continued to control the administration of Robin's firm and, through finance and accounts, much of

Brian's. The accounts function moved out of Stanmore into a new office in Harrow in April 1988. Bernard Ferguson was the accounts manager.

Bernard was assisted by Denise Windridge, Wendy Tabner, Yvonne Bolger, Dorrie Collins, Evie Anthony who dealt with wages and Carole Sales who worked as computer supervisor. The accounts and statistics IT, then in its infancy, was supplied by Roan Technology Ltd under Hartley Heaton. When Bernard retired Denise Windridge took over.

Conferences

In the early 1980s, Robin's firm started to hold an annual conference at the Selsdon Park Hotel, Croydon. Simon Walton was the driving force. It began with senior executives and partners only plus trade union guests, but soon expanded, and by 1984 Brian's firm was invited to participate. Simon explains the thinking behind it:

> In the same period, encouraged by Robin Thompson's interest, I was starting to go to American Trial Lawyers Association Conferences in America. I saw how they did things and how they shared information. We decided to try something similar, and the first conference was held of Robin's senior staff with a couple of union officers as guests in the very early 1980s. The following year we repeated the exercise, this time at the Selsdon Park Hotel, and then Brian's firm started to join in. The conference was held from then on every year until 1993. Part of the conference was designed to be educational, a venue where there would be formal lectures and seminars, where people like Andrew Dismore could share his enormous expertise in FBU matters with others from around the country who dealt with FBU cases; part of it involved guest speakers from the trade union world; and part was social where our lawyers and the trade unionists would have a chance to mingle, meet and talk to each other.

The weekend conferences combined work sessions and contributions from invited speakers and were highly successful, not least in giving Thompsons' lawyers from all over the country the chance to meet. These conferences continued until the 1990s and a great deal of course material was compiled by the seminar leaders.

The conference was normally held in the second weekend in June, and without fail the weather would be glorious. The work related aspects were important, but just as important was the social side. The facilities included an outdoor swimming pool, tennis courts and a large piece of ground where an impromptu game of football would be held – usually the Celts versus the rest. For the many Thompsons' lawyers who had moved offices, some more than once, it was particularly enjoyable to meet up with friends and colleagues.

These conferences continued annually until 1993. That year the plenary sessions included talks given by Jeffrey Burke, QC, Brian Langstaff on *The Direct Enforcement of European Law with Special Reference to Health and Safety*, Professor Brian Bercusson of the European University Institute, Florence on *Social Policy after Maastricht*, Manfred Bobke of the EMF on *The Future of Collective Bargaining in Europe*, Professor Frances H. Miller of Boston University on *Health Care and Education Issues*, assisted by panels including John Chowcat of MSF and Rory Murphy of the RCM, David Triesman General Secretary of the AUT, and Nigel de Gruchy General Secretary of NASUWT along with his Deputy General Secretary Eamonn O'Kane.

John Tomlinson MEP gave a talk on *Funding for Trade Unions in the European Community*, and other guests included Bill Jordan President of the AEEU together with his wife and a number of EC members, Roger Lyons General Secretary of MSF, and other senior members, Ken Cameron, General Secretary of the FBU, and others. It was

Induction Course Newcastle 1992
The photograph is of both trainers and trainees. Some of the trainers shown are Colin Simpson, Pauline Chandler, Jane Litherland, the writer, Stephanie Clarke, Eddie Solomons, Rose Malcolm, David Wallen, Nigel Tomkins, Chris Chapman and Mark Berry. Robin can also be seen on this picture.

a high powered gathering.

The firms also began to hold induction courses every couple of years for all new starters. Where Simon had been the driving force with the Selsdon conferences, Eddie Solomons was the main organiser for the Induction Courses, assisted by various others, notably Pauline Chandler and Nigel Tomkins.

These induction courses helped to promote a feeling of camaraderie amongst the young lawyers who joined the firms as well as the production of a large amount of training material.

Simon was also a founder member of APIL, the Association of Personal Injury Lawyers. As Rodger Pannone explained:

At the time I was chairman of the Law Society's Contentious Business Committee when Gordon Borrie, the Director General of Fair Trading, called me in to say that he was going to impose advertising on the legal profession. Having

Jersey group: Clockwise, starting from the left: *Colin Ettinger, Lawrence Lumsden, Nigel Tomkins, Eddie Solomons, Frank Foy, Mark Berry and Simon Walton. These Thompsons' partners were relaxing over lunch at the end of the Induction Course held on Jersey. Their relaxation did not last long. Robin had been otherwise engaged talking to John Stalker (whom he had bumped into) and was not invited to the lunch which had been an impromptu arrangement. He was not best pleased!*

discussed this on the committee and talked to others I set up APIL in conjunction with Simon Walton and two others including John Melville Williams who was the first president and Mike Napier.

In more recent years the firm held an Industrial Diseases Conference at Warwick University in May 2005 following on from a similar event in Newcastle and a National Conference for all their lawyers, by now numbering over 350, again in Warwick in March 2007. Tony Lawton, the firm's Director of Training and Legal education has played a key role in organising these conferences.

Chapter 24
Personal injury campaigns and test cases

The period from 1974 brought a number of major test cases. The times were changing. No longer were people so prepared to accept as pure misfortune the injuries they suffered; and the underlying legal position was improving with new regulations designed to protect workmen and women. All this was happening at a time when the consequences to health of working conditions experienced over many years were coming home to roost. The new offices opened by the firms helped cement regional relationships and were instrumental in promoting a continuing large increase in the personal injury work sent to the firms from the unions. A classic example was the intake of deafness work and the litigation which arose as a result.

Deafness

It had been known for decades that excessive noise could damage the hearing of those who had to endure it. W.H. Thompson had given talks on the subject in 1932.

Despite this, until the 1970s legal actions for compensation for noise induced hearing loss and tinnitus were almost unknown. By the latter part of the decade a trickle of cases was starting to turn into a flood, and in the early 1980s many thousands of cases were being put forward, mainly by the Association of Boilermakers, Blacksmiths, Shipwrights and Structural Workers (ASBSBSW, later to become part of the GMB) and by the Amalgamated Union of Engineering Workers (AUEW). Nearly 8,000 cases were received from the Boilermakers

(ASBSBSW) alone at the beginning of 1982, as Frank Foy describes:

The Boilermakers Union office was in Jesmond in Newcastle – close to where I lived in fact – and the Boilermakers got to know about us. Jim McFall was Executive Committee member for the Liverpool & Northern Ireland Region of the Boilermakers and was instrumental in the test cases that were brought in Northern Ireland against Harland & Wolff. One of the medical experts in those cases Ross Cole mentioned me.

At the time the Boilermakers had an arrangement with the Iron Trades, the major insurers for the shipbuilding companies and much heavy industry, where compensation figures were paid under a scale to members whose hearing had been damaged, without any input from lawyers. At the same time I in particular was pursuing cases and recovering much higher awards of compensation. There was one particularly noteworthy case in this respect, a case of Heslop heard before Mr Justice Mustill in Newcastle.

In any event, one day we got a call from Jim Murray, the General Secretary of the Boilermakers Union, seeking our advice on the prospects of success in their members' cases with a view to taking them over. It turned out that they had 6,000 or 8,000 cases waiting to be dealt with. It would also be fair to say that Geoff Thomas, a senior partner in Brian Thompson's in Cardiff, was also instrumental. He was friendly with an EC Member of the Boilermakers Union, Alan Haddon. I contacted Geoff Thomas. I knew that we would need the help of Robin Thompson & Partners to deal with this sort of volume of case … . I prepared an analysis for the union … and there was a long meeting involving me, Geoff Shears, Nick Carter, Simon Walton, David Stevenson and Geoff Thomas, as a result of which we decided that we would take on the work. I then attended the Executive

Council of the Union the following day with Simon Walton and one other, probably David Stevenson.

We were still a very small office in Newcastle. I recall that Mark Berry had just joined us but we already had many deafness cases from other unions, and I was dealing with very little else.[So] when we took the cases on many were shipped out to other offices, including substantial numbers to Cardiff and elsewhere.

Having received this huge influx of work, we then set about preparing test cases for trial. Mr Justice Mustill was assigned to deal with the cases and he requested a group of test cases to be heard. We were happy about this because he had dealt with the Heslop case in which we had received a very favourable judgment. Mark Berry and I spent a great deal of time sifting through many cases and choosing the best ones. Mark had day-to-day conduct of the cases but I was involved and we met every day and sometimes in the evenings discussing and organising how we were proceeding. Mustill J dealt with all the interlocutory applications and all these involved leading counsel. We used Richard Clegg QC, and Marrons who were also involved in another batch of the test cases used Christopher Rose QC.

The trial commenced and was lengthy. Indeed, it concluded down in London as the judge went back from Newcastle to London towards the end.

Thompson and Others v Smiths Shiprepairers (North Shields) Ltd [1984] 1 All ER 881

The six test cases [three handled by Thompsons and three by Marrons] were heard in 1983. All involved men who worked in the shipbuilding or ship repairing industry from the 1940s to the 1970s.

By the time judgment was given, Frank Foy had transferred to Birmingham office.

After starting in Birmingham office I returned to Newcastle for the judgment in the deafness test cases. We knew we would win, but the question was to what extent we would win. There were two very important issues. One was the date of guilty knowledge. We believed that it would not be later than 1963 and might be earlier in the shipbuilding industry. The other big issue was that of apportionment. We argued that the exposure to noise in the course of employment made a material contribution and that therefore the claimants or plaintiffs as they were called under the system at the time should receive compensation in full for the whole of their hearing loss. The defendants argued in favour of apportionment. There was some leading research at the time produced by academics Burns and Robinson. Robinson was the statistician and Burns was the ENT specialist. The defendants persuaded Robinson to give evidence at the trial and Mustill J, who had studied maths at university, got thoroughly involved in the statistical evidence which he understood in full. I recall during the trial our medical evidence suggesting that apportionment was not possible because it was too imprecise and Mustill J responding that "the whole system is shot through with imprecision". The atmosphere changed and it was clear that apportionment was going to rule the day.

In any event we won, but apportionment applied and guilty date was set at 1963.

The judge found that a reasonable employer would have provided hearing protection against excessive noise from 1963 when the Factory Inspectorate published a booklet Noise and the Worker, by which time hearing protection was available. The claimants were all entitled therefore to compensation. He went on to find that as it was possible to calculate that part of the damage which occurred after 1963, he would apportion the compensation accordingly. This meant that compensation would be awarded, but only for that part of the hearing damage caused by excessive noise exposure after 1963.

Following this judgment, almost all the major liability insurers agreed to a scheme of compensation for members of most of the unions on whose behalf Thompsons acted and which was negotiated by David Skidmore. David identified the fact that although the levels of compensation awarded by the judge had been less than the sums contended for, insurers faced major problems as a result of the judgment. In his words:

Some years earlier I had met John Robinson of the Iron Trades, the major employers' liability insurer for most of the defendants in the cases. Accordingly, I rang him in September 1983 to suggest a meeting. We met and nine weeks later we had the National Deafness Scheme. John Robinson involved various other insurance companies who delegated authority to him to negotiate on their behalf. I contacted various unions and solicitors, who delegated the job to me. The Scheme was set up and at the time the insurers thought it would last for a few years at the most. In the event it proved to be so successful that it continued well into the 1990s with increases in compensation levels from time to time.

It is estimated that the number of successful claimants who benefited from this case ran to hundreds of thousands.

The Deafness Scheme has proved to be the first of a number of schemes. It was a forerunner of dealing with mass claims through the legal system.

These days, cases are assessed for compensation individually. Happily the incidence of noise induced hearing loss is much less than it was. As is often the case, successful claims for compensation were followed by

Nick Carter and David Skidmore

regulation (in this case the Noise at Work Regulations, 1989), and improved safety performance by the employers.

Nurses' lifting

While big test cases such as the deafness cases dominated the landscape for several years, at the same time thousands of other cases were being pursued across the firms on a daily basis, and some of these achieved results which had a practical and widespread impact. One example was in the area of nurses' lifting

Williams v Gwent Area Health Authority [1982] Stephen Brown J –unreported

Until the 1980s large numbers of nurses and care workers suffered back injuries as a result of patient handling. However it was regarded as very difficult to bring a successful claim – unless for example it could be shown that two nurses were required and one had to do the job alone.

Mrs Williams, the claimant in this case, had to lift a large heavy patient. She was assisted by another nurse. They were using the lifting technique commonly adopted in the hospital. The patient made a sudden move during the manoeuvre, and Mrs Williams injured her back. Thompsons obtained documentary evidence that in the five years leading up to the accident there had been 136 lifting injuries in North Gwent Health District alone, 16 of which were at Blaina Hospital where the claimant worked. Evidence was called from a Nurse Adviser who had served on a working party which produced a booklet in 1979 *Avoiding low back injury among nurses*. He was able to show that the lifting technique used, known as the drag lift, was dangerous and that safer techniques could have been used. The case was successful.

Although it was not reported in the Law Reports, the case achieved a good deal of publicity. It helped to heighten awareness of the problem, and lawyers began to pursue many other cases based on lifting techniques. The employers could no longer defend cases simply by asserting the old refrains 'pure accident' and 'unavoidable'. The case was dealt with by the author.

Firefighters and 'special risks'

The development through the common law of the law relating to compensation sometimes gave rise to odd and unfair rules. One such rule was the doctrine that rescuers such as firefighters could only recover compensation when injured in the course of their duty if they were exposed to an *exceptional* risk which was foreseeable, and that compensation should not be paid if the risk was an 'ordinary' risk inherent in fire-fighting, even where the risk arose as a result of negligence.

Thompsons challenged this approach successfully in the Salmon case:

Salmon v Seafarer Restaurants Ltd [1983] 3 All ER 729
A fireman was injured in an explosion in a fish and chip shop owned by the defendants. The fire was caused by an employee negligently failing to extinguish the gas flame under a chip fryer before going home. As a result the fat caught fire; the explosion happened when the fire melted a seal on a gas meter allowing gas to escape. The defendants argued an occupier's duty to firemen attending in the cause of their work was limited to special or exceptional risks over and above the ordinary risks necessarily incidental to a fireman's job. The court disagreed, finding that an occupier was under the ordinary duty; that as the fire was caused by their employee's negligence and since it was reasonably foreseeable that a fireman would be required to attend the fire and that such an explosion might occur, the defendants were liable.

The defendants' argument on the old 'special risk' rule was put to bed for ever as a result a successful hearing in the House of Lords in Ogwo:

Ogwo v Taylor [1987] 3 All ER 961
The defendant negligently started a fire by using a blowlamp to burn off the paint on the fascia board under the eaves of his house. The fire service was called, and Mr Taylor suffered serious burn injuries whilst tackling the fire. He brought an action contending that because the fire was negligently started and because he had been injured as a result, he was entitled to damages. His claim was rejected by the judge. Mr Taylor appealed and his appeal was upheld. The defendant appealed to the House of Lords, contending that a person who negligently started a fire was only liable to a fireman if there was an exceptional risk associated with the fire which imposed an additional hazard over and above the ordinary risks inherent in fire-fighting. The House of Lords rejected their argument and decided that where it could be foreseen that a fireman

would have to attend a fire which was negligently started, the person starting the fire owed a duty of care to the fireman and was liable.

Both these cases were dealt with by Stephen Dudley one of the stalwarts of Ilford office who worked for the firm from 1968 to 1989.

These cases were two of many fought particularly during the 1980s and '90s which set precedents and improved the prospects both of bringing successful claims for firefighters and improving the levels of compensation which could be obtained. The firm has always had a team of experienced lawyers specialising in the many unusual issues in firefighter cases and a very close relationship with the Fire Brigades' Union.

Welders' lung

The human legacy and toll of injuries and diseases from old manufacturing industries was again highlighted in the welders' lung cases.

Knox & ors v Cammell Laird Shipbuilders Ltd (unreported) [1990]

In the 1980s the GMB union referred to Thompsons a number of cases relating to former shipyard workers mostly from Merseyside, who were suffering from a variety of respiratory diseases, including chronic bronchitis. They believed their condition to be at least partly attributable to exposure to copious quantities of welding fumes. Mostly this had occurred in very confined, unventilated spaces on board ships under construction or repair.

Test cases were pursued to trial involving a number of such welders. The judge found that by 1951 the employers should have realised the risks and instituted safeguards such as the provision of proper exhaust mechanisms. The employers were at fault, and for those who worked in dense fumes in confined spaces compensation was payable for the

Pauline Chandler and David Stevenson

consequences. However, the judge also apportioned the damages and discounted them because of the effects of smoking.

These test cases were expensive and high risk. They were handled by Pauline Chandler. As ever, the union funded the claims and faced the possibility of being met with a huge legal bill. Mark Berry recalls early on, before the litigation started, attending a conference with Pauline and Joe O'Hara (then the union's legal officer and later himself to become a Thompsons' partner). After discussing at length the likely prospects of success and more particularly the serious risk of failure with a crippling costs bill, Joe gave Thompsons the go-ahead to proceed, to which Pauline responded 'Right, we'll crash on then'! And of course she did, never once giving away to the defendants any hint of anxiety or concern.

The success of the cases meant that many more claimants, mostly elderly and infirm, were able to bring claims and secure some compensation for their respiratory illness.

Passive smoking

Thompsons has long been involved in a campaign in respect of passive smoking. An early boost was given by the Bland case, handled by Simon Denyer, which did not proceed to trial but resulted in an out-of-court settlement.

Bland v Stockport MBC (settlement 1993)

Mrs Bland worked for the council from 1979 in a large open-plan office with little or no ventilation. Until a no-smoking policy was implemented in 1990 she was exposed to a large amount of cigarette and pipe smoke causing persistent coughs, sore throats and catarrh. There was some improvement after 1990. A settlement was achieved in the sum of £15,000.

The case gave rise to a good deal of publicity and had a substantial impact in highlighting awareness of the problem and causing employers to evaluate their own smoking policies.

Stress

Another case which made a major impact on health in the workplace was Walker, a case handled by John Usher from Thompsons' Leeds office, and the first successful claim for stress induced illness caused as a result of work. It brought widespread publicity. Although the judgment in favour of the claimant was very much based on its own facts, it is an example of a case which has an impact well beyond the narrow area of law involved. In particular, the case affected and influenced the thinking and behaviour of personnel departments all over the country and has caused employers to consider the emotional as well as physical well-being of their employees.

Walker v Northumberland County Council [1995] 1 All ER 737

Mr Walker was an area social services officer from 1970 to

1987. He was responsible for managing four teams of social services fieldworkers in an area which had a high proportion of child care problems. In 1986 he had a nervous breakdown because of the stress and pressures of work and was off work for three months. Before he returned to work his employers agreed to provide assistance to lessen the burden. In fact the assistance provided was limited and the position was worse rather than better. Six months later he suffered a further breakdown and was forced to stop work permanently.

The court found that his first breakdown was not reasonably foreseeable; however, the council should have foreseen that if Mr Walker was exposed to the same workload there was a risk of a further breakdown. They should have provided assistance, were negligent for the second breakdown and therefore liable to pay compensation.

The Walker case has subsequently been discussed in a number of further decisions of the courts, including the Court of Appeal, and has had far reaching implications.

The Criminal Injuries Compensation Authority Campaign

In 1994, the Tory government attempted to change the Criminal Injuries Compensation Scheme without obtaining parliamentary approval. The situation was an odd one. The scheme had been running since 1964 but had never been placed on a statutory basis. This was partly remedied in 1988, but the relevant sections of the Criminal Justice Act of that year had never been brought into force. In 1994 the government decided to change the system completely and introduce a tariff system and make various other changes, without even referring the matter back to parliament.

R. v Secretary of State for the Home Department Ex p. Fire Brigades Union [1995] 2 A.C. 513

The Fire Brigades Union and other bodies applied for judicial review of Michael Howard's decision to replace the scheme with a new tariff based scheme without obtaining parliamentary approval. They were unsuccessful before the Divisional Court, but succeeded in part at the Court of Appeal. This held that, while under Section 171(1) of the Act it was for the Secretary of State for the Home Department to decide when to bring into force the relevant statutory provisions and he could not be said to have acted unlawfully by not implementing the statutory scheme, his decision to introduce a new scheme which was radically different from the scheme which parliament had approved was unlawful as long as the statutory provisions remained unrepealed. The Secretary of State for the Home Department appealed and the union cross appealed.

It was held, dismissing the Secretary of State for the Home Department's appeal, and the union's cross appeal, that under the Act the Secretary of State for the Home Department had some discretion as to when to introduce the statutory scheme and was not under a legal duty to appoint a commencement date, merely to keep the question of time of implementation under consideration. However, by announcing that the provisions in the Act would not now be implemented, the Secretary of State for the Home Department had acted unlawfully. His decision to introduce a new scheme, which was inconsistent with the statutory scheme, when the statutory provisions remained unrepealed, was an abuse of the prerogative power.

This success in the House of Lords gained valuable time for proper consideration and debate, and when the matter came before parliament a number of important concessions were gained.

The CICA scheme in fact was a regular battleground for

Thompsons. Some years earlier Simon Walton had successfully spearheaded the campaign on behalf of train drivers who suffered mental injury as a result of suicides on the lines, the result of which was that train drivers were included as victims of violent crime for the purposes of the scheme.

Damages

Winning the entitlement to compensation is only part of the story. The other is ensuring that the correct compensation is awarded. An example of a significant award was the judgment in 1987 in

Cook v Englehard Industries & Ors. [1987] (unreported)
Following a ten day trial on liability, agreed damages were awarded in the sum of £850,000 in a case sponsored by ASTMS. The previous highest known award in a personal injury case had been £675,000.

Over the following years levels of damages awards grew significantly not only in line with inflation but also because of greater awareness of and ability to recover care costs, the cost of aids and equipment and so on.

In 1994 Stuart Henderson then of Thompsons achieved a stunning success when he achieved damages of £3.4 million in a case for **Christine Leung**, believed to be another record award at the time.

Of course, behind every damages award is a story of injury and hurt. The highest awards are made to those who have suffered the most and have the greatest needs. Thompsons have campaigned over many years to increase the levels of damages for personal injuries.

Damages are made up of a number of elements – the sum for pain, suffering and loss of amenity, the sum for actual past losses, for future losses and so on. From time to time major breakthroughs have been achieved in persuading the courts to add new and additional heads or elements of damage, thus adding to the overall levels of compensation recovered.

One classic example of this is damages for handicap on the labour market, commonly referred to as Smith and Manchester damages.

Smith v Manchester Corporation [1974] 17 KIR 1
Mrs Smith, who worked in an old people's home, tripped and fell injuring her elbow. She had a continuing disability but returned to work. The employers undertook to keep her in employment for as long as they could properly do so. In spite of the undertaking, the Court of Appeal increased the award by £1000 to take account of loss of future earning capacity – in other words, the fact that she would, as a result of the injuries, find it more difficult to get another job if she ever lost her present one.

This landmark case, handled by Keith Berry, has resulted in extra compensation in many thousands of cases. In every case since this one, where there is a continuing disability leading to an increased risk on the open labour market – such as that faced by Mrs Smith, extra damages can be argued for and usually awarded.

A similar point arose in respect of awards for loss of congenial employment. Such awards are now commonplace where a claimant is forced by his or her injuries to retire early or change to less enjoyable work, and apply particularly in cases where the claimant has had to give up work involving an element of public service, for example work as a nurse, firefighter, etc.

A typical example is Hale v London Underground, one of many cases fought by Andrew Dismore, who almost single-handedly pioneered such claims as an additional award of damages in the late 1980s and early 1990s. Hale was also notable for the award of damages for post-traumatic stress in the absence of any substantial physical injury, possibly the first such case (and certainly one of the earliest) to receive such an award at trial.

Hale v London Underground [1993] PIQR Q30

Mr Hale, a firefighter, was injured during the course of duty at the King's Cross disaster on 18 November 1987. He suffered no significant physical injury (although he collapsed from exhaustion and had to be helped to the surface). His actions at the disaster were such that he received three awards for bravery. However, it subsequently transpired that he suffered severe post-traumatic stress disorder and depression, had to give up his job and would never make a full recovery. An award of £27,500 was made for the PTSD as well as all the usual awards for past and future losses and handicap on the labour market. In addition, the judge agreed that there should be a separate and additional award of £5000 for loss of congenial employment.

Andrew Dismore dealt with a number of cases arising out of this disaster in which 31 people were killed and many others injured. One of the dead was Station Officer Townsley, and a number of other firefighters were included among the injured. Within days of the disaster Dismore had briefed Ben Hytner, QC, and together they visited the scene. He recalls: 'The scene was horrendous. Above the fire was complete devastation although below it was untouched. The smell was horrific.'

After the disaster Andrew collated a lengthy report on fire service protective equipment, and took many statements which were used at the Fennell Inquiry which gave rise to the Fennell Report. One of the results of the report was a considerable improvement in protective equipment provided to firefighters including improved gloves and leggings. There was a major reform of Fire Precautions Law regarding stations although twenty years on it is interesting to note that there is a threatened move away from the prescriptive approach to a risk assessment approach. Another consequence was that the partial ban on smoking in underground stations became total.

At the time, Kings Cross was a turning point in demonstrating how to use the media as a tool to increase the level of damages, and Thompsons started to engage with the media more effectively as a result.

After Kings Cross a campaign got underway to classify corporate manslaughter as a crime, a campaign that has only recently come (partially) to fruition. Andrew was in the forefront of this campaign along with others including Tom Jones and Mick Antoniw.

Andrew worked for Robin Thompson and Partners from 1978 until 1995, the last nine years as an equity partner. For many years he handled the FBU folio and had many dealings with Ken Cameron along with many others from the union. He dealt with a significant number of major and important cases including Smoker, mentioned below, Hale and the CICA campaign judicial review case. He also worked with Stephen Dudley on Salmon and Ogwo, and was an active campaigner for example as Chairman of the APIL Damages Special Interest Group. Andrew's work as an MP [for Hendon from 1997 to 2010] included much important committee work – for example as Chair of the Human Rights Committee.

The Smoker case related to pension loss. It had long been the rule (known to lawyers as the rule in Parry v Cleaver) that if you were claiming a loss of earnings as a result of your injuries, the money you received from an occupational pension could not be deducted in assessing your loss. The reason was simple. You had paid, at least to some extent, for the pension yourself, and it was not appropriate to take into account the pension receipt except as against any actual future loss of pension itself. (In other words the receipt of pension could only be set against any claimed loss of pension). This rule came under significant attack in yet another case involving a firefighter.

Smoker v London Fire and Civil Defence Authority [1991] 2 All ER 449

Mr Smoker was injured as a result of the defendants' negligence. He was unable to return to work. He claimed a loss of earnings. The defendant employers said that in assessing his loss he should give credit for the ill health and injury pensions they paid to him under the terms of a compulsory pension scheme to which he had contributed. The defendant employers failed to persuade the judge but then appealed direct to the House of Lords.

The House of Lords ruled that since the claimant had purchased his pension, which was therefore the fruit, through insurance, of all the moneys set aside in respect of his past work, the pension to which he became entitled in respect of his illness/disablement was not deductible from the damages awarded for loss of earnings.

The case turns on what might be regarded as a technical point, but as well as being clearly correct, it has made a substantial impact in preserving decent awards of damages in all serious cases involving loss of earnings where the claimant receives an ill health occupational pension.

By the early 1990s the legislative framework for personal injury cases was starting to change, and this time the changes were prompted by Europe. A number of EC Directives led to a raft of new regulation such as The Noise at Work Regulations, 1989; the Control of Substances Hazardous to Health Regulations (COSHH), 1988; and the Control of Asbestos at Work Regulations, 1987.

New impetus was given to European safety legislation when, with the passing of the Single European Act in 1987, two new articles were added to the Treaty of Rome. Article 100A, introduced to ensure free trade in products including those used at work, required that EC proposals must be based on a 'high level of protection for health, safety, the environment and consumers'. Article 118A allowed the Council of Ministers to adopt directives aimed at 'harmonising laws on the working environment' and 'setting minimum requirements for health and safety'.

The result was an ambitious programme sponsored by the EC on safety at work. Various directives were passed laying down general duties and minimum standards and incorporated into UK law. The regulations became known as 'the six pack' and included:

The Management of Health and Safety at Work Regulations, 1992;
The Workplace (Health, Safety and Welfare) Regulations, 1992;
The Provision and Use of Work Equipment Regulations, 1992;
The Personal Protective Equipment Regulations, 1992
The Manual Handling Regulations, 1992; and
The Health and Safety (Display Screen Equipment) Regulations, 1992.

Twenty years after Robens had reported, the old piecemeal legislative framework was at last consigned to the dustbin of history, to be replaced by new regulations designed not only to be all encompassing but with teeth as well.

Booklet produced in 1993 explaining the new statutory framework

Chapter 25
Employment Law starts to bite (but sometimes its bark was louder… .)

In 1972 Dr Otto Kahn-Freund delivered the Hamlyn Lecture *Labour and the Law*. In his introduction, 'Some Reflections on Law and Power', he noted:

The evolution of an orderly and (compared with most other countries) even today reasonably well functioning system of labour relations is one of the great achievements of British civilisation. This system of collective bargaining rests on a balance of the collective forces of management and organised labour.

Notwithstanding this, the clamour for legal intervention in industrial disputes became overwhelming. The decades which followed produced not just an economic but also a legislative assault on the trades unions, matched by a vast increase in individual protections for workers. The unions turned their attention to the use of individual employment protection rights to protect their members. This shift gathered pace during the 1990s when unions increasingly redirected their services to members from the collective to the individual.

Early forms of individual protection were provided by the Redundancy Payments Act, 1965 in respect of redundancy, the Industrial Relations Act, 1971 in respect of unfair dismissal, and the Equal Pay Act, 1970 in respect of equal pay for women. These were followed by the Sex Discrimination Act, 1975, the Employment Protection Act, 1975 and the Race Relations Act, 1976. The intention was that the remedies available in what were then called

Industrial Tribunals could be obtained in an informal and non-legalistic setting with representation provided for the employees by trade union representatives.

All this resulted in a substantial increase in work sent to Thompsons arising out of employment cases such as unfair dismissal, equal pay, sex and race discrimination, redundancy and other 'individual' employment issues as well as those collective issues where new rights applied such as redundancy consultation. Thompsons brought many test cases, specialising in particular in matters which would have maximum impact for groups of workers.

The change in Thompsons' structure in 1996 when the firms of Robin and Brian merged to form Thompsons coincided with a welcome change of government, elected in 1997, which repaired some of the damage caused by anti-union legislation. The Employment Relations Act, 1999 restored to an extent the right to recognition, and there was a raft of new regulations, many owing their origin to European Directives.

Indeed the last two decades of the twentieth century saw the protection available to workers mushroom, a good deal of it on the back of European regulation but at the same time the whole area became ever more complex and legalistic.

Important cases are reported in the Law Reports either in Industrial Cases Reports or in Industrial Relations Law Reports. Despite the fact that this is a modern area of law, by January 2006 Thompsons had had well over five hundred reported cases in the Law Reports.

A few of the more important cases are recounted below, mainly to illustrate the range of issues now covered by legislation. Some of these cases were successful and have had a lasting impact; some were unsuccessful – for example some of those below on recognition – and are indicative of the problems still facing unions.

The cases fought over the years cover every aspect of employment law, with the firm representing unions or their members in tens of thousands of cases. By the late 1990s many unions which had until then instructed Thompsons only in appeal cases or particularly difficult matters such as race or sex discrimination, had decided to hive off the whole of their tribunal work to the firm, resulting in a massive expansion of the firm's Employment Rights Unit (the 'ERU'), an expansion fuelled by the welcome reduction by the Labour Government in the qualifying period of service from two years to one in unfair dismissal claims. The benefit for unions was that they were able to redirect their resources away from tribunal claims handling and towards recruitment of new members.

The firm's employment unit is now headed nationally by Victoria Phillips, having initially been led by Stephen Cavalier, now the firm's Chief Executive Officer. Victoria leads an ever expanding team of lawyers organised into regions each with its own regional head. The regional heads include lawyers such as Susan Harris in the Midlands, Mark Berry in the North East, with decades of experience of dealing with complex employment cases and liaising with the unions at the highest level.

It is impossible to do justice to the scale and diversity of cases, but worth mentioning a few of particular importance and interest.

Trade union and collective labour law

The modern regulatory state has affected trade unions more than many other organisations. The common law's hostility to workers acting collectively has been augmented by the Thatcherite restrictions on industrial action (retained in their key elements under New Labour) and by greater regulation of trade unions' internal affairs.

Industrial action

In the realm of industrial action, unions have been caught in a tangled web of excessive legislation. Any union wishing to take industrial action has to jump through numerous hoops to avoid illegality e.g. postal ballots before action; two seven-day notices to employers; appointment of independent scrutineers. Thompsons has been at the fore of advising unions and defending them against applications for injunctions, where the employer is often in the driving seat.

The Wandsworth Council case recounted below demonstrates some of the complexities faced by unions before authorising industrial action. The legal exemptions from certain civil actions still apply, but only if a number of conditions are met. More than ever unions cannot move without complying with detailed statutory procedures.

Wandsworth London Borough Council v NASUWT [1994] ICR 82

The union was campaigning for a reduction in its members' increasingly excessive workload. A ballot paper was sent to all members as follows:

In order to protest against the excessive workload and unreasonable imposition made upon teachers, as a consequence of national curriculum assessment and testing, are you willing to take action, short of strike action?

88 per cent of members voted *'yes'*. The council sought an injunction to prevent the action on the basis that it was political and the usual immunity did not apply. Thompsons represented the union both before the judge and the Court of Appeal and reason prevailed. The court found that although the union had criticisms of the national curriculum on educational grounds, the dispute was

mainly concerned with the extra working time imposed on them, and this was correctly identified in the ballot paper. Accordingly the matter was a trade dispute and the union was protected from liability.

Another well publicised and rather more recent case involved workers at Heathrow airport. It was handled by Richard Arthur and the result can probably be described as a score draw:

Gate Gourmet v TGWU [2005] IRLR 88

A bitter dispute grew out of the efforts of equity investors trying to cut costs at Heathrow Airport. The staff were prevented from leaving the canteen and many were dismissed by tannoy. The issues in court were whether the pickets at the gates and the demonstrators on land nearby had exceeded what was permitted. Although the Court imposed some restrictions, the case was notable for the successful use of freedom of speech and the right to demonstrate in a trade dispute. The High Court refused to order the complete removal of peaceful demonstrators and expressly relied on their European Convention rights – an enlightened approach that has been followed in other cases.

Recognition

A key area of collective labour law is the right to require the employer to recognise the union for collective bargaining. An example of the difficulties occurred in the Grunwick case, *Grunwick Processing Laboratories Ltd v ACAS [1978] ICR 232*, described earlier.

The right to refer matters of recognition to ACAS had been given by the Employment Protection Act 1975, and ACAS was the statutory body charged with the general duty of promoting the improvement of industrial relations.

The first test of the provision came in the Powley case which again illustrated the problem, notwithstanding the Act, of securing negotiating rights:

Brian Thompson and Clive Jenkins
(General Secretary ASTMS)

Powley v ACAS & anor [1978] ICR 124
On the day the Act came into force, ASTMS referred the question of recognition by an insurance company to ACAS. A poll a year earlier had resulted in a majority voting against ASTMS having full negotiating rights. Conciliation proved impossible, and ACAS, after making enquiries and consulting the staff association, proposed to issue a questionnaire to the company's employees. The staff association complained about the questionnaire. When ACAS nevertheless proceeded, the claimant, representing the staff association, sought an injunction.

The judge found that even though ACAS could only make a recommendation, it had misdirected itself, had posed the wrong question and did not hold the balance fairly as between ASTMS and the staff association. The injunction was granted. So much for the recognition provisions!

The 1975 provisions were repealed and a statutory right to recognition was not restored until the Employment Relations Act 1999. Whatever its defects, this legislation has met with greater success than its 1975 predecessor and Thompsons has acted for unions in a number of important cases:

R (British Broadcasting Corporation) v Central Arbitration Committee & Anor [2003] ICR 1543

BECTU applied to the Central Arbitration Committee (the CAC) for recognition on behalf of a group of cameramen and women who were engaged on freelance contracts. The Committee decided on a preliminary issue that the union's proposed bargaining unit was a group of 'workers' and not professionals within the meaning of the Act since there was no form of regulation of their activities.

The Corporation sought judicial review and succeeded. The Committee was obliged to reconsider because although the existence or otherwise of a regulatory body could be relevant or a significant feature pointing to the exercise of a profession, it was not a necessary condition, and the imposition of such a test as determinative was an error of law.

However, when the CAC reconsidered the case and applied the correct legal test as required by the Court, BECTU was again successful and obtained an award of recognition. Stephen Cavalier dealt with the case.

The next case described (also for NUJ) was handled by Richard Arthur and involved a journalist who worked at the Racing Post:

R (National Union of Journalists) v Central Arbitration Committee & Anor [2005] ICR 493

The union applied for recognition in relation to sports journalists at a newspaper publisher. Half the journalists were in the union. The CAC rejected the application as inadmissible on the ground that another union, which had at most one member in the sports division, already had a recognition agreement with the publisher.

The union sought judicial review, relying on the fact that the other union was not in a position to conduct collective bargaining, had in fact conducted no negotiations, and in any event the statutory position set out in the Act was incompatible with article 11 of the European Convention for the Protection of Human Rights.

The judge rejected the claim. He found that the written agreement the company had with the other union was binding and in force and therefore the CAC could not, under the Act, recommend recognition of any other union; further, the Convention did not impose on the state any positive obligation to grant a union the right to conduct collective bargaining with any particular employer.

Despite this set back, unions continue to use the 1999 provisions to press for collective bargaining rights when employers refuse to accept the wishes of their workers that they speak collectively on issues such as pay, hours and holidays.

Some employers have resorted to issuing individual contracts to avoid collectively-agreed terms and conditions. This practice led to landmark litigation, handled by Stephen Cavalier. It involved trade union recognition but was really about the right to trade union membership and victimisation. It took the European Court of Human Rights to sort out the mess UK law was in and impose some justice.

Wilson & NUJ v United Kingdom; Palmer, Wyeth & RMT v United Kingdom; Doolan v United Kingdom [2002] IRLR 568

By the time these cases reached the European Court of Justice they had been consolidated. The Wilson case involved Associated Newspapers who essentially wanted to get out of a collective agreement and attempted to do so by stealth by offering new individual contracts. Dave

Wilson had the courage to say no.

Mr Wilson was employed as a journalist. He was a member of the NUJ, which had for years been recognised by the employers for collective bargaining. In 1989 the employers gave notice that they were ceasing to recognise the union and were instituting a system of individual contracts. Mr Wilson refused to sign. In subsequent years, his salary increased but was never raised to the same level as those who had accepted personal contracts. Similar issues arose in the other cases.

Mr Wilson won his claim in the Employment Tribunal, relying on S.23 of the Employment Protection (Consolidation) Act 1978 which provided that

> every person shall have the right not to have action (short of dismissal) taken against him as an individual for the purpose of ... preventing or deterring him from being or seeking to become a member of a trade union, or penalising him for doing so.

The employers successfully appealed to the Employment Appeal Tribunal which held that there could be no breach of S.23 where the employee's right to remain a member of the union was unaffected by the employer's action.

The applicants appealed to the Court of Appeal which overturned the EAT's ruling and restored the original decision. However, the employers then appealed successfully to the House of Lords. The Lords decided that the word 'action' in S.23 could not include an omission (in this case the withholding of benefits), and in any event the right conferred by S.23 was limited to trade union membership and did not extend to making use of the union's services!

By this time, S.23 had been re-enacted as S.146 of the Trade Union and Labour Relations Act 1992; and in order to counteract the Court of Appeal's judgment, the government had passed S.13 of the Trade Union Reform and Employment Rights Act 1993 to provide that there was no infringement of the right under S.146 where 'the employer's purpose was to further a change in his relationship with all or any class of his employees unless the action was one which no reasonable employer could take'.

Following criticism of S.13 by the Committee of Independent Experts set up under the European Social Charter and by the ILO's Committee on Freedom of Association, the applicants applied to the European Court of Human Rights, alleging a breach of Article 11 (which provides not only for freedom of association but also bars unnecessary restrictions on that right).

The application was successful. The Court held that by permitting employers to use financial incentives to induce employees to surrender important union rights, the United Kingdom government had failed in its positive obligation to secure the enjoyment of Article 11 rights.

This case was the first case in the European Court of Human Rights where the Court found in favour of the union/ union member, and led to changes to UK law to protect workers from this kind of victimisation.

Subsequently, Iain Birrell in the Newcastle office used the new law to gain awards of compensation for GMB members whom ASDA had tried to contract out of their collective terms and conditions, and Thompsons has advised a number of other unions so that they could defeat the employers' attempts and so retain the bargaining structures their predecessors had fought so hard to establish.

Unions' rules

The new regulatory regimes impinge on the internal organisation of trade unions – who can insist on being a member; how their elections are conducted; how their financial and political activity is overseen.

A major case, involving the fundamental right of a union to decide who can and cannot be a member, reached the European Court of Human Rights in a case that was handled by Victoria Phillips (head of Thompsons' Employment Rights Unit) and involved ASLEF:

ASLEF v UK [2007] IRLR 361

A member of the train driver's union ASLEF decided to expel one of its members after he stood as a BNP candidate in local elections. This was contrary to the union's rule that individuals who hold views that are diametrically opposed to the objects of the union cannot be members. The member challenged his expulsion and two employment tribunals agreed with him, saying that section 174 of the Trade Union and Labour Relations (Consolidation) Act, 1992 bars unions from action that is due, at least in part, to membership of a political party.

The union lodged a claim at the European Court of Human Rights arguing that UK law contravened article 11 (freedom of assembly and association) of the European Convention on Human Rights. The question for the court was whether UK law struck the right balance between the member's rights and those of the trade union. Deciding that it had not, the Court of Human Rights recognised that trade unions are not bodies 'solely devoted to politically-neutral aspects of the wellbeing of members, but are often ideological, with strongly held views on social and political issues'.

Because the membership of the BNP was in fundamental conflict with the union's political objectives, ASLEF was therefore entitled to expel him. Whilst individuals have the right to participate in collective bodies, that right is conditional on abiding by their rules and accepting the outcomes of decisions they reach. Whilst very different on its facts from the ground breaking Wilson case, this case again uses European Convention rights to allow unions a greater margin of self-regulation than UK law would otherwise allow.

Finally, Thompsons has assisted unions in their dealings with the Government regulator, the Certification Officer. The Tories' legislation gave the CO jurisdiction in a number of areas, including the conduct of elections for union executives and general secretaries and the compliance with a range of rules including those relating to the discipline of members.

Redundancy, Redundancy Consultation and Transfer of Undertakings

Redundancy is a concept which sounds straightforward. But what rules should apply when it comes to choosing which employees are 'selected' for dismissal for redundancy? Roger Bent at the Cardiff office fought the first important case on the issue:

Williams v Compair Maxam Ltd [1982] ICR 157

The company decided to make a considerable number of their employees redundant as a result of financial losses. Department managers drew up lists of those to be made redundant on the basis of who would be most useful in the long term interests of the company. Mr Williams and others applied to the tribunal. The tribunal found against them, but their appeal to the EAT was successful, finding that in assessing whether an employer's selection process for redundancies is fair, the tribunal must have regard to current standards of fair industrial practice, for example whether maximum warning of impending redundancies had been given, and whether there had been consultations with unions as to the criteria to be applied in the selection process, whether these criteria were objective rather than subjective, whether suitable alternative employment could have been offered, and so on.

Many years later Mark Berry dealt with another case on the point, one which created a presumption in favour of consultation – in the absence of which a claim for a protective award under the 1992 Act will be successful, and that it was not necessary to establish that consultation would have made a difference. The case was Radin:

Susie Radin Ltd v GMB & Ors [2004] ICR 894

The employer, Susie Radin Ltd, announced that subject to any consultations, it proposed to close a factory in just over three months' time, making 108 employees redundant. Meetings took place, but the closure went ahead, and the employer failed to comply with the consultation requirements set out in S.188 of the Trade Union and Labour Relations (Consolidation) Act 1992. The tribunal hearing the case found that consultation would have made no difference, but nevertheless made a maximum protective award of ninety days in favour of all the employees. The EAT dismissed an appeal by the employer who then appealed to the Court of Appeal. The Court dismissed the appeal, finding that the purpose of a protective award was to provide a sanction for breach of the Act. It was not intended to be compensatory, and the tribunal had a wide discretion as to what was just and equitable; the focus should be on the seriousness of the employer's default.

Unfair dismissal

As a concept, unfair dismissal again sounds simple enough, but in practice many issues arise which demand a consistent approach. An example is what do you do if you, as a tribunal, cannot tell whether the decision was correct because the employers have failed to follow a proper procedure in carrying out their decision? The British Pump case founded the principle of procedural unfairness and gave the first answer to the question.

British Labour Pump Co. Ltd v Byrne [1979] ICR 348
The EAT found that where employers have summarily dismissed an employee, the onus is on them to establish that the employee would still have been dismissed even if they had investigated the matter fully.

The employee was dismissed after having knowingly shared in the proceeds of sale of goods stolen from the employer. He asked for a union official to speak on his behalf but was dismissed before representations could be made. The tribunal found that the employers should have convened a disciplinary committee to consider the matter and that had they done so they might have considered the employee's conduct to be insufficient to warrant dismissal; accordingly the dismissal was unfair, and the EAT agreed.

In truth, the rule was easy to circumvent. Employers would simply turn up at the tribunal and claim that even if they had carried out a proper investigation they would still have dismissed the applicant. A substantial improvement was obtained in the Polkey decision, but this underwent statutory amendment in the Employment Act in 2002 and the law on the issue remains in a state of flux.

Generally over the years, the growth of employment rights has been matched by the attempt by some employers to circumvent the rules. An example occurred in the Kelly-Phillips case, handled by Victoria Phillips on behalf of a BECTU member. It related to the use of fixed term contracts to avoid unfair dismissal rights.

British Broadcasting Corporation v Kelly-Phillips [1998] ICR 588
From 1993 to 1994 the applicant was employed on a fixed

Bill Jordan, Ken Gill and Ron Todd

term contract which provided that non-renewal would not constitute grounds for a claim of unfair dismissal. In September 1994 she entered another fixed term contract for a further year on similar terms, and this was extended in August 1995 to 31 December 1995. In December 1995 the applicant was told that the contract was not to be renewed on grounds of capability. She claimed unfair dismissal and succeeded at the Industrial Tribunal, who found on the facts that the employee had not been employed on a fixed term contract, and alternatively that in any event her dismissal did not consist just of expiry of the term but was partly related to capability. The EAT dismissed the employers' appeal, and the employers then appealed to the Court of Appeal.

The Court of Appeal found for the employers. On analysis of the relevant statutory provision, the contract was a varied contract for an extended fixed term and when this expired without renewal in December 1995 the exemption provided in the Employment Protection (Consolidation) Act 1978 came into play and precluded any action for unfair dismissal. An appeal to the House of Lords was about to be made, but was rendered unnecessary by legislative change in 1999 which removed the bar on a successful claim in similar circumstances in future.

Transfer of employment

Before the Transfer of Undertakings (Protection of Employment) Regulations, 1981 (TUPE) were enacted, employees often faced major problems when the business for which they worked was taken over. An example of the problem was the Rastill case:

Rastill v Automatic Refreshment Services Ltd [1978] ICR 290
At the time it was necessary to complete two years continuous employment to qualify for a redundancy payment.

The respondent company contracted with the previous operator of the canteen services to take over the running of the firm's canteen. They wrote to existing employees expressing willingness to 'continue your present contract'. Less than two years later a number of employees were made redundant, but their claim for redundancy payment was rejected on the ground that they had not been employed for two years. The EAT overturned this decision, finding that the business of running the canteen had been transferred (and therefore that employment was continuous).

A similar issue arose in Lister, one of the most important cases on the TUPE Regulations, a case which went to the House of Lords. Lister was handled by Thompsons in Scotland, supported by the GMB, and pursued to the Lords despite an adverse opinion after the Court of Session hearing from the barrister then handling the case:

Lister & Ors v Forth Dry Dock Engineering Company Ltd [1989] ICR 342

The employer went into receivership. The receiver agreed to sell the business assets, and one hour before the transfer took place the workforce were told that the business was to close and they were dismissed with immediate effect.

Within 48 hours, the applicants, learning that the transferee was recruiting labour, applied to be taken on but none was successful. They claimed unfair dismissal.

The tribunal concluded that the applicants had been employed by the company immediately before the transfer within the meaning of the TUPE Regulations, that their dismissal was for a reason connected with the transfer and was therefore unfair.

The case proceeded through the EAT, the Court of Session and then to the House of Lords. The Lords decided that the Regulations were expressly enacted for the purpose of complying with the relevant EU Directive which provided for the safeguarding of employees' rights on the transfer of a business; that the courts were under a duty to give a purposive construction, and on this basis the Regulations applied and the applicants had been unfairly dismissed.

The result was described by IRLR Highlights (an authoritative monthly journal commenting on the month's cases in Industrial Relations Law Reports) in April 1989 as 'historic … transforming the interpretation' of TUPE law, and the case, dealt with by Manus McGuire in Edinburgh, put the Scottish firm on the map as a major force in employment law issues.

This 'purposive' approach, a new concept of statutory interpretation imported into our law from Europe, also played a major part in the next landmark case, Dines, a case handled by Stephen Cavalier involving UNISON members, cleaners from Orsett Hospital:

Dines & Ors v Initial Healthcare Services Ltd [1995] ICR 12
The applicants were employed by a private company as cleaners. Following a tendering process, the cleaning contract was awarded to a different company, and the applicants' employment was terminated. They were then offered employment by the new company but on less favourable terms and with no continuity. They complained of unfair dismissal on the basis that they had been dismissed because of a relevant transfer for the purposes of the regulations.

The tribunal found that there was no transfer of an undertaking as one business had ceased and then another had commenced. The EAT agreed. However, the Court of Appeal took a more robust approach and found that, construing the 1981 Regulations as far as possible so as to give effect to the relevant Council Directive, where one company took over the provision of services from another company as a result of competitive tendering, the business of the first company did not necessarily come to an end. The tribunal had misdirected itself.

A classic victory on the interpretation of transfer of undertakings and in particular pension benefits was won in the next case, Beckmann, handled by Richard Arthur. Richard was named Pensions Lawyer of the Year for his work on the case:

Beckmann v Dynamo Whicheloe MacFarlane Ltd [2002] Court of Justice of the European Communities, Case C-164/00.
The claimant was an employee of a regional health authority. His terms and conditions included Whitley Council conditions of service, and these contained the terms of a collective agreement which were implemented in the National Health Service (Compensation for Premature Retirement) Regulations 1981 and the NHS Pension Scheme Regulations 1995. Employees over fifty who satisfied the conditions were entitled to an early retirement pension and

other benefits.

The activities of the regional health authority were transferred to the company, and less than two years later the claimant was dismissed for redundancy. The company refused to pay the Whitley Council benefits even though the claimant satisfied the conditions. The company claimed that the benefits were not transferred because they were 'old age ... benefits' and thus excluded under the Directive, and in any event arose under statutory instruments rather than the contract of employment.

The issue was referred to the Court of Justice. The company's claims were rejected. 'Old age benefits' referred only to benefits paid at the end of the normal working life, and the benefits transferred must include all benefits, even those derived by statute.

In another case involving hospital staff, this time dealt with by Mark Berry and then Bernie Wentworth, Thompsons was able to obtain a significant victory on the scope of the cases where a transfer can be held to have taken place:

RCO Support Services v UNISON [2002] ICR 752

Over a period from 1994 to 1998, a hospital trust, which operated two hospitals, moved the in-patient facilities at one to the other at which cleaning and catering facilities were supplied by RCO. The claimants were cleaners employed by I Ltd and caterers employed by the trust, to supply services at the first hospital. When the transfer of in-patient facilities was complete, most of the remaining caterers and all the remaining cleaners were made redundant. There was very little in the way of assets to transfer.

The tribunal considered as a preliminary issue whether a transfer of undertakings to RCO had taken place. The tribunal found that the need for caterers had moved from the first to the second hospital and that the cleaning and catering formed economic entities which had transferred under the regulations. The EAT agreed, and the company RCO appealed to the Court of Appeal.

The Court of Appeal rejected RCO's appeal and found that a transfer could take place even where neither assets nor workforce were transferred. On the facts such a transfer had taken place.

Equal pay

The story of equal pay in Britain has consistently shown that improvements, both legislative and industrial, emerge only after union agitation. Increases to women's wages have rarely, if ever, been secured through the largesse of employers. A rare exception occurred in the early 1920s when Poplar Borough Council under George Lansbury attempted to apply equal rates of pay regardless of sex, but that was firmly squashed by the House of Lords in Roberts v Hopwood.

One of the first signs that women who toiled in factories were not prepared to continue to suffer exploitation came in 1870s and 1880s at the Bryant and May match works in the East End of London. Sporadic industrial unrest culminated in the iconic and successful match girls strike in 1888 which lasted three weeks. Virtually all the women's demands on pay and conditions were met. This dispute was a key moment in the birth of a vast social movement which would be celebrated in labour and socialist history as the 'New Unionism' and the first TUC resolution on the issue of equal pay was passed in the same year as the match girls' strike – long before parliament or the liberal establishment countenanced such a revolutionary notion.

In 1935 Joan Beauchamp launched a withering attack in her book *Women who Work* on the disparity between the wages of men and women. In 1970 the rest of society started to try and catch up with the farsighted thinking of visionary

Robin Thompson, Roy Grantham (Gen Sec APEX) and Norman Willis

people like Lansbury and Beauchamp. The issue hit the headlines in the 1960s when Ford Motor Company sewing machinists, all female and members of the Transport and General Workers Union, walked out when a new grading scheme placed them in a particular grade but Ford decided they should be paid at 85 per cent of the grade rate. Production ground to a halt and Barbara Castle, then Employment Secretary, intervened and secured the outcome that the women would receive the full rate phased in over two years. Castle then sponsored the Equal Pay Act in 1970 to try and remedy this shocking area of discrimination.

Many cases have been fought through the courts on the issue since, but the Act was lacking in some respects, and cases take many years to jump through all the legal and procedural hurdles before reaching a conclusion. It took the European Court of Justice to force the Conservative government in 1983 to introduce an amendment which provided for equal pay where women could demonstrate they were undertaking work of 'equal value' with 'male comparators' in the same employment.

The equal value amendment was crucial in prompting Julie Hayward to bring a claim. The case was planned and set up by Tess Gill at GMB and then handled by Nick Carter at the Manchester office.

Hayward v Camell Laird Shipbuilders Ltd [1988] ICR 465

The applicant, a woman, was employed as a cook at a shipyard canteen and was classified as unskilled for the purposes of pay. She claimed under the Equal Pay Act 1970 that she was doing work of equal value to male comparators who were shipyard workers paid as skilled tradesmen. She succeeded in the tribunal following evaluation by an independent expert. However, the tribunal then went on to reject her claim on the basis that without a comparison of all terms and conditions she was not entitled to a declaration that she should receive a higher rate of pay. She appealed but both the EAT and then the Court of Appeal rejected her claim.

However, the House of Lords allowed her appeal (all five Law Lords finding in her favour) and found that the provisions of the Act referred to the specific term of the contract of which complaint was made, notwithstanding that, when looked at as a whole, her contract may have been no less favourable than the comparators. Nearly twenty years later, Hayward still stands as a landmark decision and was the first court judgment in favour of an equal value claim.

Another crucial case on the subject was Enderby, which required the input of the Court of Justice of the European Communities. It was sponsored by MSF and the Equal Opportunities Commission. The case started in 1985, eventually involved 1,200 individual claimants, and was seriously delayed by a series of technical legal arguments raised by the employers before eventually reaching a successful conclusion. It was handled by Sarah Leslie, initially as a partner with Thompsons and latterly at Irwin Mitchell's after she left Thompsons:

Enderby v Frenchay Health Authority [1994] ICR 113

There were collective bargaining agreements negotiated by the NHS and relevant unions. These provided different pay structures for speech therapists, pharmacists and clinical psychologists. The speech therapists, a predominantly female profession, was the lowest paid.

A woman speech therapist brought proceedings claiming equality of pay with two male comparators, a clinical psychologist and a pharmacist also employed by the health authority. There was a preliminary hearing to decide whether there was a defence under the Act on the basis of the difference in pay being due to a material fact other than sex. The tribunal accepted the defence that the difference in pay was due to other reasons – hours, nature of work and responsibility. However, the tribunal at the same time rejected the defence that the difference was due to market forces on the ground that although market forces had played a part, it did not account for the whole of the difference.

Both sides appealed. The EAT rejected the applicant's appeal but accepted the employers appeal that as market forces had played some part the whole of the difference was justified.

The applicant appealed to the Court of Appeal which then sought a ruling from the Court of Justice of the European Communities. The Court of Justice found that whilst normally it was for the worker to prove sex discrimination as to pay, once a prima facie case of discrimination was made out the burden of proof shifted to the employer to justify the difference in pay and that this had to be justified by objective factors unrelated to any discrimination on grounds of sex. The Court also found that the fact that the respective rates of pay of two jobs of equal value were arrived at by collective bargaining did not preclude a finding of prima facie discrimination and was not sufficient objective evidence for the difference in pay; and it was for the national court to decide whether and to what extent the shortage of candidates for a job and the need to attract them by higher pay constituted an objectively justified economic ground for the difference in pay.

Enderby was crucial as establishing the right to allow comparison of pools of claimants in separate bargaining groups, and opened the way to claims in both public and private sectors where management had used separate bargaining processes to avoid equal pay rates.

It also had a wider impact than even this. It led to the historic collective agreement Agenda for Change and the national pay structure in the NHS in 2004 providing for equality.

Another major case which went all the way to the House of Lords was Ratcliffe where the court was called on to make a ruling in a case arising out of privatisation:

North Yorkshire County Council v Ratcliffe [1995] ICR 834

The applicants were female school catering assistants (dinner ladies) employed by the county council at national joint council rates. The work was carried out almost exclusively by women and had been rated as of equal value to that of men employed by the council at various establishments. In 1989 the council established a direct service organisation for the provision of school meals, and tenders were sought in the six areas into which the county was divided. The only tender for the first area was from the direct service organisation at rates close to the joint council rates. The contract for the second area was won by a commercial company which paid much less. In order to secure the contracts in the remaining area the council declared the catering assistants in those areas redundant and re-employed them at rates mostly below joint council rates. The applicants, who were employed in those areas, sought equality of pay with their male comparators who were still employed on broadly the same terms as under the joint council agreement. The tribunal found in their favour, but the EAT decided that the tribunal had misdirected itself. An appeal by the applicants to the Court of Appeal was unsuccessful. The applicants then appealed to the House of Lords.

The House of Lords found for the applicants. Although the council's reason for paying women less than men for equivalent work was to allow it to compete with the commercial company, the tribunal had been entitled to conclude that the council had not shown that the variation was genuinely due to a material factor other than difference of sex. Ratcliffe involved 1,300 dinner ladies who won a total of £2m in back pay as a result of the award.

Ratcliffe, a case dealt with by Mark Berry, was the first big local authority equal pay case and led indirectly to the Single Status Agreement.

The Single Status Agreement in 1996 covering local authorities and the Agenda for Change deal in the health service in 2004 both sought to iron out anomalies between different jobs and to introduce equal pay. Problems arose with both because the Government failed fully to fund either. By 2007 only a third of local authorities had completed Single Status deals, largely because they did not have the resources to do so.

Whereas the details of Single Status were meant to be worked out locally, Agenda for Change was a national agreement backed by £920m of government money. In the NHS wage rates between the genders were equalised, but the funding was insufficient to cover back pay. As with the local authorities, unions increasingly opted for litigation to rectify the situation. Neither of these union-negotiated deals was perfect, but more than a million women won equal pay as a consequence.

The deals and their imperfect implementation continue to reverberate amongst employers, in the trade union movement and in the tribunals. When union representatives negotiated Single Status deals locally, they found that limited funds put a strict limit on what could be achieved. So the unions decided to negotiate a way through. Unions would not budge on the introduction of equal pay rates for men and women, but in some cases they made concessions on back pay. They did so because they knew if they pushed councils too far on back pay, services would close and people would be made redundant. All such local deals were the subject of votes among members after they were given full details of the proposed agreement. Without a Yes vote, there was no deal.

Because of the concessions on back pay, unions were able to secure equal pay rates for tens of thousands of women who did not qualify for equal pay under the law.

Occasionally councils wanted to cut the wages of men, rather than increase the pay of women to deliver equal pay. Unions pointed out they were not in the business of negotiating wage cuts (in some cases up to 20 per cent) so some men got their pay 'protected' until women caught up with them.

Thompsons' view and that of the relevant unions was that it was right to ensure that as many women as possible got as much as possible, in the shortest possible time. Hundreds of thousands of women would have languished for years on unequal pay rates if had it not been for the agreements.

In any event, the result has been that the unions have

come under pressure, and in some cases subject themselves to litigation. The GMB came under the spotlight in what was described as 'the most keenly anticipated trade union case for some years':

GMB v Allen & ors [2007] UKEAT/0425/06/DA

Following the introduction of an agreement between Middlesbrough Council and the local trade unions, manual and clerical workers were assimilated into a single pay spine. In order to implement the agreement the council carried out a job evaluation study. The union had some members who were in danger of losing pay, as a result of which the council introduced a pay protection scheme.

The claimants alleged that the GMB had prioritised the interests of its male members needing protected pay rather than the equal pay claims of the women members, the result of which being an agreement which included offers of back pay to the women which were less than what they might have achieved from a successful claim to an employment tribunal. They brought claims of sex discrimination against the union (which was represented by Thompsons).

The tribunal found no evidence of direct sex discrimination – the union's aim was not specifically to protect men's pay, but 'to achieve equality with as little collateral damage as possible'. But they found that there was indirect discrimination against the women by agreeing to a low back pay settlement in order to release money 'for the future pay line and pay protection'. The tribunal went on to find that the union had victimised Mrs Allen and her colleagues by failing to provide the women with any support or advice in relation to their claims when they instructed a 'no win no fee' solicitor to represent them.

The union successfully appealed to the Employment Appeal Tribunal. The EAT found that the objective – the new pay and grading structure – was legitimate, and therefore it was difficult to see how it could be alleged that the means were inappropriate. It also rejected the tribunal's finding of victimisation, saying that there was no evidence on which the tribunal could have come to the conclusion it did.

But the matter did not end there. A further appeal – to the Court of Appeal – was successful in part; the union was found to have been guilty of indirect discrimination: 'by agreeing to a low back pay settlement in order to release more money for pay protection and the future pay line, the union had engaged in a potentially discriminatory practice' which the union had failed to justify. The EAT had found that the union justified the practice. The Court of Appeal overturned that finding.

In any event unions have become impatient for action from the employers, and their members increasingly ready to litigate on the back pay issue – the only issue at stake. In the meantime, the Government has now released more money, £500m, so that 46 councils in England can fund back pay. Thompsons calculate that it would take £3bn to fund the shortfall in its entirety, and thousands of claims are now being processed by Thompsons, instructed by the relevant unions on behalf of affected members in an episode which bears comparison with the mass deafness litigation of the late 1970s and early 1980s.

The desperation of some employers was shown in the Derbyshire case where the employers sent letters to the 39 claimants, female catering staff, asking them to withdraw their claims and warning them that it could not absorb the cost of their claims. At the same time they wrote to all catering staff stating that the cost of school meals would rise and everyone's jobs would be at risk if the claims were successful:

St Helens MBC v Derbyshire & Ors [2007] IRLR 540
About five hundred catering staff brought equal pay claims against the council in 1998. The vast majority settled, but

39, including Mrs Derbyshire, continued to pursue their claims. The letters referred to above were sent two months before the hearing in 2001. The claimants ignored the warnings, were successful in their equal pay claims and then brought fresh claims for victimisation. The victimisation claim eventually reached the House of Lords which found that whilst the council had been entitled to send out letters pointing out the possible consequences of a successful claim, the letter sent by the council was 'intimidating' and was therefore a breach of Section 4 of the Sex Discrimination Act (which says that victimising someone for bringing a claim under the Equal Pay Act is, in itself, a discriminatory act).

The importance of the case and the wide definition given to 'victimisation' by the Lords cannot be overstated.

Generally, as Vicky Phillips has commented, the number of equal pay cases reaching the courts 'is now of almost epidemic proportions, making it well-nigh impossible for trade unionists to keep on top of the most important decisions'. And of course as well as the cases which result in reported judgments of the courts there are many which conclude with unreported judgments or out of court settlements. A few examples in this context are:

> Foster v British Gas in 1991 where UNISON won £813,000 for 16 former British Gas workers compulsorily retired in 1986 at age sixty.

> The Bedfordshire dinner ladies case sponsored by UNISON and GMB which resulted in £1.5m back pay.

> Wilson v North Cumbria NHS Trust: again sponsored by UNISON and GMB which resulted in a £300m settlement for more than 1,600 women.

Before leaving the issue of Equal Pay, the Preston case, handled by Richard Arthur is one which led to tens of thousands of cases and the recovery of hundreds of millions of pounds.

Preston v Wolverhampton Healthcare NHS Trust [1998] ICR 228

The claimant and other part-time workers who had been denied access to membership of occupational pension schemes because of the number of hours worked, appealed against the dismissal of their appeal against the EAT's ruling that the six month time limit for filing claims in the Equal Pay Act 1970 and the two year limit on the right to recover arrears applied to their claims of indirect discrimination. The EJC had ruled in an earlier case that the right to join an occupational pension scheme was covered by the prohibition of differential treatment of men and women under Art 119 and that if a higher proportion of part time workers were women their exclusion could amount to a contravention; further, that national time limits applied to the assertion of the right to membership provided that the rules were not less favourable than those applicable to similar domestic claims and did not make it excessively difficult for claimants to exercise their rights under EU law. The House of Lords referred the matter to the EJC.

The European Court found that the imposition of a 6 month time limit on the institution of proceedings under the Act was not precluded under Community Law provided the principle of equivalence was not infringed. However, the rule providing that a claimant's pensionable service was to be calculated only by reference to service after a date falling no earlier than 2 years prior to the date of claim, infringed the principle of effectiveness. Part of the claim was not concerned with arrears of benefits but rather to secure recognition of the right to retroactive membership of the pension scheme.

Two other recent examples of the problems which continue to arise under the 1970 Act are worth recounting, both dealt with by Nicola Dandridge; the first, Robertson, was unhelpful, but the second, Bailey, strongly affirms the Enderby approach:

Department for Environment Food and Rural Affairs v Robertson [2005] ICR 751

Between 1992 and 1996, responsibility for pay bargaining for civil servants had been delegated from the Treasury to individual government departments. The applicants were male civil servants employed by DEFRA. They sought equality of pay with female civil servants working in other government departments on the grounds that their work had been rated equivalent. A preliminary issue arose as to whether employees in one department could compare themselves with employees in another department. The tribunal found in the applicants' favour but this was overturned by the EAT. The applicants appealed to the Court of Appeal.

The Court rejected the appeal. The bare fact that the applicant and comparator were in common employment was not a sufficient basis for comparison; in each case it was necessary to consider whether the terms and conditions of the applicant and comparator were traceable to a single source which had responsibility for the claimed inequality and the capacity to restore equal treatment. In this case there was no such single source

Home Office v Bailey [2005] ICR 1058

The claimant employees worked for the Prison Service in administrative, executive and secretarial support grades. They claimed equal pay with comparators in other grades in the service which were predominantly occupied by men. The claim related to indirect discrimination, since the pool of employees in the claimants group were predominantly women. The tribunal found that there was a prima facie case of indirect discrimination which required to be justified. The EAT upheld the employers' appeal, and the claimants appealed to the Court of Appeal.

The Court found for the claimants. Provided the tribunal was satisfied as to the validity of the statistics and the way they were used, there was no reason why the statistical approach used by the tribunal should not be used where the only question was a pay disparity between two occupational groups, even where the disadvantaged group contained a significant number of men.

Discrimination

The law relating to discrimination is another major area where employment rights have been extended and where Thompsons has played a significant part in assisting the trades unions. A few of the many important cases pursued by the firm are described below.

Sex discrimination

Home Office v Holmes [1984] ICR 679

The employee, a woman, was employed full time as a civil servant in a grade and department in which part-time workers were not allowed. Following the birth of her second child she notified her employer of her intention to return to work but that being a single parent family she could only work part time. Her request was refused and she complained of sex discrimination under the Sex Discrimination Act 1975.

The tribunal concluded that there had been discrimination by subjecting the applicant to a detriment, namely the condition of full-time work. The Home Office appealed, but the case was upheld by the EAT.

This case, handled by Colin Ettinger, was the first case where it was held that there had been discrimination in requiring an employee to work full time.

Brown v Stockton-on-Tees Borough Council [1988] ICR 411
This was another widely publicised case.

The employee was employed as a care supervisor under a scheme. The scheme was terminated, but she was invited to apply for a position on a revised scheme. She was not offered the job, on the basis that she would require maternity leave soon after the start of the 12-month contract.

The tribunal found that she had been unfairly dismissed as she had been selected for redundancy because she was pregnant. The EAT disagreed, and so did the Court of Appeal. The applicant appealed to the House of Lords. The Lords found in her favour; the need to take maternity leave was a reason connected with pregnancy and accordingly the dismissal was automatically unfair under Section 60 of the Employment Protection (Consolidation) Act 1978.

Mobility clauses in contracts were the issue which arose in the next case:

Meade-Hill v British Council [1995] ICR 848
On promotion to a more senior grade, the applicant was required to accept a new term in her contract that she should serve wherever in the UK the employer might direct. As a married woman earning less than her husband, she would have found it difficult to move.

She sought a declaration that since a higher proportion of women were secondary earners the term constituted unlawful sex discrimination. The claim failed in the County Court but was successful in the Court of Appeal. The number of women who could comply with a direction to move their workplace involving a change of home was considerably smaller than the proportion of men who could comply; the requirement was a detriment, and was unlawful unless it could be shown to be justifiable.

However, one of the judges then went on to suggest to

employers a simple method to avoid discrimination by including a caveat to say that compliance could not be required from an employee who was unable to comply!

British Airways plc v Starmer [2005] IRLR 862

The claimant was employed as a pilot, full time as a first officer from May 2001.

In November 2000 BA introduced a policy to make part-time opportunities available to accommodate the particular personal circumstances of its employees, such as childcare. Pilots were expected to work full time for the greater part of their employment, but there was an option for part-time work on the basis of either 50 per cent or 75 per cent of normal full-time working. In April 2003, in accordance with statutory requirements, the company also introduced a procedure to request flexible working.

In March 2004, the applicant applied to work part time on a 50 per cent basis to accommodate her childcare arrangements. The employers refused but offered 75 per cent, citing various business reasons.

The applicant claimed indirect sex discrimination and succeeded in the tribunal which found that the employers' decision amounted to the application of a provision that the claimant had to work full time or 75 per cent full time, and that this was to the detriment of a considerably larger proportion of women than men.

On appeal, the EAT agreed, and said that the tribunal was entitled to reject the justification defence based on resource considerations.

This case was dealt with by Nicola Dandridge and then Rakesh Patel on behalf of BALPA.

Disability discrimination

The Disability Discrimination Act 1995 added another tranche of regulation against discrimination, and the Collins case, handled by Nicola Dandridge on behalf of

BECTU is an example.

Collins v Royal National Theatre Board Ltd [2004] IRLR 395

The claimant was a semi-skilled carpenter's labourer. He lost part of a finger in an accident at work and was left with extreme pain and sensitivity together with loss of dexterity and grip.

He wanted to return to work but refused to have further surgery. The employers carried out an assessment involving a series of typical tasks to test his capability, found that he could no longer work safely or efficiently, concluded that there was no job to which he could return and, in the absence of alternative work, dismissed him.

The tribunal upheld his complaint of disability discrimination on the basis that there had been a failure to make reasonable adjustment contrary to S.6 of the Act. The employers had focused 'on what the applicant was unable to do, and not how the situation could be created whereby he could continue to work'.

The EAT allowed the employers appeal, but the decision of the tribunal was restored by the Court of Appeal.

Discrimination in Northern Ireland

Discrimination issues of a different sort arise in Northern Ireland. A recent case pursued by John O'Neill of Thompsons in Belfast concerned the interpretation of the Fair Employment and Treatment (Northern Ireland) Order 1998.

Maurice Neill v Belfast Telegraph Newspapers Ltd [2002] Case no 00554/00FET, 03297/00

The applicant was a member of the NUJ and father of the chapel at the company. Terms and conditions of employment were negotiated annually between the union and the employer until 1995 when the company unilaterally refused to negotiate with the union.

The applicant applied to the Fair Employment tribunal claiming that he was not selected for the post of Business

Editor in July 2000 and that the post was given to a person who was much less experienced and who was not an NUJ member.

Under the 1998 Order, article 32 refers to discrimination as including religious belief or political opinion. Political opinion is not defined save that it excludes any opinion which consists of or includes approval or acceptance of the use of violence for political ends.

A preliminary issue arose as to whether the applicant's political opinion was covered by the Order, the context being the applicant's political belief that workers' representatives should be able to engage in collective bargaining to promote workers' rights and interests. The tribunal found in his favour.

The working time regulations

Classic examples of regulation promoted by European law to secure improved employment rights are The Maternity and Parental Leave Regulations etc., 1999 which were enacted following the EC Parental Leave Directive, and the Working Time Regulations 1998. Under Regulation 13(7) of the 1998 Regulations, entitlement to paid annual leave only arose after continuous employment of 13 weeks. BECTU challenged this restriction arguing that most of its members were engaged on short-term contracts and would thus be deprived of annual leave entitlement even though they were in regular employment, albeit with successive employers. Stephen Cavalier dealt with the case, an important one in the film and theatre industry:

R (on the application of BECTU) v Sec of State for Trade and Industry [2001] Court of Justice, Case C-173/99

The union maintained that Regulation 13 (7) incorrectly applied article 7 of the relevant Directive which required member states to ensure that all workers were entitled to at least four weeks' paid annual leave 'in accordance with the conditions for entitlement to, and granting of, such leave laid down by national legislation and/or practice'.

The court found in favour of the union. The purpose of the Directive was clear, the right to paid annual leave was a particularly important principle of Community law and member states could not make the existence of the right subject to preconditions.

A recent successful case, sponsored by their union PCS and handled by Victoria Phillips involved employees who had been absent from work over a long period of time during which their entitlement to any pay had been exhausted:
Stringer v HMRC [2009] UKHL 31
They claimed under regulation 30 for payment of statutory holiday pay and the tribunal upheld their claims. However, when the case proceeded to the Court of Appeal, the Court found against them, holding that a worker on long-term sick leave was not entitled to annual leave in a year when he had not been able to attend work.

After a referral to the European Court of Justice, the employers accepted that a worker's entitlement to compensation for termination of employment could not be affected by sickness absence, and that workers on long-term sickness absence and who apply to take annual leave but cannot because they have no right to carry over under the Working Time Regulations, are entitled to be paid annual leave.

The case returned to the House of Lords to decide the issue of whether unpaid annual leave under the Working Time Regulations and/or payment on termination could also be pursued as unauthorised deductions of wages claims under the Employment Rights Act, 1996.

The Lords said that it can. The important practical effect is that a worker can take advantage of the more generous time limits which apply to unlawful deduction claims.

Pensions

A recurring theme in some of the cases has been the attempt to protect workers' pensions. Very often the issue has arisen in the context of a transfer of undertakings or an attempt to secure equal pay. Sometimes the issue can arise on its own as a rearguard action to protect the general employment rights of workers. This is what happened in 2000 in relation to the Firefighters' Pension Scheme.

Firefighters were then required under their conditions of service to be fully operationally fit at all times in order to cope with the emergencies they have to face, often with great courage. They also had to pay a significant part (11 per cent) of their salary towards their pension entitlements. It had been the normal practice that if a firefighter became operationally unfit for work he could no longer continue (for example in a lighter capacity). A firefighter becoming operationally unfit as a result of an accident would qualify for an ill-health award.

In 1994 West Yorkshire Fire and Civil Defence Authority tried to change the practice and insist that such firefighters continue in employment on light duties. Two firefighters, Mr McCalman and Mr Lockwood, supported by the FBU, contested the matter.

R v West Yorkshire Fire and Civil Defence Authority ex parte McCalman and Lockwood (2000) QBCOF/1999/0798/C

Both men suffered back injuries as a result of accidents at work, and were registered by medical experts as permanently unfit to perform their duties. The authority refused to retire them. Mr Lockwood was transferred, under protest, to light duties; Mr McCalman refused such a transfer and was dismissed.

The men took their case for judicial review and were successful. The judge considered the legislation including the Firemen's Pension Scheme Order 1992 and decided that the authority was wrong. A firefighter who was permanently unfit to carry out his work could not be required to remain in employment carrying out work of a light nature (which of necessity did not include firefighting). The employers appealed to the Court of Appeal but the appeal was rejected unanimously.

In fact, the goalposts were then moved and the scheme amended so that firefighters could be moved off firefighting provided they were placed in some other meaningful role. As ever, the passage of time has given rise to new interpretations and the issue is likely to resurface in the courts once more.

A case of wide national importance reached the House of Lords in relation to part time firefighters' sickness benefit and pension rights in March 2006. It was dealt with by Richard Arthur on behalf of the Fire Brigades Union and was hailed by the union's General Secretary Matt Wrack as a 'momentous decision [which] paves the way to ending 60 years of discrimination against firefighters working retained duty':

Matthews v Kent and Medway Towns Fire Authority [2006] 2 All ER 171

The case was brought under the Part-time Workers (Prevention of Less Favourable Treatment) Regulations, 2000. The case was lost in the Employment Tribunal, failed on appeal to the EAT and failed again in the Court of Appeal.

But when it reached the House of Lords, the Lords, in a majority decision, held that part-time firefighters were employed under the same type of contract as full-time firefighters and, although there were some differences in some work activities, their work was sufficiently similar for them to have the right not to be discriminated against over sickness benefits and pension rights.

The simple 'industrial' system of tribunals for the legal resolution of workplace issues and disputes had by the 1980s and '90s become a massive growth area of law, with a growing army of lawyers to support. Trade union officials quickly had to become versed in the law and the law became ever more complex. Thompsons' role was to try and assist with advice wherever necessary and to take over and pursue those cases which proceeded to the higher courts or which involved issues of particular complexity. After many years when the vast majority of Thompsons' lawyers dealt with personal injury cases, increasing numbers started to specialise in employment cases. This process accelerated when, increasingly from the late 1990s, unions sought to delegate the handling of all their tribunal cases to their lawyers – partly at least as a quid pro quo for the allocation of personal injury work.

The law itself has become complex and legalistic. The tribunals are full of lawyers armed with masses of legislation and case law. For the employee with a case to pursue, trade union backing provides the only free system for access to justice, and the unions have responded by making their lawyers such as Thompsons available to them.

Chapter 26
Preparing for life after Robin and Brian

The success of the firms after 1974 could not mask forever the underlying problem of what was to happen after the brothers retired. While they were involved they would always ensure that the firms did not diverge or splinter. But what once they were gone?

As time went on, the structures of the firms had become closer, partly by design and partly driven by events. The problems they faced, as ever, were shared.

In Robin's firm the structure was relatively traditional. In 1988, aged fifty, David Skidmore became co-ordinating partner when Robin stood down as senior partner in his favour.

The management system in Brian's firm was different. The firm continued to operate through an Executive Committee, but this was eventually recognised as being too unwieldy to operate at anything other than a policy level and in February 1990 management of the firm was delegated to a management subcommittee, the 'MSC'. In 1993 the MSC was replaced by a Managing Partners group, very similar to that which existed in Robin's firm, and David Skidmore masterminded joint groups whose function was to achieve better financial planning and effective financial administration on a joint agreed basis.

Financial planning was critical. In the early 1990s following the conclusion of large numbers of deafness cases and at a time when word processing functions on typewriters along with a greater standardisation of work methods had become the norm, it became clear that, in

Brian Thompson's in particular, there was a significant excess of support staff (together with a more modest excess of case handlers).

Negotiations with the union (the GMB) followed, including agreement of a redundancy procedure agreement and a redundancy programme went ahead in January 1994, achieving its aim through volunteers.

In 1993, Brian's firm took space in Congress House, and closed down the Pimlico office the following year. The two firms now existed side by side in London, and another important step had been taken to bring them back together.

A strong supporter of merger and a prime mover in the background setting the scene for it to come about was David Skidmore.

David's contribution to Thompsons was remarkable. As co-ordinating partner he was in overall charge of Robin's firm and continued in this role until 1993 when he retired aged 55 on a three year consultancy. During that period of three years he assisted with the process that was to lead to the amalgamation of the firms into Thompsons in 1996. When David retired, he still had energy enough to obtain a full private pilot's licence in 1997, to run the Law Society's Personal Injury Panel, when it was set up in 1993, as Chief Assessor, and to devote a great deal of time to charitable works. In his 'retirement' in October 1994 he was appointed Consultant Director of Finance, a position he held until the firm appointed its first non-lawyer finance director. David also had an embryonic film career! He starred in a film made by ICI to demonstrate the use of artificial limbs which he described as

quite an experience – "banger" lights on the floor to keep the shadows off my face and soap on the metal parts of my arms to stop reflective glare. Then, after the Star Wars film I went to Elstree Studios to audition for the part of a robotic doctor

David Skidmore with his aeroplane, July 1997

in the sequel *The Empire Strikes Back*. I met the producer and saw all the props used for Star Wars. However my socialist/trade union conscience got the better of me and I suggested the part could easily be played by a member of Equity. Silly me, I could have retired earlier.

Frank Foy took over the role of Coordinator in Robin's firm in October 1992:

It was clear to me that Geoff Shears and David Skidmore had agreed that a merger was desirable and that Nick Carter agreed.

My own feeling was that a merged firm was essential but would be very big. It could not be a simple merger of the two cultures. It had to be a new firm with a new culture, and to achieve this would take a great deal of work. To fail would be disastrous.

I went out and found a facilitator, Professor Martin Read, a renowned expert in solicitors' practices and author of a large book on the subject.

In 1994, Frank and Geoff (Shears) set up a joint portfolio review, and then a Strategy Group as the firms began to move decisively towards re-amalgamation. Brian decided to retire from his firm as at 30 April 1994, following on from a similar decision by Robin a year earlier, but they both continued to perform a valuable role as consultants. Geoff Shears took over as the lead partner in Brian's firm:

The legal business environment changed radically during the nineties. It was about to change even more. Trade union finances were such that it was vital to reduce unit cost in order to maintain service quality. The two firms had to merge in order to play to their strengths, and there had to be great changes in the way most of the work was done. Brian was enthusiastic and supportive, but had the sense to see that he could help the process best by becoming a consultant. After the merger he happily attended the office three or four days a week (for half a day at a time), did some work well, participated in the occasional debate, then spent time on holiday, at the theatre or down the pub with his friends. He said that he had been treated well. He said, mischievously, that we allowed him to come into the office to give him an interest in life.

The firms' Strategy Group gave rise to a Joint Coordinating Group, the members of which were Geoff, Frank, Nick Carter, David Thompson and Colin Ettinger. With the support of Robin, Brian and David (Skidmore), all of whom continued to take a keen interest, the stage was set for the firms to join together again.

In the lead up to the merger, Simon Walton left and moved to the USA in 1994, and Andrew Dismore departed on 28 April 1995. Andrew's work for the FBU, not to mention his work on cases and massive cost (fee) recovery for the firm, and campaigning work generally, were all outstanding. He left on good terms, to join Russell Jones and Walker, and subsequently secured a seat as MP for Hendon, a seat he held for over ten years.

Colin Ettinger also departed in 1995 and was joined by two other partners, Alison Eddy and Sara Leslie. Together they opened an office for Irwin Mitchell in London. Sara, who had dealt with a number of train crash enquiries including Clapham Junction and Purley, took the Enderby case with her.

Simon Walton's departure was a watershed. He made an outstanding contribution to Thompsons over thirty years and was one of the key players in the firms for the majority of that time. He emigrated to America, having met his new wife Nicole, requalified as an attorney and lived and worked in Baltimore for Schultheis and Walton, P.A. until his untimely death on 20 November 2008 aged just 66.

In America he continued to represent people injured in workplace accidents and in public interest litigation. After the 9/11 terrorist attacks he championed the 'Trial Lawyers Care' programme where members of the Maryland Association for Justice joined with lawyers across the US in providing free legal representation to the victims and their families.

Simon brought in lawyers from Thompsons' offices to work with him in representing the families of six UK nationals killed in the World Trade Centre, and in 2004 the firm's conference suite in Congress House was the venue for the UK hearing of the September 11 Victims Compensation Fund. Presided over by Special Master Kenneth Feinberg, it was the first time a civil hearing had taken place in the UK presided over by a US judge.

Colin Ettinger:

One of the things that Simon Walton was very keen on was getting some of our female partners involved in women's issues ... . Alison Eddy and Sara Leslie in particular did so and it has been very successful. It was typical of Simon who was innovative and imaginative.

Geoff Thomas, having supported the merger, retired on a consultancy on 30 April 1996, aged 54. Geoff had been a stalwart of Thompsons since he joined the Serjeants' Inn office in 1965. He became managing partner in Cardiff on Ted Lewis' death, and forged a number of important and long-lasting links with the unions, particularly the AEU, and notably John Weakley. Geoff moved to London and became an A partner in Robin's firm in 1985 and was managing partner in what was then called Bainbridge House for a period. On retirement he moved to West Wales with his new family hoping for an academic career. Regrettably he did not have the chance to enjoy his new life for long. He was diagnosed with a brain tumour and died on 9 February 2000 aged 58.

The author spent over a decade in the room next door to Geoff in Cardiff office and was supervised by him for several years. In those days he was a formidable litigator; he could, and did, reduce opponents to apoplexy on occasions.

Another senior partner in Robin's firm was Colin Simpson. Colin remained with the firm through the merger process but did not stay for long thereafter, leaving on 30 April 1998. Colin had joined in 1971 and spent most of his time at Ilford office where he succeeded David Skidmore as managing partner. He also succeeded David as the partner responsible for the finance function in Robin's firm, a position he held for about ten years.

It was an important role, because we largely ran Harrow on behalf of not only Robin's firm but also Brian's. I spent a lot of my time in Harrow. The accounts department in Harrow had great staff including, of course, Bernard Ferguson,

Denise Windridge and so on.

I was on the inter-firm Liaison Committee and had a place on the Finance Liaison Advisory Group (FLAG).

Following the successful implementation of the Deafness Scheme by David Skidmore, I negotiated a Vibration White Finger Scheme with Ashton West who was then John Robinson's deputy in The Iron Trades Insurance Group.

Colin was also the person in charge of costs within Robin's firm, in the course of which he dealt with a case which went to the House of Lords.
Hunt v R M Douglas (Roofing) Ltd [1988] 3 All ER 823.
The House of Lords decided that a litigant who has been awarded costs is entitled to interest on those costs from the date of judgment rather than the date the taxation (assessment by the court) of those costs is complete.

This rather dry legal point was of considerable benefit to claimants' lawyers generally, and of particular value to Thompsons in increasing costs income from defendants and their insurers (and thus reducing bills to the trade unions at a time when it was becoming increasingly important not only to provide a service which was high quality but also to do so at an affordable price).

Colin had particularly strong links with ASLEF, and along with many others made a big contribution to Thompsons over many years. He was also Chief Assessor for the Law Society Personal Injury Panel from 1997 to 2003, serving two full three-year terms.

Brian's firm also saw some significant departures.

Chris Chapman relinquished his position as managing partner of Sheffield office in 1994 and subsequently left the firm on 31 July 1995 to pursue a new career as a part-time Employment Tribunal chairman.

As well as his work with the Employment Tribunal,

Chris is now Deputy Chairman of the Central Arbitration Committee and an individual ACAS arbitrator, all work he thoroughly enjoys. He has recently co-authored *Employment Court Practice*.

Eddie Solomons, another important partner in Brian's firm, left in 1994 to pursue a career with the Treasury Solicitor. Eddie had been folio holder for the law folio in Brian's firm for a number of years and was managing partner in Pimlico. An outstanding lawyer, it was not surprising that he progressed in government service to become Deputy Official Solicitor and Public Trustee, a position he gave up at the end of April 2006 to take a new role as Director of Legal Services at the Metropolitan Police. Eddie also now holds a senior role at the Law Society as a member of its regulation board and chairman of the rules and ethics committee.

In the mid 1990s the legal environment was about to present a major challenge with the proposed changes to the way personal injury cases were handled – the Woolf reforms. The industrial environment was already in a state of upheaval with the decline in manufacturing and the growth of the service sector – this had important implications for the firm in terms of its core caseload; and society was daily becoming more consumer driven.

In *SOGAT: A History of the Society of Graphical and Allied Trades* by John Gennard and Peter Bain, the authors comment on the expansion of the union's legal services, already underway in the early 1990s:

> In 1991 SOGAT's legal services, which were among the best in the trade union movement, expanded to cover conveyancing, financial advice, wills and protection on the roads. The lawyers for the SOGAT were Robin Thompson and Partners and Brian Thompson and Partners.
> This relationship with the Thompsons dated back to 1947

Rodney Bickerstaffe, Neil Kinnock and Jacqui and Eddie Solomons at the Thompsons' Reception to celebrate Rodney Bickerstaffe becoming Chairman of the TUC and Tom Sawyer becoming Chairman of the Labour Party, 29 September 1991

when the NUPB and PW employed W.H. Thompson Solicitors. This was the same year that Robin and Brian Thompson joined the firm. Through nearly 45 years of change the relationship grew and strengthened. It survived various amalgamations. The 1991 changes meant Thompsons were not just there to help members when they suffered an injury at work but also to protect members and families in other ways.

It was now time to step up the pace of change. Leading the way were Geoff Shears and Frank Foy, together with David Thompson who had transferred from Nottingham to Congress House in October 1995 as managing partner of the London office for both firms.

Geoff Shears' role was pivotal. By then, he was the most important link with the trade unions, and had a key role with a number of them, not least UNISON and various regions of the GMB. He helped the firms acquire a great deal of additional work, and formed lasting relationships with the union movement at the most senior level.

Brian Thompson and Robin Thompson
Equity Partners 1974 -1996

Those marked with* transferred to Thompsons in 1996

Brian Thompson; Brian Thompson & Partners	Robin Thompson & Partners
1 March 1974	**1 March 1974**
Brian Thompson retired 30.4.94	Robin Thompson retired 30.4.93
Ted Lewis left for BT Cardiff 1978	David Phillips retired 5.4.82
John Lebor retired 30.4.94	Victor Nicholls retired 31.4.88
Nick Carter*	Ivor Walker left 27.6.80
John Pickering left 1979	David Skidmore retired 30.4.93
Mike Osborne retired 30.4.92	Simon Walton left 30.4.94
Geoff Thomas left for BT Cardiff 1978	
Roger Bent left for BT Cardiff 1978	
	1 March 1978
	Barry Samuels left 30.4.94
	Colin Simpson*
BT & P Cardiff	
Ted Lewis 1.9.78 – 80 (retired)	
Geoff Thomas 1.9.78 – 30.4.85	
Roger Bent 1.9.78 – 30.4.85	
Andrew Herbert 1.9.78 – 30.4.85	
Chris Short 1.9.78 - 85	
Steve Allen 1.9.83 -30.4.85	
	1 May 1982
	Stuart Carroll left 31.8.82
	Graham Dickinson left 30.9.83
	Colin Ettinger left 17.11.95
1 May 1983	
Geoff Shears*	
Pauline Chandler*	
Chris Chapman left 31.7.95	
Eddie Solomons left 30.9.94	

Brian Thompson; Brian Thompson & Partners	Robin Thompson & Partners
	1 May 1984
	Frank Foy*
1 May 1985	**1 May 1985**
Philip Ballard*	Geoff Thomas retired 30.4.96
Mark Berry*	Roger Bent*
Steve Allen*	Andrew Herbert*
	15 October 1985
	David Thompson*
	Lesley Wicks left 31.3.87
1 May 1986	**1 May 1986**
Jane Litherland*	Tony Lawton*
Mike Humphreys left 30.4.91	Andrew Dismore left 28.4.95
	Sarah Goodman*
	Paul Llewellyn left 31.12.87
1 May 1987	**1 May 1987**
Tony Briscoe*	Alison Eddy left 17.11.95
Roger Maddocks*	Karen Mitchell*
Francine O'Gorman*	Elisabeth Roth*
1 May 1988	**1 May 1988**
Pam Kenworthy left 30.4.92	Neville Filar*
Rosalind Wilson left 30.9.94	Sara Leslie left 17.11.95
Janet Allan – relinquished equity partnership on 31.12.94 (but remained as a salaried partner)	
Caroline Humphreys left 1.11.90	
Keith Roberts left 30.4.89	
Alicia Rendell*	
Julie Wood*	
	1 August 1988
	David Wallen left 17.11.95

385

Brian Thompson; Brian Thompson & Partners	Robin Thompson & Partners
	1 November 1988
	Alan Jones left 28.4.95
1 May 1989	**1 May 1989**
Virginia Kerridge left 30.4.93	Mick Antoniw*
Gaenor Stuart-Murray – joined RT & P 29.1.90	Philip Brooks*
Sally Gold (reverted to salaried partner on – but was reappointed to equity on 1.5.1995)*	Rhod Griffiths left 1.12.95
John Usher*	
	3 July 1989
	Keith Roberts left 21.12.1995
	29 January 1990
	Gaenor Stuart-Murray left 14.3.92
	1 May 1990
	David McPherson left 30.4.94
1 May 1991	**1 May 1991**
Stefan Cross*	John Skinner*
Stephanie Clarke left 28.2.96	
David G Thompson*	
Stephen Cavalier*	
Ed Myers left 31.8.1994	
Keith Patten*	
Simon Denyer left 30.9.1994	
Martin Harvey left 31.10.95	
	1 May 1992
	Phil King*
	Stuart Henderson left 30.12.94

Brian Thompson; Brian Thompson & Partners	Robin Thompson & Partners
1 May 1993	
Steve Cottingham*	
Peter Bamford*	
Steve Pinder*	
Vicky Deritis*	
Matthew Tollitt*	
Phil Smith*	
Rob Wood*	
1 November 1994	
Judith Gledhill*	
Gill Owen*	
John Myles*	
1 May 1995	**1 May 1995**
Sally Gold (See above)*	Peter Mulhern*
Tom Jones*	Nigel Saunders*
Mary Stacey*	Richard Woolley*
Paul Jackson*	
Katrina London*	
Ian Kinnear*	
Kate Ross*	

Chapter 27
From 1996 – change, challenge and campaigns

The last twenty years has been a period of upheaval in the legal framework within which personal injury work is conducted. This was a key driver in the decision to remerge the firms in 1996.

Doug Christie, a member of the firm's Executive Board:

… there have been numerous changes in the way personal injury cases are dealt with procedurally and how they are funded.

Some big changes happened a number of years ago when the procedure was changed to require disclosure and exchange of medical reports followed by disclosure and exchange of witness statements a little bit later; there were also changes to the way damages were calculated and in particular in the way DSS payments were taken into account with the new Compensation Recovery Unit being set up.

Next came the review by Lord Woolf of the personal injury system:

His first remit was simply to amalgamate the Rules of Practice in the High Court and County Courts, as embodied in the White and Green Books respectively. However, Woolf decided to shake up the system.

His interim report recommended fixed costs at 18 to 20 per cent of damages – and that was if you went to trial. That would have been disastrous to union legal services and to Thompsons since costs would normally be a greater proportion of the damages – because of the way defendants defend cases. Woolf also talked about raising the small claims limit. Fortunately, we had some success there since by the time of his second report in 1996 he exempted personal injury work from the small claims limit increase (which otherwise went up to £3,000 and later £5,000). That was a victory which was at least partly attributable to David Thompson's efforts following his involvement and links that he had built to the consumer lobby. Nonetheless, it was a very anxious period, not knowing how the system was going to be changed and how costs were going to be dealt with.

By the time the Labour government was elected in 1997 the issue of fixed costs was still to be decided. But it was then possible to lobby Government for some changes. Geoff Hoon took up the issue as the relevant minister. He was very anxious about the costs of Legal Aid which were spiralling out of control, and his big idea was to extend the use of conditional fee agreements (CFAs). We encouraged him in this and were involved in the early discussions and meetings. Together with us, he then came up with the concept of recoverability of success fees under CFAs together with recoverability of the ATE insurance premiums.

Tom Jones and I regularly visited a senior civil servant…who was the policy maker, and we put to him the concept of collective CFAs [CCFAs] to enable a level playing field for membership organisations such as trades unions. We also put to him the concept of self-insurance for unions. We helped with the drafts in the Access to Justice Act, 1999 which brought all of this into effect although there were aspects of the legislation which we were unable to change. But the net result of the change of government together with our efforts was that we turned round a potential disaster.

By 1997, when the Woolf reforms were being prepared for implementation, the pace of internal reform within the firm

Tom Jones speaking at Thompsons' National Conference, Warwick, March 2007

was stepped up to meet the challenge. Team working was introduced along with a computerised case management system.

It was a race against time to get the new systems in place to meet the challenges of the changes in practice and procedure; and it cost money. The cost of the new IT system and the training needed to help hundreds of non IT literate lawyers use it was considerable, but even that was dwarfed by the cost of reductions in mainstream staff on the one hand, the increase in less profitable employment work on the other, not to mention the expansion costs associated with the large influx of coal miners' chronic bronchitis and vibration white finger cases.

While all this was going on the firm tried to surf the

wave of a new threat – the emergent claims companies which were riding on the back of the new funding regime. Tom Jones:

A major initiative was in relation to telephone access. At the time trade union members who wanted legal assistance would have to find their branch secretary or other union representative, obtain a form for legal assistance and fill it in, and then rely on the union to send the form to head office where it would be allocated. They would then wait to hear from the solicitor. Weeks could go by. At the same the claims companies which were springing up and advertising heavily on television and elsewhere, were offering immediate telephone access. The unions feared a loss of control that came from a move away from the paper based system. However, we were successful in overcoming the concerns of the unions and set up the Trade Union Call Handling Centre (TUCH) under the control of Liz Wood.

Free legal advice had been offered to unions as a system for a number of years, but essentially it was paper based and office based within all the local Thompsons' branches. Free legal advice matters that were not personal injury or employment cases would get passed around in offices and were difficult and time consuming to deal with. The free legal advice system we set up with Liz involves a specialist department in Sheffield and now handles 20,000 free legal advice queries a year.

In July 1999, the firm opened a related practice The Thompsons Partnership, in Plymouth, to handle wills and conveyancing.

Most importantly, in 1999 an office was formed in Belfast, when the firm joined forces with McClure & Co to form Thompsons McClure, thus ensuring that Thompsons had offices in every part of the UK. Paul Shevlin was

Tony Lawton at the Thompsons' National Conference, Warwick, March 2007

appointed the regional managing partner.

From early in the new millennium the financial position improved. Success fees – the additional element of costs allowed to solicitors in successful cases under conditional fee agreements to cover the shortfall of nil costs recovery in unsuccessful cases and to fund investigations into cases that are ultimately turned down because they do not have reasonable prospects of success – began to have an impact, though this silver lining came with its own cloud. As Doug Christie explained:

The backlash then occurred because defendants' liability

Rodney Bickerstaffe, Neil Kinnock and Geoff Shears at the Thompsons' Reception to celebrate Rodney Bickerstaffe becoming Chairman of the TUC and Tom Sawyer becoming Chairman of the Labour Party, 29 September 1991

insurers started fighting back on the recoverability issues and the costs war started. The defendants started peddling the myth of a compensation culture and ran a smart campaign in 2003. Employers' liability premiums shot up, the real reason for that being structural in the industry, but the line was peddled that it was because of the increased costs of litigation caused by compensation culture and CFA recoverability and that the increased premiums were damaging small businesses. The small businesses affected by the increase in premiums were told to go and lobby government, and they did.

The costs war has rumbled on ever since … . Obviously, Tom has been very much involved in this campaign and in many other campaigns. My main involvement has been in the area of costs and funding since the whole viability of union legal services and of Thompsons depends on this. Tom has effectively been dealing with campaigns now for ten years, and has been involved with MPs, ministers, civil servants and government generally on a whole range of issues.

Tom Jones, Thompsons' Head of Policy and Public Affairs:

A classic example is the Corporate Manslaughter Act. Our involvement there was helped by the firm's friendship with a number of MPs. Mick Antoniw was also much involved. We attended numerous meetings, attended the committee stages of the Bill and advised on any adverse points. The net result is not perfect, but we have achieved a result.

An example of a current campaign is the campaign Thompsons is running for improvements in the compensation regime for asbestos victims in England and Wales. The point here is that bereavement damages are much more favourable in Scotland than they are in England and Wales and we are campaigning to secure a similar level of benefit across the UK.

These comments give little more than a snapshot of the context within which the firm has been operating in recent years. Campaigns, challenges and changes continued at a rate that would dismay the fainthearted. As ever, and wherever possible, campaigns were supported by test cases, and the next chapter attempts to describe some of the more important cases pursued in the last few years.

Chapter 28
More test cases

As we moved towards and beyond the millennium, the human cost of the country's industrial legacy showed no signs of abating. Asbestos related injuries continued to rise but were met with increasingly sophisticated defences. Areas of work such as asbestos claims were given their own specialist units within the firm, and Thompsons was involved in many leading cases, including the Fairchild decision in the House of Lords.

Not surprisingly, one of the groups of workers whose health continued to be most affected by their work was coal miners. Test cases were brought, followed by a major undertaking to pursue thousands of cases of former miners suffering from emphysema and/or vibration white finger.

Vibration White Finger
Armstrong & Others v British Coal [1998)] (unreported)
Following meetings which took place in 1988 at Vane Tempest pit in Durham between Thompsons and the Durham Area NUM & Durham Mechanics Trust it was clear there was a significant problem with coal miners working in the industry suffering from the condition known as Vibration White Finger 'VWF' now commonly referred to as Hand Arm Vibration syndrome or 'HAVS'.
Backed by the Durham Miners Association and Durham Colliery Mechanics Trust together with support from other unions, a series of test cases was brought against British Coal (BCC) culminating in the judgment of HHJ Stephenson on 17 January 1996 on two preliminary issues:
   a the date from which BCC ought to have recognised that working with tools which caused excessive

vibration gave rise to a risk of injury (1 January 1973) and

b that warnings of the dangers and examinations ought to have been introduced to protect the workforce from 1 January 1975 and job rotation introduced by 1 January 1976.

This ruling was appealed by BCC and the appeal was effectively dismissed by the Court of Appeal on 28 November 1996.

The hearing of the test cases resumed before HHJ Stephenson on 3 March 1997 in Newcastle upon Tyne and judgment on the lead cases was given on 30 September 1997 when the judge found BCC liable and negligent in respect of vibration induced injury suffered after 1 January 1975. Of the nine lead claimants four were clients of Thompsons and members of either the Durham NUM or Durham Colliery Mechanics Trust. Of those four cases, three were successful.

Again the judgments were subject to appeal by BCC but the appeals were largely dismissed on 31 July 1998.

Respiratory Disease Litigation
Griffiths & Others v British Coal [1998] (Unreported)
The second major piece of litigation in the late 1990s involving BCC was a series of eight test cases brought by former BCC employees suffering from the effects of exposure to coal dust whilst working underground.

Thompsons' involvement in these cases was with the generic work only.

Judgment was given by Mr Justice Turner on 23 January 1998 in which he found BCC liable to pay damages in respect of in particular chronic bronchitis and emphysema where the claimant had been exposed to coal dust working underground after 5 June 1954.

Apportionments would be made to damages awarded for matters such as a claimant's smoking history, the extent of his exposure, the extent of his exposure before June 1954 and his use of a respirator.

Given the numbers of potential claimants awaiting the results of the test cases in the two actions, BCC entered into handling agreements with the claimants' representatives to deal with the many thousands of expected claims. The VWF scheme closed for most Claimants on 30 September 2002 and the Respiratory Disease scheme on 31 March 2004. Thompsons handled claims on behalf of union clients, in particular the Durham area NUM, the Durham Mechanics and the South Wales area NUM.

Regrettably the operation of these schemes became embroiled in controversy. Tom Jones commented:

One event that has caused considerable difficulty is the Coal Board claims on behalf of former mineworkers suffering from chronic bronchitis and emphysema and/or vibration white finger. Thompsons of course ran/was involved in the litigation that resulted in a successful outcome and then negotiated the scheme before setting up our own in-house systems to run the cases. On behalf of our clients we have been highly successful in recovering substantial damages for many thousands of mineworkers, their widows and their families. Unfortunately, what should have been a success for everyone – miners and their widows and the government, has been turned into a PR disaster by greedy lawyers who, despite having been paid by the government under the scheme and despite the damages they won having been poor, took additional money out of the injured miner's compensation.

John Mann and Kevan Jones, both MPs, started to run campaigns critical of the way deductions from damages were made in miners' cases. Thompsons got caught up in the maelstrom. Essentially a member's returned contribution went to the union as the mining unions had no working members and therefore no income. Thompsons took nothing from the damages but the mining unions used the money to build up a fighting fund for the next big battle (miner's knee litigation) and to provide welfare services to their elderly and often infirm members. We have been criticised for taking the deductions and passing them on and the criticism has really stung because of our political heritage and the results we achieved.

In 2010 Thompsons, through their Chief Executive accepted a severe reprimand for breaches of the Solicitors' Practice Rules, a finding which took account of regulatory breaches but which also noted that the firm had been proactive in providing compensation, had been cooperative and constructive.

Asbestos

The past several years have been marked by a rear guard action by the insurance industry in the area of asbestos disease compensation.

Ian McFall, Thompsons' Head of Asbestos, has been involved on behalf of at least one of the claimants in many recent leading cases, some of which are as follows:

Fairchild & ors v Glenhaven Funeral Services & ors [2002] 3 All ER 305 HL

This involved five similar cases, one of which concerned Robert Pendleton, a Thompsons' client.

The defendants in each case tried to avoid liability entirely on the basis that although they had negligently exposed the claimant/deceased to asbestos dust, it could not be proved that it was their dust which was responsible for the fatal cancer – mesothelioma – as the claimant/deceased had also been exposed to asbestos dust by one or more other parties. They persisted with this argument even when all relevant companies had been sued.

It took the House of Lords to sort out what to lawyers

was a legal conundrum relating to the burden of proof but to ordinary people seemed like nothing other than a cynical ploy to deny damages to the most deserving cases. The cases were ultimately successful, and hundreds of cases which had been held up in the courts while this litigation was pursued were paid out.

Barker & ors v St Gobain Pipelines Ltd & Ors [2004] PIQR P34
In this case, in which Thompsons again acted for one of the three claimants, the defendants tried to revisit the Fairchild point, this time trying a different form of attack. They argued that the compensation should be reduced where part of the exposure occurred during a period of self-employment or during a period of employment not pursued as part of the proceedings. The defendants failed in their arguments in the High Court and the Court of Appeal, but succeeded before the House of Lords. The judgment gave rise to much criticism and a concerted campaign to reverse the decision.

Tom Jones:

After the decision of the House of Lords there was a demonstration close to the House of Commons which I attended. I saw Dave Anderson MP there, briefed him, and he went in and asked a question of the Prime Minister at Prime Minister's Question Time. The Prime Minister expressed concern about the decision. Within three days John Hutton the DWP Minister, had condemned the decision. Lord Falconer became involved, and the campaign snowballed. Subsequently we helped with some drafting of the relevant provision – Section 3 of the Compensation Act 2006 – which retrospectively overturned Barker.

Ian McFall noted that the issue

was "resolved" as a result of a campaign involving

everything that I feel is good about trade unions, the labour movement and claimant specialist law firms. The government deserves great credit for acting swiftly and decisively in reversing the House of Lords decision in Barker.

Fortunately only a small minority of those exposed to asbestos are unlucky enough to suffer a mesothelioma or asbestos related lung cancer. Some suffer no disease at all; some contract asbestosis with disabling respiratory symptoms; and many incur pleural disease, usually pleural plaques which cause no symptoms but are a sure sign of past asbestos exposure and frequently a cause of anxiety about what the future might hold.

The right of claimants to claim damages for pleural plaques had been established in a series of cases in the 1980s (one of which, Patterson v Ministry of Defence [1986] was a Thompsons' case). The courts would normally award a modest sum in damages for this condition, usually with a proviso that the claimant could return to court for a further award in the unhappy event of contracting a serious asbestos condition (the provisional damages system).

The right to claim for pleural plaques came under attack in *Grieves & ors v FT Everard & Sons & ors [2005] EWHC 88 (QB)* There were ten similar cases, two of which were dealt with by Thompsons, all involving workmen who were exposed to asbestos and had been diagnosed with pleural plaques. The employers attempted to resist the cases saying that pleural plaques do not cause any injury and should not be compensated. The judge rejected this argument but set levels of compensation at a level below that which had become the norm in recent years. The insurance industry was still not satisfied and appealed to the Court of Appeal. The appeal judgment was given on 26 January 2006 and found against the claimants. In a majority verdict of two to one the court decided that the physical changes to the body

Ian McFall at the Thompsons' National Conference, Warwick, March 2007

caused by pleural plaques were not sufficient to amount to damage giving rise to a cause of action even where the underlying asbestos exposure carried a risk of causing significant injury and gave rise to anxiety. One of the judges disagreed, and four of the cases, including the two handled by Ian McFall were taken to the House of Lords in July 2007. In its judgment of 17 October 2007, the Lords agreed with the defendants and dismissed the appeal.

The Scottish Parliament decided to take steps to pass legislation to overturn the judgment, and the Ministry of Justice issued a Consultation Paper to review the issues. The Ministry eventually decided not to follow suit (and to deal with those who had outstanding claims with a one-off payment).

Turner & Newall PLC (in administration)

The desperation of some employers to avoid having to pay for the injuries and disease they have caused (or more particularly for insurers to avoid paying claims notwithstanding their acceptance of premium income over many years) is no better shown than in the case of Turner and Newall PLC. They adopted a novel (for this country) approach and mimicked the tactic of some American companies by filing for administration. The effect of this was that no legal proceedings could be commenced against them pending the resolution of insurance issues, and all the cases where proceedings were already underway were 'stayed', i.e. stopped in their tracks. This even applied to cases where settlements had been agreed and all that was awaited was the cheque for compensation. Indeed in some cases the cheques which had been issued bounced, literally adding insult to injury and increasing the distress of the injured and in some cases widows. In the meantime there was complex litigation involving the existence and scope of relevant insurance which the relevant insurers fought for all they were worth.

Ian McFall secured a position on the Creditors Committee of the company as the best place from which he could influence events, and a scheme was eventually agreed and approved by the court which ensures that the injured and bereaved receive at least some compensation.

The 'Trigger issue' litigation – Durham v Builders Accident Insurance (Run Off) Ltd [2008] EWHC (QB) 2692

Yet another massive attack on the right to compensation related to the so-called trigger issue, and this time it involved insurers fighting it out with one another as well as with claimants.

The important legal issue in this test case was to determine the true meaning and effect of the terms of insurance policies that were sold to employers at a time when workers were being negligently exposed to asbestos. A number of insurers argued the policies they sold, to insure employers against liability for workers who were injured or suffered illness as a result of their work, were 'triggered' by the development of the disease rather than by the exposure to asbestos. The challenge, if successful, would have deprived many mesothelioma victims and their families of compensation, because by the time the disease develops many employers have gone out of business and no longer have any insurance cover. One of the cases in the test litigation was handled by Joanne Candlish from Liverpool office.

The Background

Until 2006, employers' insurers had always accepted that the policies meant that an insurer on cover at the time of the asbestos exposure would pay the claim even though the worker developed mesothelioma many decades later.

Following a Court of Appeal decision in a Public Liability insurance claim in 2006, a number of employers' insurers decided to refuse to pay out in mesothelioma claims. Those insurers were Builders Accident Insurance (BAI), Independent Insurance Company Limited (IICL), Excess Insurance Company Limited (EICL) and Municipal Mutual Insurance (MMI). They argued that, despite the universal custom and practice that had always operated throughout the Employers Liability market, the policies really meant that the insurer was not liable if the mesothelioma developed after the period of insurance cover ended.

The central issue the court had to decide was whether the policy trigger was:

a) the inhalation/exposure to asbestos, or

b) the development of the mesothelioma tumour some forty or more years later.

After a trial lasting two full calendar months of evidence and exhaustive legal argument, including ten days of opening and nine days of closing submissions, the High Court decided in a judgment running to over one hundred pages that the policy trigger was the inhalation/exposure and therefore the insurers on cover when the exposure occurred were liable to pay out.

The decision of the High Court was as a victory for fairness, justice and common sense in which the support of the trade union Unite played a pivotal role. As Derek Simpson, Unite Joint General Secretary, commented, this was

> a hugely important victory for the victims of this deadly dust … . Thousands of men and women across the UK have been negligently exposed to asbestos by their employers but insurers have tried and failed to use legal technicalities to escape their responsibility to pay compensation under the policies they sold to employers. They sought to avoid their liabilities while pocketing the money.
>
> We are prepared to take on the big cases and fight for our members' rights to justice … . Without trade unions many of these cases would never have been fought. Unite has been in the forefront of the legal and political campaign to win compensation for the victims of asbestos.

This decision was partially overturned by the Court of Appeal but was subsequently reinstated by the Supreme Court.

All these cases are evidence of a powerful and concerted effort by the insurance industry and the financial institutions which support them to minimise the financial effects to themselves of the negligence and breaches of duty of the companies whose premiums they gladly took, notwithstanding the injuries suffered and despair caused to the workers whose efforts made them the companies they were.

The need for a strong and concerted defence to the attack on protections fought for over so many years has never been more evident. In Ian McFall's words:

We still consider that the only effective way of obtaining proper compensation for sufferers and their families is to pursue a policy of assertive litigation. We haven't noticed any general willingness on the part of the insurance industry to deal with claims any more efficiently than they may have done in the past.

Before leaving the subject of asbestos disease there is one further case which merits a special mention and in which a remarkable victory was achieved.

Dawson v The Cherry Tree Machine Company Ltd & anor [2001] EWCA Civ 101 CA

The case, handled first by Pauline Chandler and then Judith Gledhill and heard by the Court of Appeal in 2001, established an important point of interpretation in respect of the Asbestos Industry Regulations 1931.

Mr Cherry was employed by the company as an apprentice fitter from 1945 to 1949. The company manufactured dry cleaners' presses. From 1946 to 1948 part of his job was to seal the platens of the presses with asbestos to stop steam escaping. He would take a couple of handfuls of asbestos flock, put it in a bucket and mix it with water and then apply it. He alleged that the employers were in breach of the 1931 regulations.

The employers argued that the 1931 regulations only applied to the asbestos industry and not the incidental use of asbestos in other industries. The judge disagreed, a finding upheld in the Court of Appeal, a decision of considerable importance to anyone suffering from an asbestos related disease from such exposure before the Second World War.

Another recent case, again a disease case but this time not involving asbestos, struck a significant blow in favour of the protection afforded to workers under a rather more recent regulatory framework applicable to dangerous substances.

Dugmore v Swansea NHS Trust and another [2003] 1 All ER 333 CA

This case, handled by Mick Antoniw, is one of the most important disease cases of recent years. It concerns the interpretation of the Control of Substances Hazardous to Health Regulations, 1988 (the COSHH Regulations).

The claimant worked as a nurse. She had suffered eczema and asthma all her life. Between 1993 and 1995 she developed an allergy to latex as a result of using powdered latex gloves in the course of her work.

There was no published evidence before 1993 that the use of latex gloves could result in latex allergy. In 1996 the hospital provided her with vinyl gloves after she suffered a serious reaction whilst performing a procedure using latex gloves. In 1997 whilst employed at a different hospital and using vinyl gloves she suffered an anaphylactic attack when picking up an empty box which had contained latex gloves. She had to give up work.

The court held that the duty under the COSHH Regulations was absolute: to ensure that exposure was prevented or adequately controlled. The defence of reasonable practicability qualified only the duty of total prevention. The employer could have provided vinyl gloves. The purpose of the regulations was protective and preventative and the claimant therefore succeeded in her claim against the first hospital.

The battle for compensation for the victims of asbestos and other diseases rightly achieves a high profile in the media. But there are many cases which are in the mainstream of personal injury work which have a lasting impact – not just on the compensation payable to an individual or indeed a whole class of claimants, but on the whole approach to health and safety to be taken by employers across the board.

One such case, pursued by Henrietta Phillips recently achieved such a result. It was an exceptionally difficult case:

Adequate training under the Health and Safety at Work Regulations

Allinson v London Underground [2008] EWCA Civ 71

The claimant was a tube train driver who suffered tenosynovitis due to prolonged use of the traction brake controller (TBC), a lever that has to be pressed at all times for the train to go forward. When the TBC was introduced, a grooved end was added on the suggestion of experienced drivers to make the handle more comfortable. This was done without expert advice. The claimant adopted a grip with her thumb against this grooved end, and this caused her repetitive strain injury.

She brought her claim under the 1998 Provision and Use of Work Equipment Regulations, Regulation 9 of which requires the employer to ensure that all persons who use work equipment have received adequate training for purposes of health and safety. There had been training in avoiding the known risk of such injuries through flexion of the wrist, but there had been no training as to where to place the thumb whilst driving.

The county court judge found that the training had been adequate in all the circumstances – it dealt with the known risk. The Court of Appeal disagreed and found for the claimant, finding that

the test for adequacy (of training) for the purposes of health and safety is what (training) was needed in the light of what the employer ought to have known about the risks arising from the activities of his business. To say that the training is adequate if it deals with the risk which the employer knows about is to impose no greater a duty than exists at common

law. In my view the statutory duty is higher and imposes on the employer a duty to investigate the risks inherent in the operations, taking professional advice where necessary … .
– per Lady Justice Smith.

The court went on to link the need for adequate training to the risk assessment required under the Management of Health and Safety at Work Regulations.

Risk assessments are meant to be an exercise by which the employer examines and evaluates all the risks entailed in his operations and takes steps to remove or minimise those risks. They should be a blueprint for action … . It seems to me that insufficient judicial attention has been given to risk assessments in the years since the duty to conduct them was first introduced.

The court drew a parallel with the Dugmore case where again the court made the distinction between the common law duty to take reasonable care to avoid unnecessary risks and the more onerous duty under the regulations to go out and discover the risks and to take the appropriate steps.

The international dimension

Thompsons' international work has links which can be traced back to its earliest days – for example in the Meerut conspiracy case, but which lay dormant for many years. More recently and often in conjunction with progressive trade unions, there has been a resurgence of initiatives in other jurisdictions.

South Africa

In South Africa, despite knowledge of the lethal dangers of asbestos, mining companies continued to excavate the mineral, exposing thousands of mainly itinerant workers. Come the end of apartheid, the companies closed their mining operations. Using the skills and experience drawn from their fight for justice in the UK for victims of the mining and asbestos industries, Thompsons was able to assist in securing compensation for South African asbestos miners and their families in landmark multi-million pound settlements.

The firm reinvested all profit from the settlement back into further projects in South Africa. The funds were used to help establish a law firm there, Narian and Associates, working on the same principles as Thompsons. This firm has been processing claims into the £45 million trust fund set up as a result of the settlement.

Further research is being sponsored to investigate the prospect of litigation for gold miners suffering from silicosis, and to prepare a potential claim in the Constitutional Court challenging the parallel system of benefits for workers suffering from silicosis. One covers mineworkers (mainly black), and the other covers workers in other industries (mainly white). As Tom Jones commented: 'no prizes for guessing which pays out more'.

China

In China, Thompsons is supporting a joint TUC/ International Miners Association initiative aimed at improving health and training standards in Chinese mines. Funding is being supplied with part of the proceeds from the UK Coal Scheme cases.

Columbia

It is said that more trade unionists are killed in Colombia each year than in the rest of the world combined. In the vast majority of cases, no one is ever held accountable.

The firm has worked with NGO Justice for Colombia in their political prisoner campaign, as a result of which a number of trade union activists were released in 2008; but hundreds remain in prison, and the campaign in conjunction with regional trades unions and trades councils continues.

The firm has been working to support FENSUAGRO, the Colombian agricultural workers union, with the establishment of a new legal unit for the union designed to assist in two key areas:

1. Providing legal defence to members of the union imprisoned for their union activities
2. Strengthening the capacity of the union to document and disseminate information about human rights abuses against members.

There has also been work with FECODE, the teachers' union and largest in the country, by way of a project sponsored by the three British teaching unions ATL, NASUWT, NUT and Thompsons to fund regional seminars and other recruitment initiatives designed to raise awareness of the union and the benefits of joining.

A recent project, sponsored by CWU, NIPSA and GMB Southern Region, along with Thompsons, has been run in partnership with the Permanent Committee for the Defence of Human Rights, the largest and one of the oldest human rights organisations in Colombia. Professional experts such as psychologists, post-trauma therapists and social workers have been engaged to work with displaced people and their families who have been the victims of violence.

In 2008, a number of the firm's lawyers took part in a delegation that went to Colombia as part of a Law Society initiative to investigate the situation faced by Colombian human rights lawyers, and generally the firm supports many fringe meetings at conferences and speaks on platforms to highlight the plight of trade unionists in Colombia.

Cuba

Thompsons works with the Cuba Solidarity Campaign in the defence of the Cuban people's right to self-determination, against the US blockade, and for the freedom of the Miami Five.

When the Soviet Union collapsed, Thompsons worked with UNISON and other unions to deliver supplies, and in particular ambulances, to the Cuban health service. The links established then and since have been used to work with individual unions and the TUC to develop solidarity work with the CTC (the Cuban equivalent of the TUC).

Venezuela

The firm has been involved with the Venezuela Information Centre, a broad-based UK campaign launched by the unions in May 2005 to support the rights of the Venezuelan people to determine their future. Its aim is to provide accurate, objective information about trade union and political movements in the country.

Palestine

In 2008, some of the firm's partners took part in a delegation to the Occupied Territories. Delegation members reported that they were shocked by the level of human rights abuses, One of the delegates was David Thompson, who recalled poignantly that his grandfather W.H. had been a friend of David Ben-Gurion, Israel's first prime Minister.

Following the trip, Thompsons affiliated to the Palestine Solidarity Campaign (PSC). Many of the firm's staff have since become involved in local PSC groups.

Thompsons – 1996 Equity Partners

NAME	DATE LEFT
1 May 1996	
Geoff Shears	
Frank Foy	31.07.02
Andrew Herbert	30.04.03
Colin Simpson	30.04.98
David Thompson	
Roger Bent	30.04.98 – retired on 3 year consultancy
Tony Lawton	
Karen Mitchell	
Nick Carter	30.04.97 – retired on 2 year consultancy
Pauline Chandler	31.08.99
Steve Allen	30.04.04
Phil King	
Mark Berry	
Philip Ballard	
Francine O'Gorman	
Tony Briscoe	30.04.01
Sarah Goodman	
Roger Maddocks	30.09.00
Jane Litherland	31.05.99
Elisabeth Roth	31.10.99
John Skinner	30.04.98
Steve Cottingham	31.10.03
Stephen Cavalier	
Julie Wood	
Alicia Rendell	31.05.99
Mick Antoniw	

NAME	DATE LEFT
Neville Filar	30.04.99
Philip Brooks	31.05.99
Sally Gold	30.03.00
John Usher	15.05.00
David G Thompson	31.08.99
Keith Patten	30.04.02 (subsequently rejoined)
Peter Bamford	30.04.97
Stefan Cross	30.09.02
Nigel Saunders	
Peter Mulhern	
Richard Woolley	
Steve Pinder	31.12.99
Matthew Tollitt	
Phil Smith	
Rob Wood	
Vicky Deritis	31.12.99
Gill Owen	
John Myles	30.04.99
Judith Gledhill	
Katrina London	31.12.99
Mary Stacey	31.12.98
Paul Jackson	30.04.99
Tom Jones	
Ian Kinnear	31.10.99
Kate Ross	31.10.04
Susan Harris	
Gavin Roberts	
Pat Andrews	04.07.03
Doug Christie	
Cathryn Davies	

414

NAME	DATE LEFT
1 November 1998	
Nicola Dandridge	30.06.06
1 May 2000	
Keith Taylor	31.12.01. Rejoined 1.5.09 – see below
Stephen Jones	
Ivan Walker	31.12.06
Rachel Sarfas	
1 May 2002	
Joanna Stevens	
Terry Loughrey	
David Stothard	
Victoria Phillips	
Richard Arthur	
1 May 2005	
Joe O'Hara	
Rakesh Patel	
1 May 2008	
Chris Strogen	
Julie Blackburn	
1 May 2009	
Jeremy Hague	
Peter Carson	
Keith Roberts	
Keith Taylor	
John Parkhouse	
Neil Johnson	
Paul Evans	
Mary O'Connor	

Accurate as at June 2009

Chapter 29
Thompsons Scotland and Northern Ireland

Scotland

When Robin Thompsons decided to open an office in Scotland they started the process from scratch, recruiting two lawyers David Stevenson and Manus McGuire. David and Manus had the benefit of taking an immediate caseload, but the challenge was to set up a successful operation within the Scottish legal framework and against a backdrop of expectation, both from the trades unions and the firms of Robin and Brian in England and Wales – a very different legal jurisdiction.

The story of Scotland could be split up and described at relevant parts of the general chronology of the firm; but it is a story in its own right, best described by David Stevenson who, together with Manus, opened the office in 1979. David retired from Thompsons on 31 October 2006 and now undertakes some work as a counsel for the office.

I was apprenticed as a solicitor at Strathern & Blair. My father knew a partner there. The firm did very little litigation when I started, but they did take on a litigation lawyer, and as it turned out a client of his was W.H. Thompson, Cardiff in respect of the SOGAT West of Scotland work; I saw what he did, and became interested in litigation.

On qualifying as a solicitor I joined Bonar McKenzie, a big litigation firm, where I undertook legal aid work and some advocacy. I did personal injury, family and criminal work and was keen on forging a career in personal injury or criminal work (but not family). I applied for a partnership at the firm but the conveyancing partners decided there were too many litigation partners and I therefore started looking round for another firm.

This coincided with Thompsons advertising for lawyers to run a firm in Edinburgh following the McShannon -v- Rockware Glass case. Thompsons were under considerable pressure to open up an office following McShannon, and some of that pressure came from the Constructional Section of the AUEW who had a lot of big cases in Scotland, cases that were not easily settled outside of litigation and which therefore now required litigators in Scotland.

I was interviewed by David Skidmore and Colin Simpson. Manus McGuire and I were chosen. Manus was from a mining family background who came late to the law after working as a probation officer. I believe I was chosen because I was knowledgeable in respect of the Court of Session and litigation generally. I knew local counsel and how to go about things.

Accordingly we opened the office on 1 November 1979. Before that the two of us spent a number of weeks in Ilford, and we initially took the Ilford Scottish work which consisted of about 400 cases including ASTMS, ASLEF, SCPS and of course the Constructional Section of the AUEW.

A number of other Thompsons' offices had Scottish work, but it was this work that we started off with. Bainbridge House, for example, had the SOGAT work, and the intention was that we would take that when we were up and running.

Manus was not that keen on administration, and from day one I dealt with most of the administration. I recruited the staff. I was able to obtain a senior secretary from Bonar McKenzie, and she became our office manager, Elaineen McAuley. She had a wealth of experience. I also recruited my own secretary and one other. We were a small operation at first but, unlike other Thompson offices which opened, we had to stand on our own two feet from the beginning. This was because the procedure is, of course, entirely different in Scotland and furthermore we were not known to the trade union movement. The Scottish TUC is very different to the TUC in England, and the CEU or Constructional Section of the AUEW did not have a significant voice in the STUC.

We soon got to know the District Organiser of ASLEF, Johnny Walker, who was heavily involved in the STUC and helped to get us accepted. Once we acquired from the English offices of Thompsons the NUPE work (which was previously handled at Stanmore) we got to know Ron Curran the Divisional Officer (DO), and Bob Thomson, the ADO, and they were also very helpful.

Obviously the reason for opening Scotland was so that Thompsons could deal with litigation in personal injury cases in Scotland without farming the litigation out to Scottish agents. It was clear that personal injury work received a low profile under the Scottish system at the time, The Court of Session mainly dealt with divorce cases and personal injury cases were dealt with poorly within the system (in contrast to the position as it had been a couple of decades earlier when there were still jury trials). It was our job to improve the profile of personal injury work, the litigation rate, solatium (general damages for pain and suffering), etc. The only area where Scottish damages were higher was in respect of fatal claims under statute (and this remains the case even now).

Bearing in mind the length of time it used to take to get a case to trial (a minimum of two years), it was essential that we pushed on hard and a lot of the pressure therefore fell on me as the litigator.

We soon acquired the SOGAT cases which by then included the SGA (the NGA's Scottish equivalent) which, unlike the NGA had a considerable membership – 20,000 in Scotland, We developed geographical regions for dealing with the cases and by the end of the first year we had accumulated about 1,000 cases, had taken on more staff including Mike Allen, a friend of mine who was also an experienced litigator.

Manus dealt with what tribunal work there was as well as litigation. The tribunal work at the time was just for SOGAT, although we did the occasional industrial work, for example arising out of the Civil Service Strike, the sit in by MLSO's at Victoria Hospital, and criminal work such as the defence (unsuccessful) of Ted Elsey, the National Officer of IRSF who was charged under the Conspiracy and Protection of Property Act 1878, the first person to be so charged for many years.

From an internal structural point of view, in law we were independent as a Scottish firm but in reality we operated as part and parcel of Robin Thompson & Partners. On joining I was an equity partner at the age of 28 and indeed at that time the number of partners was not high. Thompsons depended on many unqualified executives rather than partners. I became part of the management and joined the Liaison Committee in 1983 and became increasingly involved during the 1980s. We acquired the NUPE work, and also the Foundry Workers cases from late 1980 and we were expanding. Frank Maguire joined in 1981 and Syd Smith in 1982. We were anxious to pursue all the issues on which we felt Scotland needed to get up to speed, including Smith -v- Manchester damages, nursing lifting cases and so on. RSI (repetitive strain injury) was also on the radar. Thompsons generally were a huge help and the Court Service began to become conscious of the greatly increased amount of litigation.

1982 was a crunch year for us in more ways than one. We had been dealing with some deafness cases from the early days. At the time the Boilermakers Union were operating a direct scheme with the Iron Trades Insurance Company. Of course, boilermakers worked in multi union workplaces, and other unions and their members started to get to know about the Scheme. I was starting therefore to get a number of deafness cases, particularly from ASTMS, and had negotiated an unofficial Scheme with the Iron Trades (which was 50 per cent better, as it turned out, than the Scheme that we ended up with after the Deafness Judgment in 1984). In 1982 I got a call one day from Simon Walton. Newcastle office had had an approach from Boilermakers about their deafness cases and wanted Thompsons to take them over. There was to be a meeting in Newcastle the following night. I attended and we were told that there were 3,000 deafness cases in Scotland. The real worry was the volume of North Eastern cases. Geoff Thomas was at this meeting and was bullish about handling the problem and offered on behalf of Cardiff office that Cardiff alone would take 3,000 cases. Buoyed up by this I agreed that we should take the Scottish cases in Edinburgh. The background was that although Frank Foy and Geoff Shears were keen (as of course was Geoff Thomas) on taking these cases, Brian Thompson certainly was not. His view was that the firms had far too many cases already.

Ten days after that meeting, on 10 March 1982, I was asleep in bed at night when the police rang. There was a fire in the office and could I come in. I drove in, and as I reached Charlotte Square I saw the bay window to my office burst followed by a huge fireball. Within 24 hours I had obtained some temporary property. A rota of people came up from Congress House and Ilford to reconstruct files, and in the end we lost only about fifty files.

All that was happening when the deafness cases were about to arrive. So, the troops of executives carried on coming to assist us with those and somehow we got through it. We had to recruit, and did so well. We were fortunate to obtain John Henderson who was very experienced and knew all about administration. He was taken on to manage the deafness cases.

As the cases proceeded with litigation, the initial batch of course were being handled by Frank Foy (and finally by Mark Berry). I was due to take the second batch of lead cases, against Babcocks. It was all very heavy litigation and the Court of Session had started to become extremely anxious about the volume of it. In the midst of all this we found our present premises in Castle Street in late 1982. While all that was going on there were two relevant matters so far as staffing was concerned. Manus started to make a real name for himself in employment law, and Mike Allen unfortunately had to leave in early 1983 for family reasons.

Although the Deafness Scheme which followed the Newcastle test cases meant that the deafness cases were all then concluded under the Scheme rather than by litigation, we had another enormous amount of work on the horizon, and this arose out of the Miners' Strike. We got to know the Scottish miners, partly as a result of the contact with Johnny Walker, mentioned above. Johnny recommended us to Mick McGahey. When the miners' dispute started, the Hunterston Oil Terminal which took oil to Ravenscraig Steelworks was in the frontline. Accordingly, picketing at Hunterston was heavy, and there were many arrests. The miners contacted us to represent them.

In that period from 1984 to 1986 Thompsons effectively became the largest criminal law practice in Scotland because of the number of cases.

Organisationally it was not easy. Manus and I had dealt with criminal law in the past and we did a lot of the attendances at police stations. Our experience with the deafness work meant that we had an organisational system in place. John Henderson organised the representational side to ensure that it was all covered. At the same time Jackie Verth and others in deafness had enough knowledge to keep the deafness running. Manus dealt with the bigger cases and a lot of our solicitors were drafted in to deal with the appearances. I tried at the same time to keep the core personal injury work going.

There was a big issue during the strike when an application was made to challenge the legality of the strike, a challenge we successfully resisted. We were able to achieve this, unlike the English and Welsh counterparts, because of differences in the Rule Book as applied to the Scottish area. It was very important for the NUM because it meant that at least one part of the regional structure could carry on conducting business lawfully. At one point I was appointed as representative of the NUM Scotland in dealing with the Receiver, and had meetings with accountants in London where I was singularly unhelpful due to my total ignorance, a helpful point in the context.

The trials of miners were constant, and Mike Allen came back for a few months to assist us, his family problems having abated. I recall one particular case where we were able to have a number of convictions set aside on grounds of bias, the findings of guilt having been made by the Ayrshire Sheriff who had been unwise enough at some point to boast at a Curling Club Dinner that if any miner came before him he would soon be sorry. This comment had been heard by Roy Penny one of the other lawyers who acted for the NUM.

At the end of the dispute there was also a raft of unfair dismissal cases which we were successful with because the NCB had been unwise enough to take back some of the miners on the basis that they had returned to work before the end of the strike.

The upshot was that when the dispute came to an end the NUM gave us all their work and this, once more, included a considerable amount of deafness work. Prior to this the NUM had dealt with legal claims through their own Compensation Department. We were invited to investigate this at the request of the offices of the Scottish area and it was clear that cases were being settled for less compensation that we would have been able to recover, and that there was a cosy system in operation with NCB Claims Department involving tariffs and few investigations. The officers Mick McGahey and Eric Clark had influence and got the change through that we would deal with the compensation work direct. There was a considerable volume of it.

We also started receiving accident case work from the GMB following the amalgamation of GMBATU with ASBSBSW. Initially we were one of three firms of solicitors who dealt with the GMB work, ultimately reducing to two. We received deafness and white finger cases in huge volumes.

One of Geoff Thomas's great successes with John Weakley of the AEU was to get the Engineering Section deafness cases dealt with by Thompsons nationally so we then received the Engineering Section deafness work. Prior to that we had never received any Engineering Section work save for the Foundry Section and Construction Section (along with TASS at another date). It was another huge influx. By that stage we must have had at least eight executives plus support staff all dealing with this work under the control of John Henderson.

We struggled to find enough space for all the people we needed, and this was the final spur in persuading us on the need for a Glasgow office which we opened in 1987 with John Henderson as managing partner and Frank Maguire as his number two plus a number of executives. The opening of Glasgow office gave us a better profile, Glasgow is the centre of Scottish Trade Unionism. Indeed, the main reason for opening in Edinburgh initially was because Edinburgh houses the Court of Session. Anyway, the SOGAT deafness came in at about the same time and that was yet another big influx of work.

Again around this time a very significant employment case was going through the courts, probably the most famous Scottish Thompsons' case, Lister -v- Forth Dry Dock, a GMB employment case which changed the face of the TUPE regulations bringing in the European purposive approach. That was Manus McGuire's case and put us on the employment law map in a big way. It finally reached the House of Lords in 1988.

When Glasgow office opened my life became a little easier, and we were just settling down when Piper Alpha exploded in July 1988. Syd Smith and Frank Maguire took charge of what became a huge amount of work. The Piper Alpha disaster involved the death of 187 men on the Piper Alpha oil production platform in the North Sea on 6 July. Many of the men on the rig were non-unionised and had no organisation, and it was the trades unions and their lawyers who ran and organised the case. Very shortly after the disaster it was announced that there would be an Inquiry, and an Inquiry was duly held under Lord Cullen. The Inquiry commenced in November 1988 and was published in November 1990. It was held in two parts, first to establish the causes of the disaster, and second to make recommendations as to the future safety regime. The report subsequently made over 100 recommendations, and they were all accepted and parliament then passed regulations.

The handling of the Inquiry was lengthy and time consuming, Thompsons were instructed by ASTMS, by the Construction Section of the AEU in individual cases, by the GMB for odd boilermakers. The T&G through Ron Todd were also involved on behalf of caterers on the rig. There was a Trade Union Group set up to deal with representation, the template for this having already been set up to some extent by the work that had been done a couple of years earlier on the Chinook helicopter crash which involved ASTMS members in which I had taken the lead.

During the course of all this Syd Smith gave up his caseload to be administrator of the Trade Union Group and

Frank Maguire did the trade union co-ordination but had still to carry on with his caseload. Syd worked on it fulltime for over a year and the Inquiry was a huge success. The 1991 Regulations passed as a result of the findings of the Cullen Inquiry have also been a success. Over the years we have dealt with many compensation cases arising from accidents on rigs. After the regulations were passed, the number of accidents on rigs declined dramatically. To that extent Cullen and the work that we did (since he accepted all of our recommendations) made a difference. The case also had a big impact in raising our profile.

The other major matter which started to develop around that time was the asbestos work. I had started this off in a small way taking on cases referred to me by doctors. Frank Maguire introduced himself to the Clydeside Asbestos Group in the early 1990s and had started getting referrals from Clydeside. This has progressed massively over the years to the extent that Thompsons in Scotland deal probably now with 75 per cent of Scottish asbestos cases. We have not just dealt with the individual cases but campaigned for changes in the law and procedure. As an example, until 1993, solatium (general damages for pain and suffering) was not inheritable under Scottish law. In other words if a mesothelioma victim died before a case was concluded in the courts, the right to compensation for the victim's injuries died with him. Clydeside campaigned to get the law changed so that it fell into line with the law in England and Wales and we had a part in that campaign. Now indeed damages for asbestos victims are considerably better in Scotland than they are in England. For example, the class of individuals who can claim is much wider. The Thompsons Glasgow office has a department of eight or nine lawyers dealing exclusively with asbestos cases.

In 1990 a new management structure was introduced into Scotland and I became co-ordinator spending from then on one or two days per week in London. That lasted for about five years. As a result I was pretty involved in the merger discussions between Brian and Robin Thompsons at least in the sense of trying to bring together the partners from both firms. In due course I chaired the Robin Thompson & Partners merger meeting which achieved what was required. I was firmly in favour of the merger, I had been on the Liaison Committee which was a useful body but I had seen how limited it was in scope.

Once the merger discussions were underway it was clear that it would be a big exercise to try and accommodate the Scottish end and that this would be more than could be easily digested. It was agreed that it would be better for Thompsons Scotland to become more autonomous while the structure of the new firms bedded in. This was agreed in principle and is what has happened in practice. The result of that was that we needed a new structure for the Scottish firm. There were differing views and David Skidmore assisted in achieving a resolution. He came up with the proposal the result of which was that Scotland was run by a Management Committee including Frank Maguire in charge of client relations; Syd Smith, finance; me, staffing; and Lawrence Lumsden, case management. The Management Committee did not include a number of other partners, for example John Henderson or Manus McGuire, and there were some tensions. John in fact took ill health retirement at the end of 1996 and Manus left to become an Employment Tribunal Chairman at the end of 1995; Graham Garrett, another partner, also departed some time later.

From 1996 we still had huge volumes of deafness work which by then we were litigating and we also obtained the non deafness AEU work. When John Weakley died and John Allen became responsible for legal work for the Engineering Section he found, on enquiry, that the union's other solicitors were expensive. John Allen got on well with Frank Maguire and the result was that we got the other part of the AEU work, the majority. It was the final piece of the jigsaw in terms of the Scottish intake of work.

We were able to make progress on other fronts. I had joined the Rules Council of the Court of Session and got on to Rules Working Parties. We were able to achieve fast tracking and proper case management of asbestos cases and we were able to have considerable input into the revision of the entire rules on PI procedure.

By 2000-2001 the Scottish practice had become one of over 150 employees. It was a big firm to manage, and I dealt with the staffing side but passed my liaison role to Frank Maguire. At the same time I was having to manage the employment work, Nicola Dandridge having transferred to London.

The biggest single issue in Scotland in recent years has been handling the chronic bronchitis and emphysema and vibration white finger cases for former miners. We ended up with 25,000 cases in Scotland. Lawrence Lumsden took the lead role in dealing with these cases – a vast and lengthy process.

Today, the Scottish offices, now supplemented by an office in Aberdeen, under the leadership of Syd Smith and others, continue to flourish and continue their role as leading players in the battle for compensation in Britain for those who have suffered accidents and, in particular, industrial diseases.

Belfast

The Thompsons' associated practice in Northern Ireland, Thompsons McClure, is of much more recent vintage. The practice became part of the Thompsons' network in 1999, but already had a long and distinguished history.

The story starts with Francis Hanna & Co which Gerard

McClure joined in 1953 shortly after qualifying. In 1958 McClure set up his own practice, undertaking significant amounts of work for large trade unions including the AEU and the TGWU, as well as some smaller unions including the Ambulance Service. Some of this work was undertaken on an agency basis from Thompsons who received the initial instructions.

An important source of work was the Harland and Wolff shipyard. In the 1960s there was a major catastrophe when the gang plank collapsed on the Rena de Pacifico, causing many fatalities. Not only did the office become extremely busy dealing with the claims which arose from this disaster, but also gained valuable contacts. The firm acquired the work of the electricians union EEPTU (which subsequently merged with the AEU). Work from other trade unions also started to come their way – NUPE as it then was, after the Ambulance service merged with them, and the FBU. In the 1970s the firm also acquired the USDAW work following the retirement of their previous solicitor.

Paul Shevlin entered into partnership with Gerard McClure in 1976. As Paul commented:

Working for some of these unions during the troubles brought different challenges. McClure & Co acted for the first two firemen injured when a mob smashed the windows of the car they were travelling in and threw petrol bombs into the car because they were in uniform.

The offices of the firm had to be evacuated on numerous occasions as the result of security alerts and indeed were severely damaged as the result of a car bomb attack on the nearby Law Courts.

The firm represented all working people irrespective of political or religious beliefs and worked across the sectarian divide that existed throughout Northern Ireland.

When the office joined with Thompsons, Paul became the regional managing partner. Following his retirement Gerard McClure's daughter Oonagh has led the office as branch manager, and today it forms an integral part of the Thompsons' network.

Chapter 30
Robin and Brian Thompson

Brian Thompson died on 26 February 2000 and Robin on 31 October 2002. David Thompson, Robin's son, is a senior partner with major responsibilities working in the Congress House office, and carries the family's torch.

Brian

In his lengthy obituary of Brian, Rodney Bickerstaffe noted:

Brian Thompson continued working as a consultant for Thompsons until his death. He was a brilliant and unusual man, with a wide range of interests: particularly a love of nature and concern for the environment, before it became fashionable.

Brian was a member of the Communist Party for most of his adult life, only relinquishing membership in order to join the Labour Party when persuaded to do so by Tom Sawyer.

For a number of years Sid and Gladys Easton lived at Brian's home. Sid had been Harry Pollitt's driver (with all that this entailed) and was active in the Party and in the T & G Cab Drivers Section. Gladys, who remained there after Sid's death, worked for the Communist Party in an administrative capacity, and, like Sid, was close to Harry Pollitt. Something of a beauty in her youth, she featured in an advertisement for Skegness wearing a bathing costume and holding a beach ball above her head!

Brian was homosexual. Before homosexual activity between consenting adults was legalised in 1967, according to Ivor Walker this was not openly known – those of us who did were constantly afraid that the secret would come out. The effect on the firm would have been disastrous – we could have lost all legal work from the Catholic controlled unions.

Gerald Gardiner QC had to assist on occasion when he needed legal assistance. Certainly after the 1967 Act was passed, Brian made no secret of the fact. He lived a Spartan life in a large rambling house which was barely furnished. He liked nothing more than spending his time at Kew Gardens and enjoyed annual holidays usually on Corsica at a naturist resort.

A complex and brilliant man, he often seemed tortured by the problems he had to deal with. He wanted partners who were his friends; not easy to achieve in a complex, highly charged political firm.

In a typed letter to Eric Heather dated 10 June 1988 following Eric's retirement, he commented: 'I hope your years with Thompsons were tolerably happy and comfortable: I think we had too many problems, and not enough solutions … .' He then adds in longhand, 'Fundamentally, broadly, I feel that I failed …'

These were sentiments he expressed often. Following a response from Eric, Brian wrote to him again on 22 February 1999 thanking him for visiting Margaret Paterson (the nurse who was blinded in 1944 in the incident when the hospital in which his mother was a patient was bombed). This time he notes:

I am glad that you are so positive about Thompsons: there is a lot to be said in its favour, but I have always felt that it could and should have been so much better! I tried to make it better but failed.

Geoff Shears:

Brian was a complex and unique personality. He grew up heavily influenced by radical politics and perhaps radical everything, yet in many ways he was personally conservative. He liked the same clothes (Austin Reed) and the same hairstyle. He was fastidious in his appearance except when on holiday when he would wear his favourite jumpers with holes in the arms (thereby confirming, as we said, his vast wealth). He stood and sat straight. He utterly believed in the important things in life – health, pleasure, people. Yet he was the first to admit that his personal financial security was such that it was easier for him to oppose conventional materialism. He had a marvellous laugh, and a great way of telling a story so that it was difficult to interrupt.

It sometimes seemed by definition that he had met almost everyone who mattered. By the standards of most people, he had an encyclopaedic scientific knowledge and deployed it to great effect. Can you imagine a debate, over several drinks, in Corsica between Allan Taylor and Brian Thompson on whether or not the gleaming star in the firmament was the pole star? He had a comprehensive knowledge of and an interest in most aspects of culture, yet he carried his knowledge lightly and was the first to criticise pretentiousness and bourgeois moralising. He was increasingly concerned about green politics. He would talk endlessly, if allowed, about the interminable problems of waste and decay, hunger and over population. He could not understand progressive colleagues who collected paper for recycling and produced more than two babies. He could not really understand marriage, which was an institution he thought went out in the sixties. Yet he could be very good with children, stimulating their intellectual interest, and manifesting fascination with their honesty and insights.

He loved trees and plants and wildlife. It was impossible to go for a walk with him through the woods or mountains of Corsica without learning more within ten minutes than could

Brian Thompson
1926-2000
Lawyer and Socialist

easily be remembered.

He was gentle and vulnerable, hard and sharp. He was loyal to his friends but demanding in argument. You had to fight for your case, and if necessary deliver the coup de grace to win it.

He loved Ibsen, Wilde and Shaw. He did not like long novels or plays with no clear meaning. I do not think he would ever consciously hurt any living creature (and yet there was that story about the hammer and his brother when they were young). He loved to talk about his mother, his childhood, people whom he had met. He loved to talk about interesting legal cases, he enjoyed philosophical challenges. He argued dialectically – there had to be a victory.

He loved karaoke – Strangers in the Night, It's Now or Never, Danny Boy. To the annoyance of other members of his family he would insist on playing games for pleasure. Yet he played to win in real life on behalf of working people and their trade unions.

He was an ardent and aggressive philosopher on health. He learnt about the importance of diet in the thirties and forties. He said that he was often ill when young, so he cut out this, that and the other preferring for the most part vegetables, nuts and above all fruit. He would occasionally indulge meat, and later in life drank more wine and cider but needed very little to lose his inhibitions. He would often greet one on arrival at his flat with the news that his nuts were in the oven. He described himself as a hypochondriac. When he had a cold he would reduce his intake of food. He was utterly hostile to antibiotics and doctors. Although he was always very thin, he kept himself fit through walking and latterly through exercise at his gym … . He liked swimming, but preferred cold, fresh water and hated the sea "because it is dirty". Nonetheless he could be prevailed upon to make a splash at the beach provided enough of us were watching. He liked to make an entrance. Brian always "arrived". In the same spirit he could be persuaded to stand upon his head in the sand or on a table (falling over in the presence of the recently elected Bill Morris).

He loved his walking holidays in Corsica. He visited the island for about three weeks virtually every year since 1947. His mother had been there earlier. Some of us accompanied him in recent years and we were treated to a guided tour of the walks, paths, hills and hotels and bars. As we climbed or descended he would talk and talk about the past, present and future.

He loved to shock. In conversation or action. He loved to remove his artificial teeth and place them on the table or in a glass. It was fortunate that he did not have an artificial eye.

His sexuality was unusual and challenging. He could not have had an easy time. Nonetheless he had some close friends and many friendly acquaintances, and some people loved him. It was unfortunate, but probably predictable, that he never found a long live-in relationship on which he could depend. He said that he was often lonely in his earlier years, but came to realise that he was happy. He had his friends and his work … .

He was very tolerant of the sins of others. He had friends who stole from him but he would take no action. He would defend anyone in need of support against the police. He hated oppression, racism and brutality and, notwithstanding his personal vulnerability, would occasionally take a `calculated risk´ by standing up to those who perpetrated it. He was a brave man with too much sense to make a virtue of bravery. He was utterly consistent in his commitment to the interests of working people and very hostile to those on their own side who occasionally led them astray. The Miners' Strike was an example.

He was rich company and a good friend.

Brian's oldest friend was the artist Dorothy McGuffie. After he died, she gave these recollections:

The foundation of my friendship with Brian was laid at Dartington, he used to sit on a low wall facing the main entrance from the courtyard at Foxhole always in a green jersey of a specific colour between moss and olive, grey long shorts and bare feet. The shorts finally evolved into blue trousers.

His room was notable for its extreme order and anonymity like a monastic cell, cupboards, shelves and drawers were meticulously tidy and impersonal.

Brian had never explored the surrounding countryside and grounds. I set about changing this and after a while we used to go for long walks in the early hours and at weekends often watching at a particular pool on the Dart, late in the day badger watching. We had a common interest in animals and trees.

I remember staying at his then home, Heysham, on Naphill Common, being shown a collection of conifers which he had found attractive and which were never really a favourite of mine. We spent a lot of time collecting mistletoe berries and trying to graft them under apple tree bark. Great clusters of it were in the elms on the Beaconsfield Estate.

Brian's father, on hearing I was born in Yorkshire, immediately started playing Gracie Fields' records. Later we all went to Amersham to see Orson Wells in *Citizen Kane*.

One of the very first walks from Dartington was to a quarry that Brian could just see from the window of his room. We had to cross the main railway from Totnes Station. To my surprise Brian nipped smartly down the embankment to the track beneath the bridge and laid three pennies on the rail, we watched the next train thunder below the bridge and I can vividly recall the flattened copper discs that he salvaged, a curious but indelible incident.

When Brian visited Lannacombe and later Plymouth and Dartmoor he always complained about the cold. Equally praising the warmth of Corsica and the pleasures of climbing mountains there.

When I lived and worked in London and visited his home in Hampstead I remember him practising Beethoven Sonatas on a baby grand. We used to walk on Hampstead Heath taking Khan the German Shepherd dog sometimes, [also in] Holland Park, Richmond Park and riverside often as my aunt lived on Richmond Hill and she and Brian became friends. I can remember walking in Kenwood in late springtime and there was snow everywhere and the cream magnolia flowers looked strangely dingy against the dazzling white. Brian wore a very long brown overcoat almost to his ankles.

We visited the valley gardens to look at the holly collection and trees in general, also Cliveden and frequently Kew, where Brian surprised me again by voraciously eating rather succulent yew berries and saying it was quite safe if one spat out the pips. Brian commented that he found the evergreen Holm Oak trees dull and oppressive and disapproved of the geese poaching the ground around the lake.

We occasionally visited galleries and art exhibitions together, notably the large Van Gogh exhibition where I was shocked when Brian said he preferred the photographs of the places to the artist's impressions. After queuing to get into the great Turner Exhibition at the Royal Academy Brian seemed to enjoy the immediacy of the open sketch books and sunsets. Monet brought recollections of warmth and the London river landscapes he was familiar with at Pimlico. Stubbs was a failure seen only from a sociological point of view and not appreciating his skill with anatomy and paint. I should have known better!

Latterly I used to stay at Queensgate Gardens whilst visiting Crufts and Smithfield to draw animals. We frequently went to the Natural History Museum to see `Wildlife Photographs of the Year´ and always enjoyed that. Brian kept a pile of wildlife magazines for me to look at on arrival at the flat, saying he never had time to look at them himself. We watched Attenborough programmes and Brian insisted on having the colour tuned the very brightest, most unnatural hues. This applied to any programme and I often wondered if he saw colours quite differently.

It would be impossible not to miss profoundly Brian's integrity and great qualities as a person and a friend, staunch, rational and intelligent.

The burst of song, the head stands, the vagaries of diet all made him essentially Brian, and unique.

Two or three years ago showing me some photographs in a so tidy drawer I was touched to see small pen drawings of mice I had sent him over fifty years ago.

The flowering cherry was Brian's favourite tree and I shall be planting one for him at Lannacombe this year.

Robin

If Brian was his mother's son, so Robin was his father's son. His style, personality, good looks, and sporting prowess all bore an uncanny resemblance to those of his father.

Rodney Bickerstaffe's obituary of Robin noted Tony Benn's comment that he was 'one of the most important figures of his generation'.

Robin was never a member of the Communist Party, but he was active in the Labour Party for many years, including a period as a councillor, and serving on committees. Robin's last few years were blighted with failing eyesight, but his mind remained as razor sharp as ever. These comments were typed for Robin by Pat Hone, one of his carers, in August 2002.

Soon after the war commenced, I think my father considered

my school reports. They were not very good concerning academic subjects. John Platts-Mills had just been stationed and had lodgings in Loughborough College. He told my father about the college. My father did not know the difference between a screwdriver and a spanner and as I looked after all maintenance needs in the house and built a path in the garden etc., he thought that perhaps I should be an engineer and sent me to Loughborough College. After a few weeks the RAF took over our accommodation and I was in lodgings for the rest of the three years. The son of my landlady, slightly older than me, became Sir Denys Wilkinson FRS, late Vice Chancellor of Sussex University. He was outstandingly good at everything except that he was infuriated as he could not beat me at chess.

REME was formed in 1942 and they searched for officer potential around the colleges. I was selected for a War Office Selection Board, which meant a few days away being tested. I passed. Meanwhile at college I had joined the Home Guard which was not very exciting. I think my only claim to glory was that on an exercise I was behind someone's garden wall with my rifle and on pulling myself up, I pulled over an ornament and half the garden wall. I rushed off to join my fellow defenders of the country.

Robin reported for army service in 1943 aged 19. He firmly stated his religion as 'atheist'. He spent time at Aldershot and recalled being on a course in Stoke-on-Trent in 1944:

My father visited me and took the opportunity of visiting some Irish friends who lived nearby and who he had not seen since he was in prison with them. I found the visit an interesting occasion but my father found that their politics were not very progressive and was rather unhappy with the visit. Soon afterwards I was notified that my mother had been badly injured by a V1 bomb and I was given a day's leave to see her in London and to visit my father.

It was not long after this that Robin was on a course in Croydon and met up with Wilfred Clayton, Harry Thompson's right hand man, and decided to join the firm. Before that could happen he was posted to India where he contracted dengue fever. He recalled:

My year in India had been interesting but depressing. I was depressed because there was so much poverty around and I could not see any solution to India's problems. There were great religious differences and so far as the Hindus were concerned, there was the caste system. I found it strange that Ghandi was held in such high regard. My mother in her book on India, written in the British Museum, was very critical of the support for Ghandi … all the political interpretations and Ghandi's publicity made me feel that India would remain on the whole a poverty stricken country with little real future despite its enormous population.

Robin left the army in 1947, and shortly afterwards was called for an interview at The Law Society at which he turned up in his captain's uniform with a Sam Browne belt. They decided that he should do only two year's articles and should be exempt from all examinations except the final and accounts.

Robin also recalled:

The problems relating to our union clients were legend. We also had problems when the leadership of unions changed. Bill Carron whose executor I was, was succeeded by Hugh Scanlon who I played golf with quite a bit. This was a traumatic change and although we got on with Hugh very well, he certainly did not like receiving legal advice which annoyed him as he made very clear.

To confirm our political image, I decided to stand for the new GLC and was elected for Bexley and became Vice Chairman of Finance, only to be defeated in the next election three years later.

At about the same time the Winn Committee under Lord Justice Winn, concerning the Reform of Personal Injury Procedure, was appointed, with myself as a member. Ultimately, I presented a minority report that Brian helped me with, which I think was referred to by various law colleges in subsequent years. By doing a minority report I think this guaranteed that I would not be appointed to any similar committee in the future.

In fact the minority report was widely admired. Robin was a founder of the Trial Lawyers for Public Justice and a life member of the Association of Trial Lawyers of America. As Rodney Bickerstaffe's obituary subsequently noted 'he was respected by the legal establishment but never part of it'.

After Robin retired he retained a keen interest and involvement in the firm. In his later years he suffered from poor health and declining eyesight. Again, to quote Rodney Bickerstaffe's words, 'He was still as entertaining, mischievous and sometimes as cantankerous as ever. Always a source of historical insight, anecdote and – when he wanted to be – wisdom.'

In Robin's words:

Eventually I got the office out of my system and thought of some other matters, for example: because of my blindness, I listen a lot to Radio 4 but on a Sunday the programme is filled with religion. We are offered prayers, etc. There is never an alternative view put. Sometimes a person is referred to as an atheist but it is never developed. For example, some atheists like myself consider all religions as harmful, but I have never heard this view put forward on the radio.

There is also the fact that a woman's position in several religions is almost non-existent. They are organised and dominated by the men.

I found it appalling when Tony Blair suggested that there should be more faith schools. I think the existing faith schools are harmful enough and should be abolished as soon as possible. Religion, if it is taught in schools, should be taught as a subject reviewing different religions. Certainly the school should not be subsidised just because they are supporting some religion or other, this will lead to obvious problems.

Then there is the other matter which is never properly developed over the radio and that is: the arguments of those of us who are against the monarchy. It is merely confined to whether or not you are in favour of the Queen. The main point of course is that we still live in a class ridden society and the Queen is at the top of the class system. The monarchy is full of hangers on and people like Lord Lieutenants, High Sheriffs and others who are in some way related to the monarchy. We have, for example, a ridiculous system of getting the Queen's Speech read in Parliament. We have the farcical situation where the House of Lords is assembled in their robes and MPs are summoned by one of these figures from the past and assemble as though they are some second rate group at the end of the chamber and stand to hear the speech.

This type of idiotic ceremonial is repeated in the name of royalty throughout the year.

It is repeated in different ways throughout our society. For example: the Lord Chancellor in secrecy aided by his civil servants appoints all the judges. At the end of the day, we finish up with a set of High Court Judges, more than 80 per cent of which went to public schools and Oxbridge. I could go on forever.

Before I became blind I started to make enquiries

PERSONAL

Rt Hon Tony Benn
12 Holland Park Avenue
London W11 3QU
England
Tel: (44) (0) 207 229 0779
Fax: (44) (0) 207 243 0009
e-mail: tony@tbenn.fsnet.co.uk

November 6 2002

Dear David

I have just got your letter telling me the very sad news of your father's death, and this is to send my sincere condolences to you and all his family.

Robin was, in my opinion, one of the most important figures in our generation, but so he was so modest that he may not have realized it himself.

Unfortunately I cannot come to his funeral on Friday, but attach a poem which was sent to me when my wife died and which gave me great comfort.

I read it at her graveside recently when we interred her ashes.

I shall be thinking of you on Friday

Yours Tony

Do not stand at my grave and weep
I am not there, I do not sleep.
I am a thousand winds that blow
I am the diamond glint on snow
I am sunlight on ripened grain,
I am the gentle Autumn's rain
When you awaken in the morning's hush
I am the swift lifting rush
Of quiet birds in circled flight.
I am the soft star which shines at night
Do not stand at my grave and cry
I am not there,
I did not die.

Author,
An American Indian

concerning the EU and the Common Agricultural Policy. I found it difficult to try and get information from the EU and I sought the assistance of Neil Kinnock that was helpful. I had already tried one of our MEPs and she did not even reply to my letter. I think the situation of the MEPs is quite appalling because they are not selected on a local basis but are imposed upon us by headquarters. I really wonder what they do except draw substantial expenses.

Robin noted that, 'Twenty years ago there were sixteen Thompson first cousins', but now he was the last one. He also said that having prepared some comments he only wished his mother and father could have done something similar. He was deeply aware of the firm's heritage.

Robin was married to Queenie on 21 August 1954, and they had one child, David, who joined the practice. The relationship broke up in 1971, and Robin subsequently met and lived with 'Bee' (Barbara). They had a child, Natasha, who has a successful career as a Picture Editor for a popular magazine. Queenie died on 16 April 2008.

Towards the end of his life Robin and Bee parted and he lived alone in Primrose Hill. He remained in contact with friends in the firm, including some who had left many years previously. One such friend was John Bowden. After leaving the firm in the early 1980s John had worked for Seifert Sedley's for a period where he eventually qualified as a solicitor and then managed his own firm before retiring to Devon. John appeared as a civil rights lawyer in countries all around the world:

Even after I left Thompsons I kept in close touch with Robin and Brian. They were both good fun. Towards the end of his life when Robin was going blind it was sad and difficult for him. Robin sometimes rang up during the night saying he was fed up and asking if there was any chance I could come to London and read to him. On occasions I said I would come down the following day and Robin would ask me to come up on the "milk train". Robin would tell me how pleased he was that I had continued the Thompsons tradition in civil rights cases.

The brothers, so different in many ways, but each so difficult in their own special way, inspired this loyalty.

Robin Beauchamp Thompson
1924-2002
Solicitor and Socialist

Chapter 31
My story

'Choose a job you love and you will never have to work a day in your life'. **Confucius.**

In the early 1970s it was still common for solicitors to charge trainee solicitors - articled clerks as they were then known – a premium or fee for the privilege of joining their practice, working for them and hopefully qualifying as solicitors. There was no question of actually paying them for their services. Some more enlightened firms had abandoned this archaic practice and were even paying a modest sum towards living expenses. As I was to discover, W.H. Thompson was unusual. There was not only no charge, but a living wage was paid.

In the summer of 1972 after finishing my degree course I was working at the newly opened University Hospital in Cardiff cleaning operating theatres when my labour law lecturer John McGlyne contacted me. He had got talking to a lawyer from a firm that sounded 'just up your street', and did I want an interview? At that time I was not sure if I wanted to be a solicitor, and in any event how I could afford it, but I went to the interview. I was looking for a temporary job until February 1973 when I was due to start at Law School to take the professional examinations.

Despite the short term nature of the job I was looking for I was given the third degree by Ted Lewis and Freddie Oaten, mostly on my politics and background. Part way through this grilling I had to leave the room while they dealt with a call from Hugh Scanlon about some aspect of the developing crisis arising out of the engineering workers' union's refusal to recognise the National

Industrial Relations Court (which was sitting in Cardiff at the time).

I was offered a job at £16.20 per week (the junior general clerk rate for a 21 year old and more than enough to live on), with the prospect of a training contract – articles of clerkship, with pay at an even higher rate – after my forthcoming stint at Law College, provided I passed the exams and had shaped up successfully. I couldn't believe my luck. It got even better when I started and discovered that the person whose room I was sharing was the lawyer who dealt with Paris v Stepney Borough Council, Wardlaw v Bonnington Castings and numerous other significant cases which I had studied as a student. This was Fred Oaten. He gave me very little work to do, but spent a lot of time telling me about the firm and its cases. I was spellbound. Fred and his wife Edna invited me and my wife Ros (we had married in 1973 at ages 22 and 23 respectively) to his house.

I started to learn about the firm and the role it had played in the politics of the labour movement and in civil liberties, and in opening the door of legal rights to the oppressed, the poor and disadvantaged.

I was away at Law College in Bristol from February to September 1973. When I returned, I discovered the big news that the sons of W.H. Thompson, Robin and Brian, had decided to split the practice, and a note had been sent to relevant unions on 25 June 1973. The split took effect in 1974, and the separate firms of Robin Thompson and Partners and Brian Thompson came into being.

I started my training contract to become a solicitor in September 1973 as an articled clerk to Ted Lewis. In fact though, all my training was given by Roger Bent for the first year and then Geoff Thomas for a couple of years. I learnt a great deal from both of them.

I acquired my own room, and a secretary, first Ruth Nash

for a year or so and then Clare Mullins who worked as my secretary throughout the remainder of my time in Cardiff.

The firm operated in a modest way. Whenever someone left, the first thought of a newcomer like me was to see if I could acquire a better piece of furniture – maybe a telephone table or a better chair! Beryl Westwell, the office manager, treated everyone well but ran a tight ship. Pencils, biros, notebooks and so on were dispensed on a strict basis.

I was given an area to cover – Gwent and Gloucestershire – and had to learn the ropes in all types of cases and industrial environments: various hospitals, engineering works, the steel works at Ebbw Vale and Llanwern, foundries and so on, and all sorts of cases including asbestos and other diseases as well as accidents.

Most clients were seen on regional visits to union offices and workplaces. Conveners and branch secretaries would make an office available and their members would be seen wherever possible at the place of work. It was easy and natural to get to know the union officers and build a rapport with them. We all dealt with hundreds of cases. Some stick in your mind, mostly the ones which were lost, but sometimes the successful ones as well. I had many cases for example from the Gloucester Foundry. One of these was for a young man involved in some horse play who lost an eye as a result of some sand being thrown at him. After a monumental battle we were able to recover a substantial sum for him from what was then the Criminal Injuries Compensation Board, as well as securing on appeal industrial injuries and disablement benefit.

A few years later Brian Salt, the full time officer for the Foundry Workers union, asked me to represent the convener Wally Hall who had been dismissed for throwing some sand in the foundry. We won the case because we showed inconsistency by the employer – the man involved in the earlier incident had been disciplined but not dismissed, even though that incident had been much more serious. The image of Wally, a large man, dancing down the corridor at Gloucester Law Courts, where the tribunal case was heard, arms aloft, singing on hearing the verdict, is one which will live with me forever.

In early 1982 we acquired a vast number of deafness cases. I already had a caseload of 400 or so and was by then assisted by an articled clerk (David Tye). There were so many deafness cases that the Cardiff office took cases from outside the region, and I was allocated Wearside. [In my ignorance I had to check where it was]. Within days of the decision a box load of new deafness cases arrived for me – about 750 of them! Over the next year I spent six weeks in Sunderland with David, interviewing one boilermaker after another. Every evening we went back to the Mowbray Park Hotel to dictate all the statements, instructions to counsel and other work on each case where the client had been seen so that when we returned to Cardiff at the end of the week we had all the work well in hand. I recall on the first journey up reading and re-reading the Ladybird book in the series 'People at Work' called *The Shipbuilders* – a useful if somewhat rudimentary initiation into how ships were built. During the first week we were taken by the conveners on tours of two shipyards, including the modern and covered plant at Pallion. Sadly all the yards are now long since closed down.

By the beginning of 1984 I had court proceedings underway in 289 of these cases (I still have my old handwritten records). The clients ranged from fairly young men to the very old. There were a few who had fought in the First World War (and were exposed to gunfire and explosions – a relevant fact in deafness cases)

My expericnce was repeated throughout both the Cardiff office and a number of others. In Cardiff, Andrew Herbert dealt with even more cases from Teeside, and Roger Bent and Geoff Thomas also dealt with vast numbers. Rather than serving the court proceedings as they were prepared we saved them up and served them in large batches all on the same day. As each case usually involved more than one defendant it meant that on each 'D Day', as we called it, literally hundreds of sets of court proceedings would be served, a tactic obviously designed to cause maximum difficulty to the defendants and in particular their insurers (mostly the Iron Trades Employers' Insurance Association). The defendants adopted their own tactics in response. It was truly attritional.

On 15 February 1983 the firm held a conference in London on deafness cases and the issues that arose from them. A couple of weeks before the conference Geoff Thomas asked me if I could speak at the conference on the problem of issuing court proceedings against dissolved and defunct companies. After a frantic few days spent at the Law Library a paper was prepared and the speech delivered. Over the years I extended and updated the paper – the Company Restoration Manual – from time to time, and it now lives on all Thompsons' lawyers' computers in their Case Management Notes on Screen. The other speakers at that conference were Frank Foy, David Stevenson, Keith Spicer, Geoff Thomas and Nigel Tomkins, all of whom went on to make big contributions to the firm. One side effect of the deafness litigation from my point of view was that I got to know many colleagues from other offices. We were all in the same boat and a lot of lasting friendships arose in this period.

The mass litigation of deafness came to an end with the Hearing Loss Scheme dated 11 January 1984 negotiated by David Skidmore after the test cases were heard.

No sooner had the deafness litigation ended, and during the period when we were concluding vast numbers of the cases on the scheme settlement terms, than the miners' dispute started, and it was all hands to the pumps once more.

The Cardiff office, like the others, was full of talent. Lawyers who were there when I joined included Ted Lewis, Fred Oaten, Geoff Thomas, Roger Bent, Andrew Herbert, Ted Constable, Chris Short, Gareth Thomas, Norman Edwards and Don Berkshire. I stayed there until 1985, becoming an equity partner in 1983. Even in those days Thompsons had a comprehensive supervision system. Everyone from top to bottom had a supervisor. For most of my time in Cardiff I was supervised by Andrew Herbert. Andrew was an aggressive litigator unfailingly calm as well as being incredibly knowledgeable. I learned a huge amount from both him and Roger.

While I was in Cardiff I dealt with the first patient handling case which succeeded at trial on a faulty lifting technique. Before that it had sometimes been possible to win cases for nurses and other carers who injured themselves handling patients, but only in obvious circumstances – for example where it was clear that two nurses were required and one had to try and do the job alone. In this case two nurses were lifting a heavy patient using a method known as the 'drag lift'. One of the nurses, Mrs Williams, was injured. I found a nursing expert who had recently produced a booklet *Avoiding low back injury among Nurses* who reported that this technique was outdated and dangerous. He was supported by a consulting engineer, and we obtained by court order the defendants' injury books for the whole of North Gwent for a period of five years leading up to the accident. The injury books showed a large number of back injuries. I recall receiving a note from Brian Thompson, not long before the trial, enquiring whether the union (NUPE at the time) knew about the case, what it was going to cost, and so on – not very reassuring. Although the case did not have a high monetary value I instructed J. Hampden Inskip QC, a highly experienced senior barrister. The defendants could not counter our expert evidence, and we won. The case was not reported in the Law Reports, but it received a lot of publicity in nursing journals as well as among lawyers in practice, particularly in Thompsons, and it opened the door to bringing successful claims. These days patient handling injuries are uncommon. After the Williams case, there were many further claims and it became increasingly possible to win them. In due course hospitals and homes changed their practices, lifting aids started to be provided and used and the statutory framework changed. I was lucky with this case; if I had not had the case someone else in Thompsons would have brought a similar case with a similar outcome. But I doubt that any other firm would have done so. We dealt with our cases to win for the (union) member, our client, but also to win for working people as a whole and sometimes we made a difference.

In the late 1970s the Cardiff office, which had been part of Brian's firm, fell out with Brian. The main reason was a clash between Brian on the one hand and Geoff Thomas in particular on the other. The resolution in 1978 involved Cardiff becoming financially independent, with Brian as a nominal partner and payment of a modest annual sum under a seven year agreement from the Cardiff office to Brian's firm for the work. Cardiff office retained the title 'Brian Thompson and Partners'. The arrangement worked well enough, but by 1984, Geoff had decided that he wanted to move to London to join the 'A' partners in Robin Thompson and Partners, and in the course of negotiations it was agreed that Cardiff would rejoin the fold, but as part of Robin's firm rather than Brian's (to Brian's disappointment).

The first problem Robin had to contend with was how to accommodate the Cardiff partners, particularly as the office seemed to them to have rather more of them than seemed necessary. Geoff's position was clear – he was to move to London. Roger Bent was to become managing partner of the office and Andrew, like Geoff and Roger, would be offered an equity partnership with Robin. I was more of a problem; I would only have fitted into their structure at the time as a salaried partner, and in any event they were keen for me to move to an office where the need was greater. Birmingham was mentioned.

With all the feeling of a free agent on a 'Bosman', I decided to write to Brian, suggesting that I would be keen to join his practice in Sheffield (recently opened under Chris Chapman). I was particularly friendly with Eddie Solomons and Philip Ballard and they encouraged me. Needless to say, Brian either did not receive my note, or mislaid it, but when Brian's firm got wind of my feelings Nick Carter contacted me and asked if I could meet him at the Hotel Russell. I did so and was persuaded to consider Manchester. Ros, my wife, and I made the decision simply on the basis of which city we liked best after spending two or three days visiting both, and Manchester won.

I transferred to Manchester office in May 1985.

I brought just one case with me from Cardiff, the Cook case. I got the case in late 1982 as part of my usual allocation. From the union schedule it looked serious, but I did not realise how serious. Mr Cook had been working for a company which reclaimed the precious metal from items such as silver oxide batteries. As a result of a mix up the wrong material was emptied into a vat, and the result was the emission of a large quantity of hydrogen sulphide. Mr Cook was overcome and suffered cerebral anoxia causing permanent brain damage. In hospital he appeared to be conscious but in a vegetative state. However, the medical staff soon discovered that his cognitive function was intact. He had lost the movement of his four limbs, the power of speech and hearing, but by holding up letter cards he could answer questions by moving his head at letter boards so as to formulate his replies.

The case was not straightforward on liability; there were three defendants and eventually there was a ten day trial on liability which we won. But the amount of damages was even more difficult. Apart from all the usual calculations there was a major issue on life expectancy, with different opinions ranging from ten years from the date of the accident on the one hand to 25 years on the other. Mr Cook was provided with a computer which consisted of a BBC basic with a memory of 32k – computer technology was in its infancy and this was state of the art at the time. A head set was made, with the result that he would read written questions (his sight was unimpaired) and then generate the replies on the computer screen using head movements. Expert evidence was needed not just from medical experts but also a housing expert, an expert in aids and equipment, an actuary and a computer expert amongst others.

A team of carers was organised to enable Mr Cook to go on holidays. (He would go for a week at a time with a team of carers – I recall asking him why he only went for a week. The computer generated reply read: `after 7 the slaves are knackered´.)

During the trial on liability in 1987, with a trial on quantum due to follow straight after, there were many discussions about value, and the parties settled on a figure of £850,000. This represented a compromise between the differing estimates of life expectancy. The settlement was noted in open court by the judge the day after his judgment on liability and there was a blaze of publicity with a lengthy televised press conference, radio interviews, etc. The case was front page news in every daily paper.

In any event, the award smashed the record for the highest personal injuries damages award (although the figure was bettered in another case within a few months).

I missed all the television and most of the radio coverage except what I heard on the car radio on the way home, but years later a colleague Eddie Solomons congratulated me on my comments he had heard on the radio. I was somewhat intrigued as I had not given an interview the previous evening. In fact the BBC was recycling remarks I had made in the Cook press conference about the cost of disability. Such is the way the media works.

I heard about Mr Cook again twenty years after the judgment. He was still alive, but the money had run out, and he wrote to his union to see if anything could be done. Of course, it could not, but it reminded me that it was a classic example of a case where periodical payments of part of the award – not possible for the judge to award at the time – would have been far preferable to a final award.

The union which sponsored that case was ASTMS, Clive Jenkins' union, which subsequently became part of MSF and is now part of Unite. As ever, the case did not cost the claimant a penny, he bore no risks in relation to costs and he received the full award with no deduction.

I received further insight into how the media works in the course of the miners' dispute. We found that even the news bulletins would not let the facts get in the way of a good story. If it made better TV to show miners throwing stones first and then follow it with a charge by mounted police, so be it. The fact that it happened the other way round was apparently not the point. I recall in one of the trials an issue arising about the soundtrack to the footage of an incident, only to discover that the soundtrack was not the actual soundtrack of what happened – that had not been recorded. The news media simply added their 'riot' soundtrack from their sound archive. I don't suppose I was alone in assuming that what I saw and heard on the news was a faithful and accurate recording of events. Is it any wonder that some people consider some parts of the media to be biased and unreliable?

The miners' dispute gave rise to some big trials. One morning, just after arriving at my desk in Cardiff I was advised that some miners had been arrested in Newport and could I go over to the police station. I discovered that forty miners had been arrested after effectively hijacking the transporter bridge. I and a colleague Paul LLewellyn got them bail (though a number were subsequently charged with major offences and tried in the Crown Court). As we left court we were then advised of an incident – I think at Swansea. Paul lived over that way so said he would deal with it. When he arrived he discovered that a number of miners had gone up the tower crane above the docks. Paul ended up climbing this to negotiate on behalf of the miners the terms on which they would come down. Having brokered the deal with the British Transport Police, Paul went back up to tell the men. Some came down, but some jumped straight into the river and swam away.

I transferred to Manchester in 1985 as an equity partner but had no seat on the firm's Executive Committee. The committee was made up of a mixture of equity partners, elected representatives, and appointees. At some point shortly after I joined, John Whelan one of the appointees, in a typically generous gesture, agreed to stand down for two years to allow me to attend. When the two years were up I simply carried on attending. No one ever mentioned or queried it. In truth, the Executive Committee (EC) was no way to run a law practice. Some of those who attended owed their allegiance to Brian and would rarely say anything or do anything except to put their hand up to support Brian in the event of a vote. And there was a clear and unequivocal split between Brian and his friends on the one hand and those he thought did not support him on the other.

I knew very little of Nick Carter before I came to Manchester in 1985. The atmosphere in the office itself was stunning, with an emphasis on court litigation. Much of the training was given by Pauline Chandler with her unique style. Nick ran the office with calm efficiency, and a healthy emphasis on good case management systems and procedures.

I thoroughly enjoyed the work and loved the office. But matters at a national level in relation to the firm's management were more difficult. Disputes and personality clashes seemed to be the order of the day. No doubt the same is true of most workplaces but I suspect the political nature of the firm tended to amplify it all.

In 1993 Mike Humphreys, the partner in charge of Liverpool office, had left the firm and Tony Briscoe had taken over, assisted by Dave Armitage. The office was struggling. I offered to go there for two years on secondment. Coincidentally Phil Smith and Rob Wood two outstanding young lawyers from Newcastle volunteered to transfer. I duly transferred in May 1993, fully expecting to return to Manchester two years later. After I had been in Liverpool for a year or so, Tony returned to London and I was appointed Managing Partner there.

At around that time, the firm had a major redundancy problem. It fell mainly to me to conduct the difficult negotiations which were necessary, starting with a Redundancy Procedures Agreement and ending with the redundancy, all achieved voluntarily, of about one hundred mostly support staff. Indeed, over the years I spent a great deal of my time on staffing issues, as a folio representative in Manchester and then folio holder in Brian Thompson's responsible for the technical (support) staff, as part of the staffing group in Thompsons and finally in my role as Director of Operations (PI and Staff) from 2002.

In late 1997 I was appointed Regional Managing Partner

with responsibility for both Liverpool and Manchester, and spent my time (when I wasn't in London) equally between the two.

The most difficult time professionally was in 1999. The firm needed to restructure and a decision was made that there were too many equity partners. A redundancy package for partners was devised, and a number left. The situation was particularly bad in Manchester where there were a lot of partners and where not only was I in charge but also on the firm's Policy Group. Pauline Chandler was one of those to leave. Her contribution as a lawyer was awesome. Other partners who left included Alicia Rendell, Sally Gold, Elizabeth Roth, Katrina London and Jane Litherland, along with a number of others all of whom had made significant contributions.

Two other longstanding partners and good friends had by then already departed. In 1997 and 1998 respectively Nick Carter and Roger Bent retired from the partnership but remained working for Thompsons on three year consultancies undertaking case work.

More changes occurred with the advent of the corporate structure. I became one of the Regional Managing Directors, and my local North West responsibilities diminished to an extent with the appointment of local Branch Managers, Julie Wood in Manchester and Matthew Tollitt in Liverpool.

A particularly sad event was the death of John Whelan on 2 December 2001, aged just 58. John had joined Thompsons on 29 March 1971 and worked throughout in Manchester office. John was an outstanding litigator, well known both inside and outside the firm for his exceptionally hard work and the very high level of damages he recovered for clients (and costs income for the firm). He could deal with all types of case, no matter how complex. John was also extremely popular with the unions, particularly the AEEU and UNISON, with whom he forged strong relations, and for many years along with Francine O'Gorman carried the Manchester office's efforts in this area. He was a good friend.

In 2002 when a vacancy arose for Chief Operations Officer I applied. I was not successful – the position was given to Phil Smith – the candidate I would have voted for had I been on the interview panel. Phil had worked with me for a year or two in Liverpool from 1993 and we got on well. I was appointed Director of Operations (PI and Staff). I had particular responsibility for personal injury work, the staff portfolio and the IT department, and reported to Phil. I had a seat on the firm's Executive Board which at that time consisted of Geoff Shears, Phil Smith and me. We were soon joined by Carolyn Hurley as Chief Financial Officer and then Stephen Cavalier as Client Director.

It was a satisfying period. After a shaky period financially, the firm made real progress. Income from the miners' chronic bronchitis and emphysema and Vibration White Finger cases had started to come in, the benefits of the computerised case management system were becoming apparent, and there was a welcome period of stability. The operations team with Phil Smith at the helm and Carolyn Hurley in charge of finance was the strongest that I had known in my time with the firm.

But all good things come to an end. I retired from the partnership on 30 April 2004 after nearly 32 years, over twenty as an equity partner. An opportunity arose for me to take charge of a group of companies, including a medical reporting company, an insurance intermediary and a copying company. Thompsons is the major customer and my knowledge of the firm remained of value. Life in a normal commercial organisation was a good deal less pressurised if not quite as exciting as Thompsons, but I was able to assist them by producing an Asbestos Manual and various other guides and documents.

I have always been lucky with my secretarial support. In Manchester my secretaries were Linda Arrowsmith and then, when Linda became office manager in place of Cynthia Palmer, Jacqui Dodd. Both were excellent. In Liverpool I had Theresa Nelson, now one of the lawyers, then Marina Glinos and, for many years the brilliant Ann Flanagan. Back in Manchester again I inherited Nick's top team of Val Watson and Mary Clark, with Val as my PA.

The size of the firm is huge now – over 1,000 staff and partners. It has come a long way in the past forty years; some say it has lost part of the family atmosphere that existed, but this is inevitable. What certainly remains is the ethos which makes it a special practice; a firm united in its endeavour to act for the trade unions, for working people and the disadvantaged and oppressed. It has never acted for insurance companies, and the central tenet of the partnership deed remains – to assist trade unions and their members and not to maximise income for its partners.

In the last year alone the firm recovered £150 million in compensation in personal injury cases, dealt with and advised on over 4,000 employment cases including unfair dismissal, sex discrimination, race discrimination, redundancy, pensions, whistle blowing, human rights, as well as a significant number of industrial disputes.

Where does it go in the future? The manufacturing base of the country – the part which gave rise to most accidents and diseases - has been severely reduced, while at the same time the personal injury market has been opened up to severe competition, some of it wholly undesirable, in the nature of claims farmers. Over the years the firm has survived by acquiring more trade union clients but that type of expansion cannot be guaranteed.

The last few years has seen a major increase in the employment work the firm has undertaken for the unions. A lot of the work, particularly but not exclusively that done in Congress House, is cutting edge. Very little of it generates significant income, but it adds a major dimension.

Acquisition of private work is one way of filling any potential gap: private work for those who would otherwise be denied justice. The firm has already built relationships with several of the asbestos support groups around the country. Maybe there is room again for the civil liberties work which formed the basis of the firm under Harry Thompson. The remarkable work of Public Interest Lawyers under Phil Shiner (who worked at one time for Thompsons) may point the way. Another pointer may be the work presently being undertaken in South Africa and elsewhere. But the essential bedrock of the firm's work will remain acting for trade unions and their members.

The new Chief Executive Officer Steve Cavalier has a heavy burden of leading the firm over the coming years, but, assisted by David Thompson and others, the firm is in good hands.

The first major case W.H. Thompson worked on was on behalf of the aldermen and councillors imprisoned in Poplar in 1921. After the successful outcome engineered by W.H., one of the aldermen published a pamphlet *The Rate Protest of Poplar*. He concluded it with the following:

'All who shared in the fight can feel proud of their achievement. We have to gird our loins for the next struggle'.

*The author speaking at the Thompsons' National Conference,
Warwick, March 2007*

Bibliography

Ed. Victor Bailey, *Forged in Fire. The History of the Fire Brigades Union*. Lawrence & Wishart; 1992

Joan Beauchamp, *Women who Work.* Lawrence & Wishart; 1937

Joan Beauchamp, *British Imperialism in India*. Martin Lawrence; 1934

Various. Ed Joan Beauchamp, *Martin's Annual.* Martin Lawrence; 1935

Ed. Joan Beauchamp, *Poems of Revolt.* Labour Publishing Company 1924; Reprinted 1987 Labour Research Department

Ed. by Joyce M Bellamy and John Saville, *Dictionary of Labour Biography Volume 10.* Palgrave Macmillan; 2000

Noreen Branson, *George Lansbury and the Councillors' Revolt: Poplarism 1919-1925.* Lawrence & Wishart; 1979

Dominic Carman, *No Ordinary man – A Life of George Carman.* Hodder & Stoughton; 2002

Barbara Castle, *The Castle Diaries 74-76.* Holmes & Meier Pub; 1982

Margaret Cole, *Growing up into Revolution.* Longman Green and Co Ltd; 1949

John Gennard and Peter Bain, *SOGAT: A History of The Society of Graphical and Allied Trades.* Routledge; 1995

JW Graham, *Conscription & Conscience: a history 1916-1919.* G Allen & Unwin Ltd; 1922

Clive Jenkins, *All Against the Collar. Struggles of a White-Collar Union leader.* Methuen; 1990

Mervyn Jones, *Michael Foot.* Victor Gollancz; 1994

Otto Kahn-Freund, *Labour and the Law.* Stevens & Sons; 1972

Ronald Kidd, *British Liberty in Danger.* Lawrence & Wishart; 1940

David Marquand, *Ramsay Macdonald.* Jonathan Cape; 1977

Various. Ed Julia L Mickenberg and Philip Nel, T*ales for Little Rebels.* New York University Press; 2008

Charles Nevin, *Lancashire – Where Women Die of Love.* Mainstream Publishing; 2006

Robert Dale Owen, *Threading My Way: 27 Years of Autobiography.* Trubner & Co; 1874;

OH Parsons, WH Thompson and his Cases

Ann Pettitt, *Walking to Greenham.* Honno; 2006

DN Pritt, *From Right to Left. Autobigraphy of DN Pritt; Part 1.* Lawrence & Wishart; 1965

Sylvia Scaffardi, *Fire under the Carpet. Working for Civil Liberties in the Thirties.* Lawrence & Wishart 1986

John Scurr, *The Rate Protest of Poplar.* Caledonian Press; 1922

Gary Slapper, Times Online

AJP Taylor, *AJP Taylor – a personal history.* Hamish Hamilton; 1983

Martyn Thomas, *Blaina Riots.* Martyn Thomas

WH Thompson, *Civil Liberties.* Victor Gollancz; 1938

Chris Wrigley, *AJP Taylor – Radical historian of Europe.* IB Tauris & Co Ltd; 2006

Newspapers and periodicals

The Friend
Daily Mail
Lansbury's Labour Weekly
The Tribunal
The Times
Daily Worker
Morning Star photo
Stockport Express

Index of Thompsons' cases referred to

Case	page
Allinson v London Underground [2008] EWCA Civ 71	407
ASLEF v United Kingdom [2007] IRLR 361	344
Armstrong v British Coal [1998] (unreported)	395
Barker v St Gobain Pipelines [2004] PIQR P34	399
Beckmann v Dynamo Whicheloe MacFarlane Ltd [2002] EJC Case C-164/00	351
Bland v Stockport MBC [1993] (settlement)	324
Bonnington Castings v Wardlaw [1956] 1 All ER 615	171
British Airways plc v Starmer [2005] IRLR 862	367
British Labour Pump Co. Ltd. V Byrne [1979] ICR 348	347
British Broadcasting Corporation v Kelly-Phillips [1998] ICR 588	347
Brown v Stockton-on-Tees BC [1988] ICR 411	366
Central Asbestos Co Ltd v Dodd [1972] 2 All ER 1135	173
Collins v Royal National Theatre Board Ltd [2004] IRLR 395	368
Cook v Englehard Industries Ltd [1987] (unreported)	327
Cory Lighterage v TGWU [1973] 2 All ER 341	246
Cowan v Scargill [1984] ICR 647	284
Dawson The Cherry Tree Machine Co Ltd [2001] WCA Civ 101	405
DEFRA v Robertson [2005] ICR 751	364
Dines v Initial Healthcare Services Ltd [1995] ICR 12	351
Dugmore v Swansea NHS Trust [2003] 1 All ER 333	406
Durham v Builders Accident Insurance (Run-Off) Ltd (the "Trigger issue" litigation) [2008] EWHC (QB) 2692	402
Elias v Passmore [1934] 2 KB 164	112
Enderby v Frenchay Health Authority [1994] ICR 113	356
Fairchild & Ors v Glenhaven Funeral Services [2002] 3 All ER 305	398

Gate Gourmet v TGWU [2005] IRLR 88   338
GMB v Allen [2007] UKEAT/ 0425/ 06/ DA   360
Griffiths v British Coal [1998] (unreported)   396
Grieves v Everard [2005] EWHC 88   400
Grunwick Processing Laboratories Ltd v ACAS [1978]
    ICR 232   280
Hadmor Productions Ltd v Hamilton [1982] 1
    All ER 1042   247
Hale v London Underground [1993] PIQR Q30   329
Hayward v Cammell Laird Shipbuilders Ltd [1988]
    ICR 465   355
Home Office v Bailey [2005] ICR 1058   364
Home Office v Holmes [1984] ICR 679   365
Hunt v R M Douglas (Roofing) Ltd [1988] 3
    All ER 823   380
King-Emperor v Spratt [1932]   103
Knox v Cammell Laird Shipbuilders Ltd [1990]
    (unreported)   322
Leung   327
Lister v Forth Dry Dock Eng. Co. Ltd [1989]
    ICR 432   350
MacShannon v Rockware Glass Ltd [1978] 1
    All E R 625   304
Matthews v Kent and Medway Towns Fire Auth. [2006] 2
    All ER 171   372
Meade-Hill v British Council [1995] ICR 848   366
Moss v McLachlan [1985] IRLR 76   287
Neill v Belfast Telegraph Newspapers Ltd [2002]
    Case no 00554/00FET, 03297/00   368
News Group Newspapers Ltd v SOGAT '82 [1987]
    ICR 182   291
North Yorkshire County Council v Ratcliffe [1995]
    ICR 834   357
Ogwo v Taylor [1987] 3 All E R 961   321
Paris v Stepney Borough Council [1951] AC 367   166
Pickles v National Coal Board [1968] 2 All ER 598   173
Powley v ACAS [1978] ICR 124   339

Preston v Wolverhampton Healthcare NHS Trust [1998] ICR 228	363
R (BBC) v Central Arbitration Committee [2003] ICR 1543	340
R v Mansfield Justices ex parte Sharkey [1985] 1AER 193	287
R (NUJ) v Central Arbitration Committee [2005] ICR 493	340
R v Sec of State for Home Dept Ex p FBU [1995] 2 AC 513	326
R (BECTU) v Sec of State for Trade and Industry [2001] EJC, Case C-173/99	369
R v West Yorkshire F & CDA ex p McCalman & Lockwood COF/1999/0798/C	371
Rastill v Automatic Refreshment Services Ltd [1978] ICR 290	349
RCO Support Services v UNISON [2002] ICR 752	352
Roberts v Hopwood [1925] All E R 24	67
Rookes v Barnard [1964] 1 All ER 367	242
Salmon v Seafarer Reastaurants Ltd [1983] 3 All ER 729	321
Smith v Manchester Corporation [1974] 17 KIR 1	328
Smoker v London F & C D A [1991] 2 All E R 449	331
Spencer v British Steel Corporation [1979] CL 703	300
St. Helens MBC v Derbyshire [2007] IRLR 540	361
Stratford v Lindley [1964] 3 All ER 102	243
Stringer v HMRC [2009] UKHL 31	370
Summers v Frost [1955] 1 All ER 870	168
Susie Radin Ltd v GMB & ors [2004] ICR 894	346
Thomas v NUM (South Wales Area) [1985] ICR 887	286
Thomas v Sawkins [1935] 2 KB 249	114
Thompson v Smiths Shiprepairers (North Shields) Ltd [1984] 1 All ER 881	316
Thompson v Deakin [1952] 2 All ER 361	241
Wallhead v Ruston and Hornsby Ltd [1973] 14 KIR 285	177

Walker v Northumberland CC [1995] 1 All ER 737   324
Wandsworth LBC v NASUWT [1994] ICR 82   337
Williams v Compare Maxam Ltd [1982] ICR 157   345
Williams v Gwent Area Health Authority [1982] unreported   319
Wilson & NUJ v United Kingdom [2002] IRLR 568   341

Other cases (non Thompsons)
Cartledge v E. Jopling & Sons Ltd [1963]   172
Duncan v Jones [1936] 1KB 218   116

Acknowledgements

thanks to

David Skidmore for his recollections and for interviewing Ron Smith.

David Thompson for his recollections and for providing numerous documents, photographs and other material.

Tony Lawton for his recollections and photographs.

Victoria Phillips and Joe O'Hara for their assistance on the employment law section.

Mark Turnbull for supplying a copy of the O.H. Parsons manuscript

Anthony Patterson for providing the material for the British Coal test cases.

Roger Bent, John Bowden, Terry Butterfield, Nick Carter, Stephen Cavalier, Pauline Chandler, Chris Chapman, Doug Christie, Dorrie Collins, Ted Constable, Marg Craner, Andrew Dismore, Colin Ettinger, Miriam Edelman, Frank Foy, Peter Gornall, John Harris, John Harwood, Eric Heather, Andrew Herbert, Pam Holman, Tom Jones, Tony Lawton, Margery Lewis, John Lebor, Brenda Long, Rosina Newton, Rodger Pannone, John Pickering, Freda Phillips, Edna Scharts, Sir Stephen Sedley, Geoff Shears, Paul Shevlin, Colin Simpson, Ron Smith, David Stevenson, Bruce Tyrer, Simon Walton and Ivor Walker and for their recollections.

Professor Chris Wrigley for sending me the early chapters of his draft manuscript of a biography of AJP Taylor – from which I have quoted liberally in the early part of this document, and to I.B. Tauris & Co Ltd for allowing me to reproduce the same from the published book *AJP Taylor – Radical Historian of Europe*.

Martyn Thomas for his permission to use material from his article The Blaina Riots 1935.

The TUC website.

Nick Mansfield, Director of the People's History Museum, for his assistance in tracing the documents relating to the Meerut

Conspiracy case.

The Working Class Movement Library, Salford for various documents.

The Morning Star, for use of the Grunwick photograph and obituary of WH Thompson in *The Daily Worker*.

The Stockport Express at MEN Media for permitting the use of their photographs of the Roberts Arundel dispute.

Taylor & Francis for permitting the use of the quote from *SOGAT: A History of the Society of Graphical and Allied Trades*, published by Routledge, 1995.

Elibron Classics for permitting the use of the quote from *Threading My Way – 27 Years of Autobiography* by Robert Dale Owen, reprinted by them in 2001

Thompsons for allowing me to use their photographs.

The Times obituary by DN Pritt by permission – The Times/nisyndication

Lawrence and Wishart for permitting the use of various quotes from *British Imperialism in India, Poplarism 1919-1925, From Right to Left – Autobiography of DN Pritt, Forged in Fire – The History of the FBU, British Liberty in Danger, Fire under the Carpet – Working for Civil Liberties in the Thirties*, and photographs/graphics from *Women who Work* and *Martin's Annual*.

David Higham Associates for permitting the use of quotes from Growing up into revolution and AJP Taylor – a personal history.

Routledge for permitting the use of quotes from *SOGAT: A history of the Society of Graphical and Allied Trades*.

Thomson Reuters for permitting the use of a quote from *Labour and the Law*.

Professor Gary Slapper for his interview by Laurie Flynn and for allowing me to reproduce the same along with his *Times Online* list.

Laurie Flynn for carrying out a great deal of research, writing parts of the text and interviewing Miriam Edelman.

Val Watson for proof reading the text and correcting many grammatical errors.